AMERICAN THEATRE ENSEMBLES

VOLUME 2

RELATED TITLES

AMERICAN THEATRE ENSEMBLES
VOLUME 1
978-1-3500-51546
Edited by Mike Vanden Heuvel

MODERN AMERICAN DRAMA: PLAYWRITING IN THE 1930s
978-1-4725-7187-8
Edited by Anne Fletcher

MODERN AMERICAN DRAMA: PLAYWRITING IN THE 1940s
978-1-4725-7186-1
Edited by Felicia Hardison Londré

MODERN AMERICAN DRAMA: PLAYWRITING IN THE 1950s
978-1-4725-7142-7
Edited by Susan C. W. Abbotson

MODERN AMERICAN DRAMA: PLAYWRITING IN THE 1960s
978-1-4725-7220-2
Edited by Mike Sell

MODERN AMERICAN DRAMA: PLAYWRITING IN THE 1970s
978-1-4725-7175-5
Edited by Mike Vanden Heuvel

MODERN AMERICAN DRAMA: PLAYWRITING IN THE 1980s
978-1-4725-7246-2
Edited by Sandra G. Shannon

MODERN AMERICAN DRAMA: PLAYWRITING IN THE 1990s
978-1-4725-7247-9
Edited by Sharon Friedman and Cheryl Black

MODERN AMERICAN DRAMA: PLAYWRITING 2000–2009
978-1-4725-7147-2
Edited by Julia Listengarten and Cindy Rosenthal

STAGING AMERICA: TWENTY-FIRST-CENTURY DRAMATISTS
978-1-3502-0092-0
Christopher Bigsby

GOOD NIGHTS OUT: A HISTORY OF POPULAR BRITISH
THEATRE 1940–2015
978-1-3500-4621-4
Aleks Sierz

AMERICAN THEATRE ENSEMBLES

POST-1995: THE BUILDERS ASSOCIATION,
PIG IRON THEATRE, RUDE MECHS,
RADIOHOLE, THE CIVILIANS, AND 600
HIGHWAYMEN

VOLUME 2

Edited by Mike Vanden Heuvel

methuen | drama

LONDON • NEW YORK • OXFORD • NEW DELHI • SYDNEY

METHUEN DRAMA
Bloomsbury Publishing Plc
50 Bedford Square, London, WC1B 3DP, UK
1385 Broadway, New York, NY 10018, USA
29 Earlsfort Terrace, Dublin 2, Ireland

BLOOMSBURY, METHUEN DRAMA and the Methuen Drama logo are
trademarks of Bloomsbury Publishing Plc

First published in Great Britain 2021

Cover design by Holly Bell
Cover image © Gem Lauris

A catalogue record for this book is available from the British Library.

A catalog record for this book is available from the Library of Congress.

ISBN: HB: 978-1-3500-5163-8
         ePDF: 978-1-3500-5165-2
         eBook: 978-1-3500-5164-5

Typeset by Integra Software Services Pvt. Ltd.

To find out more about our authors and books visit www.bloomsbury.com
and sign up for our newsletters.

For Sally Banes

CONTENTS

Notes on Contributors viii

Series Preface x

Acknowledgments xv

1 **Historical and Cultural Background** *Mike Vanden Heuvel* 1

2 **American Theatre Ensembles, 1995–Present**
Mike Vanden Heuvel 35

3 **The Builders Association** *James Frieze* 95

4 **Pig Iron Theatre** *Kathryn Mederos Syssoyeva* 121

5 **Rude Mechs** *Jane Baldwin* 147

6 **Radiohole** *Steve Luber* 171

7 **The Civilians** *Sara Freeman* 193

8 **600 Highwaymen** *Rachel Anderson-Rabern* 217

Notes 239

Bibliography 244

Index 261

NOTES ON CONTRIBUTORS

Rachel Anderson-Rabern is Associate Professor of Theatre and Performance at Franklin and Marshall College. Her recent work is *Staging Process: The Aesthetic Politics of Collective Performance* (2020).

Jane Baldwin is an actress, critic, and scholar. Her publications include *Michel Saint-Denis and the Shaping of the Modern Actor* and *Vies and morts de la création collective*, coedited with Christiane Page and Jean-Marc Larrue. She edited Michel Saint-Denis's *Theatre: The Rediscovery of Style and Other Writings*. Her essay "Michel Saint-Denis: Training the Complete Actor" appears in Alison Hodge's *Actor Training*. She recently published "Raising the Curtain on Suzanne Bing's Life in the Theatre" in *Women, Collective Creation and Devised Performance*. She has also written two chapters on the Canadian actor and director Jean Gascon: "Klondyke: Une Tentative de créer une dramaturgie nationale," which received the André Bourassa prize, and "Jean Gascon's Theatricalist Approach to Molière and Shakespeare," which appears in *The Oxford Handbook of Dance and Theatre*. Her most recent publications include two chapters on Michel Saint-Denis, which appear in volume I of *The Great European Stage Directors*, edited by Peta Tait for Methuen Drama.

Sara Freeman is Associate Professor in the Department of Theatre Arts at the University of Puget Sound. She coedited *International Dramaturgy: Translation and Transformations in the Theatre of Timberlake Wertenbaker* (2008) and *Public Theatres and Theatre Publics* (2012) and has published chapters in *Working in the Wings: New Perspectives on Theatre History and Labor*; *The British Theatre Company: From Fringe to Mainstream*; *Decades of Modern British Playwriting: The 1980s*; and *Readings in Performance and Ecology*. She is editor of the annual journal *Theatre History Studies*, a publication of the Mid-America Theatre Conference, and assistant editor to Bloomsbury-Methuen's new *Encyclopedia of Modern Theatre*. As a director, she most recently staged *Mr. Burns: A Post Electric Play* by Anne Washburn, *The Force of Habit* by Guillén de Castro, and *In the Next Room (or, The Vibrator Play)* by Sarah Ruhl. Past favorite directing projects include

Steven Sater and Duncan Sheik's musical of *Spring Awakening*, Sarah Ruhl's *Eurydice*, Shakespeare's *Love's Labour's Lost*, Timberlake Wertenbaker's *Our Country's Good*, Susanna Centlivre's *Bold Stroke for a Wife*, and Caryl Churchill's *Blue Heart*.

James Frieze is the author of *Theatrical Performance and the Forensic Turn* (2019) and *Naming Theatre: Demonstrative Diagnosis in Performance* (2009). He is editor of *Reframing Immersive Theatre: The Politics and Pragmatics of Participatory Performance* (2016). Senior Lecturer in Drama at Liverpool John Moores University, he teaches devising, improvisation, performance theory, and contemporary practice. His theatre-making centers on the conception and direction of site-responsive performances and the adaptation to theatre of novels, poems, satirical newspapers, picture books, and role-playing games.

Steve Luber is Associate Director of the Ammerman Center for Arts and Technology at Connecticut College. He specializes in multimedia performance history and has published work in *TDR, PAJ, Scene, Theatre Survey*, and the *International Journal of Performance and Digital Media*.

Kathryn Mederos Syssoyeva is coeditor of a three-volume series on collective creation and devised theatre practice: *A History of Collective Creation*; *Collective Creation in Contemporary Performance*; and *Women, Collective Creation, and Devised Theatre: The Rise of Women Theatre Artists in the Twentieth and Twenty-First Centuries*. She is co-artistic director of AnomalousCo, a transdisciplinary theatre collective, and teaches directing, acting, and collaborative creation at Dixie State University in Utah.

Mike Vanden Heuvel is Professor of Interdisciplinary Theatre Studies and a member of the Classics and Near Eastern Studies Department at the University of Wisconsin-Madison. Author of *Performing Drama/Dramatizing Performance: Alternative Theatre and the Dramatic Text* (1991) and editor/contributor to *Modern American Drama: Playwriting in the 1970s* (2018), his teaching and research are centered on modern and postdramatic theatre as well theatre and science. His essay "Devised Theatre and the Performance of Science," appears in *The Cambridge Companion to Theatre and Science* edited by Kirsten Shepherd-Barr.

SERIES PREFACE

In 2006 Deirdre Heddon and Jane Milling published a key text on the history and practice of collective creation, *Devising Performance: A Critical History*. Despite a laudable attempt to encompass work from the UK, Canada, Australia, and the United States, the authors overstated the case when they asserted that "[t]he relative scarcity of contemporary devising companies in the USA is all the more marked when placed beside the vibrant scene in the UK, where there are too many companies to mention" (247, fn. 3). This view repeats a line of thought initiated by Richard Schechner in *The End of Humanism* (1982), and repeated by Arnold Aronson in his *American Avant-Garde Theatre: A History* (2000), that American artists, retreating from the counterculture ethos of the 1960s and seduced by the lure of individual success and the quickest route to Broadway or television, were by the end of the 1970s no longer interested in collective work (Schechner has since amended his view; see 2010). As for the comparison made by Heddon and Milling, it is not supportable and requires remediation.

The misapprehension stems, in part, from the very different funding strategies pursued by artists in different locales. Support for devised work in the UK and Commonwealth nations is more centralized and overseen by national arts councils, which not only results in a relatively higher profile for ensemble creation but also provides a ready archive of the extent of its practice. As well, in the UK a comparatively stable record exists made up in part by the archives from these state funding agencies as well as research they have supported. For instance, the project *Giving Voice to the Nation: The Arts Council of Great Britain and the Development of Theatre and Performance in Britain 1945–1995*, undertaken in 2009 by the University of Reading and the Victoria and Albert Museum, became

> a unique and, up until recently, unexplored resource for the study of theatre companies active in those years: materials include minutes of company meetings, funding proposals for projects, records of tour dates, statistics on box-office takings and audience attendance,

newspaper and magazine reviews, and publicity materials, as well as Arts Council memos, letters and records of meetings.

(Bull and Saunders 2016, ix–x)

The UK online archive "Unfinished Histories" under the supervision of Susan Croft has also gathered scholar- and practitioner-contributed research and interview material devoted to fringe companies, as well as placing hard copies of materials in central archives.

In the United States, on the other hand, without a central funding agency whose records define the true scale and range of such work, the practice of ensemble creation is scattered. Much activity goes unnoticed, in part because most collectively created work is not, for reasons of aesthetic style and sometimes a textual animus, intended to be, or valued sufficiently to be, published. Especially with regard to ensemble-created work from the last quarter of the twentieth century (and the subject of the first volume), the material record of the work is fast disappearing. The vast number of companies that began in the 1970s and 1980s are no longer operating and—with few exceptions—had neither the means nor the desire to archive their activities, so the collective memory of this work is threatened.

It is easy to mistake this lack of hard evidence for want of activity, but as research for this series has proved, there has always been a tremendous amount of collaborative theatre-making happening both on and off the radar in the United States, and this has been true since the 1970s. The period selected for attention in this series was chosen, in part, to rectify this misinterpretation. Especially for the timeframe of the first volume (1970–1995), scant critical attention has been given to the history of collective creation, in part for reasons discussed in the introduction. These include the general acceptance of what I refer to as the "declension hypothesis" and its conclusion that after the early 1970s, creative collectives had all but disappeared.

So, while critics have directed considerable attention to US ensemble theatres more recently, little has been done to establish historical trajectories or to situate this work in broader historical and social contexts. While *American Theatre Ensembles* does not attempt such an epic project, the hope is that it might inspire others to contribute to imagining such an endeavor. The initial case study in the first volume by Curtis L. Carter, on Milwaukee's critically neglected Theatre X, complete with reflections from former company members and collaborators, provides an example of the kind of reclamation project that might fill gaps in the historical record and convey the true extent and diversity of collective creation activity in the United States.

The two volumes of *American Theatre Ensembles* represent the first collection of critical assessments devoted to US companies between 1970 and the present that create and produce theatre work through collective means. The series both supplements and marks a departure from the compilation edited by James M. Harding and Cindy Rosenthal, *Restaging the Sixties: Radical Theatres and Their Legacies* (2007). While picking up roughly where that volume ends and extending the chronology of collective creation to the present, this series questions the assumption that ensemble-based theatre must be seen only in light of those radical legacies. For this reason, too, the series departs from the approach used by Mark Weinberg in his groundbreaking *Challenging the Hierarchy: Collective Theatre in the United States* (1992) because his focus is on the continuation of the collective work of the 1960s rather than the diversification of collective practice represented in *American Theatre Ensembles*. The more recent trio of books on the longer and transnational history of collective creation edited by Kathryn Syssoyeva and Scott Proudfit—*A History of Collective Creation* (2013); *Collective Creation in Contemporary Performance* (2013); and *Women, Collective Creation, and Devised Performance* (2016)—more substantially reflect the orientation of this series concerning historiography, chronology, and theoretical models. Recent work by Rachel Anderson-Rabern (*Staging Process* 2020) and others have further elaborated this historiography and also question the simple line of descent from the 1960s to the present. Yet, the nature of legacy and succession is a complex one, and there is value in attending to the continuing dialogue between past and present.

Of course, eliminating the single criterion of direct legacy from the 1960s and opening up the history of collective creation to its many and diverse expressions mean quickly becoming overwhelmed by the sheer number and variety of ensembles that merit attention. Thus, it is important to state at the outset that the series does not pretend to "cover" US ensemble-based creation over the last fifty years. A growing but scattered critical literature is emerging that addresses the many forms of collective creation and devised theatre in theatre for youth and young adults, theatre-in-education, grassroots and community-directed theatre, a wide assortment of applied theatre forms, a variety of constituency-directed theatres, game-based performance, immersive theatre, and many, many more. While my introductions to the two volumes attempt to construct a partial ecology of these diverse practices and place many of these forms of ensemble creation within the broader trajectory of collective creation broadly conceived from 1970 to the present, I do not attempt to be comprehensive. Rather, the main goal is to establish contexts that scaffold the kinds of work represented in the series.

With regard to the companies chosen for individual case studies, the aim was not to make them in any sense representative of the variety and range of practices that fall under collective creation, a goal that would surely founder under the weight of evidence. Instead, the guiding principles for selection directed focus toward the most prominent ensemble practices over the past fifty years, those that have helped to distinguish and define what is generally understood as modern and contemporary collective creation and devised theatre in the US context. As these definitions remain imprecise, the intent was to feature ensembles whose work was diverse enough to elicit a wide range of individual essays and approaches. Companies that have endured for long periods were particularly attractive, as these allowed contributors to begin at the founding date of the ensemble and track developments and the evolution of practices over many years and in changing contexts. "Significance" is always a slippery concept on which to hang choices, but effort was made to find a balance between repeating material on companies that have already received substantial critical attention and recognizing that such consideration is a sign of an ensemble's vitality and importance. A special case arose concerning the Wooster Group, whose singular importance to developments in ensemble theatre-making in the United States can hardly be overstated. Given their unique contributions to the field, I felt these would be better contextualized in the editor's introductions to both volumes rather than in a single case study restricted to one timeframe or the other.

Even so, during the process of organizing the series it was impossible not to be sensible of what has been left out. In the interval between proposing the series and its publication, some companies, such as Rachel Chavkin's The TEAM, Big Dance Theatre, and The Nature Theater of Oklahoma, have seen their critical profiles raised substantially. Fortunately, their work has received robust critical attention elsewhere. More concerning, as issues surrounding equity, diversity, and inclusion (EDI) in the field have rightfully moved to the forefront in 2020, the series most certainly lacks diversity and features companies led by, and largely made up of, white, middle-class. When I first proposed the volumes some time ago, I had in mind to render the apparent disproportion of mainstream ensembles (what I will define as "broad remit" companies to distinguish them from forms of applied theatre) led by white artists a problem to be accounted for and addressed. I thought it necessary at the time not to paper over the lack of diversity by presenting inclusivity as a value-added feature of ensemble-created theatre of the kind represented in the series, when evidence pointed to the contrary. But in light of recent statements by BIPOC (Black, Indigenous, People of Color) artists such as the "We See You, White American Theatre" open letter, I recognize this as a strategy based in my own unexamined privilege.[1] Even though I have maintained the premise and pointed to possible reasons for the relative lack of ethnic-led and/or queer ensembles among the mainstream of American ensemble theatres, a further act of exclusion does not productively advance the cause of broadening diversity in this significant sector of American theatre-making. While compelled by logistics once the project was underway to abide by my initial selections, I regret and apologize for not including a company like Universes, which in every sense represents the type of broad remit ensemble featured in the volumes, and whose work deserves the recognition to which scholarship can contribute. And, taking nothing away from the excellent contributions made by the scholars represented in the case studies, I regret the absence of the voices of BIPOC scholars whose perspectives would undoubtedly have enriched this study.

Still, it is my hope that these two volumes of essays will pave the way for future studies that broaden and diversify our understanding of the exciting work, past and present, that collective creation has contributed to American theatre.

ACKNOWLEDGMENTS

I thank the contributors to the two volumes in this series, whose acuity and obvious passion for the work they write about made this a most satisfying project. Mark Dudgeon, whose enthusiasm for theatre and scholarship first launched this series, has my respect and gratitude. Lara Bateman assisted at every stage of the undertaking and guided the project to its conclusion.

I gratefully acknowledge the research support provided by the University of Wisconsin-Madison Office of the Vice Chancellor for Research and Graduate Education. The Howe-Bascom Professorship, bestowed by the Integrated Liberal Studies Program at UW-Madison, allowed me to conduct necessary research in New York City.

I dedicate these volumes to the memory of my father, Norbert, and younger brother John, as well as my mother-in-law, Caroline Wolenec, whose company was taken during the completion of the project but whose memories I cherish.

To Tracy: 'til the wheels come off.

CHAPTER 1
HISTORICAL AND CULTURAL BACKGROUND
Mike Vanden Heuvel

The historical overview provided in the first volume of *American Theatre Ensembles* began with the rise and fall of President Richard Nixon following his landslide election to a second term in 1972, touching upon his strategies for dividing the electorate to consolidate political power. While certainly not the first politician of any party to pursue this strategy, Nixon vigorously set about creating the divisions that continue to most affect US politics and elections today. Most memorably, he addressed a putative "silent majority" of white, middle-class conservatives threatened by the counterculture, civil rights movement, and feminism. Moreover, he used his office to achieve these aims while engaging in unconstitutional abuses of power that would lead to his resignation in the face of certain impeachment in August 1972.

Later, the first actual modern impeachment of a sitting US president occurred during the period represented in this volume, when Bill Clinton—the Oxford-educated, antiwar, and pot-smoking (if not inhaling) antithesis to Nixon's quiescent majority—was prosecuted for perjury and obstruction of justice during his second term in 1998. Amid a strongly partisan environment that pitted the "Contract with America" hard-Right Republicans headed by Congressman Newt Gingrich against Clinton's New Democrats, the president was acquitted in the Senate trial mostly along party lines and served out the remainder of his term.

Contemporaneously, on the cusp of the third decade of the new century, impeachment proceedings were initiated against President Donald Trump (for abuse of power and obstruction) in December 2019 before his acquittal in the Senate in early 2020. Claims of bias and partisanship were freely exchanged once again, at Democrats for having failed to prove the president's actions amounted to an impeachable offense and at Republicans for voting to disallow key witnesses and testimony at the trial. The country found itself, as it had at each of these historical moments, further divided and painfully aware that the upcoming 2020 election will be more rancorous and partisan than ever. President Trump, in fact, has recycled Nixon's overture by appealing to another "silent majority" as a strategy early in his campaign.

Such recurring situations convey the widespread sense that American history straddling the twentieth and twenty-first centuries can indeed seem a period of perennial crises. Especially since the turn of the millennium, the main historical events and themes defining the American experience center around foreign and domestic terrorism, endless wars and occupations, financial meltdown, sexual violence and its consequences, gun violence on the streets and in the schools, an existential crisis concerning climate heating that somehow goes unaddressed decade after decade, and a growing fractiousness among American citizens and the consequent rise of populisms both benign and violent that threaten democratic institutions and processes. After a period of hopefulness following the fall of the Berlin Wall in 1989 and the collapse of the Soviet Union in 1991, political tensions have relocated to the Middle East, and the threat of nuclear war has not abated as weapons proliferate while autocrats in North Korea, Iran, and elsewhere conduct foreign policy over the threat of developing weapons. Domestically, an opioid drug epidemic, caused in part by large pharmaceutical companies pushing dangerous levels of prescriptions, has ravished US urban and rural communities. Even the once-exalted internet revolution, destined (it was said) to unite humanity, stands exposed today as, among other things, the most severe invasion of personal privacy in human history and a platform for sowing discord and confusion alongside selfies and cat memes.

Little wonder, then, that Julia Listengarten and Cindy Rosenthal begin their *Modern American Drama: Playwriting 2000–2009* by asking, "What else could have gone wrong in the first years of the twenty-first century?" (2018, 1). Although writing amid the Great Recession following the banking collapse of 2008, the authors were still able to find hope in that year's election of Barack Obama, the first African American president in the country's history, as well as in the growing social equality granted to some groups through progress toward marriage equality (the Supreme Court ultimately legalized same-sex matrimony in 2015) and transgender rights. Yet since then, many of the advances gained through democratic means have mainly served to unleash a series of backlashes that drive the country further toward illiberal and nondemocratic, even authoritarian, forms of leadership and a sense of hopelessness for anyone invested in progressive principles.

After the prospect of a "post-racial" America opened up following Obama's election and ensuing two terms of office, the election of Donald Trump in 2016 signaled a refutation of that (admittedly problematic) discourse and the rise of new and even grimmer racial tensions. With regard to economic policy, the Tea Party within the Republican caucus ascended soon after Obama's election, initially pushing mainly for tax cuts and reduction of the national debt. But under Trump, these and other hard-Right factions have turned to mobilize white discontent against entitlement programs—even those primarily serving the nation's poverty-stricken white citizenry—while no longer opposing the ballooning national debt. Owing to partisan gerrymandering, population shifts, and restrictions on voting, most local and state elections are decided in advance as red states become redder and blue states bluer, furthering the deep political divides that fester from coast to coast. Because social media companies like Google, Twitter, and Facebook remain unregulated, they brazenly publish and profit from targeted political advertising based on falsehoods and unproven conspiracy theories mounted by disruptive domestic fringe groups and foreign powers, such as Russia, who benefit from US political instability. Such tribalization enhances forms of voter suppression that have become almost a platform within the Republican Party since the Supreme Court decision on *Shelby County v. Holder* in 2013, which rolled back the 1964 Voting Rights Act and cleared the way for individual states to purge voter rolls, gerrymander election maps with greater impunity, limit early and absentee voting, and set up byzantine voter ID laws. The selective disenfranchisement of American voters, by any measure directed predominantly at communities of color, has become a widely accepted norm. With Americans essentially refusing to share a common reality and establish mutual ground, it is by no means an exaggeration to state that the country faces a series of existential threats in its near future that might well reshape the nation in unforeseen but perilous ways.

Even in the midst of preparing this volume, the succession of life-altering events has continued unabated. First, as described in detail below, the worldwide COVID-19 pandemic of 2020 struck the United States with deadly force, killing well over 100,000 citizens in just four months and current projections estimating at least twice that number before a vaccine can be developed. Under the pandemic and the forced closings of schools, restaurants, and offices, the US economy has suffered greater contraction and unemployment than in any period since the years of the Great Depression. Worldwide, the effects of the virus have profoundly disrupted trade and threatened the intricate ecologies of globalism. All forms of live art are endangered by the extended shutdowns of mass gatherings, and collective creation is particularly vulnerable given the fundamental need for physical proximity in order to improvise and create.

Second, a new wave of police killings of people of color in the United States, particularly the brutal slaying of George Floyd in Minneapolis, Minnesota, on May 25, 2020, set off an unprecedented surge of social unrest across the nation, with protesters demanding social justice, police reform, and a sustained national discussion regarding the value of Black lives. In the immediate aftermath of the protests, the Black Lives Matter (BLM) movement (which rose to prominence after the "Ferguson Unrest" of 2014) regained traction and small but important changes have taken place: a number of monuments celebrating racists and the Confederacy have been removed (some by force, others by legislation), corporate America has nominally joined the calls for reform, and some local governments have moved toward defunding and demilitarizing police forces. Whether these most recent calamities will produce even greater chaos and division in American culture or enable new and more equitable social and economic systems to emerge will be the great question not only for the November national elections but for the future of the republic.

Social and Political Contexts

The era began with the relatively orderly transition of power from the Republican Party (which had dominated the Oval Office between 1980 and 1992) to the Democrats under Bill Clinton. But after Clinton defeated Bush in 1992, the Democrats were beaten badly in the 1994 midterms when House conservatives under Congressman Newt Gingrich launched their "Contract with America" that united candidates behind a national platform based in Reaganesque goals for thwarting Clinton's agenda. Gingrich's pugnacious style helped establish the toxic partisanship that now dominates American politics, establishing the mantra of every reality TV politician succeeding him from both parties: "Conflict equals exposure equals power" (Ziegler 2020). Republicans won the House for the first time in forty years, making Gingrich the Speaker, and flipped the Senate. Even so, Clinton won a second term handily in the 1996 election over Senator Robert Dole but invited another setback when his sexual relationship between 1995 and 1997 with a 21-year-old White House intern, Monica Lewinsky, became public in 1998. The House impeached Clinton on charges of lying under oath and obstructing justice on December 19, 1998. At trial, the Senate acquitted the president on both charges.

Clinton's two terms, despite the partisan roiling and failures on many fronts to steer the country back toward the center from the Right-leaning conservatism of the Reagan and Bush terms, are often evoked nostalgically as a period of relative civility and incremental progress on economic and social issues. The period saw the recovery from the "Black Monday" market crash of 1987, when world markets plummeted and the Dow Jones Industrial Average lost a record 22.6 percent of its value, causing the ensuing recession of 1990–1991. President Bush's inability to find a quick fix for a faltering economy provided Clinton with the needed focal point on which to run his successful campaign. Once Clinton assumed office, signs of recovery were almost immediate, fueled in large part by the new dotcom market which, after the introduction of functional HTTP-based internet browsers in the early 1990s and the first true smartphones, exploded across virtually all sectors of the economy. By 1996, new telecommunications legislation was passed that opened up investment opportunities, and venture capital angels rushed in to fund hundreds of start-ups. Clinton's well-timed Taxpayer Relief Act (1997) combined with historically low-interest rates to invite middle-class speculation in "e-commerce" as well. Microsoft introduced Windows 95 and quickly cornered the operating system market, while Google began indexing the now-centerless World Wide Web in 1996. Many fly-by-night companies made an initial splash and were quickly overvalued. Returns on these investments were unrealistically robust (even hapless Yahoo's IPO set NASDAQ records), and valuations quickly exceeded rational appraisals. Most notoriously, the internet provider America Online (AOL) was able to purchase the Time-Warner Corporation (the most extensive media conglomerate in the world at the time) in 2000 because its valuation was so high ($47.23 per share). By the time the sale was completed, the dotcom bubble burst and AOL shares dropped to $9.64. The sale consequently went down as one of the worst mergers in corporate history.

Nevertheless, the economy steadily grew into the late 1990s, so Clinton is remembered today as the last president to oversee a budget surplus (of 2.3 percent) upon leaving office after the federal deficit had grown to 5 percent of GNP by the late 1980s (it returned to that level in 2019 and, following stimulus funding occasioned by the COVID crisis, will likely double by the next fiscal year). Despite failing to pass national health care legislation in its first term, the Clinton administration still brought the matter to public and Congressional attention and laid the foundation for the Affordable Care Act (or "Obamacare") in 2010. Yet Clinton grudgingly signed the Defense of Marriage Act (DOMA) in 1996 and compromised on a policy ("Don't Ask,

Don't Tell") that restricted gays from openly identifying in the military while allowing them to serve. And, owing to his generally neoliberal advocacy of open international markets and the continued deregulation of the financial industry, the Clinton economy did little to staunch the growing income equality that had begun in the 1970s and accelerated under Reagan, and in some ways widened the gap. Clinton signed the repeal of the Glass-Steagall Act, which had governed banking practices since 1933, thus allowing some investment and retail banks to consolidate and be overseen by the Federal Reserve. These would eventually become the institutions deemed "too big to fail" during the 2006–2008 economic crisis and thereafter on the receiving end of massive government bailouts.

Concerning domestic and international politics of the late 1990s, war and terrorism dominate the record. Despite the euphoria of the Berlin Wall coming down and the eventual collapse of the Soviet Union by 1991, conflicts overseas mounted during the following decade. In response to the US invasion of Kuwait against Iraqi occupation under Bush in 1991, the United States suffered the loss of military lives and international prestige over skirmishes in Somalia and terrorist bombings in Saudi Arabia, Iraq, and elsewhere. Many of these were sponsored by the newly formed al-Qaeda jihadist group (which had bombed the World Trade Center in 1993). Although NATO-based airpower eventually intervened in the decade-long Yugoslav Wars (1991–2001), the intercession came only in 1995 after a series of ethnic genocides and rampant war crimes had become public. Matters were not significantly calmer at home: perhaps emboldened by Timothy McVeigh's 1995 destruction of the Murrah Federal Building in Oklahoma City, domestic terrorists bombed the Olympic Village in Atlanta during the 1996 Summer Games, as well as abortion clinics and gay and lesbian nightspots.

Most troubling was the school shooting at Columbine High School in Colorado in April 1999, when two heavily armed students murdered twelve classmates before committing suicide. Mass shootings at schools were not unprecedented before Columbine—witness the University of Texas shooting in 1966, which claimed eighteen lives—but usually these were perpetrated by disturbed individuals with little connection to the school. While such seemingly random mass murders committed at schools would continue to take a horrific toll into the twenty-first century, Columbine marked the beginning of a disturbing outbreak of students taking on the role of active shooters. Along with the body count, each event brings with it difficult questions regarding gun ownership, mental health, school bullying, and a host of additional social ills.

Despite the buoyant economy, Clinton stepped down at a volatile moment in American history, and the election of his successor was a harbinger of events to come. The 2000 presidential race pitting Clinton's vice president, Al Gore, against George W. Bush, governor of Texas and the eldest son of former president George H. W. Bush, was notable not only for the razor-thin margin by which Bush won (537 votes in the bellwether state of Florida decided the vote in the Electoral College) but also for the fact that for the first time since 1888 a president was elected after losing the popular vote. The unprecedented intervention of the Supreme Court to adjudicate the decision whether to continue recounting ballots in Florida seemed to confirm for many that even the highest court in the land had become explicitly partisan.

President Bush's first year in office focused on a massive tax cut program and the Republican education reform program No Child Left Behind, which accelerated school privatization. In Spring 2001, the Enron scandal broke, involving a major energy corporation (ranked as "America's Most Innovative Company" by *Fortune* for six straight years beginning in 1995) engaged in high-risk trades that started to falter in 2000. However, propped up by byzantine and illegal accounting practices (conducted by the top-five firm of Arthur Andersen), their stock value reached a peak of $90.75. But after losses began to mount, analysts demoted the company's investment ratings. By October, employees of Arthur Andersen were shredding files, and the SEC began investigations. Enron's stock closed the year at $0.26 and soon filed for bankruptcy while the Andersen firm surrendered, temporarily, its CPA license. What might have been a warning for similar practices by investment banks leading up the 2007–2008 subprime mortgage crash was dismissed as an aberration rather than systemic corporate accounting practice.

Before President Bush could establish a legislative agenda, however, the United States was attacked on September 11, 2001 (hereafter, 9/11), by factions of al-Qaeda, who succeeded in skyjacking four domestic flights and sending two planes into the World Trade Center, or Twin Towers, in lower Manhattan. Another plane was piloted into the Pentagon in Washington, DC, and the last went down in an empty field in Pennsylvania after passengers attempted to stop the terrorists from returning to Washington. With a worldwide television audience following events in real time, the Twin Towers collapsed, killing thousands of civilians and first responders. Hundreds more died in the attack on the Pentagon and the failed suicide mission in Pennsylvania. The death toll reached nearly 3000, and tens of thousands of survivors have been treated for PTSD and a variety of health-related issues caused by the attack.

While generally admired for his initial decisiveness in responding to the deadliest terrorist attack in history and the most significant loss of life on American soil since the Civil War, Bush's formulation of a "War on Terror" and passage of his Patriot Act have haunted American domestic and foreign policy ever since, given their focus on a tactic rather than a specific nation or military force. He ordered the invasion of Afghanistan in 2001, which successfully toppled the Taliban regime providing cover for al-Qaeda. Using authorization passed by Congress in 2002 to use military force against Iraq if he deemed it necessary, Bush ordered an attack in March 2003 based on faulty evidence that Saddam Hussein was producing weapons of mass destruction. Joined by the UK and a small coalition of allies, US troops quickly defeated the Iraqi Army and deposed the ruling Ba'ath Party and Hussein. Infamously, on May 1, Bush visited a returning aircraft carrier wearing a flight suit, and although he cautioned that dangerous work remained to be done in Iraq, a banner declaring "Mission Accomplished" appeared behind him during the speech. Bush was then heavily criticized when civil unrest and a counterinsurgency erupted in Iraq. The American invasion of Afghanistan has since grown into America's most prolonged military occupation, and neither war prevented the rise of the Islamic State of Iraq and Syria (ISIS), the imagined caliphate proposed by Sunni jihadists inspired by al-Qaeda, from being proclaimed between 2014 and 2018.

The cabinet-level Department of Homeland Security created by Bush following 9/11 has now grown to be the third-largest department in the federal government, with a 2018 budget of just under fifty billion dollars. Despite some success in calming the original fears of the populace following 9/11, the agency regularly draws criticism for its labor practices (having stripped 180,000 federal workers of their union rights at its inception), government waste and inefficiency, its record on cybersecurity protection following foreign meddling in the 2016 elections, its surveillance practices over foreign journalists and US citizens via data mining, and most recently for the practices (such as separating children from parents) associated with border security and immigration and customs enforcement (ICE). The recent weaponizing of Homeland Security for immigration control under President Trump is currently one of the most divisive issues in American society.

Nevertheless, Bush turned back the challenge by Democratic Senator John Kerry to earn a second term in 2004, winning a simple majority of the popular vote (the first time for any president since 1988 and the last Republican to win the popular vote). Kerry waged a tepid and wavering campaign and saw his reputation unfairly tarnished by being "swift-boated" by a Republican political action group that fabricated narratives that undermined his status as a Vietnam War veteran and Purple Heart honoree. Such activities by PACs were later fueled by the 2010 Supreme Court decision in *Citizen's United v. Federal Election Commission*, which effectively upheld the rights of corporations and unions (as citizens) to donate with little oversight to political parties and causes. The ruling opened the doors to a massive influx of corporate money to support "super-PACs" that, because they are ostensibly not affiliated with either major party, can promote more strident messages. In 2010 when the decision was read, corporate political donations totaled just over $200 million: in 2016, the figure had risen to just under $1.5 billion, with the highest share supporting action committees committed to conservative and libertarian candidates and causes. That level of spending is expected to rise to $6 billion for the 2020 elections.

Throughout his second term, Bush pursued traditional Republican initiatives (he attempted but failed to privatize social security and signed several international trade agreements) and focused, unsuccessfully, on ending US involvement in Iraq. In April 2004, CBS News revealed photos of Americans torturing and demeaning Iraqi prisoners of war in violation of human rights accords. Despite claims that these acts constituted aberrant behavior, further abuses at prisons housing al-Qaeda suspects at Guantanamo Bay (Cuba) and in Afghanistan placed the US military and the president on the defensive. Although the United States was eventually successful in capturing Saddam Hussein and turning him over for trial and execution by the new permanent Iraqi government in 2006, the insurgency continued and in 2007 Bush approved a US troop increase. American forces remained in Iraq until 2011. On the domestic front, Hurricane Katrina struck Florida and Louisiana in August 2005, devastating the cities of Gulfport, Mississippi, and New Orleans and eventually claiming more than 1800 lives and causing more than $126 billion in damages. Failures at every level of government to adequately prepare for and address the consequences of the tragedy reflected poorly on Bush and his cabinet. Bush's support declined steadily after, with the Democrats taking the House and Senate in the 2006 midterms (eventually making Congresswoman Nancy Pelosi the first female Speaker of the House).

Concerning the economy, the single most consequential development was the subprime mortgage collapse that began in 2006 and started making headlines in early 2008. After more than a decade of descending prime interest rates and inflated home valuations, lenders began offering exotic mortgage contracts to people whose credit history precluded them from obtaining prime rate loans. These were initially marketed disproportionately to people of color and others long frozen out of prime lending opportunities. These "subprime" mortgages were then bundled and sold to investment banks that profited from these risky derivatives while rates stayed low and home values continued to skyrocket. The repeal of the Steagall-Glass Banking Act under Clinton had removed one of the few firewalls to such activity. But the bubble began to deflate as early as 2006 despite warnings from Warren Buffet regarding derivatives in 2003 and red flags from the International Monetary Fund in 2005. When home values fell up to 11 percent in 2006, this triggered higher interest rates for homeowners that resulted in massive defaults, rendering, in turn, the mortgage-backed securities almost worthless. Banks lost confidence (in part because they were aware that rating agencies had been downplaying their risk posture for many years) and stopped lending to Americans now swallowed up in debt (the ratio of household debt reached 127 percent entering 2008). By 2008, the entire world financial system bordered on collapse. The venerable investment banks Bear Stearns and then Lehman Brothers folded, sending shock waves through the financial sector even as other firms were scooped up in hasty mergers, and government lending agencies like Fannie Mae had to be federalized.

Bush initiated the Troubled Asset Relief Program (TARP) late in 2008 to buy up toxic assets from failing banks by increasing the money supply, but the Great Recession had settled in and would straddle the next election cycle. More than 6 percent of the US workforce would be laid off between 2008 and 2009, while the housing market's value declined by 30 percent and the stock market by 50 percent. The recovery would last four years and cripple the world economy, as well as causing the US federal deficit to climb back to historic heights. Eventually, the global banking collapse contributed to the sovereign debt crisis across the European Union, as governments could no longer secure loans to cover rising interest payments. By 2009, Greece, Spain, Cyprus, Portugal, and Ireland all needed massive EU bailouts to stabilize the euro. A wave of austerity measures, often set by the IMF, followed and even nations that had not felt severe economic decline (such as the UK) began cutting back social services in order, some would say, to balance budgets and maintain strong credit ratings. Others perceived an ideologically motivated justification to implement neoliberal economic and cultural policies.

The economic shock coincided with the 2008 elections, which because it featured no incumbent (for the first time in fifty years) and occurred just as the housing collapse came into view, favored Democrats. Surprisingly, Illinois senator Barack Obama was able to overcome the presumptive favorite, Hillary Clinton, who, after leaving her role as First Lady, had been elected Senator for New York. Obama's 2004 keynote address at the Democratic convention nominating Kerry had been well received and presented him as a unifier who could bridge the racial divide. His canny campaign was the first to solicit online donations from all parts of the electorate, further establishing his grassroots image. Obama was also able to tap into growing American dissent against the wars in the Middle East, as he (unlike Clinton) had voted against the 2002 motion handing war powers to President Bush to move against Iraq. He astutely selected Senator Joe Biden as his running mate to offset his youthfulness and lack of international experience. Dogged by internet-fueled conspiracy theories that questioned whether the Hawaiian-born Obama was a natural-born American citizen (many such "birther" theories were funded and repeated by the New York real estate tycoon Donald Trump, who would succeed him as president), Obama nevertheless energized the Black vote and captivated young voters with a series of stirring public speeches that directly addressed issues of race and the economy.

The Republican nominee, the conservative and Vietnam War hero Senator John McCain of Arizona, had supported the war against Iraq and later troop surge. As well, to assuage social conservatives while also confirming his "maverick" status, he selected as his running mate the relatively unknown Alaska governor, Sarah Palin. The choice likely hurt McCain in the election; Palin performed poorly on the campaign trail by presenting herself as singularly unprepared to assume the powers of the presidency and thereby distracted from Obama's lack of experience. She was mercilessly mocked in the media, particularly on the long-running variety show *Saturday Night Live!* But Palin's nomination also opened the door for a robust populist faction to arise within the Republican Party during and following the election. She remained in the public eye as a media pundit for the next decade.

Obama easily defeated McCain, winning 53 percent of the popular vote and tallying the highest number of votes (69.5 million) ever cast for a presidential candidate to become the first African American elected. While his campaign often felt like a social movement directed toward substantial change, Obama's first term was decidedly cautious in most regards. In response to the ongoing economic crisis, he extended Bush's TARP plan and committed to the federal bailout of banks considered "too big to fail," eventually overseeing a long period of quantitative easing to increase the money supply artificially. While addressing America's racial problems more passionately and articulately than anyone since Martin Luther King, many in the Black community felt he accomplished little of substance in alleviating racism and white privilege. This indicated that a post-racial America was a national fantasy, as when Obama took even tentative steps to address the country's racial scars (such as commenting on the Trayvon Martin murder, detailed below) and many whites who had voted for him reacted with outrage.

Yet, in his first term, Obama achieved a long-standing Democratic goal with the passage of the Affordable Care Act, which provided basic medical coverage to millions of uninsured Americans by extending Medicaid eligibility, creating health insurance exchanges, and preventing denial of coverage based on preexisting conditions. A signal reform in US political history, it nevertheless became a rallying cry for Republican opposition that regenerated the Tea Party faction of the party and deeply divided the electorate. Obama also successfully repealed Clinton's "Don't Ask, Don't Tell" policy, allowing openly gay, lesbian, and trans people to serve in the military (President Trump has since used an executive order to bar transgender troops). The president also publicly supported the landmark Supreme Court decision in *Obergefell v. Hodges* that sanctioned gay marriage.

Despite the cataclysmic effects of the 2008 downturn, it was a period of rapid technological progress. Advances in computing speed propelled the Human Genome Project to complete the sequencing of human DNA in 2003. The dotcom bubble had burst, but real innovation took off over the next decade as Web 2.0 technology with its greater online interactivity arrived. BlackBerry had introduced the first functional mobile phone with texting in the early 2000s (it was still popular enough that President Obama fought to retain his after the 2008 election, thus becoming the first texting president), but that market took off when the iOS and Android smartphones hit the market: the iPhone arrived in 2007 and the Samsung G1 in 2008. Soon, iOS and Android systems were battling for market share in the booming smartphone industry, and providers like Sprint, Verizon, and AT&T drove competition to create new and better generations of cellular service in rapid succession (5G appeared in 2020). The iPod had been on the market since

2001, and the iPad first appeared in 2010. Web 2.0 technology was refined by 2002 and introduced blogs and podcasts, opening up new and powerful platforms for free speech and civic engagement while also ushering in the era of a weakened civic press, internet trolls, and behemoth corporations like Facebook and Google that resist regulation: Facebook went live in 2004, YouTube appeared in 2005, with Twitter following in 2006, and Instagram in 2010. Online shopping took off, with Amazon opening its virtual doors in 1995 and growing exponentially into one of the most powerful companies on the planet while making its founder, Jeff Bezos, the world's wealthiest individual. Video gaming on multiplayer platforms reached new heights with the arrival of PlayStation in 2000 and Xbox 360 in 2005. All these developments would combine to create the foundation for the transmedial, multi-platform, and thoroughly virtual social media universe that the globe now inhabits (or vice versa: estimates report that in America people now spend an average of 153 minutes per day on social networks alone, putting it behind only sleeping and watching TV).

After eight years of a centrist governing with unusual civility and articulateness under Obama, very few anticipated that the 2016 election would be momentous. The Republicans began with sixteen candidates, most of them handpicked by the party or affiliated donors and organizations and running the gamut from moderate to ultra-conservative. The Democrats, on the other hand, seemed to have a natural successor in Hillary Clinton, the former First Lady, Senator from New York, and Secretary of State under Obama. She confronted a strong challenge from the Independent Senator from Vermont, Bernie Sanders, who ran on a progressive and traditionally liberal platform that now seemed radical. Clinton unethically but expertly maneuvered the machinery of the Democratic primaries in her favor and eventually defeated Sanders for the nomination. On the Republican side, however, the populist candidacy of Donald Trump, the New York City real estate magnate and former television host, accelerated in ways few had foreseen. After announcing his candidacy late and using it to attack current immigration policies in overtly racist language, Trump went on to dominate his Republican opponents in the debates through a strategy of name-calling and mockery. He easily defeated them for the nomination and then commenced on one of the most unconventional campaigns in modern politics, holding raucous "MAGA" (Make American Great Again, the slogan Reagan had invented) rallies in which he continued to attack communities of color, the media, and especially Obama and Clinton (shouts of "lock her up!" became the signature event at these events). He survived the release of a scandalous audiotape on which he exulted in serially assaulting women, as well as the revelations from a former porn star that he had paid her hush money to keep silent regarding a sexual encounter while he was married. In debates, he often misstated facts, revealed a lack of experience and understanding of the essential functions of government, and seemed utterly careless of international relations. Rejecting both liberal and conservative labels and policies, Trump promised as a populist to return the United States to relative international isolation, to void international trade agreements such as NAFTA, and to "put America first" in every instance. Led by his campaign manager, Steve Bannon (a figure with deep connections to "alt-right" news and internet outlets such as Breitbart), Trump cobbled together an incoherent platform based in a reactionary populist nationalism and his own capricious predilections. Using a combination of brashness and appeals to white voters who perceived themselves disenfranchised by a long line of liberal elites, Trump established a base consisting of 38 to 42 percent of the electorate who remained loyal despite the massive negative press he received from both the Left and Right and who agreed that the media (except for Roger Ailes's conservative FOX News Network and alt-right outlets) were spawning "fake news" to a gullible electorate needing to be shaken out of its delusions.

Throughout the campaign against Clinton, almost all polls and commentators predicted a Democratic landslide; however, she made many tactical mistakes and never presented herself as more than an extension of the center-right beliefs and policies that Bill Clinton and then Obama had upheld. In one of the most shocking upsets in US political history, Trump dominated the electoral vote, although he lost the popular vote by almost three million ballots (which he immediately ascribed to voter fraud). He turned many white, male Obama voters to his ticket to carry 52 percent of that demographic and managed to temper Clinton's support among women by making inroads across class categories. Even though Clinton took the female vote by a 54–39 percent margin, white women predominantly went with Trump by 47–45, and only female voters of color going overwhelmingly for Clinton kept her from losing the gender demographic. Another sign of the increasing divide among American voters was revealed when college graduates voted 57–36 for Clinton while the noncollege votes were 50–43 for Trump. But unsurprisingly, the racial divide in the electorate was most telling: Trump received just 6 percent of the Black vote (his support from Black women did not even register in the final numbers) and 28 percent of the Hispanic, but, importantly, was able to depress turnout.

While his divisive rhetoric and eccentric leadership style mark Trump as unique, his election took place within a global context of a rising illiberal populism and discontent at the reigning liberal and social-democratic political hegemonies. The Brexit situation in the UK and the rise of Right-wing parties and authoritarian leaders across the EU, along with populist strongmen such as Jair Bolsonaro in Brazil and Rodrigo Duterte in the Philippines, were all exacerbated by the large numbers of immigrants fleeing violence and poverty in the Middle East and North Africa and seeking asylum in the West. Anti-immigration parties arose in Latin America and Asia as well, and Trump yoked himself to these groups. Collectively, these events exposed the core of such global developments as a growing nationalism, often based on racial differences and economic anxieties.

Since his inauguration in 2017, President Trump has been successful in making over the Republican Party in his image, despite being denounced at one time or another by the previous three Republican presidential candidates (Bush, John McCain, and Mitt Romney). On international relations, Trump has met with and expressed admiration for several former "bad actors," foreign autocrats formerly considered toxic by both US parties such as Kim Jong Un of North Korea and, preeminently, Vladimir Putin of Russia (despite overwhelming evidence that Russian meddled in the 2016 election to Trump's advantage). In terms of economic policies, while the first two years of his presidency seemed to conform to the Republican and neoliberal playbook (with his 2017 tax bill that reduced corporate rates while the administration pursued policies cutting back on social services), he has since dictated policy from a position of economic populism that has kept both majority parties off balance. Former conservative budget hawks remained silent as the tax cuts and additional spending sent the federal deficit soaring to record heights even before the COVID crisis. After the Democrats captured the House in the 2018 elections, Trump voided both the North American Free Trade Agreement and the Trans-Pacific Partnership, which elements of the Left had been demanding for years. Against traditional Republican tendencies and in violation of foundational neoliberal beliefs, he initiated a protracted trade war with China and campaigned against cuts to social security and Medicare (with reelection on the horizon, he has signaled his willingness to consider cuts to entitlement programs). At the same time, he has worked to undo his predecessor's signature health care policies, cut many entitlement programs that directly affect the working poor, and stacked the federal judiciary and Supreme Court with judges whose views on reproductive rights, religious liberty, and gay marriage and trans rights, among a host of other issues, guarantee that freedoms and rights gained since the 1990s will continue to face critical challenges.

Like any populist, Trump cuts across traditional Left-Right cleavages, and in the United States this has solidified a base of disenchanted voters whose approval ratings for both parties and most civic and political institutions more generally, especially Congress, are at an all-time low (24 percent for the latter in 2019). His poll numbers (never high) have remained unshakable even during impeachment, and many party leaders who have run for reelection against his platform have been soundly defeated when his base rises in sufficient numbers. Meanwhile, evangelicals have flocked to Trump in great numbers despite his casual history with religious faith and his three marriages, drawn to his regular appeals to a cultural nationalism that speaks, directly and indirectly, to issues of race and entitlements as the most significant problem in the country. Some evangelicals refer to him as "a modern-day Cyrus," evoking the sinner who was nevertheless anointed by God to free the Jews from captivity.

Notoriously, even after white supremacists staged a violent "Unite the Right" rally in Charlottesville, South Carolina, in late 2017 that resulted in the murder of a counter-demonstrator, Trump commented publicly that there were "fine people on both sides," leading many to perceive an overt racism in his views (which he has denied). Nevertheless, his presidency was already marked by a spike in racial tensions not seen in the United States since the late 1960s before these exploded anew in 2020. Similarly, his selection of deeply conservative judges for federal courts and the Supreme Court has also angered many women, although he continues to be supported by female Republicans, older white females, and many non-college-educated women.

The Trump presidency has more deeply divided the country than perhaps any time since the Civil War. Indeed, the day after his inauguration, more than three million women marched in protest around the country, the single most massive one-day mass demonstration in the nation's history. The impetus achieved by the marches played a significant role in the reawakening of the #MeToo movement after it was revealed later in 2017 that the Hollywood mogul Harvey Weinstein had engaged in serial sexual abuse of female actors. The hashtag had originally appeared on MySpace in 2006 to bring notice to the pervasiveness of sexual assault. Now transferred to Twitter in 2017, #MeToo went viral, and in the following months, several prominent artists, sports figures, and businesspeople were accused of sexual aggression. Weinstein himself was convicted of sexual assault in 2020. In the era of partisan divisiveness, however, the movement also became a lightning rod among conservatives as an example (like BLM) of the overreach of a liberal political correctness that Trump would stamp out with his authenticity and directness.

Meanwhile, hate-crime violence reached a 16-year high in 2018, and to many, the decade seemed poised to end with traditional democratic values and institutions under attack. Whereas the 2010s began with Lin-Manuel Miranda's stunningly hopeful musical *Hamilton* (2010), as the decade wore on popular culture turned to expressing troubled anxieties:

> Dystopian fables and horror-driven films and television series— including *Black Mirror* (2016) ... *Joker* (2019), *Get Out* (2017), *Watchmen* (2019), *The Handmaid's Tale* (2017) and *Westworld* (2016)—spoke to the darkening mood in the second half of the decade, as drug overdose deaths in America rose to nearly half a million by the decade's end, life expectancy fell in the United States and Britain, and many of us started to realize that our data (tracing everything we viewed, bought and searched for online) was being sold and commodified, and that algorithms were shaping our lives in untold ways.
>
> (Kakutani 2019)

Supporters of the president maintain that he is a populist addressing their concerns and a badly needed outsider to Washington, whose ability to shake up business as usual in the Capitol reveals how deeply entrenched the ruling elites were. In extreme versions, the conspiracy of a "Deep State" that involves all US intelligence agencies is sometimes cited as a threat to his presidency. Polls show that Republicans rank him a better president than Lincoln, and many refer to him (as does the president himself on occasion) as "the chosen one." His attacks on the media have been relentless, and he often refers to them publicly as "the enemy of the people," even as those same media tracked more than 15,000 public misstatements and outright fabrications during his first three years in office. His travel bans specify ethnic and religious groups (mainly Muslims), and his policies at the Mexico-US border include demands for a border wall and the detainment of families seeking asylum that involve separating children from parents. Meanwhile, Trump's peculiar fixation with engaging in relentless Twitter feuds with celebrities, his cozy relationship with, and call-ins to, the FOX punditry shows he watches endlessly, and his language tics, gaffes, and general inarticulateness generate a 24/7 news cycle with the president firmly at the center.

After rumors began circulating that Russia had interfered with US elections in 2016, Congress launched an investigation that included inquiries into whether the Trump campaign had colluded with election meddling. After almost two years, the Mueller investigation closed and verified that interference had taken place and that Trump could neither be exonerated nor (as president) charged with an offense. Then, in the lead-up to the primaries for the 2020 election, whereas Trump would face no serious challenges, in typically aggressive style he attacked some potential Democratic candidates. He seemed particularly concerned by the threat of former Obama Vice President Joe Biden (then the presumptive nominee), and in 2019 launched a series of efforts to discredit him by linking one of his children to corruption with the government of Ukraine. After one phone call in which the president appeared to demand a quid pro quo, trading Congressionally approved defense funding in exchange for political dirt on the Biden family, Trump was investigated by the Democrat-controlled House. Two articles of impeachment were brought forward for abuse of power and obstruction of Congress (because his administration did not allow former Cabinet members and other appointees to testify), and on December 18, Trump became the third sitting president to be impeached. Even before the mandatory trial in the Senate, the majority Republicans had promised a full acquittal (going so far as to report publicly that they would coordinate his defense with the White House, in violation of due process).

Upon acquittal on February 5, 2020, pollsters gave President Trump a better-than 50 percent chance for reelection; if so, he would be the first impeached president to retain office in US history. However, Trump's fumbled handling of the COVID-19 pandemic as well as his "law and order" response to the racial unrest spurred by police murders of Black citizens (see below) have somewhat undermined his poll numbers, and by June he was trailing the now-confirmed Democratic challenger, Joe Biden. As further evidence of the parlous state of national politics, commentators are asking openly whether Trump would even accept the results of an election sure to be affected by the ongoing pandemic and social unrest.

Social Issues: Gun Violence

Mass murders have rocked the United States in increasing numbers in the twenty-first century: indeed, they have become so commonplace that a sense of futility has poisoned efforts to address the problem. In 2019, for instance, there was an active shooter alert, on average, every two weeks. Most never attain the notoriety of the "high yield" shootings, but even these typically now excite merely a moment's outrage, a good deal of mourning in the affected communities, and political inaction by members of both parties but particularly the NRA-funded Republicans led by Senate Majority Leader Mitch McConnell. (America now has more guns than people, owns 40 percent of the world's firearms, and keeps 100 times more guns than its military forces.) Sadly, in the wake of these tragedies, internet trolls and conspiracy theorists compound the agony of survivors by spreading rumors that they were staged by hired "crisis actors."

Meanwhile, the toll continues to rise: in 2007, a mass shooting occurred at Virginia Tech University in Blacksburg, where the shooter took thirty-two lives before killing himself. In 2016, the gay Pulse nightclub in Orlando was attacked by a jihadist who killed forty-nine before being killed by police. The deadliest single shooting in US history took place in 2017 when a man equipped with dozens of semiautomatic weapons (legally purchased) opened fire from a Las Vegas hotel room at a crowd of concertgoers, killing fifty-eight (and himself) and wounding an astounding 422.

Perhaps the most stunning mass murder occurred in 2012 at the Sandy Hook Elementary School in tiny Newtown, Connecticut, when a disturbed man gunned down twenty-seven children and adults before killing himself. Many of the shootings seem randomly motivated, such as the student shooting at Stoneman Douglas High School in Parkland, Florida (seventeen dead), and the Sutherland Springs Church in Texas that claimed twenty-six lives. Yet, hate crimes have added to the toll: these include the Charleston Church shooting of 2015 that murdered nine Black worshippers (including State Senator Clementa Pinckney) and a 2019 mass shooting at a Wal-Mart in El Paso, Texas, in which Latinos were targeted and twenty-two were killed.

The second symptom of the nation's inability to address the roots of gun violence has manifested in the increasing number of killings of BIPOC people by police. Whereas in previous decades such homicides were treated as individual events with unique causation, activists in the African American community have made the case that the shootings are part of a systemic racism spread across all sectors of American culture. They posit that such state violence should be understood in conjunction with the ongoing mass incarceration of people of color (heightened by the 1994 crime bill and fueled by the privatization of the prison industry into a for-profit enterprise) and widespread racial profiling exacerbated by "stop-and-frisk" policies introduced into urban police methods, particularly in New York City, in the early years of the twenty-first century which dramatically targeted Black and Latino youth. Several high-profile cases of police brutality (such as the Abner Louima case in New York City in 1997) and deadly police shootings of unarmed Black men received moderate media attention. Still, when in 2012 a neighborhood watch captain in a gated community in Sanford, Florida, shot and killed seventeen-year-old Trayvon Martin, who was unarmed, national media responded. During the lead-up to the trial, the liberal petition website Change.org received more than 13 million signatures demanding that the shooter be charged, and President Obama weighed in by saying that "if I had a son he would look like Trayvon." Following local and federal investigations, the gunman was tried for second-degree murder but acquitted. The activist group #Black Lives Matter formed after the acquittal and almost immediately became a lightning rod for new racial tensions in the United States.

Their influence grew immensely when the issue of police shootings culminated in Ferguson, Missouri, in August 2014. There, during a scuffle, a policeman shot and killed Michael Brown, an unarmed eighteen-year-old, firing twelve times. The killing was followed by mass protests in Ferguson and other communities, some organized by BLM, that sometimes turned violent over the months of investigations that ensued. State police stocked up on military equipment, and the image of armored vehicles (many purchased by federal funds tied to the Bush Patriot Act) rolling through the streets created painful associations with the worst moments of the civil rights movement from almost fifty years earlier. The police officer never faced trial, but in 2015, the Department of Justice released a report critical of the Ferguson Police Department, citing patterns of racial profiling and civil rights violations of Black citizens.

The Environment

Following the disputed 2000 election, former Vice President Al Gore became involved with the environmental movement and began sharing a PowerPoint on the subject of impending climate change (then called global warming) during a lecture tour that eventually extended to over a thousand venues. Ultimately it became a documentary film and a book in 2006. Amassing both anecdotal information and somewhat incongruent scientific data, Gore's homely PowerPoint formed the core of the film, which went on to win an Academy Award for Best Documentary and a Grammy as a spoken word performance, becoming one of the highest-grossing documentaries in US history. The former vice president, along with the UN Intergovernmental Panel on Climate Change, was awarded the Nobel Peace Prize in 2007. The ripple effect of these public statements reenergized the environmental movement and brought a new urgency to the consequences of global carbon-based economies.

The first president to address climate change was the Republican George H. W. Bush in 1988, who termed it a bipartisan problem that required collaboration to solve. The harmful effects of carbon dioxide and greenhouse gases were known since the 1960s, and documents made public through the Freedom of Information Act show that energy companies were aware of the harmful consequences of fossil fuels since at least the 1970s and then cut funding for research in the 1980s. By the late 1980s, Exxon Corporation was funding front organizations like the Global Climate Coalition to spread doubt and lobby for their corporate interests, and their efforts were successful to the extent that by the mid-1990s, the divide between pro-business Republicans and pro-environmentalism Democrats had already begun to widen. President Clinton kept the issue front and center by signing the Kyoto Protocol in 1997, although by the time it evolved to a specific action plan, George H. Bush (a former oilman) was in the White House and declined to attend the Buenos Aires Convention.

This left the United States and China as the only major powers not to sign off on the treaty. Bush and Gore debated climate change during the 2000 election, by which point it had become a strictly partisan issue: it may have cost Gore the dependably Democratic state of West Virginia, which would have given him the presidency. Bush, himself, faced a stern test when Hurricane Katrina was linked to global warming. When Obama took office in 2008, he signed on with the Paris Accord that obliged signees to cut emissions sufficient to keep the increase in warming below 1.5 degrees Celsius. Without signs of real progress toward that goal, and with climate deniers entrenched in all the key Cabinet posts, President Trump officially took the United States out of the Paris agreements in 2019. Although corporate America has recently presented itself as increasingly "green," sometimes contesting the president's policies, to this date and with temperature thresholds almost certain to be passed in the next five years, the United States and most of the world lack any coherent energy policy that involves mitigating or addressing climate heating. Meanwhile, weaker consensus-driven organizations with no mandate to effect change continue to grapple with ever more vehement denials that the science is absolute despite overwhelming data-backed evidence. Today more than 90 percent of research that disputes the science of climate heating is produced through conservative-funded think tanks in the United States and then spread across the world by conservative media moguls like Rupert Murdoch, aided by online "bots" that crank out misinformation to RSS and social media feeds.

Crises of 2020

The most recent decade began calamitously when the COVID-19 pandemic struck the United States in January; and, even while the country struggled with stay-at-home orders and restrictions on social interactions, a series of ongoing encounters between police and citizens of color resulted in physical abuse, emotional trauma, and even death. The callous murder of George Floyd by a Minneapolis police officer in May, who kneeled on his neck for almost nine minutes while bystanders pleaded with him and other policemen to intervene, was caught on tape and set off a wave of revulsion across the country. Both events have substantially impacted the US theatre ecology in general and ensemble creation more particularly.

The pandemic caused by the novel coronavirus, believed to have originated in China, spread quickly across globally interconnected nations with frightening speed and intensity. Italy saw the first major surge by February, and soon the national health care system was overrun by cases that would eventually surpass 240,000 by June, including almost 35,000 deaths. Europe's situation varied tremendously, with Spain and the UK suffering high incidence rates and mortalities, while countries like Germany had greater success limiting the spread. Iran was quickly compromised, although mortality figures were not made public. By late February the virus was spreading across the United States, but in part owing to slow and incoherent planning and lack of national political leadership, a state of emergency was not proclaimed until mid-March. Within a week of the declaration, the United States had more confirmed cases than any nation in the world.

Shortages in personal protection equipment, intensive care beds with ventilators, and, most crucially, adequate testing revealed widespread lack of pandemic planning. It was soon revealed that, upon assuming office in 2017, President Trump had disbanded the federal pandemic response unit and rejected existing policies and procedures laid out by previous administrations. His actions lurched from proclamations of absolute authority to direct responses to the crisis to federalist arguments that state governors and legislatures bore responsibility to acquire medical supplies and enact stay-at-home orders (which he then sometimes sought to undermine by supporting local antigovernment protests against mandatory social restrictions). The president and White House officials, with an eye toward the November election, made a point of appearing in public without masks and often violating social distancing guidelines in order to boost faith that the disease was manageable and that the country could soon return to normal. By May, debates were raging as to whether more harm was being done by maintaining the pandemic response than by reopening the stalled economy. Lacking a strong federal response, individual states enacted their own widely varied procedures for relaxing business closures, public gatherings, and prophylactic measures (such as mask-wearing). Some initially appeared to have weathered and contained the initial spread of the disease, but troubling surges of cases in other states, particularly those with weak responses, have created fears of continued restrictions and even a second wave of infections later in 2020.

As a sign of the present state of national will and cohesion, the pandemic quickly became politicized: citizens following protocols devised by scientists and the Center for Disease Control (CDC), such as wearing masks in public and observing social distancing, were soon interpreted as expressing anti-Trump sentiments. By mid-April, anti-lockdown protests were staged in several states, supported by white power organizations and conservative organizations. In Michigan, heavily armed second amendment advocates and supporters of the president occupied the state legislature for a day. The president himself tweeted support of these actions and then began holding campaign rallies in June, in which little attempt to recognize the ongoing pandemic were evident. Often his supporters and some libertarians described social masking as "the new muzzle." Contrarily, those observing health guidelines sometimes engaged in acts of social shaming against those choosing not to, arguing that pandemics do not respect conventional definitions of personal liberty. Most dispiritingly, when the prospect of a vaccine arriving by sometime in 2021 has been offered, polls show that between 30 and 50 percent of Americans may opt not to receive it, and, alarmingly, only a quarter of African Americans polled report they will do so.

The last statistic is particularly troubling, because COVID data quickly revealed that minorities in the United States were suffering morbidity and mortality rates roughly five times those of white persons. These are caused by "long-standing systemic health and social inequalities" that have been recognized for many years yet left largely unaddressed (Centers for Disease and Control and Prevention 2020).

Growing awareness of such race-based health inequalities had already raised alarm, but while in the midst of the pandemic suffering, several police killings of BIPOC citizens rendered even more starkly the manifest racism that continues to haunt the nation and maintain white privilege. Coupled with past instances of police brutality, such as the unrest in Ferguson, Missouri, in 2014 after the police shooting of an unarmed Black youth, and recent hate crimes, such as the murder in February 2020 of Ahmaud Arberry by a former police officer and two accomplices in Georgia, the George Floyd killing in May sparked national outrage. While still in the midst of the COVID pandemic, protesters took to the streets in cities large and small to demand police reform and a larger acknowledgment of the systemic racism ingrained in American social, political, economic, and cultural life. While local governments ruminated on defunding their police departments and reinvesting in preventative care, a national debate erupted after several monuments celebrating Southern figures with racist connections to the Confederacy were toppled by protesters. After many failed attempts to do so in the past, the Mississippi legislature finally removed the rebel battle emblem from the state flag. Such actions inspired hope for more than incremental changes, but also stirred responses from the far Right, which began to appear at local protests brandishing weapons and at rallies for the president shouting white power slogans. A recent report by the Center for Strategic and International Studies think tank predicts that Right-wing terrorism will continue to far outpace perpetrators from abroad and is likely to increase following the presidential election (Jones et al. 2020). Rarely has the country found itself in more perilous or uncertain times, with prospects for the November election running the gamut from ballot interference by Trump and voter meddling by Russia to an unprecedented turnout (despite the ongoing pandemic) and an opportunity for the Democrats to return to power.

The Larger Picture: Neoliberalism and Precarity

The overarching historical trajectory on which all the events mentioned above can be plotted concerns the slow and uneven entrenchment of neoliberalism. As detailed in the following chapter, this also provides a context for understanding developments in collective and devised theatre, which evolve within the logic of neoliberalism in complicated and ambivalent ways. On the one hand, the nature and formation of ensembles alter under the economic and cultural circumstances produced by neoliberalism, challenging older ideals of collectivity and moving ensembles to adopt varied structures for collaborating that sometimes mimic, and at other times contest, prevailing labor trends. This as much as any aesthetic or ethical ambition creates the diverse creative procedures that cause the term "collective creation" to become too restrictive and usher in the more generic term "devised theatre" to define the broader practices operating after the 1980s. But even as neoliberalism is built upon more flexible forms of labor and organization that reward innovation and entrepreneurship (which, too, have always been affirmed in ensemble theatre-making), it also is responsible for destructive consequences that many contemporary artists seek to address and resist. Perhaps most directly, collective and collaborative ensembles respond to the prevailing condition of precarity that intensifies under neoliberalism and other historical factors in the twenty-first century. These conditions have spurred companies to address directly the increasingly complex ethical and political realities of the twenty-first century by investigating new means of unsettling conventional audience responses and moving spectators to engage more critically with the form and content of their work.

Neoliberalism, of course, has existed as an idea since the Enlightenment, forming around the core ideals of classical liberalism as espoused by Adam Smith, John Locke, and David Ricardo before being refined by John Stuart Mill in the nineteenth century. But the theories had been mollified considerably following the First World War. They underwent significant change during and after the Great Depression when President Roosevelt instituted the modern liberal welfare state in the United States (while also excluding Blacks and others from reaping many of its intended benefits, such as low-interest housing loans). Following the Second World War, the Bretton Woods compacts organized international finance around Keynesian notions of stable global monetary exchange rates, open markets, and active state control over market volatility and inflation. In contradiction to classical liberal theory, which depended upon markets to adjust and correct themselves internally, in Keynesian terms, the state and strong labor unions were understood to be responsible for protecting the welfare of citizens, acting as a bulwark against market swings and predation. Low unemployment, mild recessions, and public ownership of those parts of the economy susceptible to monopolization ("the commons") were all stabilizers that, while they restrained the economy from explosive and expansive growth, allowed governments to work toward providing Roosevelt's "four freedoms" (from want, fear, and the loss of free speech and religious worship). These were the foundations for the liberal consensus in the United States that dominated policy and cultural production for twenty-five years. It evolved a set of social welfare policies intended to buffer society from the most dramatic effects of the market and to protect those least able to benefit from it even when it was functioning smoothly. Most dramatically under the Johnson administration (1964–1968), the liberal consensus promoted Great Society programs like Medicare and Medicaid, the War on Poverty, Head Start, and support for civil rights through fair housing laws and other initiatives.

The liberal consensus was questioned continuously by conservatives and, later, the counterculture, and was subject to constant theoretical critique by economists (in the United States, primarily associated with the Chicago School under Milton Friedman who deployed the theories of the Austrian economist F. A. Hayek). Still, it only began to founder when Keynesian principles proved unable to address the crisis of stagflation— the combination of high inflation and low economic growth—during the 1970s. The revival of the neoliberal elements of classical liberalism begins in earnest at this moment, as the crisis of capital accumulation (when consumer demand could not keep up with supply) resulted in the grinding stagflation that resisted Keynesian interventions and created a long period of inflation, unemployment, and low productivity. Exacerbated by the oil crises of the mid-1970s and a general loss of confidence in American power following Vietnam, under the Democrat Jimmy Carter, the United States began tentative steps toward dismantling the liberal welfare state by deregulating the transportation industry and calling for increased defense spending. At around the same time, business interests began to take more proactive steps to influence US policy: in 1972, there were 60,000 firms associated with their local Chambers of Commerce, but by 1982 the number had grown to a quarter million. New lobbying groups such as the National Association of Manufacturers and the Business Roundtable were formed, and think tanks supporting market-based solutions to political and economic issues such as the Heritage Institute joined older organizations like the Hoover Institute and the American Enterprise Institute in pressing conservative causes. Foundations and NGOs (nongovernmental organizations) were established by the Pew, Scaife, Olin, and Koch families to provide funding for new or expanding schools of business at major universities that would espouse and support neoliberal economic theories.

The rise of neoliberalism was not solely an American phenomenon and ultimately parallels the advance of globalism more generally. In the UK, the ascent of Margaret Thatcher to Prime Minister in 1979 resulted in several conservative economic reforms and the weakening of labor unions and other liberal collectives. (Thatcher notoriously devised and deployed the acronym TINA—"there is no alternative"—to the market economy.) China began implementing market socialism in the late 1970s to integrate the communist nation with the global economy. But the economic theory produced the most significant political changes in the United States, paving the way for Reagan's election in 1980 and the transformations it wrought. He set out to deregulate a wide swath of economic sectors, placing particular emphasis on extractive industries that would help return US sovereignty over its oil and gas supplies. As well, Reagan followed Thatcher's lead in liberating the finance industries and speculative capital, opening up and privatizing new markets in what had formerly been understood as the commons: land, water, education, health care, social security, and the like. Such financialization would utterly transform, for instance, the urban fabric and power structures governing New York City following its near-bankruptcy in the 1970s, shifting authority to bondholders and lending institutions (Miller 2016; Phillips-Fein 2017). Finally, Reagan steadily curbed the power of labor, first by breaking the 1981 strike of the federal air traffic controllers by firing over 11,000 employees. In the longer run, he supported tax breaks on investments that moved capital from the union-heavy manufacturing centers of the Northeast to the less regulated and lower-wage Southwest (or simply shipped manufacture abroad).

As much as anything, Reagan laid the foundation for neoliberalism by instilling a national ethos that shifted the understanding of freedom from the "liberty from" conceptualization that underlay the New Deal liberal welfare state to the idea of "liberty to." The latter emphasized not collective responsibility but individual autonomy free of collective judgment and government intervention. From the neoliberal position, the overriding concern is economic freedom (based on Friedman's 1962 *Capitalism and Freedom*), and the obstacles are policies that curtail this through taxation, welfare entitlements, tariffs, and regulation. Touting the morality of markets, the citizenship of corporations, and evoking traditional US myths of manifest destiny and the "city on a hill," Reagan energized a new Republican base that expelled most of its remaining liberal members. To rebuild an electoral base, Reagan cannily began to court the previously neglected and politically inactive Christian Right. Making connections to Jerry Falwell's

Moral Majority (formed in 1978), Reagan effectively mobilized evangelicals by appealing to their conservative beliefs on family values and responsibility (particularly on abortion), their sense of being marginalized by urban liberal elites, and their cultural nationalism tinged with a moral righteousness often formed from their own previous experiences of poverty and neglect.

The new order, wonderfully encapsulated in Martin's excited (and in retrospect, highly prophetic) speech in Scene Six of Tony Kushner's *Angels in America, Part I: Millennium Approaches*, would exalt supply-side economics that focused on investment and production (rather than the liberal millstone of taxes and spending), tax breaks for the wealthy based in trickle-down theories, and freedom for workers to pursue forms of labor and compensation with greater flexibility to order to innovate and practice private entrepreneurship. Companies triaged pension plans so that, rather than working toward a secure but staid retirement package, workers could compete for lofty incentives and perhaps step away at a younger age. Increasingly, the role of the state was redefined to serve the needs of the market rather than to provide social welfare programs against its worst excesses. An ethos of extreme competition and a belief that applying market-based solutions to every context began to dominate in the United States and, progressively, the global economy. By 1996, leading up to the Olympics in Atlanta, the shoe manufacturer Nike could proclaim that "you don't win silver, you lose gold," thus capturing the national mood.

While Democrats sought to oppose most of Reagan's policies, by the time he was succeeded by George H. W. Bush the Left's options for resistance were diminishing. Needing to counter the new Republican fund-raising and electoral juggernaut, Democrats felt they could not afford to turn their backs on big business by openly criticizing the short-term economic gains that conservative policies had generated. At the same time, they needed to maintain ties with their traditional mixed base, made of up Blacks, Latinos, women, environmentalists and social justice advocates, and unskilled workers, all of whom suffered under the predatory economic policies of a nascent neoliberalism. As a result, the Democratic Party, under the influence of the Southern-based Democratic Leadership Council (headed by Arkansas governor Bill Clinton), began tacking toward the center-right. The so-called New Democrats continued to support their base by recognizing their needs and causes (such as multiculturalism, environmentalism, feminism, and diversity), yet primarily by linking these to neoliberal ideals like meritocracy and the individual freedom to innovate and succeed in existing socioeconomic structures. Such beliefs would help propel, for instance, market-based ideas for fighting environmental degradation with cap-and-trade policies, and post-feminism's notion of "leaning in" to break the glass ceilings of business as a marker of individual progress that would nevertheless benefit the standing of women in general.

Turning away from the structural model for understanding the bases of poverty, racism, patriarchy, homophobia, climate change, and other social disorders, the New Democrats increasingly adopted the language and, eventually, under President Clinton, many of the policies of neoliberalism. As recorded above, under constant pressure from the Republican-controlled Congress, Clinton generally acceded to demands that "failures" from all races, genders, sexualities, and political orientations be disciplined (or disinvested in) if they failed to exercise their freedom to act responsibly within the neoliberal order and lift themselves out of poverty and the margins. This would result, for instance, in the 1994 crime bill that continues to bedevil Democrats in recent and upcoming elections and fracture their base, as well as Clinton's welfare reform policies, the most far-reaching of which utilized neoliberal language in its very title: "The Personal Responsibility and Work Opportunity Reconciliation Act of 1996." While progressives among historically Democratic constituencies continued to push for meaningful structural changes, the media fixated on the glamorous examples of success within capitalist terms. They helped the New Democrats remain in power to oversee the prolific economic expansion of the 1990s before the dotcom crash.

Thus, by the year in which this volume begins, neoliberalism had become the de facto economic and cultural hegemony in the United States. Although not reducible to a specific ideology and evolving unevenly as a hybrid practice, neoliberalism provided the framework for the gradual dismantling of the liberal welfare state, the increased privatization of welfare operations, and the global free trade agreements that proliferated during the 1990s. It developed, somewhat like collective creation itself, haphazardly and in response to similar anxieties and desires: the mistrust of authority, particularly the federal government following Vietnam and Watergate; the muscular strain of individualism and self-reliance that characterizes American self-identity; and the acclaim of values such as innovation and entrepreneurship (and the corresponding consequence of increased status and capital, material or symbolic). And, like ensemble theatre in its contemporary form, neoliberalism promised new and more flexible arrangements of labor that rewarded experimentation and risk. This was seductive during a period of unconstrained growth and innovation but would face reassessment after 9/11, the 2008 Great Recession, and in the face of rapidly increasing economic inequality and precarity throughout the 2000s.

Perhaps most significantly, forms of labor and production were undergoing monumental changes as the country moved away from Fordist modes of producing and disseminating goods. The post-Fordist or "Toyotaist" economy rewarded flexibility, non-specialization, and just-in-time production that could respond nimbly to changing buyer demands and react to a developing niche consumerism. Workers were expected to multitask and develop a portfolio of skills that were easily transferable both within a company and across different business sectors in anticipation of the mobility that such skills would enable. (Of course, this weakened union membership, a significant development given what was to follow.) In line with neoliberalism's rendition of all social and economic life to a market logic, labor became something of a commodity to be branded and exchanged on the open market of employment: the lither the brand, the more opportunities for advancement. Especially as production shifted from manufactured goods to the "immaterial" and "affective" labor that produced the curated services of the growing experience economy, job security was positioned as a worn-out ideal that limited one's agility to move quickly to the best next opportunity. Temporary contracts and forms of ad hoc employment began to displace the notion of a settled career, which appeared now discredited and a recipe for stagnant income. Risk had its rewards but playing by the old rules almost guaranteed a sedentary and unrewarded existence. In the workplace, a premium was placed on communication skills and an ability to produce knowledge and affect in the service of productive team dynamics and marketing: "celebrating," as Shannon Jackson summarizes, "the spontaneous and flexible in lieu of the planned and anticipated" (2012, 13).

The post-Fordist economy arrived after decades of union-mandated work regulations that, along with forms of job training available to unskilled laborers, prepared them to perform a single or narrowly proscribed task. And so, after a period of adjustment, it was warmly embraced by many, particularly those just entering the workforce. It afforded greater opportunity for quick advancement and flattered job seekers to be in demand and thus in control of their prospects, as well as facilitating the adventure of constant changes in location, work responsibilities, and status. Ironically, it may have been the Democratic neoliberals under Clinton and to some extent Obama who provided the sense that flexibility and lack of old-fashioned job security was sexy and chic in the fast-moving, high-tech economy in which a select few might win big in the risky exchange of security for flexibility. The notion profoundly influenced the art market and the status of the artist, now seen as a proverbial canary in the coal mine who had invested in flexible and immaterial labor before it became trendy.

The arts, in general, played a significant role in these transformations. As the following chapter explains, these massive changes altered how theatre ensembles would form, structure their collaborations, and sustain themselves in the new order. Several studies from the last decade address the new relations between art and economics that have emerged from neoliberalism's penetration into the cultural sphere. The nature of performance's labor practices, the many instances of immaterial labor involved, the marketization of cutting-edge work in the "creative economy," and the effects on funding and support have been scrutinized to map out complex and still-evolving interactions between the performing arts and neoliberalism (Wickstrom 2006, 2012; Jackson 2012; Nielsen and Ybarra 2012; Rideout and Schneider 2012; Harvie 2013; Walsh and Causey 2013; Tomlin 2015a; Fragkou 2018). These have rarely been addressed in discussions of ensemble-created theatre, yet they play a significant role in the shift from collective practice to the more diverse and heterogeneous forms of collaboration that emerge as "devising" just as neoliberalism is becoming established.

However, neoliberalism is hardly impregnable from the shocks of modern life, and already in the late 1990s was being shaken by events like the dotcom bubble collapse. Fundamentally, classical liberalism claims that the market, not the state, has access to the information required to set the accurate value of a commodity. But with online pet food vendors becoming "disruptive innovators" whose stock values soared into the billions before ever turning a profit, the market's claim to verisimilitude was challenged. When the bubble burst in 2000, more than five trillion dollars in market capitalization was lost, and many investors and pension funds suffered as the stock market plummeted 78 percent from its artificial highs. To give some sense of the scale of confidence lost in the internet bust, university enrollments in computer-related degrees dropped considerably.

Those degrees would surely have retained their value moving into the first decades of the twenty-first century. But while computer-based industries and the United States as a whole recovered from the dotcom bust, even more significant shocks would follow. After 9/11, President Bush urged the country to unite, not as citizens but as consumers: "Get down to Disney World," he exhorted: "Take your families and enjoy life, the way we want it to be enjoyed" (Schiller 2012). On the brink of recession before the terrorist attacks, personal consumption spending skyrocketed later in the year to stave off the decline. But a deeper pathology existed in the economy that had been festering since the mid-1990s, and it finally metastasized just as Bush was about to leave office. The subprime mortgage crises, explained above, had created the most massive housing bubble in US history. When it began to crumble near the end of 2006, it remained hidden only because minority and low-income homeowners were the first to feel the effects. By the time it was fully unleashed in 2010, it nearly took down the global economy and was staved off only by a massive bailout, funded by taxpayers, of the very institutions that brought it about. Globally, the crash caused the EU to adopt draconian austerity measures, often at the behest of the IMF and World Bank, that prioritized servicing financial institutions, creditors, and bondholders by keeping interest rates low (benefiting large corporations rather than private individuals) at the expense of national social welfare programs.

In the years following, many looked back at decades of risky adventurism that had produced hundreds of millionaires but very little economic progress for the lower and middle classes, who faced stagnant wages, sometimes exorbitant debt, and reduced employee benefits and social welfare options. The Occupy Movement, which flared into existence in 2011, popularized the slogan "We are the 99 percent," bringing the scale of neoliberalism's inequalities into stark belief by calculating the disparity in global wealth. Conceived by the editors of *Adbusters*, an online magazine engaged in new media campaigns that performed guerilla tactics against marketers, Occupy formed around opposition to neoliberal economic policies and the global financial system that had undermined democracy and instituted austerity governments in the United States and abroad. Based on earlier widespread protests like the EuroMayDay events in Milan in 2001, and uprisings such as the Arab Spring revolts of early 2011, the first US event took place at Zuccotti Park near the Wall Street financial district in New York City in September of 2011, soon spreading to dozens of other US cities and towns. Similar protests erupted globally, eventually sweeping over 900 cities worldwide. Famed for forming as a leaderless organization, Occupy, in some respects, revivified the ideals of participatory democracy that characterized the 1960s counterculture. Although now amped up by pervasive social media, it was still based in the physical presence of bodies gathered to reclaim a lost commons. Often criticized by many on the traditional Left for failing to present a coherent set of demands, Occupy lingers in the collective memory as a possible model for future resistance. However, it has since 2012 become more splintered and diffused. For ensemble-created theatre, Occupy is sometimes cited as a model for the new forms of collectivity and ethical practices pursued by contemporary companies (Harvie and Lavender 2010; Syssoyeva and Proudfit 2013b).

In the face of such crises, the only feasible response that would maintain neoliberalism's hegemony was to double down on the core austerity policies that shaped its theory (these were much more draconian in the Eurozone than the United States). Taking a page from the same playbook that had transformed New York City in the 1970s into a neoliberal stronghold, a discourse arose preaching a gospel of never-ending austerity, of limited mobility and precarious work, of historically high levels of debt, of greater social and personal levels of stress and fewer social welfare institutions to address them. The situation is largely responsible for the election of a populist president (it might have been so even otherwise, as the Bernie Sanders campaign in 2016 offered a liberal-based populism) who has, however, so far has governed mostly as a neoliberal—causing some commentators to evoke "zombie neoliberalism" (and Occupy demonstrators to march as the walking dead) that continues to take all the air out of the room despite its seeming demise as a credible economic theory more than a decade ago.

Neoliberalism produces precarity as a means to an end; it renders the vast majority of citizens as losers in the market of accumulation while also endorsing continued risk even as it weakens the social safety net. "Precarization," according to Isabell Lorey, has evolved into a form of governance under neoliberalism, an "instrumentalization of insecurity" based in austerity policies that maintain and governmentalize hierarchies of power and wealth. Having constructed a set of internalized values based on moral principles like responsibility and self-management, neoliberalism advanced to hegemonic status by its ability to direct citizens to accept economic inequalities as the natural result of one's own failures. Nancy Fraser sums up the results as follows:

> In the United States, those blockages include the metastasization of finance; the proliferation of precarious service-sector McJobs; ballooning consumer debt to enable the purchase of cheap stuff produced elsewhere; conjoint increases in carbon emissions, extreme weather, and climate denialism; racialized mass incarceration and systemic police violence; and mounting stresses on family and community life thanks in part to lengthened working hours and diminished social supports. Together, these forces have been

grinding away at our social order for quite some time without producing a political earthquake. Now, however, all bets are off. In today's widespread rejection of politics as usual, an objective systemwide crisis has found its subjective political voice. The political strand of our general crisis is a crisis of hegemony.

(2017, 9)

The following chapter will detail how ensemble-created theatre companies are both somewhat captive to these market logics while also fomenting resistance to them. As some commentators have avowed, precarity is not only a condition of inequality grounded in biopolitical hierarchies of power but also a liminal site of activism and resistance, one which many ensembles "Occupy."

CHAPTER 2
AMERICAN THEATRE ENSEMBLES, 1995–PRESENT
Mike Vanden Heuvel

The first volume of *American Theatre Ensembles* traced the transitional stages that followed the revival of US collective theatrical creation in the 1960s, represented by pioneering companies like the Living Theatre, the San Francisco Mime Troupe (SFMT), the Open Theater, El Teatro Campesino (ETC), and the Performance Group, among others. Those that succeeded the radical companies developed more diverse and heterogeneous ensemble practices between 1970 and 1995, which continue to evolve today. As the 1960s companies dispersed, ideologically based notions of collectivity that conveyed a strong countercultural orientation, forged in the white-hot political and underground art contexts of the 1960s, began to give way to more open forms of collaborative theatre-making. While some companies continued to experiment with collective arrangements and aspirations, many new ensembles shed the utopian ideals of egalitarian company structures and nonhierarchical forms of creation (seldom if ever actually attained by the radical collectives of the 1960s). This aligned with a broader shift in transnational ensemble practices recognized by earlier commentators (Oddey 1994; Heddon and Milling 2006; Syssoyeva and Proudfit 2013a). While in the American context one sometimes heard that a "second generation" of ensembles such as Mabou Mines, the Wooster Group, and the Ping Chong/Fiji Company had arrived to succeed the first, this terminology incorrectly positions the 1960s companies as the origin of collective creation in the United States and establishes them as the touchstone by which later creative ensembles should be measured.

Such unsound historiography, among other consequences, has encumbered the history of US collective creation with lineages that align it solely with radical politics and avant-garde ambitions that are often out of step with the actual objectives of many contemporary companies. Such approaches take for granted that conditions shaping the 1960s collectives and fashioning their theatrical responses still obtain, when in fact they have been significantly transformed. As shown in the first volume, devising emerges and evolves from a number of contexts and lineages which create the more equivocal field of ensemble practice the further development of which will be the focus of this introduction.

As with the first volume, here I will adopt the more comprehensive historiography and chronology provided by Kathryn Mederos Syssoyeva and Scott Proudfit in their coedited collection, *A History of Collective Creation*. They position the radical 1960s companies as only one part of a more comprehensive "second wave" (a term that avoids the narrower affiliation of "generation") within the longer history and transnational contexts of collective creation whose first wave emerged at the turn of the twentieth century (2013a, 1–12). The second wave, emerging in the early 1950s, crested and began to decline in the United States by the early 1970s, leading to new directions in ensemble methods and goals. The ensemble-created work addressed in the first volume of *American Theatre Ensembles*, then, belongs to the initial currents of an emerging "third wave" that, while it certainly drew inspiration and influence from the second—including practices from sources other than the US collectives, such as the Nuevo Teatro Popular and *creación colectivo* of the Global South as well as the ensemble traditions of Jacques Copeau, Ariane Mnouchkine, Eugenio Barba, and others—was stimulated and directed by myriad additional tides as well. (Indeed, it might be better understood as a "third weave.")

For these reasons, the overview of US ensembles in the previous volume covered a wide variety of forms that reflected this transitional stage of diversification after 1970, including ethnic-directed companies, feminist collectives, physical theatres, postmodernist performance, and the burgeoning community- and constituency-based forms of applied theatre. This comprehensive overview was necessary, in part, to counter the pernicious myth arising from an older critical discourse on US collective creation that the ensemble theatre movement had collapsed or gone into decline after the withdrawal of the counterculture and the radical 1960s collectives (Schechner 1981, 2010; Aronson 2000). That view was not amended by the manner US collective creation was initially treated within the wider international field of practice, for instance in the seminal work by Deirdre Heddon and Jane Milling, *Devising Performance: A Critical History* (2006). There, one reads of the "relative scarcity of contemporary devising companies in the USA," where, compared to activity in the UK and Australia, devised work "remains the exception" (2006, 247, fn. 3). That argument was certainly erroneous when the first edition of the book came out, and wildly so when the authors chose not to update the 2015 reprint and left the sentiment lingering in the critical literature.

Indeed, so expansive has been the growth of US ensemble-created theatre in the last twenty-five years that a broad history of its many lines of flight is becoming an urgent need. While the development of the German *freie Szene* ("free-scene") movement of collaborative theatre formed the foundation for theorizations of the postdramatic, and the history of devised theatre in the UK has been not only addressed in critical studies but archived as part of the "Unfinished Histories" website moderated by Susan Croft, substantive treatment of US collective creation and its specific evolution has hardly begun.[1] This is certainly not for lack of scale, for as Ferdinand Lewis observed fifteen years ago, "there may be as many ensembles in this country as there are many other kinds of professional theatre" (2005, xii). Soon after this observation was recorded, yet another period of explosive growth followed and today it is more likely that self-producing ensembles, in their many manifestations, have effectively exceeded in sheer number the scale of the professional nonprofit theatre sector. While the consequences of the emerging global pandemic of 2020 may radically reshape this entire theatre ecology, the fact remains that for the last quarter century ensemble theatre has been the dominant growth sector of American theatre.

Owing to the proliferation of devising ensembles and the brief space allotted for this overview, then, this chapter can only address the trajectories that most directly shape the forms of ensemble theatre included in the selected case studies, although this history is entangled with many others. That said, even the groups selected for inclusion in the two volumes, while they share a number of methods, aesthetic pursuits, and collaborative structures, are hardly mirror images of one another. They were selected, in part, because they all operate within a broad remit, developing their aesthetic practices and artistic identities by constantly experimenting with new forms of collaboration, text generation, performance, and audience relations as their primary pursuits. By virtue of this broad remit, such companies have shed some of the countercultural ethos associated with the 1960s radical ensembles and have opened up new lines of affiliation with the professional nonprofit theatre sector. In these ways, such ensembles are somewhat distinct from community-directed companies and ensembles pursuing applied theatre goals, and thereby seeking to address or intervene in support of specific needs or constituencies. Broad remit companies typically pursue multiple communities of interest and rarely interpose on behalf of local issues or concerns.

Such distinctions, albeit more expedient in theory than in practice, nevertheless have been helpful in registering differences between ensembles primarily devoted to applied theatre goals and those that pursue broadly aesthetic ends. However, as explained below, the trajectory of the work covered in *American Theatre Ensembles* troubles this very distinction through historical processes that bring the two modes of collective practice into new, and sometimes unstable, forms of exchange. Thus, the work of the broad remit companies featured in *American Theatre Ensembles* roughly parallels the UK and EU companies and art practices addressed in Jen Harvie's *Fair Play*, in that each "commonly emphasizes artistic output, and its 'social agenda' is often ambiguous or at least more open than applied [theatre] agendas tend to be" (2013, 20). This very ambiguity of goals and purpose among broad remit ensembles has complicated the very definitions of collective creation since the 1990s, while also providing a means to disentangle the practice from the linear history that bound it solely to the radical companies of the second wave. As collective creation becomes, in method, organization, and production, less homogenous, former binary delineations such as those pitting a political and avant-garde practice against an apolitical (or "postmodern") and mainstream style no longer obtain. Broad remit companies, by inclination and by virtue of their historical moment, are avid experimentalists set upon developing a multidirectional and multifaceted scene of practice.

While their engagement with pop culture and postmodern pastiche can be delirious, such companies are not focused on simple diversion, as might typically be the case, for instance, with ensemble-based immersive entertainments that utilize formulaic structures (such as escape rooms and interactive mini-dramas). Looking at the work of Radiohole and the Vampire Cowboys, for example, one immediately recognizes how their engagement with popular culture indexes broader and more critical concerns with its absorption into a wider culture of spectacle even as it provides a demotic source of energy for their work. Many broad remit companies, like the peripatetic PigPen Theatre as well as the Civilians, adeptly branch out to produce not only plays but albums, bespoke performances, workshops, and films. Companies such as those represented in the case studies are also, for various reasons, the ensembles that draw the greatest academic and critical attention, perhaps because they combine experimentation, more conventional "culinary" theatrical pleasures, and forms of social address in ways that commentators find compelling. As Rachel Anderson-Rabern points out, such companies also self-consciously "contend with the long tradition of collaboration in performance making, both resisting and embracing its implications as they establish their own working process" (2020, 8). This, alone, makes them significant to the development of collaborative creation in the United States because they offer examples of how ensemble creation both emerges out of and differentiates itself from the example of the radical 1960s companies. Significantly, in light of this volume's trajectory, broad remit companies are also involved in the shift from a relatively stable notion of what constitutes collective creation to ensemble practices that elude stable positioning, and so are complicit in the terminological distress this has occasioned (between "collective," "collaborative," "group," "theatre-makers," and "devising," for instance) and the political and ethical implications of each rubric. Finally, in a development that begins in the 1980s but accelerates considerably going into the new millennium, broad remit companies are at the vanguard of investigating relations with the mainstream professional resident theatre network, interactions that are currently reshaping both the practices of this alternative art practice and to some extent even the broader field of the US professional nonprofit theatre.

Entangled Trajectories and Confluences

In the introduction to the first volume, one reason for establishing multiple taxonomies of ensemble-created theatre that emerged from the decline of the 1960s radical collectives was to highlight how some forms of collective creation, such as feminist, constituency-based, and community-directed theatres, did in a sense continue the legacy of the more political and emphatically collectivist companies of the 1960s. However, they accomplished this not by slavishly modeling their practice on the earlier ensembles but by identifying weak points in their collective structures (which often masked hierarchies that sometimes were gender- and race-based), their putatively nonhierarchical creative methods, and their politics. Many of the constituency-directed companies of the 1970s and 1980s, especially feminist collectives, engaged in what today could be considered applied theatre (a term without much circulation until the mid-1990s). Such practices looked back to and beyond the 1960s collectives to previous forms of ensemble creation's second wave, grounded in drama in education, documentary theatre, and worker's theatre. Many of them responded in one way or another to the arrival of Forum Theatre techniques in the United States that began after Boal's

Theatre of the Oppressed was first translated into English in 1979. The locale shifted for many of these collectives from an urban underground scene to neighborhoods, feminist enclaves, and small towns in rural America. Their politics, too, generally moved on from those of the 1960s (which gathered around the New Left's participatory democracy, the anarcho-pacifism of the Living Theatre, and the more explicitly revolutionary and nationalist ideals of the Black Power Movement) to less ideological forms based in identity politics and social justice activism. Yet these companies were still involved in overtly political forms of collective creation. Importantly, they maintained connections between earlier collective work and activist politics.

Meanwhile, a new strand of ensemble-created theatre aligned with more formal and aesthetic pursuits emerged during the late 1970s. This trajectory is sometimes grouped under the rubric of "postmodernist performance" and headlined by the Wooster Group, auteurs like Richard Foreman, Ping Chong, Martha Clarke, and Robert Wilson, and members of the emerging solo performance art scene (Auslander 1994; Kaye 1994; Aronson 2000). These would generate in turn, as did also the constituency-based theatres, several physical-based ensembles and the various manifestations of visual theatre covered in the previous volume. Among other factors distinguishing different trajectories, those ensembles pursuing primarily aesthetic rather than applied goals had their identities shaped by the different training members received: unlike theatre-makers in early applied theatre, for instance, in postmodernist ensembles dance backgrounds were more common, connections to Lecoq-inspired forms of creative collaboration were more pronounced, and, increasingly, artists working with digital technologies were drawn to this work.

As argued in the first volume with reference to Antenna Theatre, the Wooster Group, Herbert Blau's Kraken company, Lin Hixson's collective the Hangers, and the Ghost Road Company, the postmodernist style is one manifestation of ensemble theatre's response to a cultural dominant that had its origins in the 1960s. Such work played the important role of establishing points of departure from the approach to collective theatre-making developed by the 1960s companies, while at the same time breathing fresh life into aesthetic practices grounded in the postmodern dance that emanated from the Judson School and in the Cagean legacies of the 1960s avant-gardes (Aronson 2000; Harding 2015). Receptive to some of the innovations being developed in these practices and in early performance art in ways that applied forms of collective creation could not be, the emerging third wave of ensemble-produced theatre fashioned a more robust response to postmodernism by setting aside strong ideological commitments and depth-based models of training and practice in favor of greater eclecticism and hybridity (see chapter 2 in the previous volume). Although Artaud and Grotowski remained common sources of inspiration and reference points for experimentation, the "cruelty" and "holiness" of their respective theories were in retreat.

But as postmodernism began to align more closely with neoliberalism starting in the 1990s, and in the wake of the culture wars of the late 1980s and the funding cuts that ensued (which nudged many companies to redefine themselves as community development entities to secure support), a subtle but consequential shift becomes evident. To generalize, under these changes some elements of third-wave collective creation operating mostly within the community-directed and applied theatre sectors, as well as select companies belonging to the postmodernist strand of ensemble creation, began to undergo an uneven amalgamation.[2] Such convergences were not limited to US companies, as witnessed by Harvie's positioning of the artists referenced in *Fair Play*:

> The work I do focus on could perhaps best be identified as "aesthetically turned" socially turned art and performance. That said, part of what this book aims to demonstrate and explore is that boundaries between contemporary "applied" and "fine" art practices, and between art and activism, are very porous or have broad overlaps, and that much art and performance which is apparently "aesthetically turned," or that appears to prioritize art practices and outcomes, is vigorously engaged in complex social work.
>
> (20)

Eventually, by the 1990s the work of broad remit companies exploring relations between applied and aesthetic pursuits helps bring about the contemporary status of devised theatre as a thoroughly mixed, even compromised, practice that operates in the equivocal space between late capitalism and the historical yearning of collective theatre to operate as an alternative site of resistance. These transformations removed many of the remaining vestiges of a political definition of collectivity that might govern a company's organizational structure, its modes of collaboration, and its open antipathy to the "other" theatre of the professional mainstream. What emerges are hybridized practices that, lacking in the purity of purpose required of any notion of an avant-garde, make virtues of mobility and the capacity to innovate rapidly by eschewing strict collectivist structures.

The companies selected for *American Theatre Ensembles* occupy this equivocal space and shape its evolution: those companies in the first volume that began by emulating the 1960s collectives (such as Theatre X and Mabou Mines) eventually responded in the 1980s and 1990s to cultural and economic shifts that altered their organizational and creative practices in these new directions. Others, like Goat Island, formed on the cusp of such changes and adopted new creative structures from the outset (such as electing a permanent director, Lin Hixson, rather than following a nonhierarchical model) that earlier collectives like Schechner's Performance Group and the Open Theatre had resisted. By the time ensembles such as the Builders Association, Pig Iron Theatre, and Rude Mechs appeared in the mid-1990s, collaborative practices were being diversified and the traditional definitions of both "collective" and "ensemble" were being tested.

One can see the emerging consolidation of the applied and formalist trajectories of ensemble creation as companies like Lookingglass, Goat Island, Ghost Road Company, Headlong Dance, and the SITI Company (which all formed in the late 1980s and early 1990s) began to establish their style by adapting postmodernist aesthetic strategies to address new and pressing social and cultural realities. A key element in this transition is the "social turn" occurring around this time in the arts more generally, occasioned in part by contemporary conditions of precarity that will be discussed below. Feminist, educational, and community-directed group theatres had been exploring deeper involvement with their constituencies throughout the 1970s and 1980s and this, along with the arrival of Boal training and other activist forms of performance, generated new forms of audience participation and engagement. Later, in response to the AIDS crisis and the homophobic backlash that followed, the revived interest in devised documentary theatre (especially after the success of Tectonic Theatre's *The Laramie Project* in 2000) further galvanized new forms of performance research on social issues (Favorini 2013). By the mid-1990s, many aesthetically turned companies were tapping into these developments, evolving mixed creative practices that melded applied and formalist methods, most notably directed at breaking down the frontality and ironic distancing effects of much postmodernist performance and seeking new forms of audience address and engagement.

The social turn, as it was originally theorized and debated (often rancorously) by Nicholas Bourriaud, Claire Bishop, and Grant Kester in the early 2000s, generates forms of relational art which, in the case of ensemble performance, may utilize formalist aesthetic strategies (such as decentering, indeterminacy, site-specificity, the blending of representational and live elements) but toward the end of opening up an intersubjective social space and interaction with the audience. The cool, distancing effect of early postmodern performance begins to give way to more intimate and complex forms of address and relationality. These spaces may produce forms of ethical praxis (allowing the spectator to ask, as in Bourriaud's formulation, "does this work permit me to enter dialogue? Could I exist, and how, in the space it defines?") and/or the kinds of relational antagonism and dissensus favored by Bishop to provoke critical dialogue (Bourriaud et al. 2002, 109; Bishop 2004, 2012).

If not political theatre as traditionally conceived, such work was nevertheless directed at generating new, or revivifying culturally repressed, forms of sociability. The strategy is common as well to much postdramatic theatre, which Hans-Thies Lehmann had begun to theorize in the 1990s based on relational aesthetics taught at the University of Giessen since the 1980s. These pursue, in his words, a "politics of perception" that questions ideological formations in and of themselves, rather than promoting one or another, and thereby fracturing once-stable identities and ideologies across various intersectional configurations (Lehmann 2006). Such practices productively collapse, or reconfigure, distinctions between applied theatre and formalist, postmodernist performance to create art that connects spectators to the precarious condition of late capitalism and opens up the prospect of new socialities (Bourriaud 2002; Bishop 2005; Rancière 2007). However, this also brings some forms of ensemble creation into ongoing debates regarding the efficacy of the social turn and whether such art can maintain a radical edge or is foredoomed to be absorbed in the late capitalist "experience economy" (Harvie 2013, 8).

Goat Island, earlier and perhaps most explicitly among companies of the late 1980s and early 1990s, signals the new direction when the ensemble begins to enact through their process and performances "small acts of repair" that, while continuing to call upon postmodern performance strategies, engage directly with ethical dimensions of collaboration and performance and explicitly mount a response to the increasingly precarious conditions of late twentieth-century culture (see the essay by Nicholas Lowe and Sarah Skaggs in the first volume; see also Ghoulish 2002; Bottoms and Ghoulish 2013). Andy Lavender has argued that such new forms of commitment give rise to "performance after postmodernism," where "after decentering we found ourselves diversely centered ... After the clarion calls of modernism, and the absences and ironies of postmodernism, come the nuanced and differential negotiations, participations and interventions of an age of engagement" (2016, 21). Social performance allows communal and aesthetic ends to be conceived, as James Andrew Wilson says, "in tandem," and the tentative and uneven integration of applied versions of collaborative creation with those practices focused on form and aesthetics direct the work of the companies represented in this volume to respond differently to the altered conditions of postmodernity as these exist today (2012).

These changes register in ways both material and abstract: for instance, in the past, a company might retain an identity as a community-directed theatre to distinguish itself from others primarily pursuing aesthetic experimentation—that is, those that validated their professional identities by the number and quality of commissions received and by establishing themselves on the domestic and international fringe theatre festival circuit. Today, however, community-directed and applied theatre companies such as Sojourn Theatre (founded by Michael Rohd in 1999) and Cornerstone Theatre (1986) regularly tour and perform at regional, national, and international festivals to expand their influence and share their work. They are also more likely than in the past to collaborate with "postmodernist" companies, such as Sojourn's work with The Theatre of the Emerging American Moment (The TEAM) on the 2013 *Waiting for You on the Corner Of ...* (a work commissioned by a mainstream regional theatre, Kansas City Rep) or Philadelphia's New Paradise Laboratories' collaboration with Children's Theatre of Minneapolis in 2004. Applied ensemble practitioners often work on a project basis depending upon the communities being addressed, which necessitates different models of collaboration for each project. These malleable company structures have increasingly been picked up by mainstream ensembles as well, another point of amalgamation.

Conversely, ensembles not connected to or addressing a regular or specifically locatable community (except perhaps the arts community broadly conceived), whose work might be described as formalist and whose professional goals are directed at touring, residencies, and the festival circuit, are no longer, themselves, absolutely distinct from constituency- and community-directed theatres. With few (and declining) exceptions, even the highest-profile ensembles in the United States—the TEAM, Ghost Road, Builders Association, Rude Mechs, Out of Hand, and older ensembles like Mabou Mines and Beau Geste—today offer educational and outreach programs intended to connect to local communities, create collaborative partnerships with local nonprofits and civic organizations, and host school residencies to teach devising methods for use in everything from anti-bullying programs to conflict resolution, team building, and diversity training. Granted, these sometimes serve ambivalent goals: as Syssoyeva and Proudfit note, the original motivation to develop these programs was in many cases financial and strategic. The nonprofit status of many ensembles allowed them to secure educational funding or grants from the constituencies they serve in order to supplement receipts from earned income and other forms of external support (Syssoyeva and Proudfit 2013b, 37, fn. 35). In other instances, community outreach has been exchanged in negotiations for rehearsal and performance space. But these once-marginal activities have become more thoroughly integrated with the development and production of many ensembles' main shows, mostly as a result of new economic realities and the social and artistic needs that have spawned the social turn in the arts. Even a cursory overview of ensemble theatre websites across the spectrum of community-directed and aesthetically inclined companies reveals hybrid mission statements grounded in community development and ideals of equity, diversity, inclusion, social justice, and sustainability while also highlighting aesthetic freedom and experimentation. Supporting arts presenters and umbrella organizations like the National Performance Network adhere to similar goals. In the midst of the 2020 #BlackLivesMatter protests and other expressions of social unrest, many companies are doubling down on these commitments and aligning their missions to serve the goals of antiracism.[3]

These conjunctions help account for what Syssoyeva and Proudfit, in the second volume of their trilogy on collective creation, *Collective Creation and Contemporary Performance* (2013b), refer to as the journey of ensemble creation from "margin to center" between the 1990s and into the new millennium. Although the media often attributes the growing popularity of devised theatre to factors like the Gen-Z pursuit of all things hip, and academics are fond of pointing out the iniquitous mainstreaming of radical art in general, the movement of ensemble-created theatre toward the center is triggered by many causes and produces complex consequences that are still unfolding. Indeed, by the opening of the new millennium, ensemble-created theatre had already arrived at a knotty three-body problem: even as devised theatre appeared to be shifting from the margin toward the center, simultaneously the cultural center itself was moving toward the alternative, and this occurred even as both were being influenced by the considerable gravitational effects of an evolving neoliberalism. The complex interplay of these transformations establishes a signal moment in the evolution of the third wave of US ensemble theatre-making (it may well prove to signal the arrival of a fourth), shifting its position from a flamboyant alternative to mainstream practices to a participant—sometimes willing, sometimes recalcitrant—in their development and potential transformation.

The Wooster Group

One way to track these developments is by noting both continuities and transformations taking place in what is still the best known US ensemble, the Wooster Group. By 1995 the Group was entering its twentieth year of ensemble creation (and the fifteenth by that name) under the directorship of Liz LeCompte. There were everywhere signs that the company had by this time achieved the peculiar status of an avant-garde classic or had joined what David Savran calls the "consecrated avant-garde" and Richard Schechner names the "conservative avant-garde" (Savran 2010; Schechner 2010).[4] LeCompte received a MacArthur "genius" award in 1995, and the year included three full-length shows running simultaneously in repertory, on tour, and in development (*The Temptation of St. Anthony* [created in 1986 and on tour in São Paulo], *The Emperor Jones* [1993], and *The Hairy Ape* [in development, premiered 1996]). The fact that Willem Dafoe had taken the role of Frank Dell in the touring show of *Saint Anthony* signaled another consequence of the company's endurance: Ron Vawter, who joined the ensemble in 1977 and whose illness formed the core of that show, had passed away of AIDS-related causes in 1994. Dafoe, himself, had achieved film stardom after his Academy Award nomination for *Platoon* (1986) and his work with Martin Scorsese on *The Last Temptation of Christ*, and was therefore often absent from the Performing Garage. Spalding Gray, a founding member, ceased performing with the company in 1984 to pursue his solo monologist and film career. In 1992 he published his novel *Impossible Vacation*, a thinly veiled autobiography that included the story of his first encounter with LeCompte and their founding of an experimental theatre group. After suffering severe trauma in an auto accident and falling into sustained depression, Gray committed suicide in 2004.

Fast forward to 2020, and *Impossible Vacation* is now one of the source materials for the Group's current work-in-progress, *Since I Can Remember*. The piece travels back in time to revisit *Nayatt School* (1978) from the first trilogy by the company (it is also the work in which Gray delivered his first solo monologue). The company website explains: "We're thinking of this piece as the first in a series of Wooster Group theatrical histories that explore our previous pieces, how they were made, and how we work."[5] The retrospective nature of the new work signals, first, that despite constant turnover the company has established creative processes that maintain its signature style over decades, even to the extent that they can be deployed to reflect on these same practices from more than forty years ago. In a strange but illuminating way, *Since I Can Remember* will take its place among the company's previous explorations of avant-garde practitioners from the past as seen in *L.S.D.* (1984), *House/Lights* (1998), *Poor Theatre* (2004), *The Town Hall Affair* (2017), and *A Pink Chair* (2018); only this time, rather than featuring the work and thought of Burroughs, Stein, Grotowski, Forsythe, Ernst, Greer, or Kantor, it will be the ensembles' own place within that history. *Since I Can Remember* will commemorate a moment before their work became institutionalized, when it was in some sense truly avant-garde and before it became recognizable as a style: one so enduring that the same methods for constructing the new piece can be built on a repetition of the methods that produced *Nayatt School*. The new work signals a profound recognition of the altered status of US alternative art practices since the 1980s, when under the influence of postmodernism and market forces, the very oppositionality of alternative art was, itself, branded as a mainstream value or lifestyle choice and marketed successfully as hip consumerism. As will be seen below, this is intimately tied to the rise of neoliberalism and the role that alternative culture plays in that ascent.

The Wooster Group plays an integral role in these developments as they touch upon US collective creation more broadly because they were the first, along with Robert Wilson, to be recuperated by the ascending "Nobrow" culture that neoliberalism would help produce (Seabrook 2000; see also Savran 2004a). Without premeditation and owing to several unpredictable factors (such as Gray's and especially Dafoe's unexpected stardom), the Group found itself by the late 1990s no longer the renegade ensemble that lost 40 percent of its state arts funding for its use of blackface (in the 1981 *Route 1 & 9*). Instead, they became the focus of admiring academic theorizing on the nature of postmodern identity owing *to* its repeated use of blackface, for instance, in *The Emperor Jones* (1993, revived 2006: see Monks 2005). Soon, their work was drawing celebrity crowds at the many international festivals to which they were regularly invited. Alongside the new (and unsolicited) fame arrived greater academic recognition and, given the number of new ensembles forming while at university, more interest in their work by nascent and developing artists. And as many have reported, the number and variety of contemporaneous ensemble artists who have interned or otherwise collaborated with the Wooster Group—collaborations built, as longtime member Kate Valk reminds us, "by attraction and not solicitation"—provide the best evidence for the influence they have exerted on ensemble practice up to the present (Gordon 2020; see also Anderson-Rabern 2020).

This imposing artistic tree of contemporary ensemble artists, however, is not grafted steadfastly to its roots: the Wooster Group, after all, remains unique in part because it has owned and operated the Performing Garage since 1980. Contemporary ensembles rarely enjoy that privilege, and so their need to remain adjacent to the professional theatre ecology in the United States, while based on several related factors, is ultimately an issue of space and control over their creative processes. US ensembles have existed traditionally in diasporic space, constantly in search of both short- and long-term residencies and the support of presenting organizations (these have multiplied exponentially after the 1990s, but the competition remains fierce). For these reasons, the Wooster Group's role in the development of ensemble-created theatre is transformed somewhat during the period of this volume. They remain torchbearers of a nominal global avant-garde and a company revered but not particularly resonant in the new directions that ensemble practice is heading. The Group shows little interest in pursuing relational forms of performance, and even less enthusiasm for establishing affiliations with the US professional theatre network, preferring to remain staunchly "alt" and perhaps even in some sense avant-garde, or at least, as above, to devote their work to commemorating those historical junctures and artists who flourished when such a position carried real cultural significance.

But while it is true that the status of alternative art has changed markedly in recent decades, we should also recognize that so, too, has the mainstream. Here as well, the example of the Wooster Group is pertinent. Steven Leigh Morris, in conversation with Mark Russell (former executive artistic director at P.S. 122 and then artistic director at the Public Theatre), writes that "if you were to write a history of the theatre, the role played in the 90s and early 2000s by the Wooster Group ('the Rolling Stones of experimental theatre') would be very important—but equally important was that group's failure to connect with the regional theatre system" (Morris 2013, n.p.). From Russell's view:

The regional theatres have resources, capacity, audiences, yet all these companies like the Wooster Group were being handled by presenters, not theatres. The foundations were asking "What's up with that?" Why were these intriguing ensembles not intersecting with these slow-moving institutions? Can we take some of this energy and raise all boats?

One wonders whether such openness to the Wooster Group taking up a residency or presenting their work at a major regional theatre in the 1990s actually existed, or if it is more likely that this new retroactive openness to producing their "intriguing" work is occasioned by their newfound celebrity status (the Rolling Stones, too, had trouble getting booked early on). Nevertheless, these comments mark the distance the mainstream may have traveled since the 1980s and suggest that contemporary ensembles may find this new potential appealing.

Of Margins and Centers

At any rate, under vastly different circumstances than obtained before the 1990s, broad remit companies increasingly have shown more willingness to connect with the nonprofit professional sector. The changing relationship between center and margin became legible, for instance, by the founding of the Network of Ensemble Theatres (NET) in 1996, which, significantly, brought together traditional repertory theatres, community-directed collectives, and many devising companies like those in this volume, signaling an important stage of amalgamation.[6] New associations were formed, and perhaps somewhat unconsciously, many broad remit ensembles (but not all: see, for instance, Steve Luber's essay on Radiohole and Jane Baldwin's on Rude Mechs in this volume) diversified their working methods to both encompass and supersede the narrower category of collective creation that, in theory, assumed egalitarian principles of shared administrative and creative powers and methods of composition. Although many companies continued to generate new material through collective creation utilizing nonhierarchical structures, even these methods were being reshaped by the 2000s as collaborative teams broadened. Whereas in the 1980s and into the 1990s performers and directors made up the core of the creative team, moving into the new millennium we see, with companies like the Builders Association, designers and even entire design firms, especially those specializing in CAD, digital and live feed technologies, and new media, expanding the creative ensemble (McGinley 2010, 14). New collaborative methods were explored by director-led companies, by ensembles who make temporary or permanent use of in-house playwrights, and by groups working in looser affiliations such as core-and-pool collaborations or associations built upon short-term artists' contracts that allow numerous creative artists to move in and out of the ensemble as particular projects demand.

It is thus common today for a single company to experiment with all these arrangements depending upon the needs of the current project, and indeed, given the lengthy period of development of some ensemble work, companies might utilize several structures during a single project. Ensembles like the Builders Association and Detroit's Hinterlands, for instance, regularly bring in individual artists and design firms whose expertise align with the needs of a particular show (Liza Bielby, codirector of Hinterlands, provides an apt analogy when she writes that "Hinterlands is kind of like a band, with each performance and area of work being an album with a unique set of musicians" [2014, n.p.]). The Hook & Eye Theater of Brooklyn has developed an elaborate structure around a "hub" consisting of the two artistic directors (Carrie Heitman and Chad Lindsey) who run the business and oversee individual projects, within an eight-person "core" of artists who may come and go but are considered regular contributors, all supported by a "cloud" of more than 250 performing and visual artists (Heitman and Lindsey 2014, n.p.). Working at "the intersection between playmaking and script writing," Hook & Eye fully embraces open-source creative structures and takes for granted the transience of their collaborations. These, then, are certainly not classic ensembles defined by their stability over time or by the ethos of what Robert Cohen describes as "a day-in, day-out collaboration in shared living, thinking and creating" (2010, 17).

These more variegated practices help push the broader term "devising" into the lexicon, which begins to gain traction internationally by the late 1980s but in the United States only in the early 2000s.[7] By then, even US ensembles that previously self-identified as collectives were moving to the broader term in marketing and funding applications to reflect the many different creative structures they explored. A company like the National Theatre of the United States of America (NTUSA) might have begun by observing strictly democratic principles in which shows were developed by consensus reached through constant debate, but eventually found it necessary to develop more hierarchical models as productions grow in scale or when regular touring affected development schedules (Krumholz

2013). These shifting creative structures cause ensemble practices to realign somewhat less as a strict and ideologically defined alternative to conventional production methods (although importantly, ensemble creation mostly maintains its longer development schedules), opening up both new avenues of exchange between margin and center and the potential for the former to effect change in the latter.

The prospects for these new affiliations are far from certain, for as Harvie writes, mainstream theatre remains based in ensemble *production* rather than *creation* and therefore has evolved in ways that are "hierarchical and fundamentally resistant to the practices of devising and/or collaboration" (2005, 117). Yet signs of change are evident: for example, collective creation and new play development were for many years quite distinct practices in the United States, the rigid borders shaped in part by the debates over the authority of the dramatic text that roiled the 1960s collectives who sometimes adopted (and often overcooked) Artaud's anti-textuality (London et al. 2009). But early in the 2000s, Theatre Communications Group (TCG) began to investigate work being sponsored by the National Performance Network (NPN), which was founded in 1985 but undergoing restructuring in the late 1990s. NPN supported interdisciplinary art forms and advocated for marginal artists and communities in particular, and represented many applied theatre ensembles. Funded by a TCG development grant and additional support from the Doris Duke Foundation, Olga Garay-English, and other cultural producers convened a "New Work, New Ways" event in Portland in 2000 that revealed in stark relief the increasingly broad spectrum of new writing and collaborative creative practices. Mark Russell (then at P.S. 122) recalled the meeting as a seminal moment between producing organizations and artists: "People from TCG theatres were saying 'I make new work—I have readings of plays.' 'No no no, *we* make new work,' other people were saying, 'We're *ensembles!*'" (Morris 2013, n.p.). These encounters would produce several significant new developments. Firstly, bringing TCG and NPN together may have contributed to the turn toward social art in what were previously fine art-directed ensembles. Secondly, such meetings not only caused ensemble creation and new play development to merge more closely but also led Russell to initiate the Under the Radar Festival in order to host both new writing and ensemble-created theatre at St. Anne's Warehouse in New York in 2005, before moving it to the Public Theatre the next year.

As regional theatre programmers vested in curating new play development became more familiar with and open to ensemble-created work, the boundaries eroded to the point that, today, even the venerable Dramatists Guild representing playwrights ("Your pen. Our sword.") now publishes *Devised Theatre: A Resource Guide* that includes information on joint authorship, contracts, copyright, and a glossary of devising terminology.[8] When the Theatre Development Fund sponsored Todd London's research into US new play development, it included participation by Lookingglass Theatre and San Francisco's Z Space, among other ensembles (London et al. 2009). At the other end, as more companies like Chicago's New Colony Theatre came to express dissatisfaction with even the generic rubric of "devised theatre," commentators began suggesting broader terms that combine new writing with devising, such as "creative development" and "nontraditional new play development" (Janiak 2014; Linder 2016). An ambitious ensemble like the Civilians, which formed in 2001 under Steve Cosson as a self-producing company, today commissions work from other ensembles and has initiated its own new play development program, practices heretofore assumed by nonprofit theatres and presenting organizations (Kozinn and Cosson 2010, 204–5; see Chapter 7 of this volume).

Given such changes, one begins to understand the impulse behind Meiyin Wang's 2011 vision of "The Theatre of the Future," alluded to in the first volume of *American Theatre Ensembles* and worth repeating:

> There will be no titles of playwrights, directors, actors, designers, managers, producers. There will be theatremakers. That will be all that is allowed on a name card. "Theatremaker." People you meet will include a writer/designer. A director/electrician. A sculptor/actor. A film editor/musician. A cook/dramaturg. A plumber/poet …

> The notion of authorship, sole authorship, will change rapidly. Theatre will be made in duos—like Big Dance Theater's Annie-B Parson and Paul Lazar, in trios—like Alec Duffy, Rick Burkhart, and Dave Malloy in *Three Pianos*, in ensembles and collectives, like the Rude Mechs, Universes and SITI Company—where you will not be able to see the edges of creation, generation, and execution.

> (2011, n.p.)

As new writing, devising, and creative development began to amalgamate, a space of negotiation opened up between center and margin, leading, for instance, to the recent practice of major regional theatres inviting devising ensembles to their festivals: these include the Actors Theatre of Louisville's

Humana Festival, which has hosted Pig Iron Theatre, Universes, New Paradise Laboratories, and Rude Mechs, among others. Some regionals commission ensemble-based work for their regular seasons, as has been done by the Walker Center in Minneapolis, Portland Center Stage, Yale Rep, the Public, Kansas City Rep, La Jolla Playhouse, South Coast Rep (which now hosts a series dedicated to presenting ensembles), the Center Theatre Group running the Mark Taper Forum and Kirk Douglas Theatre (Los Angeles), Oregon Shakespeare Festival, and Woolly Mammoth (Washington, DC). Perhaps based on the long-standing success of European theatres commissioning American creative ensembles, but also owing to the popular success of physical, immersive, and visual-based performance styles that many ensembles employ, devised theatre has proved popular as a crossover brand for larger theatres seeking alternatives to standard fare and opportunities for audience development (Carr 2015).

These developments have occasioned legitimate unease among artists and critics who prefer to maintain distinctions between the margin and the center, and who consider that "although devising practitioners continue to subscribe to a generalized collective ethos, collection creation *per se* takes place in a compromised form" (Horwitz 2012: see also Horwitz 2013; Mermikides 2013).[9] That third-wave devising is a compromised practice, however, is stitched into its very history, even leaving aside the extent to which collective creation in its second-wave manifestations may have been so as well. What will matter, ultimately, is whether ensemble-created theatre follows historical precedent and allows the center to reshape its marginal position, rather than forging an equal basis for exchange. The "artistic kleptomania" of which Grotowski and Peter Brook accused the "rich theatre" has a long and distinguished history: as Jessica Silsby Brater's essay in the first volume shows, Lee Breuer of Mabou Mines has long been calling attention to the role of alternative theatre as the "research and development arm" of the mainstream and has (half-) jokingly argued that Broadway should be funding it. And, of course, critics have thoroughly analyzed the many and sometimes nefarious ways that, under capitalism, all forms of avant-garde energy are eventually recuperated and commodified (Mann 1991; Savran 2004, 2005; Schechner 2010; Harding 2015). Fewer, though, have considered how that unstable commodity might disrupt the center even as it takes up residency there. As Shannon Jackson points out, speaking of the Builders Association and the German company Rimini Protokoll, creative ensembles have begun "to grapple with art's imbrication *within* rather than valiant separation *from* the social formations they critique" (2011, 168).

This movement is certainly essential in the transition from the second to the third wave of collective creation in the United States, yet the linear equation of "margin to center" fails to capture the complexity of such exchanges. The mutual influences and feedback loops between devised work and new play development and experimental playwriting, for instance, are only beginning to be explored, a particularly intriguing situation that encompasses not just recent examples of playwrights like Young Jean Lee, Suzan Lori-Parks, Jillian Walker, and Naomi Iizuka who have strong connections to devising but also a previous generation of writers like Adrienne Kennedy, Sonia Sanchez, Barbara Molette, and Ntozake Shange, the latter of whose work with the choreopoem inspired forms of devising (Kolin 2010; Persley 2015; Forsgren 2018). Coming at the issue of margin and center from another angle, in 2011 Rachel Chavkin (founding artistic director of the Brooklyn-based the TEAM) responded to an open blog sponsored by TCG based on the prompt "What if …?" Her post, entitled "What If … Devised Theatre Moved to the Mainstream of Theatre Making?," showed that in some respects the tables could be turned, with devising ensembles assuming a position of leverage in the exchange with conventional producing entities and potentially effecting transformation in mainstream practices.

> If devising moved to the mainstream … producers would sit down with the artists … and ask how they want to approach MAKING. Unions would have to make significant adjustments, and this would be enormously difficult since a union's power in part rests so much on the shared needs of a specific group. Devising takes longer and we'd have to accept that a three-week rehearsal period is not enough. Rules and practices that fit well for one project, simply might not translate. I think this would be healthy for institutions, though also place an increased demand on their time and resources. But from my limited experience working on new plays, this holds no less true for that world; one writer's and play's needs are vastly different from another's.[10]

Rather than an overtly oppositional stance pitting a marginalized collective creation against a playwright-centered and hierarchical production method in the center, Chavkin's musings reflect a new confidence that— especially following the devastating effects of the Great Recession of 2008– 2010—ensemble creation might positively alter the long-standing methods for funding, supporting, and developing theatre in the United States. This dynamic will certainly bear watching as all forms of theatre emerge from the social quarantines imposed by the COVID-19 crisis of 2020. Yet, whether one embraces it or not, Chavkin's position reflects a brand of entrepreneurial thinking that can hardly be imagined in earlier manifestations of collective creation by, say, the Living Theatre (which would insist that the transformation could only happen after the anarcho-pacifist revolution had been realized) or later from the Wooster Group (which would wish to maintain the separation between Uptown and Downtown theatre).

And while Chavkin's question remains an open one to this day, her query has been followed by new points of contact and mutual negotiation between resident theatres and devising ensembles. Certainly, a period characterized by miscomprehension and even suspicion is noticeable as the new terrain is explored. The Director's Guild of Great Britain and Actor's Equity Association (AEA) held a conference at the Barbican in London in 2004, and even though it set out to define ensemble creation, it focused solely on organizational structures and solicited almost no input on US practices. AEA, itself, which has long complicated the lives of its members who choose to work with ensembles, has shown greater openness to working toward more sustainable contracts (Louloudes 2012).[11] Major convenings have been held to discuss how best to support ensemble-created work by the New England Foundation for the Arts (2009), the Director's Circle (2009), and the Alliance of Resident Theatres (2012). Arena Stage hosted a conference in 2010 sponsored by the American Voices New Play Institute on "Theater Outside the Box: Devised Work" that brought together artists from Rude Mechs, Pig Iron Theatre, Universes, and other ensembles with producers and presenters from across the nonprofit sector to discuss common goals and obstacles (Sobeck 2010).

And while it is disconcerting to find how little regional theatre and arts organization administrators and curators knew about (or valued) ensemble creation until well into the twenty-first century, it is hardly surprising—especially after the 2008 Great Recession and its culling of the nonprofit theatre sector—that professional theatres are today willing to look "outside the box" to resuscitate their programs and galvanize new audiences. But even such self-regarding goals sometimes produce interesting results. Beginning after 2010, organizations like the Center Theatre Group in Los Angeles were actively developing programs for hosting, commissioning, and supporting ensemble-made theatre. They recognized that new play development had to move beyond single-authored plays and began designing hybrid support mechanisms for ensembles and "hyper-collaborators," including "completion commissions" that provided backing at earlier stages of project development (Rodriguez 2012). Ensembles like Rude Mechs (for *Never Been So Happy*) and Universes (*Party People*) used funding by CTG to develop their work at their home base or another theatre, with CTG retaining an option to produce it in Los Angeles. Interestingly, both ensembles allowed CTG to give notes at initial productions and even to bring their dramaturg in on occasion. Despite appropriate concerns over such interventions, this provides evidence that even as ensembles compromise with larger presenting organizations, collaborative creation itself is shaping the practices of the mainstream, enriching it aesthetically and expanding its repertoire. One wonders whether a breakout work like the (semi-)immersive *Natasha, Pierre, & the Great Comet of 1812*, directed by Chavkin from its opening at Ars Nova in 2012 through its Broadway run of 2016–2017, might be a sign of future crossovers.

But movement is not restricted from margin to center: as already noted, a full accounting must recognize that the center, too, has been in transit. Most developments bringing the center into closer proximity to the margin took place alongside, and in complex interactions with, dramatic changes taking place in American society. The new dynamic between center and margin results largely from a new sociopolitical and economic context, one that did not substantially influence the work of the second-wave collectives from the 1960s. As well, it was not decisive (if still present in embryonic form) during the transition into the third wave of collective creation addressed in the first volume. While these altered circumstances affect every form of ensemble-created theatre after the 1990s, they are especially dynamic with respect to broad remit companies like those represented in this series, ensembles that operate robustly alongside professional theatre networks and must constantly negotiate with the economic, social, and cultural conditions of late capitalism.

Given such challenges, perhaps their greatest claim to be represented in these volumes is simply that they have survived such conditions long enough to provide opportunities to alter the mainstream. Four of the six companies from the first volume (as well as the Wooster Group) are still producing today, pending the effects of the 2020 pandemic: Mabou Mines, founded in 1970; Lookingglass (1988); Elevator Repair Service (1991); and SITI Company (1992). Theatre X survived for thirty-five years, opening in 1969 and only shutting down in 2004, while Goat Island had the briefest (albeit an intensive) run—still twenty-two years—between 1987 and 2009. All the companies represented in this volume, except for the more recently formed 600 Highwaymen, remain active after at least twenty years. From their extended careers, a richly detailed longitudinal study emerges of the forces shaping and transforming ensemble creation and its relationship to the mainstream during a turbulent period in American and global history.

The Rise of Devised within Neoliberalism

While space precludes diving deeply into these details, this chapter will now attempt a panoramic view of the contexts that shaped ensemble-created theatre after 1995. The uprights that support the structure, as touched upon in the previous chapter, are the rise, eventual entrenchment, and potential decline of neoliberalism as the dominant economic and social order of US, and increasingly global, culture. Equally important is the consequent manifestation of a pervasive precarity that neoliberalism produces to maintain its hegemony, what Isabelle Lorey calls the "State of insecurity" (2015). One of the characteristic features ascribed to third-wave collective creation is its "nonutopic" nature, which distinguishes it from the radical 1960s companies, and precarity is itself defined by the way it limits prospects and desires.

Under the aegis of neoliberalism and precarity, then, new ways of understanding the practices of ensemble creation (including organizational structures as well as how such work is circulated within US and global culture) are required. First, one must account for the already-mentioned fact that ensemble practices have returned creative labor somewhat back toward the freelance model operating in most US regional theatres. Second, how such work is supported and circulated as part of a global economy must be placed in a contemporary economic scenario, focusing on what Bojana Cvejić and Ana Vujanović call, regarding EU practices that nevertheless resonate with US ensembles, "festivalization and the coproduction of projects that atomize and multiply work without end or limit; the proliferation of small-scale projects that rejuvenate the labor force under cheap labor contracts" (2010, 167). Finally, the domestic support of devised theatre needs to be understood within institutions of neoliberalism, for instance, concerning the role played by the academy, itself undergoing massive changes that influence the way devising is taught within, and supported by, higher education. Finally, lest the emphasis fall too heavily on devising's incorporation into the neoliberal order, a full account must also address how US ensembles working within that context have found methods to contest and resist its mandates. Despite the discouraging picture of art practices that sometimes emerge when they are viewed panoramically, US ensemble artists with boots on the ground have proven themselves shrewd tacticians in negotiating the precarious landscape of US culture in the twenty-first century.

On the cusp of the millennium, American ensemble-based theatre found itself in a unique position. Due to the proliferation of performance forms that began in the New York underground scene of the 1950s and 1960s and which expanded across the country in the intervening decades, an entire ecology of alternative practices had become, if not normalized, then at least acceptable within a widening environment of independent art production. By the late 1980s and early 1990s, ensembles like the Wooster Group, Goat Island, Elevator Repair Service, Lookingglass, SITI, and Big Dance Theatre were exploring new methods of devising that continued to question and test the ideologies of strict collectivity while still maintaining robust collaborative creation. Boosted by new channels for circulating the methods and practices of ensemble creation via academia and a growing network of alternative art venues as well as domestic and international fringe festivals, this current of third-wave collective creation helped propel the upsurge in new companies arriving in the early years of the new millennium, such as The Nature Theatre of Oklahoma, Ex. Pgirl, rain pan 34, Strike Anywhere, the Civilians, and Mondo Bizarro.

But it is certainly no coincidence that at around the same time collective creation was giving way to the looser models of collaboration that would expand into devising, neoliberalism was becoming institutionalized in many areas of the US economy and political culture. Even while the Wooster Group was "breaking the rules" (evoking the subtitle of David Savran's seminal study of the Group's work from the 1980s), Reagan was deregulating them; and both acts of disruption emerged from a common context. Although US arts in general have played an activist, resistant role in the onset and development of neoliberalism, one cannot assume naïvely that they have remained unaffected by it. As the conditions of production changed across the economy and affected all forms of labor by breaking up historical solidarities and forms of collective organization, the manner by which creative ensembles were being formed, supported, and given opportunities to work and produce were being altered under neoliberalism. Today, a robust body of work on the labor of performance more generally within neoliberalism, which often cites the practices of international as well as US ensembles, can be called upon to explore these effects (Wickstrom 2006, 2012; Bailes 2011; Jackson 2012; Nielsen and Ybarra 2012; Rideout and Schneider 2012; Harvie 2013; Mermikides 2013; Walsh and Causey 2013; Diamond et al. 2017; Ybarra 2017; Fragkou 2018; Tomlin 2015a).

As outlined in the previous chapter, the steady growth and expansion of a neoliberal political and economic order that began in the mid-1970s shadowed the emergence of devised theatre out of the traditions of collective creation in complicated ways. The radical collectives of the 1960s could claim that their egalitarian and nonhierarchical company structures positioned them as an alternative to, and as an implicit critique of, the existing US economic, political, and social order. But once those utopian desires were exposed in practice and the next wave of ensemble-created theatre assumed the "postutopic" position, the third wave was induced to move toward the looser structures of "collaborative" performance and, ultimately, devised theatre. This certainly compromised the claim of ensemble theatre to be an alternative formation and, as we have seen, has sanctioned forms of rapprochement with the professional nonprofit theatre. Especially as long-standing ensembles like the Wooster Group, Mabou Mines, Lookingglass, and SITI have become less stable in terms of company structure and membership, and younger groups form from the start with core-and-pool and temporary contract structures, their forms of labor come to more closely mirror not just those of the regional repertory theatres but even in some instances the gig or temp economy that characterizes the present working conditions of global unskilled labor.

By the 1980s the US workforce was undergoing substantial transformation. Both before and during the Reagan presidency (1981–1988) and continuing into the twenty-first century, neoliberal theory began to influence economic planning and policymaking in the United States and, increasingly, around the globe. Along with other consequences, this transformed the relationship between capital and labor by creating incentives for companies to move away from "Fordist" modes of production that concentrated the means of production in centralized locations, where limited kinds of goods were produced. But by the 1970s and in pursuit of greater flexibility, mobility, and market agility, corporations became placeless and began distributing production of their increasing varieties of commodities to multiple locations both domestic and international. As deregulated capital flowed across borders, so too did labor need to become more itinerant. Now unfettered from specific centers of production tied to a stable local labor force in whose future well-being corporations had to invest, capital was no longer bound by the reciprocal relations that had incentivized it to create and manage pensions, health care programs, and stable wages. Temp work and short-term contracts allowed corporations and businesses to turn over their workforce depending on the product or project needed (known as "just-in-time" production) and to shift some of the risk involved in market volatility to labor. Workers consequently found it necessary to become trained and credentialed across several skills to keep pace with the changes. This in turn led to the demise of centralized management systems, which depended on a stable pool of workers with similar skills to direct, and the emergence in their place of less hierarchical structures that granted greater freedom to individual employees and project teams to innovate and meet quotas. Although this granted workers relative autonomy, their efforts were closely monitored and evaluated (and often quantified by initiatives such as Total Quality Management [TQM] and New Public Management [NPM]) as the basis for continued employment and for paying out incentives or profit-sharing, which had largely replaced regular wage increases.

Thus emerged what John McKenzie has dubbed the "perform or else" ethos of the neoliberal order, which

> attunes itself to economic processes that are increasingly service-based, globally oriented, and electronically wired. Since the end of World War Two [management theorists] have argued for decentralized structures and flexible management styles, styles that, rather than controlling workers, empower them with information and training so that they may contribute to decision-making processes. The principles regularly cited in management are not uniformity, conformity, and rationality, but diversity, innovation, and intuition.
>
> (2002, 6)

Of course, McKenzie's point is that the shift in labor practices hardly stops at promoting diversity and innovation. The price paid for these more flexible management structures is greater surveillance, less job security, fewer mandated benefits, and the anxiety to perform or else in the competitive workforce.

Ferdinand Lewis, who worked with Cornerstone Theatre Company in Los Angeles and wrote their *Cornerstone Community Collaboration Handbook* in 2003, draws an interesting contrast between what he terms "the dominant 'Broadway' or 'specialist' model of play development and production" and the methods employed in ensemble creation. In the former, he writes, "most of the authority in the organization resides at the top:"

Authority over the artistic process is divided among many categories of specialization, such as the playwright, director, actor, producer, designer or stage manager. There is collaboration between the specialists, of course, but it is particular and specialized. Although the specialist model may streamline the administration of theater and encourage a high level of specific craft technique, it reduces the amount of artistic control that any one specialist has over the final product, and also reduces the amount of influence one craft tends to have over the others during the development process. It makes collaboration in its truest sense impossible.

(2005, xi–xii)

By contrast to the Fordist nature of the specialist/Broadway model, he goes on to say, "ensemble theaters tend to be composed of *generalists* who create work in full collaboration, with each contributor directly responsible for a number of production and organizational elements, if not the entire production" (xii).

These statements are familiar within an authorized discourse of ensemble creation that marks and maintains important distinctions between the center and the margin. Nevertheless, they neglect to contextualize these "alternative" practices within the shifts in labor structures and thereby to recognize that center and margin had begun, under neoliberalism, to meet somewhere in a muddled middle. Under new management systems, "the organization is a fleeting, fluid network of alliances, a highly decoupled and dynamic form with great organizational flexibility" (Martin 1994, 209). As such supple management systems were installed and production dispersed across the globe, firms experimented with less centralized and hierarchical structures, in some instances inviting employees to become (often in symbolic form only) part owners and coproducers. But they were also asking them to assume a portion of the economic risk attached to any business endeavor by linking their labor and compensation to the company's latest venture.

As post-Fordist production began to affect the nature of labor, it was often packaged, as McKenzie and others show, as a great liberation from the highly regulated schedules dictated by labor unions, fixed company leave policies, and time-served-based salary advancements of the traditional workplace. And there were many advantages gained: under a variety of rubrics (peer production, commons-based production, and—after digital technologies had penetrated the workplace—open-source, user-generated content, and crowdsourcing), post-Fordism presented a path toward greater worker autonomy, flexibility, and freedom. Workers were encouraged to develop a portfolio of skills and credentials that would facilitate movement within an organization or laterally into other forms of work. Labor would gain mobility by becoming (like Lewis's ensemble artists) "*generalists*" and thus be freed from narrow specializations that inhibited such agility. The priority was to release innovation and the individual worker's sense of entrepreneurship as she/he worked closely with decentralized project teams. Like a slippery signifier in poststructuralist theory, the point was for the worker not to be pinned down to a single denotation. Increasingly, it appeared that the mainstream was adopting forms of labor similar to those explored in certain artistic practices, slumming (as it were) with DIY culture and the "alt."

One can thus well imagine the model post-Fordist worker and ensemble theatre practitioner of the mid-1990s having more in common than differences between them concerning the nature and aspirations of their work. Indeed, it is around this time that the relative autonomy of cultural production, itself, comes under scrutiny and artistic production begins to be treated as another form of labor in the neoliberal marketplace. Under neoliberalism, notions of art as a public good or element of the commons are reshaped to position (and fund) art as another expression of economic productivity. While more transparent steps in this direction were initiated in the 1990s in the UK under New Labour's support for the "creative industries," the notion of the arts as economic drivers in the United States were being explored as part of neoliberalism's ambitious pursuit of new markets within what traditionally had been the commons: art, education, health care, water, and the like. Such thinking received a significant jolt when the sociologist Richard Florida published *The Rise of the Creative Class* in 2002.[12] According to a logic that Gregory Sholette later termed "enterprise culture," Florida argued that artists were invited into the post-Fordist order by locating their exchange value in an ability to mobilize creative capital to revitalize downtrodden urban neighborhoods and districts. Artists, he envisioned, would bring—along with the software engineers, hairstylists, postpunk fashion designers, and peripatetic chefs who would similarly gravitate toward such reparable spaces—a gentrifying energy to refresh and rebuild what had become economically dormant (Sholette 2011). The freelancing artist, ironically, became the poster child for the new enterprise culture by virtue of a commitment to constant innovation, a willingness to be flexible regarding work and location, and the immateriality of their labor. There arose an unstated compact in which artistic autonomy and the self-identification of "alternative" status were given in exchange for dashing any hope of ongoing material support in the form of regular arts funding, pensions, health care, and steady employment.

Indeed, as Shannon Jackson, Liz Tomlin, and Aras Ozgun and others have pointed out, the marketing of the flexible neoliberal workplace in the 1980s and 1990s as a site of freedom and flexibility has a particular history that intersects with the evolution of alternative art practices more broadly in the United States, including those of collective creation. Nicholas Ridout and Rebecca Schneider summarize the process in the introduction to a special issue of *TDR* devoted to "Precarity and Performance":

> In what might be regarded cynically as a spin on this state of affairs, neoliberal rhetoric promotes "creativity" as the font of economic promise. The cynicism of this discourse is that the value it claims is appropriated from sincere (even, perhaps, romantic) attempts to make a life at some distance from the demands of work. By appropriating these romantic impulses, such rhetoric compels an ever more frantic psychic investment in the constant audition that has become the work of getting work. All of these connections can be made to point to the embodied balancing act of the live performer.
>
> (2012, 7)

The discourse of ensemble creation is certainly not void of romantic impulses and rhetoric, and this sometimes shapes how collaboration is sanctioned as a method built upon creative risk and how the performer's body, especially absent the conventional structure of a predetermining text, is positioned as vulnerable and susceptible to failure (Bailes 2011). Perhaps most emphatically, in collaboratively created theatre that operated at the fringes, the values of risk and insecurity were touted as the basis for distinguishing this form from the staid professional theatre and its mitigation of risk.

An enterprise culture defined by risk is by definition also precarious: for instance, although Florida left this part of the tale of the creative class untold, once property values rose in the districts revivified by artists, these marginally or unwaged disrupters would usually be nudged along by economic necessity to the next project/location. The situation of former Downtown ensembles in New York City having to relocate to, successively, Brooklyn, Williamsburg, Red Hook, and DUMBO (Down Under the Manhattan Bridge Overpass) is just the most visible example. (The recent closing of the beloved Collapsable Hole space in Williamsburg, home to Collapsable Giraffe and Radiohole until 2013, along with the street bacchanal staged to protest its passing, drew attention to such transience [Bruin 2017]). Jane Baldwin's essay on Rude Mechs in this volume also details that company's loss of their Austin performance space, The Off Center, under similar processes of gentrification in which the ensemble's status as an alternative company plays an important, if uncompensated and transient, role. For a time, professional real estate companies like Two Trees in Brooklyn would even lease space at reduced rates to ensembles because they recognized their presence would lend the desired edge to neighborhoods under development (Pogrebin 2008).

Moving into the twenty-first century but especially so after 9/11 and emphatically following the Great Recession of 2008, US artists in general and ensemble theatre companies in particular were forced to reassess the consequences of identifying with enterprise culture. As Jackson writes, "The paradoxical advancement of a kind of 'institutionalized individualism' celebrated privatized models of creativity and life management, so that 'risk' could become synonymous with thrill and creative speculation rather than with precarity and insecurity … what we now, in 2012, call 'precarity' is the other side of a coin that used to be celebrated as 'flexibility'" (2012, 22). Of course, precariousness has always been part of the DNA of alternative art, and theatre ensembles from every wave of development have faced a hardscrabble existence. But "precarity," a term popularized by Pierre Bourdieu that enters critical discourse during the chronology of this volume, indicates a particular formation of contingency, one located in capitalism's reliance on sustained instability and inequality: Lauren Berlant describes this as "the way that capitalist forms of labor make bodies and minds precarious, holding out the promise of flourishing while wearing out the corpus we drag around in different ways and at different rates, partly by overstimulation, partly by understimulation, and partly by the incoherence with which alienation is lived as exhaustion plus saturating intensity" (2011, 166). Ensemble theatre companies across the spectrum of styles, organizational structures, methods, and degrees of success face these kinds of precarity simply by choosing to create as they do, engaging in displaced work, temporary work, project-based work, and other kinds of insecure or irregular labor that Greig de Peuter enumerates as part of the "creative precariat": "income instability, lack of a safety net, an erratic work schedule, uncertainty about continuing employment, the blurring of work and non-work time, and the absence of collective representation"

(2014, 419). However, ensemble theatres also counter these effects, as we shall see further on, by deploying collaboration and forms of solidarity as a hedge against incoherence and exhaustion, and further, by making incoherence and exhaustion important elements of their method and aesthetic. "Precarity exposes our sociality," says Judith Butler, "the fragile and necessary dimensions of our interdependency" and thus becomes not just a condition to suffer but an enabling discourse on how to effect repair through the mobilization of relational aesthetics (2016, 170).

Although Bourdieu had proclaimed in 1997 that "precarity is everywhere," during a time of economic expansion and low unemployment the enterprise economy enabled the American middle class (and especially its white members who disproportionately feature in broad remit ensembles) largely escaped the growing precariat.[13] But 9/11 and then the 2008 Great Recession created new forms of debt, occasioned by the austerity policies worldwide that further propagated the consequences of precarity. Lorey notes that "by the 2000s it becomes obvious that for cultural producers and knowledge workers, because of freedom and autonomy in comparison with full employment, self-chosen precarious living and working conditions are no longer 'alternative,' resistant, or unusual to the majority of workers" (2015, 164). Retrospectively, many artists and critics questioned the wisdom of the exchange by which job and wage security were exchanged for the potential rewards of capital (for artists, mostly symbolic rather than material) based on flexibility and risk. Speaking of the situation in the EU, which although unique still in many aspects reflects the situation in the United States, Bojana Cević and Ana Vujanović are even more direct:

> Performance workers in Europe have looked at current forms of freelance work, as well as lifestyles, conditioned by the neoliberal market, and mistaken them for innovative and creative formats …. An undying individualism prevents performance workers from reflecting on their conditions in terms of political economy, the post-Fordist condition is seen by many as a positive attribute of an avantgarde with which they overidentify.
>
> (2010, 167)

They even go so far as to take a position, echoed by Liz Tomlin, that performance practices like devising, if left unexamined, may inadvertently supply a training ground for the subjects of neoliberal capitalism (2015a, 2015b).

Circulating Ensemble Practices

Whether one accepts these judgments or not, it seems clear that to appreciate the forms of resistance and critique that ensemble-created theatre may mount within the current order, one must first acknowledge the proximities between performance and contemporary forms of labor. If nothing else, changes in the structures sustaining capitalism since the 1970s make comparisons between the radical 1960s companies of the second wave—which could confidently assert alternative performance's ability to evade commodification and retain vanguard status—and the situation of third-wave ensemble theatre nearly untenable. In addition to changes in the workplace, one can look at the effects of the contemporary international festival circuit in shaping current ensemble practices or how the academy, through training in and material support of devised theatre, now influences its development, particularly as educational institutions in the United States are increasingly affected by neoliberal reforms.

Regarding the first, the globalized placelessness of capital under neoliberalism is reflected in the burgeoning fringe festival sector which today runs constantly throughout the year and has come to play a major role in establishing the reputations and marketability of contemporary companies. During the 1960s and early 1970s, opportunities for international showcases for US alternative theatre were limited. Then as now, some US companies premiered work at the Edinburgh Fringe Festival (founded in 1947) in hopes of finding a theatre to produce their work; but compared to the steady stream of new ensembles making the trek today to Scotland (as, in their early years, did the TEAM, Pig Iron Theatre, the Builders Association, and the Civilians), few US companies from the 1960s pursued this route. Ellen Stewart uniquely brought her La MaMa ETC troupe to Paris and Copenhagen in 1965, mostly to drum up positive press in hopes of spurring interest in her company back in the United States (Bottoms 2006). Perhaps intrigued by that work, Jean Vilar invited the Living Theatre, in exile in Europe since the closing of *The Brig* in New York City in 1964, to perform at Avignon in 1968; notoriously, the performance was canceled by local authorities and eventually "Avignon Off" evolved by the 1980s as a showcase for more radical work. Beginning in 1965, Amsterdam's Mickery Theatre, under the direction of Ritsaert ten Cate, began hosting US companies like Theatre X (see Curtis L. Carter's essay in the first volume), La MaMa ETC, Robert Wilson, and the Wooster Group. This would evolve into the robust network of state-sponsored theatres in the EU that today do not just invite US ensembles to perform but often commission premieres of their work. While the faint heartbeat of a future international fringe festival circuit could be detected during and after the 1960s (the Adelaide Fringe in Australia opened in 1960, followed by others including the Festival d'Automne in 1972), the first gathering of alternative theatre-makers in North America did not arrive until 1982 with the Edmonton International Fringe Festival, in Alberta, Canada. But under the influence of the competition for global tourism, international state support for fringe festivals has since grown more robust. The EU, for instance, established a European Festival Association funded by the EU Directorate-General for Education and Culture that oversees more than five hundred events (many, but not all, fringe-based). Bonn, Montreal, Toronto, Rome, Athens, Kassel (Documenta) Paris, Hong Kong, London, Cairo, Singapore, Kampala, Dublin, Lagos, Morocco, South Africa, South Korea, and Japan all host biennales or annual festivals that regularly feature US ensembles.[14]

Festival circuits were slower to develop within the United States. The first community theatre festival (Festivals of American Community Theatre) opened in 1969 to adjudicate productions to send to overseas events. In 1988, the American Association of Community Theatres began its biannual festival in Kalamazoo, Michigan. The event went international in the next cycle and continues to this day. Dell'Arte Company's Mad River Festival began in 1991 and has since hosted dozens of US and international devising ensembles who feature physical-based and cabaret-style productions. Among alternative art venues, the Next Wave Festival at the Brooklyn Academy of Music (BAM) launched successfully in 1981 (it has hosted SITI Company, the Builders Association and the Civilians, among other ensembles). Seattle Fringe Festival opened in 1991 and the Orlando International Fringe Theatre Festival in 1992. But under the influence of national tourism boards and local municipal councils, and in support of the growing number of multimedia, mixed-use art centers across the United States (such as REDCAT in Los Angeles, the Wexner Center at Ohio State University in Columbus, On the Boards in Seattle, and the newly opened Shed in the Hudson Yard neighborhood of New York City), the number of non-juried showcase festivals in the United States began to climb steadily, opening in Minneapolis (1994), Philadelphia (1997), Chicago (2008), and elsewhere. Niche festivals, such as the site-specific Without Walls Festival sponsored by the La Jolla Playhouse, the Portland Time-Based Art Festival, the Yale

Boundaries Fest, and the recently opened NYC: Up Close Festival devoted to immersive theatre for young audiences, are becoming increasingly popular.

New York was somewhat slow in developing its fringe festival scene, but after Robert Lyons launched a summer fringe event in 1994 (the Ice Factory) at the Ohio Theatre in Soho to produce his own company's work and that of other Downtown ensembles, the pace picked up considerably. (Ice Factory, which won an OBIE in 2003, relocated to the New Ohio Theatre in the West Village after the original closed during the 2008 recession.) The New York International Fringe launched in 1997 as a juried event, but after twenty years introduced Fringe BYOV (Bring Your Own Venue) as an open-access festival spread across all five metropolitan boroughs. Complementing the International Festival, the Public Theatre's Mark Russell inaugurated the Under the Radar Festival in 2005, which has traditionally drawn many established and up-and-coming ensembles as well as cross-disciplinary artists (it is also shrewdly scheduled to coincide with the annual conference of the Association of Performing Arts Presenters). Eventually, the Devised Theatre Working Group at the Public developed a "festival within the festival" (called "Incoming!") that was added to feature in-progress work by devising ensembles and workshops where companies could share training methods. Under the Radar expanded to the West Coast in 2011 with Radar LA, hosted at REDCAT.

Today these New York-based festivals are complemented by American Realness (hosted by the Abrons Art Center), the pop-up event festival Special Effects, and Prototype (hosting theatre and new music), among many others. In 2000, Kamilah Forbes, Clyde Valentine, and Danny Hoch founded the Hi-Arts Hip-Hop Theatre Festival in New York and Washington, DC, and today it has spread to Chicago and San Francisco. Similarly, across the country and largely in response to the potential for using the arts for economic revitalization projects, both small arts venues and major regional theatres began to host alternative festivals or include experimental work within larger events. They proliferate especially in locales with existing infrastructure such as the 99-seat theatre scene in Los Angeles that formed mostly to mount Hollywood showcases, or around major universities (for instance, UCLA Live). Physical theatre festivals are becoming increasingly popular, especially in cities like Chicago that have a robust training and performance scene. More recently it has become common for established ensembles to host fringe festivals in support of other groups, such as the FURY Factory Festival of Ensemble and Devised Theatre, hosted annually by the San Francisco-based FoolsFURY. In line with the rapprochements between regional theatres and devising ensembles, several major repertory theatres now host fringe festivals, such as the Emerging America Festival initiated in 2010 at the American Repertory Theatre in Boston. All told, at present, the U.S. Association of Fringe Festivals lists close to fifty events, and an even greater number of unaffiliated festivals celebrating LGBTQ+ (like Bailiwick Theatre in Chicago), feminist, and politically activist fringe art come and go each year.[15]

Perhaps as a sign of the times, in 2012 Cara Blouin and Forearmed Productions opened the Republican Theatre Festival in Philadelphia to foster dialogue with conservative perspectives she felt were being ignored by the generally liberal-leaning alternative theatre scene. After an uneven premiere, that festival was revived in Atlanta in 2018 (two years into the Trump administration) with the same name but under different sponsorship and headed by Colt Chambers, a Young Republican with aspirations to one day lead the NEA. Robert Cooperman, a playwright and professor of literature at Ohio University, formed Stage Right Theatrics to mount the first Conservative Theatre Festival in Columbus, Ohio, in 2017 (featuring a production of David Mamet's *The Anarchist*) under his copyrighted logo "Disagreement Doesn't Equal Hate" (Horwitz 2017).[16] These festivals have thus far welcomed only new writing and have not yet featured devising companies, but although no explicitly conservative or populist ensembles have emerged into the limelight to date it seems more likely than not that this will change in the current political climate (despite the potentially embarrassing collectivist history of the form).

The results of the flourishing festival circuit have been mixed: on the one hand, artists benefit profoundly from the aesthetic and intercultural interpenetration that occurs throughout the residencies, performances, workshops, and symposia attached to most festivals. US ensembles often earn or expand their reputations with domestic audiences by their record of international tours, invitations, commissions, and recognition. Nature Theatre of Oklahoma, for instance, regularly received invitations to perform in Vienna and Hamburg as they were establishing their aesthetic and continue to tour widely in Europe. The TEAM, following a venerable road to success, made their mark first at the Edinburgh Fringe by winning several Fringe First awards in their early years, creating the basis for later European funding and development. The National Theatre of Scotland coproduced the 2008 *Architecting* (which was eventually produced at the Barbican), and this was followed by development support from the Almeida Theatre in London for *Mission Drift*. Sometimes, as with the recent case of Adriano Shaplin's Riot

Group, a company might spend years building a reputation abroad before being "discovered" in their home base of New York. As well, residencies abroad enhance the international influence of American ensemble-created theatre and thus helping to shape work globally, as when the Wooster Group and Goat Island first performed in the UK and significantly impacted the work of Forced Entertainment and other companies (Freeman 2007).

But concerns have been raised regarding some of the consequences of this growing international process of fringe arts exchange. Sponsors for such festivals sometimes have deep corporate ties or affiliations with autocratic regimes that trouble the shifting relationship between alternative theatre and hegemonic institutions. International touring also complicates the abiding commitments to local communities that many devising ensembles espouse in their vision statements and presents ethical questions regarding the relocation and decontextualization of local issues and content to the multinational places and globalized audiences of the festival circuit. A certain unease arises when ensembles find themselves, perhaps unconsciously, originally creating work for local audiences the underlying aim of which is to showcase it internationally to a very different kind of spectator. As Shannon Jackson points out:

> The economy of the [international] "tour" depends upon the particular distributions that value the new, the limited run, and the temporary contract; the "tour" is thus a place where the nomadic sensibilities of flexible citizenship meet the economic precarities of flexible citizenship. In such a space, mobility is not always "volitional." It is a model of theatre-making that cannot count on the value of home-grown theatre sustained by a community over time—i.e., the repertory model of theatre ... The politics of "globalization"—in both its cultural and economic associations— are addressed theatrically ... in part because of how globalization is lived as an itinerant artist on a limited contract.
>
> (2011, 180)

We see again concerning the festival and touring circuit how ensemble theatre must both operate within enterprise culture while sometimes also deploying its methods to critique it from within. Given the affiliation, ensemble theatres are certain to be adversely affected as this international performance scene is devastated by the 2020 COVID pandemic, as travel is curtailed and the local support environment of bars, hotels, restaurants, and galleries that contribute to "making the scene" suffer decline.

As Proudfit and Syssoyeva note, the festival circuit cannot be disentangled from the influence of the academy: "many successful theatre collectives today present almost exclusively for a 'circuit' of international festivals and university-affiliated theatres" (2013b, 27). Traditionally, collaborative theatre-making circulates through the academy both as an element of departmental curricula and training as well as in terms of productions and residencies. Readers of both volumes in this series will note how often the core of a company is forged from experiences and common training received at university, and a closer look reveals that this is becoming more often the case moving into the twenty-first century (this, too, may contribute to the mostly white, middle-class demographic that make up broad remit companies).[17] As mentioned in the first volume, as the work of the radical collectives of the 1960s was slowly and unevenly incorporated into the research and training curricula of select US colleges and universities, a new generation of artists and scholars took inspiration from that legacy. Sally Banes has argued that the sparse number of institutions housing programs that featured avant-garde theatre and performance during the 1950s and 1960s (centered mostly at Black Mountain College, the New School of Social Research in New York, and Rutgers University, among a few others) began to climb as the baby boomer generation reached college age and dramatically increased the number of students attending university in the 1970s (Banes 2000). This contributed to the number of MFA programs in the United States doubling by the late 1990s. By the early 1970s, the Association of College, University and Community Arts Administration (later the Association of Performing Arts Professionals) was active in facilitating arts education programs on campus, which included workshops, productions, and residencies. Banes's argument, that for the last quarter of the twentieth century US universities acted as a "liminoid" space that welcomed dissident art into the curriculum, faculty, arts residencies, and campus performances, helps explain the rapid growth of courses in the history, theory, and practice of US neo-avantgarde performance, often featuring the work and legacy of the 1960s radical collectives and their international (mostly European) counterparts.

The initial influx of training and research touching upon collective creation accelerated as universities began to explore interdisciplinary (and later, intercultural) studies through new department structures, centers, and institutes which brought the heretofore disconnected histories of dance, art performance/performance art, experimental music, new media, and theatre together (Carlson 2001). One can only speculate as to the influence of someone like Andrzej Wirth, who roamed the United States (without, as Matthew Cornish reminds us, a passport) for more than a decade teaching in various institutions and promoting the mutual influence of theatre training and theatre studies that, in 1982, he would take back to install at the Giessen Institute for Applied Theatre Studies (which would go on to yield companies like Gob Squad, Rimini Protokoll, and Showcase Beat Le Mot) (Cornish 2019, ix).

US theatre training, too, had been significantly influenced by the renewed emphasis on the artist's body as the source of primary meanings in performance that undergirded the work of the Judson Dance Theatre, Happenings, early performance art, and of course the somatically based collectives of the 1960s. As academic theatre training sought models for such work, the traditions of collective creation that had formally occupied only a marginal position in university curricula assumed more importance. Grotowski's work and writings, preeminently, circulated in classrooms and maintained the legacy of ensemble creation and a non-textual, physical style of training and performance. Chaikin's *The Presence of the Actor* was published in 1972, arriving at the same time as Julian Beck's *The Life of the Theatre*. Ronnie Davis produced the first book on the SFMT in 1975; by that time scholarly studies on the Open Theater and the Living Theatre had been published to complement a decade's worth of articles in *The Drama Review* and newer work coming out of the recently launched (1976) *Performing Arts Journal* (Biner 1972; Pasolli 1972). Arthur Lessac published *Body Wisdom* in 1981, collating his training techniques in kinesics, while Moshé Feldenkrais's *Awareness through Movement* came out in 1977. Jacob Moreno's *The Theatre of Spontaneity* appeared in 1983 to spread the word regarding psychodrama and theatre-as-therapy. Passed along anecdotally since the 1950s through countless workshops by the Compass Players and then Second City in Chicago, the first edition of Viola Spolin's *Improvisation for the Theatre* was published in 1985. Keith Johnstone's *Impro!* (1979) circulated in the UK and Canada before becoming popular in the United States. Also significant for the dissemination of collective practice was *Taking Part: A Workshop Approach to Collective Creativity*, collated by Lawrence and Anna Halprin in 1974. (Brian Clark's study of British practices, *Group Theatre*, had been available since 1971.) And the fascination during and after the 1970s with body-centered self-help regimens such as Rolfing and Esalen, as well as the theory and practice of encounter groups, the use of play for therapy, conflict resolution, and to promote creativity, all produced countless popular books that complemented more scholarly work. These and other readings quickly found their way on to syllabi in theatre research and practice, setting off a series of studies on the new acting and directing methods and their theoretical and practical foundations (Wiles 1980). Eventually, these developments led to professional recognition, such as the Literary Managers and Dramaturgs of America (LAMDA) hosting panels on collective creation by 1989.

Students attending US universities in the 1980s and 1990s, then, were more likely than in the past to be introduced to the work of the 1960s collectives and previous manifestations of second-wave collective creation, sometimes by artists who themselves had taken teaching positions, and to absorb this legacy in several ways. After publishing *Environmental Theatre* in 1973 and beginning to step away from his work with the Performance Group in the late 1970s, Richard Schechner devoted more time to his theoretical writings on performance, establishing the most visible and consistent voice in performance theory. The work sustained interest in collective creation and community-directed work. Les Waters left the UK Joint Stock company and traveled to the United States to direct plays like Caryl Churchill's *Fen* for the Public Theatre. In 1995 he and his wife, the costume and set designer Annie Smart, arrived at the University of California-San Diego, where he would head the MFA program in directing for almost a decade (passing along the Joint Stock method to Steve Cosson of the Civilians, among others). After leaving San Diego, Waters was named the artistic director of the Actor's Theatre of Louisville in 2012, where he was responsible for commissioning ensemble-created work and inviting a number of companies to take part in the Humana Festival. Earlier, in 1976, Ron Argelander founded the Experimental Theatre Wing at New York University (NYU) and brought in dance and theatre faculty from the metropolitan art scene (Syssoyeva and Proudfit 2013b, 28–9). As the essay by Scott T. Cummings from the first volume of this series details, this included Mary Overlie, who had performed with Judson artists like Yvonne Rainer and, while still on the West Coast, SFMT. One of her first student collaborators in the ETW was Anne Bogart, who graduated in 1977 and then was retained as a faculty member in 1979. Bogart's adaptation of Overlie's dance training method, "the Six Viewpoints," became the basis for her own Composition and Viewpoints training. The method circulated informally before the collection *Anne Bogart: Viewpoints* arrived in 1995, followed by Bogart and Tina Landau publishing *The Viewpoints Book* (2005), after which the method became tremendously influential in the training of future ensemble theatre artists such Shawn Sides and ensembles like Radiohole and Rude Mechs. In part owing to the widespread popularity of the Viewpoints in universities as well as in conservatories, new forms of collaborative creation were generated that would fuel the third wave in the United States and pave the way for the explosion of devising companies that emerge after 2005. Universities and conservatories responded in kind (and in response to earlier developments in the UK) by launching degree programs in devised theatre and ensemble creation (sometimes assembled under rubrics like "contemporary theatre" and "writing for performance") and these are now quite common and found at Berklee, NYU, Columbia College, the University of Missouri, and elsewhere. Perhaps the cutting edge of this practice is the MFA in Devised Performance at the University of the Arts in Philadelphia, based on a partnership with the Pig Iron Theatre (see Chapter 4).

Already embedded in some US universities and colleges were existing programs devoted to theatre and drama in education.[18] Many of the methods of "second wave" collective creation grew out of developments in these alternative education fields, which also emphasized embodied learning and practices—nonprofessional, low budget productions, student/performers adopting several production roles and contributing to the creation of the performance, portability of venues, a pedagogical imperative of exploring relationships and issues from many perspectives to serve the goal of inclusivity, forms of audience interaction, and so on—that carried over into the radical political collectives of the 1960s and then into third-wave ensemble creation more generally. As detailed in the first volume of this series, this trajectory would most directly inform developments in applied theatre, which by the 1990s had reclaimed the history of socially conscious collective creation to become perhaps the dominant sector of ensemble-created theatre, based in levels of participation and the sheer number of companies throughout the United States (although in America the term only achieves widespread use after the late 1990s). As universities often became laboratories for theatre in education and training centers for advocates of alternative pedagogy, they produced a significant number of teacher-artists who carried forward the practice of collaborative creation and contributed to its continued presence in American culture. Before the arrival of more conservative educational policies arising in the late 1990s, luminaries like Liz Lerman, Michael Rohd, and Rhodessa Jones were trained at universities, and all shaped the practice of collective creation in applied theatre and dance. While these programs initially seldom overlapped with the history and practice of avant-garde theatre, by 1992 critics like Baz Kershaw (commenting on a similar divide in UK theatre) were making a compelling case that applied theatre and other paratheatrical forms constituted a substantial form of experimental theatre that adapted and developed vanguard practices for more explicitly political ends (Kershaw 1992, 2016). The convergence of US devised theatre and applied theatre, then, has been developing for a long time and across several contact points.

Despite the relative autonomy traditionally granted to higher education and arts education within the academy, in particular, these developments have not been exempted from the effects of neoliberalism, and thus have been inflected by the changes taking place in US education policy that arrived during the late 1990s and early 2000s. These ultimately resulted in President George W. Bush's No Child Left Behind Act (NCLB, signed in 2002), the consequences of which are still being felt and assessed. But the reforms clearly signaled neoliberal intentions, first to produce subjects in accord with market logics based on notions of efficiency and consumer sovereignty, and second to establish an administrative ethos aligned with the new management theories overspreading the US labor sector within educational institutions. As well, NCLB was transparently intended to promote the privatization of education by dramatically cutting public school funding and then arranging competition for what remained, leaving underperforming schools (disproportionately located in communities of color and low income) to be closed and combined with others. Under the strain of increased class sizes, reduced after-school programs and summer education, and the disinvestment in funding for arts education, many parents were incentivized to take advantage of the new voucher programs that shifted public monies toward support of private academies (many for-profit), often focused on faith-based learning and other conservative causes (though progressive and even arts-centered charter schools have appeared as well).

As a result, after 2002 most alternative forms of teaching in public K-12 education, including arts education and theatre in education initiatives, were backtracked as schools were driven to produce accountable metrics based on annual testing and proficiency exams. NCLB established learning on a representational or semiotic model that assumed existing canons of knowledge to be memorized and passed along more or less unchanged, and therefore amenable to standardized testing. Little support was provided for the longer developing forms of embodied learning that theatre in education and somatic-based training had long espoused, where teaching assumes a body that is sensate, always in motion, and radically in relation to the world (and thus a work in process). As NCLB remained the national educational policy between 2002 and 2015 (when it was replaced by ESSA, the "Every Student Succeeds Act," under President Obama, which modified but did not eliminate standardized testing), this meant that the generation of students that would come to comprise US ensemble theatres in the second decade of the twenty-first century often did not substantively encounter theatre in education techniques during their formative learning years.

Concerning US higher education, similar reforms have shifted public universities toward a neoliberal model, though the pace of change is more uneven when compared to the drastic results experienced in the UK after league tables were introduced by Conservatives in 1992 and then fees were imposed by New Labour in 1998 (and dramatically increased in 2006). In the United States, annual budget cuts, particularly at state colleges and universities, have increased class size, reduced research efforts, and created a new class of contingent faculty as tenure protections have been rolled back and retired positions left unfilled, particularly in the arts and humanities (Newfield 2008; Peter and Jandrić 2018). A student debt crisis has arisen in response to the skyrocketing costs of post-secondary education, instituting conditions of economic precarity for a middle class relatively unaccustomed to them. An ethos of consumer sovereignty has thus arisen, in which debt-conscious students demand programs and experiences that will credential them for decent jobs upon graduation. The resulting flight of students from the arts and humanities into STEM-related fields (science, technology, engineering, and mathematics, as well as computer sciences and digital media) since the Great Recession has decimated departments of theatre, dance, music, and related arts.

This results in devised theatre sometimes entering the academy in economically motivated rather than ethically driven ways. Some university theatres began experimenting with devising, for instance, in response to logistical rather than aesthetic or political concerns: given the increasing gender disparity among majors in many departments of theatre (exacerbated by STEM flight), and the dominance of a male-centered canon that preponderantly creates substantial roles for male performers, many college theatres struggle to cast their seasons. The same could be said with regard to non-binary students and students of color. Devising offered a means to create work by and for marginalized and mixed groups, even if these shows were not often brought to the main stage. But such impromptu responses to economic imperatives sometimes produce unforeseen, yet largely positive, consequences. Given the empowerment experienced by many student devisers based in the method's openness to multiple subjectivities and identities, devised theatre quickly became popular among students and likely contributed to the social turn in the performances that these students might later mount as members of ensembles. The academy, therefore, may have played a role in bringing applied and formalist practices closer together. As testimony to the greater status of devised theatre in higher education, even the venerable Kennedy Center American College Theatre Festival, operating since 1969, recently added a category for devised theatre performance, collaborating with companies like Blessed Unrest to incorporate more physical theatre into their programming. These developments, in turn, have pushed the academy to respond in kind with new forms of training to prepare artists for the multidisciplinary and multimedia forms of devising now being practiced, for instance, the Carnegie-Mellon MFA in Video and Media Design for Performance.

Concerning curricula related to collective creation, what Banes described as the liminoid space of the university where experimentation could thrive is somewhat in retreat, although compared to other institutions the university remains a bastion of alternative practices. In addition to training, the academy continues to play a proactive role in presenting and producing the work of contemporary ensemble theatres. While this is not a new development—Ping Chong was a regular resident artist at several campuses and created work with a mixture of his company and students at Kent State and Syracuse University, and Mabou Mines and/or Lee Breuer were often hosted by Arizona State University West, among many other examples— the practice accelerates in the 2000s. But this, too, occurs in part because universities have also been pulled into and celebrated by the enterprise culture, forming an important element in Florida's concept of the creative class and often recruited for economic revitalization. This allows institutions of higher education to continue cultivating alternative forms of learning and expression, as these are necessary to produce the disruptors whose innovations will presumably provide the acute blade for the "edge cities" of the future. In turn, such sentiments permit university theatres and art centers to host residencies of alternative theatre artists, providing sites not only for production but also the most desired commodity among ensemble theatre-makers: the time to develop their work while being sustained by an infrastructure of support, something conventional presenters and producers rarely can offer. The University of Buffalo, the Wexner Center at Ohio State University, the University of Southern California, Carnegie Mellon, Wesleyan University (Connecticut), Montclair State University (New Jersey), CalArts, the University of Wisconsin campuses in Madison and Milwaukee, and many other institutions have a regular rotation of ensembles performing or in residence.

However, as Liz Tomlin has reported concerning UK practices, in the long run the neoliberal university may contribute to the commodification of alternative art practices rather than their autonomous development (2015b). As ensemble theatre and devising practices grow more popular (and remain considerably less expensive to mount relative to mainstage shows), educational institutions look to incorporate them more robustly into both training and production curricula, often supplementing the coursework with the type of sponsored residencies just mentioned. But even the manner collective creation is taught is undergoing substantial change. The dissemination of devising methods rose rapidly near the end of the 1990s with a series of published instructional guides. Bogart's *Viewpoints* has been mentioned but Savran's Wooster Group book of 1988 included observations on the Group's devising, and these were complemented by texts arriving later, such as Goat Island's *Small Acts of Repair* (2007), preceded by their reading companions and notebooks for *It's an Earthquake in My Heart* and other works from the late 1990s and early 2000s. From the UK, Tim Etchell's *Certain Fragments*, describing some of the methods of Forced Entertainment, was published in 1999 and *The Frantic Assembly Book of Devising Theatre* in 2009 (followed by many others). The growing number of how-to guides available today assures that almost anyone can be trained to teach devising. And the promotion of devising techniques has grown exponentially in the past decade via the internet, with companies uploading teasers of their work and rehearsals, how-to videos, and sometimes captures of entire productions to YouTube, Vimeo, and performance-specific sites like OntheBoards.tv, Digital Theatre, and Kanopy. The recent appearance of open-platform portals like HowlRound Theatre Commons (based at Emerson College), Theatre Times, and Digital Theatre+, which feature a mix of written blogs by artists and researchers, podcasts, concise guides to devising principles, histories, and methods, and live-streaming events, has certainly raised the profile of many ensembles and seeded interest in alternative forms of theatrical creation.

Given such resources, however, one need not be deeply committed to ensemble creation to teach "the basics." (This becomes clear when books appear with titles like *Making Theatre: The Frazzled Drama Teacher's Guide to Devising* [Bennethan 2014].) With techniques and formulas for successful devising so widespread, commentators have expressed concerns that an ensemble "style" may have developed that merely "quotes" the work of eminent companies rather than grounding would-be artists in the ethos of collaboration and exploring new directions as a group (Heddon and Milling 2006, 215–17; Schechner 2010). Archiving formal strategies not only feeds a market for alternative theatre but also potentially dampens the search for new forms that might enact radical breaks in the spectator's perception. And although instances of this practice in the United States are not yet widespread, Tomlin describes how in the UK even the venerable "scratch nights" that showcase ensemble-created work in progress are being shaped to select market winners and losers by advancing only those works in development that meet these stylistic criteria (2015b). Critiques have also been offered that question how, by coming to devised theatre via the abstract techniques now taught widely, future artists trained in the neoliberal university will approach such work not through deep commitments to an ensemble ideal but simply as a style like any other to be put on and taken off at will, a commodity with a trending exchange value in the enterprise culture. "The student discovers collective creation, not as social or political rebellion, but within an atmosphere of institutional approval ... They do not, in the same degree, have to fight their way free of older models to discover it on their own; it comes to them as an inherited entitlement" (Syssoyeva 2008; see also Tomlin 2015b).

"Futil(ity) Is Resistance!"

To this point, the focus has been toward understanding some of the ways that neoliberalism, as a hegemonic set of beliefs and practices extending across economic and cultural production to construct a horizon of the real and the possible, has influenced developments in ensemble-created theatre. As the values and identifications produced by neoliberalism become increasingly entrenched within institutions, their effects spread steadily if irregularly across the arts and help shape the nature of artistic labor and production. Yet hegemonies are contingent and never absolute, and as much as neoliberalism and its consequences seem to have infiltrated even those institutions to which we normally ascribe relative autonomy, it is equally the case that these are sites where resistance has historically been effectively mounted. To cite just two instances, research on the neoliberal reforms of US higher education has pointed to how incompatible these market-based reforms are proving to be with the so-called Open Model emerging organically from the digital university. As digital forms of knowledge-sharing that value interconnectivity and interactivity proliferate, these have worked against neoliberalism's foundations in contractual relations, copyright ownership, the ethos of efficiency, and hierarchical leadership (Peters and Jandrić 2018). It could be argued, then, that university-trained artists have anticipated or absorbed this model and carried it into the work they create through collaboration. Second, within liberal arts training specifically, ensemble creation has become not just a training and production practice within the academy but a model for progressive reforms in theatre pedagogy and even departmental restructuring that seek to unknot the "craft or culture" divisions within many programs and reenvision learning outcomes that "foster civic discourse, critical thinking, imaginative expression, interpersonal communication, corporeal intelligence, creative problem-solving, empathic awareness, and intercultural knowledge" (Zazzali and Klein 2015, 263; see also Schmor 2004; Fryer 2010; Perry 2011; Perucci 2018). Here as above, the potential exists that collective creation may disrupt and transform the very (academic) mainstream into which it is being hailed.

Concerning ensemble theatre itself, it almost goes without saying that most US companies found themselves opposing the policies and effects of neoliberalism, especially as they helped create a culture of toxic consumerism, environmental degradation, communities riven by problems arising from the loss of investment, privatization of the commons, and grinding inequality. Many ensembles formed specifically to act out against such depredations, and a number have shifted their mission statements to state explicitly that their values run counter to those of neoliberalism, even when that term is not used. Despite this, a discourse pitting the "political" and "avant-garde" 1960s collectives against the "apolitical," "conservative avant-garde," and "arty party" devising ensembles of the present continues to ignore the substantially altered economic, social, and cultural contexts which distinguish one era from the other.

The ethics of precarity are not the ethics of utopia: as Judith Butler and others have argued, the former must discard the ideological certainty of the latter and seek "a new bodily ontology, one that implies the rethinking of precariousness, vulnerability, injurability, interdependency, exposure, bodily belonging, desire, work, and the claims of language and social belonging" (Butler 2016, 2). Similarly, the confrontational performance politics of the 1960s collectives and demands for "Paradise now!" would hardly suffice to counter the present reality, where neoliberalism itself promises its own curated paradises of experiences and immersion in the spectacle it has helped to bring into being.

Thus, while largely eschewing strong ideological positions in their work (and positively avoiding programmatic leftist thought as embodied in worker's and agitprop theatre, as well as the utopian impulses of the 1960s collectives), a majority of broad remit ensembles nevertheless engage with the social turn in the arts and address the contemporary situation of precarity both explicitly and implicitly. Among the companies represented in the following case studies, one finds work dealing with the effects of globalization on labor practices across economic asymmetries, the subprime mortgage crisis, and the entrenchment of the post-private society of surveillance (the Builders Association's *Alladeen, House/Divided,* and SUPER VISION); the juxtaposition of the existential precariousness of approaching mortality with the stark precarity of work and living (Pig Iron Theatre's *Shut Eye*); the mobilization of resistance to the spectacle (Rude Mechs's *Lipstick Traces*); the consequences of Right-wing evangelical political activity, as well as climate change denial (the Civilians' *This Beautiful City* and *The Great Immensity*); America's perilous love affair with its myth of Manifest Destiny (anything by Radiohole); and responses to the prospect of a post-Trump era of extreme populism (600 Highwaymen's *The Fever*). Reviewing the essays on US ensembles in the celebrated special topics issue of *TDR* on "New Performance" from 2010, one is struck immediately by the focus on social issues by the scholars but also, within the several interviews, among the artists. Collectively, they indicate an awareness that contemporary ensemble theatres work in what Alex Timbers, artistic director of Les Freres Corbusier, calls a "post-ironic" mode, suggesting a relationship to earlier forms of postmodernist performance that have been altered by the pressure of a changing political and cultural landscape (Savran 2010, 40). The interviews reveal changes not just in content but in aspects of collaboration, method, process, and the relationships established with the audience as these are envisioned across the spectrum of broad remit companies: in more conventional ensembles that utilize an in-house playwright like the Amoralists; companies under a single strong director like the Freres; and groups who have, or continue to, devise original works as a collective like the NTUSA, Big Art Group, and the TEAM. The latter speak in their interview of their work in explicitly activist terms, and anyone viewing the 2013 Paulette Douglas documentary *The TEAM Makes a Play*, based on the company's long process of grappling with the 2008 financial meltdown, will observe an ensemble devoted to shaping praxis in their work despite the real obstacles they faced in bringing the show to completion over five years of development (Hilfinger-Pardo 2013). This commitment to social themes and relational performance is certainly not limited only to New York companies, as evidenced by the recent collection *Ensemble-Made Chicago: A Guide to Devised Theatre* edited by Chloe Johnston and Coya Paz Brownrigg (2018), which features more than a dozen contemporary broad remit and applied theatre companies expounding passionately about the issues facing their respective communities and their efforts to confront these through ensemble creation.

Yet broad remit companies also explore more subtle and nuanced forms of political address founded on an ethic of precarity and its emphasis on vulnerability and interdependency. The first and most obvious way they respond to the logic of neoliberalism is the very act of forming, however transiently, companies of collaborative artists to produce work not just "in common" but also in support of "the commons." In contradiction to the unrelenting ethos of individual self-interest and progress that neoliberalism mounts against all forms of collective endeavor, artists choose to gravitate toward common intentions, goals, or processes determined by collective creation. One of the first changes in post-Fordist labor was the decentralization of top-down management and the widespread use of project teams whose interactions were often fleeting. While I have argued that these practices often carried over to ensemble theatres and encouraged the loosening of rigidly collectivist ideals and structures, leading to redefinitions of "ensemble" to include more ephemeral solidarities, the types of collaboration favored by neoliberal managerialism always maintained the priority of the individual within the group. Ensemble theatres, on the other hand, have largely maintained a belief that the whole is greater than the sum of its parts, and that collaborative processes are fundamental to the kind of work and experiences they envisage.

Brad Krumholz, a founding member of NACL (North American Cultural Laboratory), which formed in upstate New York in 1997, reported on the explicitly political choice involved in assuming the title of an ensemble (rather than a "theatre company") by drawing direct contrasts with the commercial model of theatre production. Foremost is the preeminence of the group over the individual, even though NACL uses a core-and-pool structure:

> Any project that strives to unseat the prominence of *the individual* is also flying in the face of mainstream cultural and political tendencies …. Especially in today's capitalist culture, which encourages privatization and discourages anything "public" (public funding,

public education, public healthcare …), placing value on the group over the individual can be seen as nothing short of a revolutionary act.

(2013, 219–20)

Explaining how he distinguishes even a transitory creative group structure from corporate organization configurations which, although decentered, retain a neoliberal ethos, Krumholz effectively discriminates between the two:

I use the term *corporate* here to emphasize the isolation of a single body from the multitude, rather than the merging of many bodies into a shared one. While a corporation, in the sense of an identity created to operate with certain rights and protections with the capitalist marketplace, is certainly made up of the many individuals working together to give it strength, its primary characteristic concerns its *distinction* and *isolation* from other such bodies; the bodies that "work for" a corporation are, by definition, forbidden to become identified with it. It is this built-in mechanism that ultimately prevents shareholders from personal, legal and financial liability for the acts of the corporation by which they are employed.

(220, fn. 1)

Another way to understand this is that the temporary collaborations that form within corporations have no *ethical* basis, while the artistic ensemble is bound together by a shared ethos of responsibility concerning what, with whom, and for whom it creates during each project. As the following essays show, broad remit companies "work for" one another and also for their audiences, cultivating "a culture of creativity … through sustainable community service."

The ethics of ensemble collaboration are thus grounded in a commitment to maintain a community of practice that, while often competitive (both within particular devising ensembles and between companies competing for commissions and grants), is nevertheless built on the pluripotency of collaboration and a model of sustainability and care. John Collins, artistic director of Elevator Repair Service, has even argued that "an ensemble *method* is more essential to longevity than the maintenance of an exclusive and permanent membership" (2013, 236: see also Roger Bechtel's essay in Volume 1). Similarly, Pavol Liska of Nature Theatre of Oklahoma told Young Jean Lee, "We never have a goal in mind, we just have a process in mind"

(2009, 94). In keeping with the notion of sustainability, ensembles and other cultural workers are beginning to investigate commons-based approaches—which begin with a commitment to "being-in-common"—directed at sharing resources and practices, further cementing their community of practice through the desire, in the words of one working group, to imagine an arts field that

> brings to life the values and practices of the commons, orienting us toward societal transformation and values-based artistic practice. The commons is a living system that invites people to address their shared needs with minimal reliance on markets. The values and principles that guide the rules of community resource-sharing are based on fairness, inclusion, and responsible stewardship over the long term.
>
> ("The Promise of the Commons," 2019, n.p.;
> see also Laermans 2012)

Collaboration in ensemble theatre also distinguishes itself from neoliberal managerialism by its commitment to processes that repair the remorseless logic of efficiency demanded by neoliberalism. As Rachel Anderson-Rabern argues in *Staging Process*, there has been an "institutionalization of the chaos of collective creation, forging an organizational model that becomes itself through constant change" (2020, 111). Perhaps the arrival of new management theories in the 1990s built on chaos theory and theories of emergence has trickled down to ensemble theatre, whose messy and labor-intensive creative processes, as several commentators have argued, bear striking resemblance to both nonlinear systems and the dynamics of distributed cognitive systems (Hancock 1995; Kemp 2018). That ensemble theatre practice is now a dynamic system thoroughly distributed across a wide community of practice is evidenced by the dizzying combinations of artists collaborating across companies on individual projects, for which Anderson-Rabern provides ample evidence (2020, 22–3). Yet rather than viewing this as a sign of "dis(en)sembling" and lack of commitment to a traditional collective, we might instead chalk it up to an increasingly networked culture that, in its positive valence, shows itself capable of sustaining very robust and dynamic practices across differences of geolocation (the ensemble Strange Attractor, for instance, is "based" in Providence, Philadelphia, and Juneau, Alaska), temporal discontinuity, and bodily presence. It seems unlikely that any of the 1960s radical collectives would have produced emergent effects while still maintaining their utopic collective identity: emergence requires an assembly of differences and the destabilizing effects of noise, disequilibrium, and time, as well as discontinuities across scale that keep the system from stabilizing into order.

These strategies for deploying the structure and collaborative methods of ensemble creation against the prevailing neoliberal understanding of labor and production also carry over into the realm of method. Many critics have followed the line of thought established by Sara Jane Bailes in *Performance Theatre and the Poetics of Failure* (2011), which generated a productive critical approach and terminology to the ensembles she analyzed (Forced Entertainment, Goat Island, and Elevator Repair Service). Bailes recognized that the pursuit of failure through a variety of collaborative methods—setting impossible tasks, exhausting the performer or spectator (or, conversely, chasing a state of boredom), pursuing miscomprehension, layering material in constellations so complex that semiosis becomes unmanageable, slowing theatrical production (both the preparation of shows and moments in individual performances) to a crawl, incorporating misfires and moments of awkwardness as central performance concepts—was a response to a neoliberal ethos that had not yet been named, that the "social and political landscape against which these groups emerged describes a specific socio-political moment key to their development" (2010, 15). Failure, after all, is twinned with risk, and both before and after the Great Recession risk was in the air as both temptation and peril. Whereas the corporate equivalent to success in theatrical terms was virtuosity (the aptitude of the individual to exceed the efforts of the ensemble and pursue advancement that would serve private economic freedom), that term, as Shannon Jackson shows (drawing upon the work of Maurizio Lazzarato, Paolo Virno, and the Operaiso school), carries the dual connotation of a kind of failure: "not unique and exceptional but democratized and awkward, something that all of us have the capacity to access. Indeed, in Virno's frame, you can deliver a mediocre performance and still be a virtuoso" (2012, 17). By exploring forms of virtuosity that neoliberalism would mark as a failure, and further to use these to curb the frantic acceleration of the production of labor both material and immaterial in the perform-or-else economy, ensemble theatre performs poorly, awkwardly, but thereby evades neoliberalism's "or else" disciplinary machinery. When Steve Luber admires the "stunning inefficiency" of Radiohole's approach to creative labor (see Chapter 6) he recognizes the political valence of failure as a counter-discourse to neoliberalism, as does Frank Boudreaux when he discusses the "aggressive inefficiency" of the TEAM (2014, n.p.).

In a similar line of flight, Anderson-Rabern writes that "methodology is itself simultaneously political, economical, and performative" (2020, 145). In one instance, she teases out the ethical consequences of *slowness* as a method in work by the TEAM, Elevator Repair, Goat Island, and the Nature Theatre of Oklahoma. Focusing on Paul Virilio's definition of democracy as embedded in the concept of "a time to share," Anderson-Rabern places those demands against economies of production built (only) for speed, just-in-time production, and anxious consumption (2020, 10–11, 123–44). These are countered by ensemble creation's "speed-based engagement with construction, destruction, efficiency, inefficiency and care," which effectively fold third-wave devising's politics into the methods by which it comes into being (12). Another kind of ethics derived from pace and velocity is provided by Jacob Gallagher-Ross, whose *Theatres of Everyday Life* is subtitled "Aesthetic Democracy on the American Stage." He finds these currents operating across instances of experimental dramatic writing (Thornton Wilder), Method acting, and solo performance art (Stuart Sherman) as well as in the devised work of the Nature Theatre of Oklahoma (2018). In each instance, methods for slowing or interrupting the perceptions of the spectator reveal the quotidian and the everyday, "a vital source of unexhausted ideas, unnamed experiences, and un-depicted realities"—or, put another way, of objects, sensations, and processes so fleeting and lacking in value as to have escaped commodification by a regime of production directed solely toward material and immaterial exchange value (2018, 5). Such practices interrupt the embodiments that neoliberalism asks us to perform, opening up for critical assessment its failures to speed us up, wear us out, and make us coherent on its terms.

Each of these approaches is substantially more complex than space here affords, but together they signal new directions not entwined in the older binary of the "political 1960s collectives" and the "apolitical devising ensembles." With the amalgamation of formalist and applied forms of theatre-making in the present generation of ensembles, a substantial amount of work becomes, itself, precarious:

In the etymological sense: they request, entreat, supplicate, or plead. But they rarely do explicitly. In contrast to propagandistic literature, which openly flaunts its political message, leaving little room for interpretation, a precarious text eschews didacticism. Its textual mode is fragmented, jagged, and therefore unsettling. This puts its intended effort at risk of failure, which is to say, its effect is unpredictable. ...

Looking at or reading a precarious text that "makes strange" negates an immediate understanding that, at the same time, hopes to prolong one's perception of it. This in turn might give rise to an aesthetic experience in which the reader/onlooker lingers and possibly gains insights more profound than those available at first glance. A precarious text therefore activates the reader to dwell on the text without, however, allowing the reader a sense of control or mastery. This puts the reader/onlooker herself in a precarious position.

(Lemke 2016, 19)

Especially as neoliberalism was staggered by the Great Recession, and in the wake of mounting evidence of climate decline and growing income inequality, different modes of opposition to this hegemony have arisen. Among these, the precarious texts that ensemble-created theatre generates may induce important insights and perhaps the affect required to unsettle audiences to the point of resistance.

Diversifying Ensemble Creation

As mentioned at the opening of this chapter, an in-depth look at the present ecology of collective creation in its much-expanded state in the twenty-first century far exceeds the scale of this introduction and weighs against attempting a broad overview of the countless groups presently developing ensemble-produced work, even within the narrower category of broad remit companies. By way of conclusion, then, I have chosen to address both the present and future state of ensemble-created theatre by returning to an issue touched upon in the first volume of *American Theatre Ensembles*. There, I offered the generalization that US practice, from the time of its revival in the second-wave companies of the 1960s through the transitions into the third wave and up through the chronology of this volume, remained—in ensemble demographics and audience address—largely white and middle class, even despite the significant contributions made by Chicano/a and Latinx companies and other ethnic ensembles. Many contemporary ensembles are now inclusive across race, ethnicities, and sexual identities, and groups with strong historical connections to collective creation continue to create applied and constituency-based ensemble work to address these communities. Yet among broad remit groups pursuing experimentation in ensemble creation, the clear majority are formed and led by white artists with college educations (many from prestigious arts-based schools). The relative lack of BIPOC-led companies operating at the forefront of US ensemble theatre should not be ignored and normalized. This is not to argue against the widespread situation of precarity described above, but rather to acknowledge that the condition is experienced differentially across categories of difference that include race, class, and sexual identity, and that these differences register in the evolution of ensemble-created theatre.

While African American artists like Rhodessa Jones and her Cultural Odyssey company had been engaging with applied theatre projects that utilized collaborative forms of writing since the mid-1980s, such as her work with female prison inmates, *The Medea Project*, very few African American broad remit companies emerged before the 1990s. The relatively small number operating even today within the applied theatre sector began to achieve prominence only when organizations arose to support them. For example, the social justice-based National Performance Network responded to the ongoing debates over multiculturalism by focusing support toward community-directed arts (like the Local Programs network, begun after Hurricane Katrina in 2005) and launching initiatives like LANE (Leveraging a Network for Equity) in 2014. Such programs also likely contributed to the convergence of social art and an aesthetically based formalism that one can discern across ensemble-created theatre more broadly.

We can see the effects of this conjunction in the work of a new generation of artists informed by developing interdisciplinary practices such as performance studies, critical race theory, and intersectional feminism who began forming ensembles in the early 2000s. Omi Osum Joni Jones studied at the two major performance study programs, Northwestern and NYU (receiving a Ph.D. in Educational Theatre at the latter in 1993). A scholar-artist, she began developing performances and research based on her concept of jazz performance developed in conjunction with Laurie Carlos (who performed in Shange's *for colored girls who have considered suicide/ when the rainbow is enuf*), Daniel Alexander Jones, and Sharon Bridgforth. The jazz aesthetic that undergirds her creative and scholarly work creates an intersectional space (she likens it to "living in the blue note") for queer, Black, and "insurgently liminal" bodies (Jones 2015, 11). Jones's *sista docta* was first performed at the National Communication Association conference in 1993 and *Searching for Osun* toured in 2000 while she was holding academic positions. Her 2015 book *Jazz Performance* details forms of collaborative performance-making based in the Yoruba concept of *egbé*, which demands both diversity and absolute accountability within the group, placing a high value on apprentice-elder relationships. When Jones arrived at the University of Texas-Austin, she collaborated with Bridgforth and others on The Austin Project, which provided space and support for a revolving network of artists to experiment with the jazz aesthetic as a medium for social change (see Jones et al. 2010). Similar initiatives have been launched at Brown University through Rites and Reason Theatre, which combines a scholarly study of Africana performance traditions with guest residencies to translate the research into performance.

A second development that significantly impacted the participation of BIPOC-led ensembles was the emergence of hip-hop culture near the end of the 1980s. Drawing on Africanist performance traditions and Latino/a street culture, early hip-hop culture provided a stark reminder of the extent to which ensemble creation had historically arisen in conjunction with marginalized performance forms that similarly sought

> a multidisciplinary approach to enacting subjectivity, where the boundaries are blurred between sound, movement, oratory, and even visual props. One uses whatever is at one's disposal to create conjured magic that manifests a "superior mode of thought." The fact that this Africanist aesthetic philosophy is based on performance process, and the doing, as opposed to the written word—*logos*—is important.
> (Osumare 2015, 604–5; see also Zenenga 2015)

Shange's choreopoems from the mid-1970s played a singular role in combining dance and spoken word, and this, joined with the foundational elements of hip-hop emerging from the emcee/DJ-led events featuring breakdancing and graffiti art by Latino/a and African American groups in the South Bronx in the late 1970s, laid the foundation for hip-hop theatre.

But a legible "Hip-Hop Theatre" style only emerged in the late 1990s to gather under one rubric several practices that had been developing fitfully across dance, spoken word, DJ-ing, playwriting, and solo performance (Uno 2004). In some ways the foundational principles of hip-hop—what Roberta Uno lists as an "art form that provides space for artistic innovation, democratic participation, and incisive social analysis," and to which we can add its use of nontraditional venues and explorations of new spectator relations that seek a different contract with the audience—align well with the values of ensemble creation (and Jones's jazz performance). An argument could be made that collective creation *tout court* has adapted many of the same expressive forms that experiment with layered textures, juxtaposition, and fragmented narrative modes that lead to hip-hop.

Yet a strong presence of hip-hop artists engaged in broad remit, ensemble-based theatre is difficult to discern. Rennie Harris and his Puremovement troupe, founded in Philadelphia in 1992, generally perform in dance venues and festivals and rarely enter into the critical discourse of collective theatre, somewhat in the same manner as predecessors like Bill T. Jones and the Urban Bush Women. Yet, the work is assembled through collaborative means and often includes spoken dialogue and narrative. Harris's durational performance, *Facing Mekka* (2003), is essentially an embodied investigation of the historical interweaving of African and diasporic dance forms. Gabriel "Kwikstep" Dionisio and his partner Ana "Rockafella" Garcia formed Full Circle Souljahs in 1992 (incorporated as a nonprofit in 1996) as a collective arts company. Although they have produced scripted work and performed everywhere from neighborhood youth centers to the Kennedy Center, their primary remit is dance. Coming out of the developing forms of applied theatre initiated by collectives from the 1970s, Playback Theatre began in communities outside New York City in 1975 under the directorship of Jonathan Fox and Jo Salas. They embraced stories from their audiences and then improvised around them collectively (often using elements of Moreno's psychodramatic techniques) to shape performances that they brought to prisons, schools, and festivals. The format proved influential outside the United States, forming an important element of Australian applied theatre practice. Playback has since spread across America, with Fox establishing a School for Playback Theatre in 1993: today more than fifty companies are registered under the name. One, established in New York City in 1998 under the direction of Baba Israel (who trained as a youth with members of the Living Theatre) and Paul McIsaac, combines the existing Playback format with the interactive nature of hip-hop performance to improvise around its community's stories, sometimes incorporating elements of *commedia* (Israel 2009).

However, in performance proper, as Osumare points out, "solo artists are the mainstay of the hip-hop theatre movement" (611). Marc Bamuthi Joseph, for instance, often creates work during residencies that include student collaborators, yet he is best known as a solo spoken word performer, dancer, director, and playwright along the lines of Danny Hoch, Kamilah Forbes, Eisa Davis, Aya de Leon, Rickerby Hinds, and Will Power. Theatre ensembles like MPAACT Theatre in Chicago and Movement Theatre Company in New York often produce these authors, but do not devise their own work. Auteur Reza Abdoh created *The Hip-hop Waltz of Eurydice* in 1991 with his Dar-a-Luz Company, and his stunning use of layered media and performance styles strongly influenced artists who worked with him (like John Jahnke of Hotel Savant) as well as the many who witnessed the work live, on the DVDs and YouTube videos that circulated widely after his death in 1995, or more recently in the 2015 documentary by Adam Soch. Most notably, Lin-Manuel Miranda created *Hamilton* in 2015, bringing the hip-hop theatre aesthetic to the mainstream even if the show was not associated with ensemble creation.

Collaborative creation forms the basis for several ongoing hip-hop programs that do not, however, form ongoing ensembles. Roberta Uno founded the New World Theatre (NWT) in 1979 at the University of Massachusetts–Amherst to work with artists of color. In 2000, NWT launched Project 2050 to develop youth and community-directed programs to facilitate civic dialogue around the changing racial demographics of New England. The youth program was centered on hip-hop pedagogy and collaborative creation under the tutelage of visiting artists such as Guillermo-Gomez-Peña, Alice Tuan, and members of the Universes ensemble. The Oregon Shakespeare Festival developed the Nextethics initiative (the term, created at a 2003 Ford Foundation "Future Aesthetics" conference, which refers to hip-hop and spoken word performance) to host a hip-hop boot camp in 2007 and devising workshops ("Mixing Texts") between 2008 and 2011. Among those who participated was Aaron Jafferis, whose hip-hop-based work (*Shakespeare: The Remix*) has played both the Public and the Old Globe, and who developed *How to Break* with Collective Consciousness Theatre (a multicultural theatre in New Haven, Connecticut) with choreography by Kwikstep and Rokafella. Other hip-hop based programs are attached to academic institutions both as platforms for student outreach and, more fundamentally, to explore hip-hop as a form of knowledge. The first-wave cohort at the University of Wisconsin–Madison produces interdisciplinary work while pursuing "academics, art, and activism," while Robert Banks's Hip Hop Theatre Initiative at NYU's Tisch School of the Arts combines theatre training and activism (Banks 2016). Youth Speaks, founded in 1996 in San Francisco, hosts residencies across the country with artists like Marc Bamuthi Joseph to lead collaborative creation workshops and play development. The potential for these programs to launch new ensembles of color based in hip-hop is promising.

Interestingly, the most visible contemporary devising ensemble led by BIPOC artists, the Bronx-based Universes, while accepting that they are rooted in hip-hop culture, steadfastly reject the notion that they create hip-hop theatre (Uno, 28). They formed out of the spoken word movement that erupted in the 1980s by capturing elements of Black vernacular oral culture such as griot storytelling and mixing these with jazz (primarily from the Harlem Renaissance poets), revolutionary poetry (Gil-Scott Heron and the Last Poets), ethnic-based ensemble theatre techniques (from ETC and playwrights of the Black Arts Movement), and the experience of polyculturalism as these were being addressed at performance venues like the Nuyorican Café in New York (which opened in 1973). Universes began as the poetry duo and husband-wife team of Steven Sapp and Mildred Ruiz-Sapp. After meeting and working together at Bard College, they established the nonprofit arts agency The Point in Brooklyn while also competing in the then-developing poetry slams that first appeared in the mid-1980s. At a spoken word festival hosted by The Point, Mark Russell (then at P.S. 122) suggested Sapp and Ruiz shape their work for the stage. They formed Universes in 1995 when they added members and created short pieces that incorporated dialogue, spoken word, movement, and music. Jo Bonney eventually brought the company in as affiliated artists with the New York Theatre Workshop, which produced their first full-length show, *Slanguage* (based on work they had been workshopping at the Mark Taper Forum, Oregon Shakespeare Festival, and New World Theatre), in 2001. It featured the company's signature combination of remixed textual, musical, and movement material and toured for more than a decade, playing at fringe festivals, university theatres, and major regional houses.

Since then, they have produced another dozen shows, receiving commissions from the Humana Festival (2003, *Rhythmicity*, featuring Rha Goddess and Reg E. Gaines, and in 2009, *Ameriville*, based on the aftereffects of Hurricane Katrina), Curious Theatre (Denver), and the Oregon Shakespeare Festival (including *UniSon*, based on the unpublished poetry by August Wilson). *AmericUS*, commissioned by the Cincinnati Playhouse, premiered in 2019 and *In the beginning there was HOUSE!* is currently in development for the Goodman Theatre in Chicago. Touring internationally since 2008, they have developed a strong aesthetic around content that addresses such issues as the history of Black militantism (*Party People*, 2012, and still touring) and the neglect of communities of color in the ongoing climate crisis. In 2020, an anthology of their work, *The Revolution will be LIVE!*, will be published by Theatre Communications Group.

Up Next?

It can feel, therefore, like ensemble-created theatre is potentially on the cusp of a new wave that will see relatively greater diversity in its ranks, but at present (like the US theatrical mainstream) it remains haunted by the "EDI problem." Other troubling issues remain doggedly in place as well: will effective forms of social art be developed through ensemble-created theatre to continue resisting a neoliberalism that, since the election of Donald Trump, seems poised to morph into even more dangerous forms of conservative populism and cultural nationalism? Can self-producing companies effect real change in the mainstream production practices of the US resident theatre network, ranging from more flexibility on the part of Actor's Equity to season planning that can be projected forward far enough to account for devising's longer development trajectories? Finally, will the ethos of risk and experimentation that has provided collective creation its oxygen be sustained as pressures mount to find a comfortable niche within an easily replicated style that satisfies only Nobrow expectations and insipid forms of social engagement?

When *TDR* published its special issue on "A New Generation of Ensemble Performance" in 2010, the essays on individual companies were preceded by a fine overview written by Paige McGinley entitled "Next Up Downtown" (2010, 11–38). She concluded by saying that going forward, "we should pay attention to this organic community with fuzzy borders, taking note of the artistic, dramaturgical, and intermedial cross-fertilizations that are almost certain to take place" (37). Ten years on, the processes of exchange have only accelerated and the borders have grown fuzzier still; and so perhaps it is time to expect more than just "next up" ensembles who will maintain current trends. Given the foundations laid by several generations of collective creation, including those in this series, one hopes that ensemble creation is poised to generate a fourth wave of practice that emerges with greater diversity and the courage to explore new ground.

CHAPTER 3
THE BUILDERS ASSOCIATION
James Frieze

The Builders Association are a New York-based performance and media company founded in 1993 by Marianne Weems, who has remained artistic director from its inception. Their technically innovative, intermedia productions (sixteen full-scale works to date) entail extensive collaboration with guest artists and innovative agencies working in new media/architectural/video art. Often coproduced with the Brooklyn Academy of Music and the Wexner Centre for the Arts (Ohio State University), they also regularly tour the United States and internationally—most often in Europe, though they have staged work as far afield as Singapore and Australia. Unlike the Wooster Group, with whom Weems worked previously and to whom the Builders are sometimes compared, her company have never had a permanent home. Their itinerant lives chime with themes of nomadism and cultural passage in their work.

In a 2001 interview, Weems situates the company in a genealogy running from the 1960s to the new millennium:

> Schechner's generation of experimental theatre was created in opposition to mass media, The Wooster Group [are] a kind of transitional model where media are incorporated on stage but the live performer is still the center of attention, and The Builders Association (among others) is emerging as a fully-mediated theatre, where the media is the real protagonist of these productions, and mass media is the acknowledged and unavoidable context in which this work is created.
>
> (Svich 2003, 56)[1]

The Builders Association have continued to emerge as intermedial innovators in parallel with the evolution of social media. This chapter will trace that evolution.

Foundations

A variety of prior experience informs the energy, experimental sensibility, and leadership that Weems has brought to the Builders over a quarter of a century. Along with Martha Baer, Erin Cramer, Andrea Fraser, and Jessica Chalmers, she was one of the V-Girls. Formed in 1986, this quintet's performative panel discussions and presentations—including "Academia in the Alps" and a fake Lacanian reading of *Heidi*—were a mordant, feminist critique of the institutions in which they took place: galleries, museums, conferences, universities. From 1986 to 1989, Weems was Program Director of Art Matters, an independent foundation (of whose Board she has remained a member) that supports artists engaged in formal experimentation and the presentation of provocative ideas. Between 1988 and 1994, as well as being dramaturg and assistant director with the Wooster Group, she worked with Richard Foreman and Susan Sontag. Immediately before forming the Builders, she cocreated Ron Vawter's legendary solo performance *Jack Smith/Roy Cohn* (1994).

Weems cites the Wooster Group's *LSD (… Just the High Points …)* (1984) as inspirational for its integration of televisual video into performance, enfolding classic text within "a sophisticated electronic sensibility" (Svich 2003, 51). Participation in the New York performance scene of the late 1980s and early 1990s introduced Weems to an eclectic, exciting range of cross-disciplinary performance by the likes of Mabou Mines and Meredith Monk; to pioneers of mixed-media performance art like Nam June Paik and Laurie Anderson; and to feminist visual/graphic artists such as Jenny Holzer and Barbara Kruger whose work questioned and exceeded the accommodation afforded by galleries and theatres. At the Brooklyn Academy of Music (BAM), she and her peers were exposed to Pina Bausch and Robert Wilson, who worked on a scale larger than that habitual to experimental, American companies. The Builders would become regulars at BAM, their similarly large-scale works gaining the kudos of performing there, "an imprimatur, which everyone in the field responds to" (Gener 2008, 31).

The first production mounted by the company (and from which their name derives) was *MASTER BUILDER* (1994).[2] Like *LSD*, this was an iconoclastic remediation of a classic text. (As its author, Ibsen, died back in 1906, he could not object as Arthur Miller famously did to the Woosters' interpretation of *The Crucible*). Artists such as Reza Abdoh and En Garde Arts had, in early 1990s New York, "pushed the concept of 'setting' in performance to one of 'siting', lodging classic and original texts in meat markets, piers, and in other found spaces" (Jackson and Weems 2015, 27). Weems and fellow Wooster Group veteran Jeff Webster had already staged a version of another Ibsen play, *Hedda Gabler*, in her loft in the Meat Market area of downtown Manhattan; *MASTER BUILDER*, which took place in nearby Chelsea, was, in technical terms, a giant leap. The venue was a 17,000-foot industrial warehouse. John Cleater, "set designer" of the fullest kind (architect, carpenter, new media artist, sculptor), and video designer Ben Rubin (subsequent recipient of numerous awards for public artworks and director of the Center for Data Arts at the New School in New York) installed a full-size, dilapidated house, the design of which was based on a 1974 photographic collage by, and the theoretical provocations of, Gordon Matta-Clark. What confronted the audience was the eerie, voyeuristic sight of an entire, three-story house in full, architectural detail but stripped of soft furnishings. Inspired by Matta-Clark's desire to unsettle ideas of architecture as solid and static and make it sculpturally performative, the house was wired with MIDI triggers that the performers activated, setting off sound effects and musical phrases which transformed the house into an instrument. During the show, sections of the house were gradually demolished to reveal new and shifting perspectives. In the daytime, visitors could explore the MIDI triggers and the various architectural "tricks" by which the house could be transformed; at night they could see how the same installation functioned theatrically.

The team that created *MASTER BUILDER* included Dan Dobson, sound designer in, again, the richest sense: composer, musician, technician, maker of instruments, and contributor of ideas to the devising process, who has worked on every show since. It also included actor David Pence and Jennifer Tipton, who was already one of the world's most garlanded lighting designers; both have, like Dobson, remained a key part of the Builders nucleus.

Whereas actors in *MASTER BUILDER* were stationed by and largely within the house, the stage in each of the two shows that followed— *IMPERIAL MOTEL (FAUST)* and *JUMP CUT (FAUST)*—was bare except for several planted cameras, images from which were projected onto screens of various sizes within a video design by Chris Kondek. These were shows in which huge, onscreen images dissolved into one another and dwarfed the performers.

The German-speaking Swiss producers who commissioned them to produce a show for Theatre Neumarket in Zurich were keen on the Builders offering their interpretation of Goethe's *Faust* (1808 and 1832), a canonical work in Switzerland as in Germany. Weems and a team of dramaturgs did extensive research, not only on various literary and cinematic incarnations of the Faust story but on the trial of Susanna Margaretha Brandt, who had been Goethe's inspiration for Faust's love interest, Gretchen. Transcripts of the trial were handed to John Jesurun—a former CBS television analyst and producer, author of live performance serial *Chang in a Void Moon* (1982–present), and adapter of another classical play (*Philoktetes*) for Ron Vawter—who was enlisted to write a script. The text Jesurun created, *IMPERIAL MOTEL (FAUST)*, paid as much attention to sonic frequencies as the meaning of words, with sections (recalling the Wooster Group's *LSD*) sped up and slowed down like a fast-forwarded video. Jesurun knew that Weems wanted to weave his text through the trial transcripts, Mountford's English farce (1652), Marlowe's *Faust* (1588), and film versions by Murnau (1921) and Grundgens (1963). Both Jesurun and Weems testify to the collaboration's significant impact on their subsequent work. More a sketch and score than a script that dictated to actors, the text created lent itself to experimentation in rehearsal, including remediation of words by sonic and filmic apparatus.

If *Faust* seems a far cry from the contemporary stories the Builders would soon focus on, an entry in a notebook Weems kept at the time reveals that she was thinking of this classic tale in ways that anticipate what was to follow: "Faust enters a world where the promise of technology guarantees transport to a fluid, phantastical universe, where 'information' is the currency and personae are means of exchange" (Jackson and Weems 2015, 81). As its revised title hints, the second and longer-running version, *JUMP CUT* (1997), moved further away from representation of a particular, fictional world suggested by *IMPERIAL MOTEL* (1996) and referred to by Weems as the illusionary "truss" of theatrical setting. The operating systems of the stage were brought into the foreground in this new iteration, which concentrated on the Murnau film and took place in the Thread Waxing Space, a large, New York gallery in which the entire area was used as a stage and a shell for Kondek and the other designers to animate with video imagery. In performance terms, *JUMP CUT* was about actors learning to hit their mark—a complex process in this kind of intermedia performance—and to work out the intricacies of a neo-cinematic acting style.

Methodology

More precisely than terms such as "mixed media" or "multimedia," the term "intermedia" captures the way in which the various components of Builders' staging—live actors, live filming of actors, sound operated live in a semi-improvised fashion, recorded film, visualizations of data of various kinds, lighting—are interwoven in what Weems describes as a "network which connects many nodes or layers in the piece" (Marranca 2008, 199). The aim is not to create a harmony (indeed, there is often tension between the live actor and the visualized data) but to fashion a whole in which meaning crystallizes dialectically. While the collaborative, negotiatory nature of Builders' methodology is a hallmark of devised theatre, it is rare for designers and technicians to be so involved in the conception of the piece from the start and throughout, driving things forward together by experimenting. A Builders rehearsal cannot take place without Dobson's evolving soundtrack. Lighting is not grafted onto an interpretation of text but is treated as integral to its generation of the performance text. What characterizes the company's mainstay collaborators is not only specialist training and experience in a particular medium but a propensity to work synesthetically: media are deployed as a totality, their rhythmic and tonal qualities transcending the particular technical properties of each medium. Tipton speaks of lighting as being (more than just analogously) like music, describing how certain colors of light make her hear certain sounds and vice versa.

Weems is very much the director and has final say, but numerous people are heavily involved in shaping ideas and making decisions. As opposed to "scripting" a piece, Weems refers to "sketching" it. Pieces grow via rough pictures which are animated in the rehearsal lab. These are pictures in the literal sense—visual rather than verbal ideas dominate, though sound sketches (aural ideas) are also generative. In the 2000s, members describe the company's approach to technology as "artisanal," a crafting process that is adaptive, exploratory, and embodied. While many spectators perceive the work to be seamless and slick, this belies the amount of "trial-and-error ... jerry-rigging and duct tape that goes into making the production look as good as it looks" (Marranca 2008, 200). I experienced some of this trial-and-error first-hand during my only collaborative experience with the company when *SUPER VISION* came to Liverpool in 2006 and installed the show in a venue used for stand-up comedy, music, and popular theatre but not to such technically rich, experimental theatre.[3] As well as embracing the challenge, the company shared their artisanal method and energy with local artists, as they have continued to do through what are nowadays titled *21st Century Storytelling* workshops.[4] These workshops encourage and mentor participants to develop project plans via the Builders' sketching-it-out ethos.

The prevailing image of the company as high-tech wizards has obscured the dramaturgical richness of their process. The snowball that is a Builders show typically accumulates during two years of poring over documentary, philosophical, and fictional sources. This extensive research is dialogic: members will often visit sites of interest together; access specialist, archival records; hole themselves up in a cabin for viewings, readings, and discussion; use time touring one production to plan a next one. All of these activities were part of the preparation of HOUSE/DIVIDED, first mounted in 2011. A response to current events, the research process was as extensive as ever. In 2008 and 2009, while CONTINUOUS CITY toured, the world was hit by a huge economic crash. In the United States, the bursting of the housing bubble led to the foreclosure crisis that reached its peak in 2010. A Builders think tank analyzed transcripts of financial firms' conference calls about earning results, closely tracked patterns of foreclosure in specific parts of the United States, and visited abandoned, foreclosed properties. In a mournful echo of MASTER BUILDER, they cut out parts of two of these houses—sections of wall and roof, windows and gables—and repurposed them within the set of HOUSE/DIVIDED. Motifs of recycling, invoking the adaptability of those who had lost their homes in the mortgage catastrophe, were also a corollary of working with a tight budget, "which prompted the designers to repurpose old cameras and other gear" (Jackson and Weems 2015, 357). Dobson designed, built, and played (live) an elaborate, electric zither. Struck by the increasingly vivid comparisons between this crash and the Great Depression, the team watched John Ford's film, The Grapes of Wrath, and read the novel aloud. The visual language of the film is writ large in the imagery of HOUSE/DIVIDED while Steinbeck's omniscient narrator is echoed in the show's prominent, commentary voice.

That many critics fail to mention the dramaturgical richness of the company's work reflects a false perception that it is media-led. Despite the dramaturgical depth, though, it is true that the Builders have always eschewed literary script of the kind that could be published as a playtext and performed by other companies. Weems insists that this is not a rejection of narrative, which, she suggested in 1999, "has been imploded by 'experimental theater' to the point of meaninglessness," but, actually, more about "reinstating narrative in a structural sense while at the same time incorporating technology. A strong story provides the skeleton on which to hang our interactions with media" (Chalmers 1999, 60). As Randy Gener points out, however, "the stories being spun [by the Builders] come off as metaphorical hooks" (Gener 2008, 30). Angelos states that their desire has always been "to tell a story without literally 'telling,'" while Weems feels that there are "very few people in the company who actually think textually" (Schechner 2012, 45). The tension between the desire to tell stories and the desire to avoid literal telling has become increasingly evident as computer technology has, from *JET LAG* onwards, played an ever more vivid role in the work. Stories depend, fundamentally, on marking the passing of time, whereas "computer time helps construct a permanent present, an unbounded timeless intensity" (Virilio in Dixon 2005, 16). So we should ask: (how) have the Builders sought to resolve these tensions?

Fleeting references are made (at several points in Jackson and Weems) to the Builders' unsuccessful and aborted attempts to work with writers. Those writers with whom they *have* successfully collaborated—Jesurun, Constance de Jong (on *SUPER VISION*), and former V-Girls Jessica Chalmers (*AVANTI* and *JET LAG*) and Martha Baer (*ALLADEEN*)—are seen by Weems as a rare breed that enjoys "writing for a situation in which theatrical 'liveness' might be complicated by various media (surveillance images, communications technologies)" (Chalmers 1999, 59), whereas most playwrights regard the script as the architectural blueprint for a performance.

When I participated with Weems in a storyboarding workshop during their residency in Liverpool, she was not shy in asserting her desire to unchain authorship from icons of individual, literary craft. As Jackson argues, the Builders accord with Lehmann's view of "postdramatic theatre" as a paradigm shift in which "dramatic text is no longer positioned as an authority to be followed as much as material to be mined" (Jackson and Weems 2015, 27). More, perhaps, than any other company, the Builders have focused on how human beings are themselves "mined" as data by communication platforms. The dialectic fundamental to their work is not between text and performance but between data and presence. Acting, design, and writing are closely interwoven in the staging of this dialectic. Tipton reveals: "I am always bugging Marianne to make sure there is a writer involved. I find the technology fascinating, but the script does not always support it. I consider my position in rehearsals to protect the human beings in the process" (Gener 2008, 84). The challenge is being fully present in this strange, technical world which is neither a film nor a play but has elements of both, within a process that is neither improvised nor tightly scripted. It is a situation in which performers must connect without looking at one another. As Pence testifies: "It is a really interesting challenge to keep the character activated and flowing and yet to be expressed through a range of what might be about an inch and a half of head movement" (Kaye 2007, 561). Those who stay with the Builders as actors are those who see themselves within a bigger, dramaturgical picture and are adept at establishing presence through, rather than trying to work against, the framework afforded by the stationing of the actor—a framework, for Pence as for Moe Angelos and Rizwan Mirza, they themselves help to assemble as cowriters.

Key Works in Chronological Context

Given how large the company's projects are in number and in scale, we should be somewhat cautious about selecting a few pieces and positioning these as "key." With that caveat, I will focus on a trilogy of oft-cited works made during the peak of the company's impact (1998–2005). Conspicuously contemporary in their focus, *JET LAG, ALLADEEN, SUPER VISION* chart the evolution, and the social and psychological effects, of communication and surveillance technologies.

JET LAG (1998)

In 1969, British amateur sailor and failing businessman Donald Crowhurst entered the *Sunday Times Golden Globe* round-the-world, solo yacht race desperate to win the £5,000 prize. Encountering difficulty early in the voyage, he abandoned travel but pretended to continue by shutting down his radio, reporting false positions and compiling a mendacious log. Languishing near Argentina, his plan was to wait until the other boats had been around the world and back then try to make his way home in the apparent lead. The BBC provided Crowhurst with a film camera and tape deck, and he recorded tapes (used by the Builders in their research) to fake his journey. This is one of the two true stories, both dangling huge metaphorical hooks, that propel *JET LAG*. The other took place in 1971. Sarah Krasnoff had looked after her fourteen-year-old grandson, Howard, for much of his life in Cleveland after his mother died when he was three. In an effort to escape a custody battle with Howard's father and related appointments with the boy's psychiatrist, she took Howard on 167 consecutive flights between New York and Amsterdam until she died of a heart attack attributed to the exhaustion of accumulated jet lag.

These two stories were as attractive to Weems as they were to their partners in the conception and development of this production, architects, and media artists Diller + Scofidio. The decision to collaborate with Diller + Scofidio was a conscious move by Weems away from using dense texts as stimuli. Their first, collaborative decision was to "shave down a lot of the extraneous layers—much of the escape from psychiatry, the mother, the father and other minor characters' to focus on 'motion' and 'passing,' giving the story a 'larger resonance' beyond the 'freakishness' of strange people in weird situations" (Chalmers 1999, 58). Diller+Scofidio created sophisticated computer renderings of airplanes, airports, and the boy's flight-simulation game, the latter helping to tie the two stories together around an idea of retreating into fiction as a private space of fantasy, sanctuary, and purgatory. Liz Diller recounts: "For us, these two stories had a certain reciprocity: the grandmother simulates domesticity for her grandson while in perpetual motion; the sailor fabricates the bravado of movement while in constant stasis" (Chalmers 1999, 57). Noting that Krasnoff is cited by theorist Paul Virilio (1988) as "a contemporary heroine who lived in deferred time," Weems regards Crowhurst as "an early example of the fabrication of a self-image created for, and by, the media" (Svich 2003, 53). For Chalmers, too, there was something both distinctly contemporary and resoundingly timeless about both stories. While seeing them as modern manifestations of Greek tragedy, lessons in hubris couched in extreme voyages, she suggests that "lag" is "a reality of the postmodern condition, in which we are all connected, and, at the same time, newly aware of how compartmentalized we are as interlocutors" (Chalmers 1999, 60). This compartmentalization is visually rendered, the sailor (renamed Dearborn) isolated and framed by the technological apparatus that forms his boat on stage. The shortcomings of the technology are embraced as part of, not antithetical, to the magic. In a visual method that would become key to what the Builders would communicate in all their subsequent work, we see the lies told by the technology as we watch Dearborn construct his fake diaries, the image on screen (thanks to some choppy sea sound effects and a video background he uses) telling a very different story to the more pathetic one we see on stage.

JET LAG is a landmark show for several reasons. One of the first works to use CGI and computer-powered architectural modeling as a primary scenographic element within theatre, it established the company with new media and conceptual art audiences. Ironically, given its subject matter, JET LAG was a coming-together for the Builders, establishing and cementing connections between personnel and solidifying their methodology. James Gibbs (creator of computer-generated scenographic imagery) and Moe Angelos (actor, writer, member of New York-based feminist performance quintet Five Lesbian Brothers) began their Builders careers on JET LAG and have been key members of the company ever since, playing major development and authorial/dramaturgical roles in several shows.

That the Crowhurst and Krasnoff stories were yesterday's news and yet the means of re-telling these stories was conspicuously innovative is a dichotomy overlooked by most reviews of *JET LAG*. Though the Builders have always been interested in how technologies shape communication, and in the spectacular possibilities of emerging means of representation, their view is a long one: they are interested in *constructions* of newness and how these constructions erase cultural memory to promote newness as a brand. Weems was struck by the number of responses to *JET LAG* which labeled it "the future of theatre," a tag that she felt displayed "cultural amnesia about theatre's past which I wanted to explore" (Svich 2003, 55). Thematically, the show marked a shift "from the concept of the set to the concept of the network as a central staging metaphor" (Jackson and Weems 2015, 21) that would inform *ALLADEEN, SUPER VISION*, and *CONTINUOUS CITY*. Very unusually for the Builders, *JET LAG* was restaged years later, at Montclair State University in 2010.

ALLADEEN (2002)

Seated in rows before a proscenium stage, it suddenly seems as if we are here to watch a video or maybe a video game. Kaleidoscopic digital squares zoom in and around a video screen, forming grids that constantly change, their internal patterns lining up to form new symmetrical patterns. The images dance to the steady beat of techno music, accelerate and reconfigure into new arrangements of luminous, multicolored eye candy. More blocks slide in and fit together with a satisfying synthetic click. They gradually begin to form a two-dimensional busy city or street. As the techno beat continues, the iconography of LED advertising—stores, signs, billboards, buses and taxis—passes through the screened proscenium. In their pixillated luster, the digitized screens of global consumer culture advertise international clothing chains, telecommunication conglomerates, and athletic equipment. Under the banner of Virgin Atlantic, a small grid of squares appears in rows like thumbnail images on a computer screen, forming shelf after shelf of compact discs for sale. The synthesized whooshes, plops, and kerchunks mimic the soundscape of a high-end website search.

(Jackson and Weems 2015, 196)

There cannot be many performance works in which, before any words have been spoken, the audience bursts into spontaneous applause, as they did when the Virgin Megastore and its environs was built, by dazzling electronic means, before their eyes. The sequence is repeated at the end of the show, only this time the mailbox and fire hydrant common to the United States are gone and instead there is a red pillar-box, red phone-box, and other street furniture that tell us we are in the UK. Without these minor signifiers of place, there is no difference between the two images or between the two megastores, the "cloned offspring of global capitalism" (Giesekam 2007, 165). Already, there are riffs on the Aladdin story, in which, as Leslie Atkins Durham points out, virgins figure more heavily than we tend to remember given the erasure of cultural context in the story's passage, over two thousand years, from Persia to Disney. Various montage sequences of and allusions to Aladdin ensue, including magic-carpet riding and contemporary genies, co-devised and performed by Mirza.

ALLADEEN was created in collaboration with moti roti, a South-East Asian collective based in London. Sandwiched between Acts One (New York) and Three (London), the much longer Act Two portrays a call-center in Bangalore. The acts are linked: in the first, a hybrid-sounding urbanite (played by Tanya Selvaratnam) fields four phone calls in quick succession organizing travel to various destinations, including the Aladdin Hotel in Las Vegas. She cuts off a call to a car rental firm because she cannot understand the operator. As a preface to Act Two, an interview is projected in which an operator describes how he can "switch his voice on" to sound American. A training-session is portrayed, in which operators study the sitcom *Friends* as a reference point for customers in New York: the operators copy the accents and choose a character whose attributes they can base their own "character" on. We see the training in action—a comic series of attempts to "pass" despite struggling to understand certain Americans (like "smackeroony," assumed to be "macaroni") and to guide customers using computer searches and prompts from managers. While all this is happening, a huge, letter-box screen above the performers alternately displays the faces of each operator, what is on their screens as they search, and the images that the misunderstandings produce. When one tries to steer her customer from Los Angeles to Las Vegas, she tells her just to "keep going, it will be all desert"; *Lawrence of Arabia* begins to play on screen, the British emissary riding his camel through the vast expanse of sand. As Weems puts it, the (then new) phenomenon of the call-center was a kind of reversal of the appropriation of *Aladdin* from its origins in *The Arabian Nights* to its exploitation by

Hollywood, a reversal in which "fantastical geography was returned to American customers" (Weems 2016).

There is a marked tonal shift as Act Two ends in more poignant, disturbing fashion. An operator (played by Heaven Phillips) engages in flirty banter with an Indian engineer living in California's Silicon Valley who is booking flights to India for a wedding. Maintaining her disguise, she refrains from commenting when he tells her how long Indian weddings can be. When he suggests jokingly that she should move from New York to California, her disguise cracks as she asks, awkwardly, what an Indian person might make of California. He cuts her short and goes back to his flight booking. In the final act, themes of ventriloquism, and the desire for transformation, are recapitulated as we see Selvaratnam again, with Mirza, Webster, and Phillips, in an upmarket London bar, singing karaoke songs including Steppenwolf's "Magic Carpet Ride."

ALLADEEN was one of the first theatre works to use a projection screen as a computer screen. Weems reflects: "I can't believe there was a time when this wasn't obvious, but when Chris Kondek suggested that as an image, it was such an inspired, surprising way of dissecting a screen" (Jackson and Weems 2015, 386). This opened the door for more complex data display in *SUPER VISION*. Gibbs and his dbox colleagues Matthew Bannister and Charles d'Autremont created the Tetris-like opening/closing megastore sequence in a couple of weeks after Weems called them in late in the show's development; that they were there from the start on the next show would have a huge impact.

SUPER VISION (2005)

Working with Scottish set designer Stewart Laing, Weems and the dbox team enmeshed the performers in *SUPER VISION* more intricately than even *ALLADEEN* had, collapsing video space into stage space with the actors in a kind of holodeck. A huge, mobile front screen was created from Textaline, a material that allows video to be projected while partially obscuring the actors, to create various levels of dissolution of the actor into the image and making the projected image dimmable. Motion-capture imagery, tried out in residency at Wexner, was richly exploited by the three narratives that were interwoven in this network stage-space.

In the first, a father, John Fletcher Sr. (David Pence), struggles to attain credit to meet the cost of their lifestyle as "Bobos"—bourgeois bohemians, upper-class people who (as Weems describes it) strive to be funky and sophisticated as they choose "the right granite and slate and hardwoods and the right cappuccino maker and this absolutely pristine—I consider it somewhat sterile—but perfectly laid-out environment" (Weems in Kaye 2007, 563). He exploits his young son John Jr.'s personal data by pretending to be him. The father loses control and escapes, physically, but cannot evade the long reach of the datasphere. His wife (Kyle deCamp) and son are left with withered data bodies. John Fletcher Jr. is an entirely virtual presence, translucently imaged on the Textaline forescreen. He is brought to illusionistic "life" by the reactions of his parents.

In the second narrative, a solitary traveler (co-conceived and played by Mirza) of Ugandan and Indian heritage is interrogated as he crosses a number of borders within and outside the United States. The answers he gives are increasingly at odds with the data revealed on the screens that the border agents—and we—are able to survey. New information, including minute medical detail, is revealed at each checkpoint, until his whole life dances before them. Mirza was keen to make the traveler not a clear victim of a Big Brother-like gaze but an ambiguous figure, so that the audience would continually need to ask questions about what they trust and why as they try to resolve the gap between his testimony and the data. While John Fletcher Sr. tries in vain to flee the datasphere, it is Mirza who disappears, a sign that the volumes spoken about him by his data have rendered him "physically redundant" (Marranca 2008, 193).

In the third story, a young, technophilic New Yorker (Jen, played by Selvaratnam) maintains screen connection to her grandmother in Sri Lanka (Angelos) whose life she tries to archive before she slips into senility. This touching but compromised connection over distance adds another dimension to the agon of real bodies and data bodies. "Data body" is a term coined in the 1970s by sociologist David Lyon to describe the body produced by surveillance—"a disjointed, hybrid, prostheticised, multiple body, appearing and disappearing in the irregular, contradictory landscape of surveillance space" (Weems in Kaye 2007, 561). A more sardonic introduction to the idea is given at the start of the show, when Claritas software and terminology is used to tell the audience what their own data bodies look like, what sort of properties they live in, and what cars they drive, according to postcode information gleaned from their ticket purchase. Though already active in the United States, Claritas had not yet gained a foothold in Europe when *SUPER VISION* started touring.

The desire for "audience members to leave the theatre with a more visceral understanding of the data they create and carry with them" (Gibbs in Gener 2008, 87) informs the next two projects. Exploring the divide between the digital "haves" and "have-nots," *INVISIBLE CITIES* (2005) was a participatory project with at-risk teens made in collaboration with the Brooklyn College Community Partnership (January–July 2006) and the Institute for Collaborative Education in Manhattan (August 2006–March 2007). It produced photo montages and videos exploring the different versions of "New York City" that are visible to different kinds of inhabitants/ tourists. The next stage production would shine the spotlight more brightly on social media platforms.

Invoking Calvino's idea of a "continuous city" that is a "perpetual outskirt of itself," *CONTINUOUS CITY* (2007) considers how these platforms contribute to the erasure of place addressed in the trilogy. The company set up Xubu, a functionally real but invented media platform that is central to the show's narrative. Weems, Gibbs, and Angelos were among the very first users of Twitter after it became a public platform and had seen how MySpace, Facebook, and Twitter functioned as "'walled gardens' in which relationships are both fostered and 'held back'" (Jackson and Weems 2015, 251). This dynamic is portrayed in the show via thirty-two MIDI-controlled screens that appear and disappear with breathtaking speed. Structurally, there are echoes of *SUPER VISION*. The three narrative domains here are the home of a fictional father and daughter; the father's travels abroad; and the office of Xubu, where we see Mirza as J.V., an Indian transnational promising that his platform will democratize populations in the world's emerging economies. He uses it to forge romantic relationships all around the globe. While the migrants he pitches Xubu to yearn to stay tethered to their loved ones, his own relationships can only survive if he stays physically remote from the women he courts.

The book *Loving Big Brother: Surveillance Culture and Performance Space* was an important research source; Weems and Laing met and corresponded with its author, John McGrath, in developing the show. They also drew on Mike Davis's geo-economic analysis of shifting demographics in *Planet of Slums*, which maps ways in which gaps between rich and poor were becoming more pronounced as more people now lived in cities than in rural environments. *CONTINUOUS CITY* interrogates "the erosion of the quotidian character and cultural specificity of distinctive cities" and the opportunity afforded by virtual communication to gate communities, creating exclusive networks even in a world in which shantytowns sprawl around walled suburbs and glamor zones thrive next to war zones (Davis 2006).

The Frontiers of Spectacle

In a theatre lobby, audience members waiting to see the Builders' *ELEMENTS OF OZ* (2016), a live show about an iconic film, receive reassurance from tech-savvy assistants that the app they have been urged to upload to their phones to "augment" their experience will be easy to use. As the scare quotes I place around "augment" might convey, there is something both haunted and quotational about the packaging of the show as an augmented experience. Rather than a desire to drag theatre into an age of excitingly interactive technologies, the show—which, like most of their work, takes place in a proscenium theatre—is a playful but also mournful and acerbic exploration of how easy access to phones makes it *harder* to "commit" communally to a live experience (Weems 2016).

Made toward the end of the Great Depression for a staggering $2.7 million, *The Wizard of Oz* (1939) deployed Technicolor in spectacular fashion. It has become part of the American, and indeed (like Aladdin) the global, cultural imaginary. Darker stories, however, have always circulated around the film's making and meaning. Long before the movie became a cultural and subcultural reference-point, not only for "friends of Dorothy" (a clandestine term for gay men during the Second World War that became a mainstream jibe), the fantastically allegorical nature of L. Frank Baum's novel (1900) about a Kansas girl meeting a scarecrow, cowardly lion, and tin woodsman on the way to see a wizard generated a plethora of outlandish theories about what it all signified. Most mainstream critics agreed that Baum was commenting on US monetary policy of the late nineteenth century. Henry Littlefield argued in an influential 1964 article that the Yellow Brick Road represents the gold standard, and the silver slippers (changed to ruby in the film) represent the Silverites, who advocated silver coinage as the monetary standard. The city of Oz, explains Littlefield, earns its name from the abbreviation for ounces. This perfectly reasonable, prosaic explanation might have solved the riddles of the novel's encodings, but MGM's reawakening of Oz's fantastic excess paved the yellow brick road to emotional investments far more powerful than Baum could have imagined.

Invoking the performative iconicity of the film characters as conduits for role-play and pastiche, Angelos, Sean Donovan, and Hannah Heller adopt multiple roles and even switch parts freely. While there is some ironizing of the film's naïve aesthetic, enjoying the fun to be had with exchanges like "Are you a good witch or a bad witch?/I'm not a witch at all, I'm a little girl, from Kansas," the play suddenly becomes plangent. Easy distinctions between good witches and bad witches, and between the illusions of the fantasy world and the transparent realness of home, soon feel like wishful thinking. Whereas the film starkly divides Oz from Kansas, here they tussle evocatively and unsettlingly. Dobson's typically layered soundtrack pits the familiar and melodic against the strange and the dissonant. Unlike the storm that takes us from Kansas to Oz, the gather and tension of the soundtrack never resolves, often working *against* what we see in each moment in a manner that testifies to what Pence describes (in the Builders' *Decameron*) as the propensity of the auditory to render things creepy.

Watching on the giant screen behind him as vertiginously animated images of himself appear and disappear, Donovan, as Dorothy (sporting a full mustache), strolls against a series of lavish backdrops, periodically and brusquely interrupted by the bustling film crew, onstage through most of the play, who shout "cut" and "go." The crew are like Beckettian prods, super-egoistic figures keeping the laboring performers on track. Angelos appears onscreen, as if on an internet video, and we see her on stage recording herself via a selfie stick. Her Fan Lady character is full of asides that draw attention to the conditions under which the company labors. We are told that the munchkins all wanted to fly, which was considered skilled and dangerous, because they got $35 a day as opposed to the $50/week they would otherwise have received. Lest we assume that the stars had it easier, we are reminded that the acclaimed Margaret Hamilton as the Wicked Witch was not only poisoned by the copper oxide used to attain her green complexion but was set on fire for real during the melting scene. As the crew prepare Judy Garland's ruby slippers, Glenda the Good Witch cajoles her: "You have a show to do." "They're always waiting," moans Garland, unable to tear herself from her bed and escape her mental storm; "it's a sellout, I'm a sellout." Meanwhile, the snow continues to fall over the plastic wonderland of Oz—snow, we are told, that consists of "pure, crystal white asbestos."

What these and the many, many other elements of this *Oz* draw attention to is attention itself. Fan Lady tells us that it is actually Bobbie Koshay, the former Olympic swimmer who was Garland's double and personal trainer, who opens the black-and-white door of Kansas onto the technicolor world of Oz. Dissecting this moment, she recounts that Bobbie's gingham dress was sepia-dyed, and the set was painted black and sepia to emphasize the drabness of the world before Technicolor. While Technicolor was not new, she reminds us, plastic was: it is the other-worldly luminosity of the plastic objects used to build Oz that dazzles us. And this *OZ* dazzles, too, with razor-sharp video reveals and dissolves hypnotizing us until a psychedelic graphic telling us to "LOOK UP" prompts us to hold our phones in front of our eyes to enhance a twister or some flying munchkins.

This looking augments our experience but also makes us notice it, a defamiliarizing perceptual effort. It is a Brechtian device for the digital age, though the didacticism often found in Brecht is itself defamiliarized in this meditation on the role of romantic and immersive spectacle in a capitalist, attention-deficit economy. In the first of two interludes, controversial philosopher Ayn Rand argues for the power of utopian artworks like *Oz* to liberate the individual to fulfill the potential that only a capitalist system can offer. In the other, Salman Rushdie finds *Oz* Bollywood-like in its styling. As in his book on the subject, he reads the "no place like home" message as a conservative myth, the utopian lure of a migrant's dream in which Oz is a "hymn to elsewhere."

Alluding to the fact that many companies have abandoned theatres to do site-responsive works either in vast, multistory spaces (as Punchdrunk do) or in confined, one-to-one contexts, Weems asserts: "I don't believe that you have to have your body on stage or in somebody's home to make intimacy happen" through theatre (Gener 2008, 86). *ELEMENTS* explores the potential of technological interactivity in a proscenium theatre, but it is skeptical about both the pragmatics and the ethics of immersion. Reacting against shows in which interactivity "becomes only about the technology, as in, 'everybody get out your cell phones' then you're looking at your phone and not at what is on stage" (Marranca 2008, 206), the show "aim[s] to provoke an awareness of our dependence on these devices" (Builders website).

In both its tone and its concerns, this exuberant but sardonic experiment can be seen to echo a show that the Builders produced at the start of the millennium. *XTRAVAGANZA* (2000) is another piece about the making of spectacle that cuts elaborate documentary with shards of anarchic dissonance that edge toward cautionary critique. Like *ELEMENTS OF OZ*, it makes conspicuous use of computerized image-processing to translate presence into pattern and of a complex soundtrack that often unsettles what we see. Also, like *ELEMENTS*, it is both homage and mash-up. It recreates and reprocesses work by four theatrical innovators of the late nineteenth and early twentieth centuries: impresario Florenz Ziegfeld Jr., who brought the Follies to Broadway; dance and lighting pioneer Loie Fuller; director and choreographer Busby Berkeley, famous for creating elaborate geometric patterns through choreography on film; and Steele MacKaye, actor/writer/director/manager and inventor of an array of stage and auditorium devices including the folding chair, fire curtain, and double-stage system for loading and offloading scenery. *XTRAVAGANZA* layers live performance with fragments of letters and biographical sources, encasing these documentary elements in lighting and video effects that mash the nostalgic with the avant-garde to produce "a trance-induced theatre of attractions for ravers and nightcrawlers" (Gener 2008, 84) in which past, present, and future dovetail. The show is a reaching back for the origins of contemporary spectacle and a bringing forward that recognizes their inventiveness. It also reminds us that all four of these visionary highflyers died in poverty even as their experimentation was becoming mainstream.

Taken together, *OZ* and *XTRAVAGANZA* show the precarity inherent in *all* spectacle. They suggest that only by excluding the story of the labor behind the magic, the exploitation and the co-optation, can capitalism maintain the illusion of harmonious mainstreaming of production fed by experimental pioneers. If *XTRAVAGANZA* is a millennial stock-taking, *OZ* comes in the wake of companies such as Punchdrunk being criticized (Alston 2013) for "selling out" by accepting corporate sponsorship. While the Builders themselves are often thought of as makers of expensive work, they have often pointed out that their work is far less expensive than it looks. It is work that has always relied on support in kind from arts and educational organizations and the generosity of fellow innovators, like dbox and Diller + Scofidio. Even without *direct* corporate sponsorship, however, all of these organizations and companies are themselves reliant on benefactors and business deals; and, whether sponsored or not, experimental work itself is always vulnerable to appropriation. The techno music used in *XTRAVAGANZA* may have been full of cultural capital at the start of the new millennium, but its deployment is tinged with a sad recognition that "whatever subversiveness and experimentation there was became a Volkswagen commercial within two weeks of any record coming out" (Giesekam 2007, 162).

Themes and Aesthetics

As this section will summarize, aesthetic means and thematic content are closely integrated in all Builders work. The various dimensions I consider here converge around questions and ideas of "friction"—a word that comes up time and again in conversations with and about the Builders—that are worked through thematically and aesthetically: between live bodies and electronic media; pleasure and spectacle; the politics of the apparently frictionless trade/labor/exchange engendered by networked geography.

At first glance, it might seem that the journey from *MASTER BUILDER* to *SUPER VISION* is a move away from the spatial, temporal, and linguistic parameters of classical theatre. Closer inspection reveals an ongoing dialogue with these parameters. Even as many of their contemporaries have spoken of burning red, velvet seats and taking theatre to everywhere but traditional venues, this experimental, future-probing, company has kept us in old-fashioned auditoria with our bums on our seats looking at a picture-frame stage. It is a tension that, as the following remarks (made at a post-lecture Q&A in 2016) attest, Weems continues to find demanding and productive in equal measure:

> Theatre is still mired in the nineteenth century. The idea of the proscenium as an inviolable space is very strong, trying to create a theatrical experience that reaches beyond the stage is hard—harder than trying to create one that takes places entirely outside the theatre.
>
> The stage is a laboratory where you can still unpack these ideas about liveness in a very immediate way [and] problematizing that has always been a pleasure […]. We create all these channels of information that are running simultaneously, blending the elements into a seamless whole is very pleasurable for us.
>
> (Weems 2016)

These testaments to the pleasure and pain of staging myriad "channels of information in the 'inviolable space'" of the proscenium get to the heart of the Builders' mission to render sophisticated concepts in a theatrically engaging fashion that interrogates the *effects of* spectacular engagement.

As Steve Dixon theorizes, the Builders arrived on the world stage by playing place against space in powerfully uncanny fashion. The installation-performance that was *MASTER BUILDER* set a full-size home as a "place of solidity, shelter, tranquility and security" on the "ephemeral space" of the stage, where we know it can only be "a temporary structure" (Dixon 2010, 13). The house, both culturally and for the Builders, is a potent icon of how humans seek to accommodate and stabilize themselves amid change. As well as stories about escape/exile from the house (*JET LAG, HOUSE/ DIVIDED, ELEMENTS OF OZ*), they have told stories about attempts to paper over emotional cracks by building the perfect home, most vividly in *SUPER VISION*. The Fletchers' investment in the idea that "there's no place like home" is counterpointed by the aesthetics/thematics of their enmeshing in "a house constructed by illusion" (Miller 2007, 659). Reflecting back on *MASTER BUILDER*'s three-story house a decade or so later, Weems notes: "After that, and in each succeeding project since then, my interest in physical edifices has receded" (Kaye 2007, 558). But her interest in space has not waned. Since the collaborations with Diller + Scofidio and dbox, whose commercial work involves virtual modeling for innovative, architectural projects, the evolution has been away from putting *structures* on stage, set designs in a conventional sense, to the creation of *superstructures* through experimental animation. Productions from *FAUST* onwards, "especially *XTRAVAGANZA*, *ALLADEEN*, *CONTINUOUS CITY*, used a two-tier presentation of laboring bodies below a digital screen, replicating the base process of labor that supported the seemingly unfettered space of superstructural illusion" (Jackson and Weems 2015, 88–9).

As early as *MASTER BUILDER*, the Builders have addressed the emergence of a "post-private society" (Weems 2016). While *SUPER VISION* and *CONTINUOUS CITY* focus on the contemporary experience of privacy, *XTRAVAGANZA* and *ELEMENTS OF OZ* take a longer and more vocational view, reading the relinquishing of privacy in relation to the production of spectacle as they trace "how each practitioner was prey to insecurities, artistic and financial, and each ended up in personal and financial ruin of one sort or another" (Giesekam 2007, 157). Weems acknowledges the influence on this trajectory of work about privacy of Manuel Castells's theorization of networks in which "new territorial configurations emerge from simultaneous processes of spatial concentration, decentralization and connection, relentlessly labored by the variable geometry of global information flows" (Castells in Durham 2009, 522). For Weems, *ALLADEEN* shows "how the technology of fiber-optic phone lines gives the illusion of bringing people closer together when, in the case of corporate outsourcing, it's driving them further apart" (Marranca 2008, 189–90).

The Builders avoid wrapping the "tele-prosthetic experience" that is the contemporary body's relationship to the world in "a nostalgic concept that if we're in the same place, we see eye to eye and thus connect" (Weems in Gener 2008, 86). As *XTRAVAGANZA* explores, any historically aware view of technology, especially in theatre, should make it "impossible to polarize the live purity of performance with the mediatized impurity of technology" (Jackson and Weems 2015, 6). But this polarizing continues into the twenty-first century, along with the orthodoxy of theoretical discourse on performance that technological mediation elides presence. Insisting that this discourse has consistently failed to engage "with the capacity of media and mediation, themselves, to perform rather than denude both liveness and presence," Nick Kaye finds a "recovery" of liveness and presence in the Builders' work (Kaye 2007, 558–9). The presence and humanity lie, Weems argues, not only in acting and story but in the fact that there is nothing that can be plugged, played, and left on autopilot. Everything is improvised and timed live, something that she finds essential to the terror and the thrill that are integral to presence in theatre.

The ideological clarity of the Builders' work is open to debate. Distancing the company from expectations that they should offer an explicit, moral perspective, Weems suggests that the work should be seen in relation to visual art practices of "ambient criticism" and "relational aesthetics" (Gener 2008, 84; 86). Nonetheless, there are strongly anticolonial, neo-Marxist and feminist threads running through the oeuvre. *MASTER BUILDER* is suffused with feminist ideas of the "feminized space of domesticity" including allusions to the location by Hitchcock and other filmmakers of "women in hystericized space" (Jackson and Weems 2015, 37). *SONTAG:REBORN* (2012), an adaptation by Angelos of the early journals of artist/activist/intellectual Susan Sontag, is suffused with images of writing and of rummaging through the marginalia of notebooks. The "poetic video" and multilayered soundtrack are, as ever, the most distinctive forces in performance. Jessica Del Vecchio praises *SONTAG:REBORN* for "demonstrating that the small and intimate details of women's lives are worthy of examination through large and ambitious productions, and by depicting women wrestling with domestic responsibilities and career ambitions" (Del Vecchio 2012, 592). Giesekam describes how *XTRAVAGANZA* critiques the reifying way in which the "camera is used to fetishize the female leg in musicals, effectively turning the performers into mechanical objects" (Giesekam 2007, 160). Reconstructions of classic Berkeley shots in which women become "mere architectural components" are followed by original footage of sixty women playing neon-lit violins in which the women are made to disappear and only the violins and bows are left. Giesekam reads this, and other Builders work, as Piscatorian in its strategies, arguing that "a feminist critique emerges through montage rather than through explicit textual statement" (Giesekam 2007, 160).

The neo-Marxist and anticolonial critique within the Builders' work is arguably more prominent than its feminism but harder to pin down. The work always "draw[s] attention as much to processes of construction as to what is constructed" (Giesekam 2007, 152), but it is resolutely left to us to draw ideological conclusions. The politics of labor are very much a focus of the trilogy and since (in *CONTINUOUS CITY, HOUSE/DIVIDED, ELEMENTS OF OZ*). But, as Weems suggests, it is a focus drawn ambiently rather than through explicit commentary. For Durham as for Giesekam, *ALLADEEN* follows Piscator in offering various channels of information in which the documentary elements—notably, the interview with the call-center worker—are privileged because they appear authentic, unmediated, technologically "low." This privileging of the real is most pronounced in *HOUSE/DIVIDED*, which features several interviews with people who became homeless in the foreclosure crisis and with a real estate developer who bought and renovated foreclosed homes in an under-resourced part of Columbus, Ohio.

The overarching impression left by a survey of the Builders Association is not the opposition of mediation *to* humanity but our evolving struggle to find humanity *through* mediation. It is a struggle that lies behind the tonal counterpointing of openness, naivety, and exuberance with a knowing, existential anxiety. A similar combination of existential anxiety and ludic drive is found in Buster Keaton, whose *One Week* (1920), in which a man and his wife try to assemble a mail-order house, is invoked in *HOUSE/ DIVIDED*. Jacques Tati's *Playtime* (1967), in which there is a comparable tension, is a strong influence on *JET LAG*. Mirza sums it up thus: there is "a certain haunting loneliness about the quality of the Builders' shows. Even when they are funny. I think in their funniest moments there is a lonely quality" (Mirza in Kaye 2007, 571).

Critical Reception

In comparison with other companies discussed in this volume, the Builders have received considerable critical attention. Kaye's incisive, extended essay, the result of a series of interviews organized around the Builders' participation in the Presence Project, is a good place to start further research. Other valuable resources include Giesekam's chapter; Weems's eloquent published conversations with Caridad Svich and Bonnie Marranca; the *American Theatre* interview-informed article by Gener; and the interview with Schechner for *TDR/The Drama Review*. The most substantial resource, and the only book devoted to the company, is *The Builders Association* (2015) by Weems and distinguished scholar Shannon Jackson. An in-house but in-depth analysis, this large tome affords behind-the-scenes access to the creation of eight productions. Somewhat celebratory at times, it is full of detail and humanity; it offers a generous range of references to theoretical and philosophical lenses through which particular pieces may be read.

The most widely reviewed, and most hotly debated, piece is *ALLADEEN*. While Durham's essay is enthusiastic, a review article by Jennifer Parker-Starbuck finds *ALLADEEN* not critical enough, "glossing over the questions of political, economic structures." Parker-Starbuck is concerned by having found herself "seduced" and "intoxicated" by the "mesmerizing" technological feats and is left wanting more "ruptures, or moments of dissonance" (Parker-Starbuck 2004, 98–101). Though Weems is sensitive to, and has considered, such reactions (this is clear in the interview with Schechner), she rejects the idea of a more didactic approach, insisting that the work is geared "towards a smart audience" who are "computer literate ... used to taking in several streams of information all at once, and able to jump between them and synthesize" (Giesekam 2007, 171).

Some critics, however, have framed what they see as the problem with the Builders' aesthetic in starker terms. Paul Rae complains of "half-hearted attempts at character development" (see Giesekam 2007, 168). *New York Times* critic Jason Zinoman goes further, finding characters in *CONTINUOUS CITY* "thinly drawn and remote; their crucial scenes together seem lazily written, like an improvisation between strangers. Technology is a vivid character in this play, but you wish it weren't the only one." Admitting that he has an aversion to theatre that is tech-heavy, Zinoman finds the Builders' work "as emotionally starved as a robot" (Zinoman 2008).

The vast majority of reviews of the work, though, have been positive, with praise frequently lavished on its ingenuity and intelligence.

Postscript: Building in Lockdown

In Boccaccio's canonical *Decameron* (1350), ten people gather in a deserted villa in the countryside, having escaped Florence during the most fatal pandemic in history, the Black Death from which Boccaccio sheltered as he wrote. To entertain one another, his besieged characters tell stories. By turns amusing, tragic, frightening, and consoling, each tale is appraised and appreciated by the party. Locked down in 2020, the Builders' *Decameron* is a self-reflexive cover version, broadcast live online and available for viewing thereafter. In each of the five, half-hour episodes, Pence and Angelos are joined by two guest artists from among the Builders' roster who bring tales of events that took place during rehearsals and tours. Work and works are referred to only in passing (*"CONTINUOUS CITY?* Yes, but we first worked together on SUPER VISION"), productions becoming fixed stars by which contributors orient themselves and their connectedness. Angelos is Pampinea, the character made "queen for the day" by Boccaccio's group, entitling her to set briefs for each tale such as "a traveler encounters the unexpected and finds gladness of heart" or "an abundance that is not satisfying." Pence provides the ritual glue by reading (at the beginning, middle, and end of each episode) from the frame story in which Boccaccio sets the scene around and within the villa. Unwinding during a residency in Columbus, Ohio, Donovan recounts, he encounters an intense bingo session in a converted barn; transgender actor and playwright Jess Barbagallo recalls the excitement at discovering a primarily lesbian bar in the same city on a different production. In another installment, managing producer Claire Hallereau and actor Harry Sinclair tell scary tales of being awoken in hotels by ghostly presences. Drawing out similarities and differences between the tales' milieux and the assembled group's various current locations, Angelos and Pence are warm and witty hosts of this project-in-quarantine.

Picture-in-picture effects are deployed in the video editing: the background image occupying the whole frame is of the verdant countryside around the notional villa, while the guests and hosts appear within small, overlaid circles. Each teller occupies a fixed central circle that is slightly larger, while Pence, Angelos, and the listening guest occupy smaller bubbles, orbiting the teller like planets around a sun. Two other orbiting bodies make up this solar system: in one, a live camera feed called "cat relaxation" provides close-up footage of robins, finches, and other domestic birds, an internet-age iteration of Boccaccio's description of birds around the villa in Florence; in the other, hands operate consoles, laptops, and other equipment in what looks like crew preparation for a technical rehearsal. In the bottom right-hand corner is a small rectangle labeled "second screen," which reactively displays illustrative photos and CCTV footage of locations described in the current tale.

For me, the Builders' *Decameron* is a fertile exploration of nostalgia. Like all Builders projects, it underscores tensions inherent in human existence that are manifest acutely during lockdown and the memories that lockdown precipitates, remembering that is both celebratory and wounded. The humanity exuded by Pence and Angelos counterpoints the severity of the ritually methodical approach. The videographic conjunction of close-up and satellite views supports oscillation between detail and perspective in the tales, such as Selvaratnam's recollection of gorgeous, handmade salt and pepper shakers in a family-run restaurant that enchanted her in her only brief visit to Colombia, a country, she recounts, that the company were warned against touring because of criminal gangs. Now that thebuildersassociation.org has begun presenting itself as a "legacy website," this latest project crystallizes a tension the examination of which the company's oeuvre has performed in unique ways. It is a tension inherent in theatre and fundamental to the Builders' phenomenological interrogation of staging technologies: the painstaking yet magical experience of going somewhere while going nowhere. In the *Decameron*'s most telling reference to the work sessions, Laing remembers with wonder and yearning how, in rehearsals in which he participated, it would appear for hours that "nothing was happening," then everything would just click into place and "your eyes would pop."

Production Resumé

Staged from:
2020 *DECAMERON*
2018 *STRANGE WINDOW*
2016- *ELEMENTS OF OZ*
2012–2014 *SONTAG:REBORN*
2011–2014 *HOUSE/DIVIDED*
2010 *JET LAG 2010*
2007–2010 *CONTINUOUS CITY*
2005–2007 *INVISIBLE CITIES*
2005–2006 *SUPER VISION*
2003–2005 *AVANTI*
2002–2005 *ALLADEEN*
2000–2002 *XTRAVAGANZA*
1998–2001 *JET LAG*
1997–1998 *JUMP CUT (FAUST)*
1996 *IMPERIAL MOTEL (FAUST)*
1995 *THE WHITE ALBUM*
1994 *MASTER BUILDER*

CHAPTER 4
PIG IRON THEATRE
Kathryn Mederos Syssoyeva

Pig Iron Theatre Company of Philadelphia has been going strong for nearly a quarter century—impressive longevity for a regional troupe committed to collective creation, physical theatre, and ever-evolving experimentation. Founded in 1995 as a "dance-clown-theatre collective," the company specializes in the creation of original works of physically dynamic, frequently music-driven theatre, devised by a group of actor-creators typically collaborating with a playwright and always facilitated by a director. This chapter traces Pig Iron's story backward and forward in time: backward to the company's antecedents in mid-twentieth collective creation lineages emerging from the United States, France, and Poland; forward along its path of continual exploration and periodic metamorphosis. By way of example, I analyze a handful of significant productions from among the more than thirty-five original works the company has created. In concluding, I consider the company's role in seeding future generations of artists committed to physical theatre and devising—through its network of collaborative relationships; through the continued commitment to devising of former company members who have gone on to establish independent theatre-making careers; and through the Pig Iron Theatre School, founded in 2011.

Foundations

The roots of Pig Iron's aesthetic lie in a series of artistic encounters, first at Swarthmore College, and subsequently, as founding members sought out rigorous postgraduate training in Paris, New York, Minneapolis, and San Francisco.

Pig Iron's seven founders met, in the early 1990s, while still undergraduates at Swarthmore, a four-year liberal arts college south of Philadelphia. This originary group included Quinn Bauriedel, Dan Rothenberg, Dito van Reigersberg, Suli Holum, Telory Williamson, Nate Read, and Jay Rhoderick

(Bauriedel 2004). They were drawn together through the influence of theatre professor Allen Kuharski, an artist-scholar whose teaching emphasized the work of American director Joseph Chaikin (1935–2003), Ariane Mnouchkine (artistic director of France's Théâtre du Soleil since 1964), and Polish experimental theatre-makers Jerzy Grotowski (1933–1999), Tadeusz Kantor (1915–1990), and Włodzimierz Staniewski (artistic director of the Gardzienice Center for Theatre Practices since 1977). Beneath surface distinctions of style, methodology, and directorial ethos, what Chaikin, Mnouchkine, Grotowski, Kantor, and Staniewski shared in common was *collective creation*: ensemble-based generation of original works of theatre. The students' encounter with this legacy of experimental performance practice would prove formative, generative, and lasting.

In 1992, Kuharski invited Joseph Chaikin to Swarthmore for a teaching residency. Prior to Chaikin's visit, the students had explored his practices via his writings and video recordings of *The Serpent* and *Terminal*.[1] Chaikin's call for a reinvestigation of the theatre made a deep impression. Looking back a quarter century later, Dan Rothenberg would write:

> Here are some words from Joe, circa 1973: "*The study of character, like any study where one aims to go to the root, requires a new discipline. Since there is no existing discipline to use, an acting company must invent its own.*" This was Pig Iron's touchstone, our reason for being. I'm surprised to find that it still seems true to me now, more than 20 years after I first read it.
>
> (Rothenberg 2016)

During the residency, Quinn Bauriedel and Dito van Reigersberg worked with Chaikin on explorations of *Medea* and *The Misanthrope* (Rothenberg et al. 2004). These workshops exposed them to some of the practices underpinning Chaikin's directorial approach—and laid the groundwork for a future collaboration with Chaikin.

Among exercises Chaikin shared was "Open Canvas," an improvisational structure for collectively generating theatrical material. A group of actors is divided in two and sent to either side of the stage; the empty space between them is their three-dimensional "canvas." A theme is proposed, and on impulse, actors (one or severally) enter that space and respond to the theme through action: movement, a song, a scene—some "little thing," some form of theatrical "offering" (Sobelle 2017). Performers join on impulse, either building upon existing action or creating parallel action. A teacher, director, or experienced performer remains in the house as outside eye and facilitator. As the action develops, that facilitator winnows or expands the group, calling one or more actors to the side when the work is becoming muddied or something interesting needs space and focus to develop—or conversely, sending a few actors back on. Periodically, she or he calls "all off," clearing the space to start anew or begin discussion about moments meriting further development. Open Canvas would become central to Pig Iron's devising methods (Rothenberg 2017; Sanford 2017).

The following year, Kuharski hosted the San Francisco Mime Troupe. The Mime Troupe holds a peculiar place in the interweave of twentieth-century collective theatre-making practices. Though rooted in a distinctly American lineage of New Left protest theatre emerging from civil rights movements of the 1960s, the Mime Troupe's street-theatre aesthetic and clown-based gestus have French antecedents; founder R.G. Davis trained in Paris with Etienne Decroux—who, in turn, along with Jacques Lecoq and Ariane Mnouchkine, was part of a physical theatre lineage stretching back through Jean Dasté and Michel Saint-Denis to Jacques Copeau, Suzanne Bing, and the Copiaux (Baldwin 2008, 41–2; 2016, 29–50). This encounter, too, would leave its mark on Pig Iron.

Van Reigersberg and Bauriedel graduated in the summer of 1994. Rothenberg, with one year left of college, headed for San Francisco to intern with the Mime Troupe; van Reigersberg took off for New York, entering the two-year program in Meisner technique at the Neighborhood Playhouse; and Bauriedel left for Minneapolis, to spend a year interning with Théâtre de la Jeune Lune.

Théâtre de la Jeune Lune (1978 to 2008) was one of the country's most celebrated physical theatre companies in the period when the collective creation methodologies of the 1960s were transitioning to what would come to be known as devising methods in the 1990s, and the drivers of collective creation in the United States were shifting from an emphasis on social and political change to something more predominantly aesthetic (Syssoyeva 2013, 23–7). The company was founded in Paris by three graduates of the École internationale de théâtre Jacques Lecoq—Dominique Serrand, Vincent Gracieux, and Barbra Berlovit—moving to Minneapolis in 1985. Jeune Lune specialized in a mix of original works and inventively reimagined classics—Moliere, Shakespeare—and a performance style built upon principles of imagistic physical expression learned from Lecoq, inflected by theatrical clown, *commedia*, French mime, and a Brechtian sense of epic structure. The company operated as a collective, with three (later five) artistic directors. For Bauriedel, the internship proved formative as much on the business level as on the artistic.

> I started by helping out with a strike for one of their shows, then sat in on some dramaturgical meetings for a show that was nearly a year away. Then I started helping out in their Development Department and eventually wrote fundraising appeals to both individual donors and foundations. I sat in on staff meetings and artistic meetings, watched performances multiple times, and was part of a 6-month training they offered to develop their next generation of performers. In truth, it was an artistic awakening to see an ensemble with 4 artistic directors, each acting in one another's projects, designing for one another, and each heading up one administrative department.
>
> (Bauriedel 2019)

The lessons of that year would inform the foundation of Pig Iron:

> As we were setting up our own artistic leadership structure, a number of key decisions were made with info I gleaned from my time with Jeune Lune. It helped with both administrative decisions as well as some big picture "what it means to shake up the artistic make-up of a city and to really dare to operate differently than what came before."
>
> (Bauriedel 2019)

Equally important: the Jeune Lune team encouraged Bauriedel to go to Paris and train with Jacques Lecoq.

In spring 1995, Bauriedel completed his internship, Rothenberg graduated, and the Swarthmore seven launched Pig Iron, premiering an original staging of *The Odyssey* at the Edinburgh Fringe (Bauriedel 2004). With this first show, Pig Iron attracted the attention of *The Guardian*, which gave the young company four stars in its festival write-up. In September, the troupe scattered for a time, and Bauriedel and Rothenberg headed for Paris to enroll at École Jacques Lecoq, while van Reigersberg returned to the Neighborhood Playhouse—and the Martha Graham School of Contemporary Dance. Van Reigersberg had encountered Graham work in his first year at the Playhouse, where it served as stage movement training. Continuing his full-time Meisner studies during the day, he began a three-year program of modern, jazz, and ballet on nights and weekends at the Graham school.

While van Reigersberg developed the dancerly expressivity of his body and rooted himself in Meisner's particular approach to psychological realism—moment to moment truth derived from close observation of the behaviors of one's acting partners and a deliberately cultivated emotional vulnerability—Rothenberg and Bauriedel immersed themselves in the study of mime, acrobatics, juggling, and stage combat; neutral, larval, and expressive mask; bouffon and the grotesque; observation of people, animals, and the natural world; and character, environment, and scene creation: Lecoq's *auto-cours* ("self-course"). The *auto-cours* consists of the assignment of weekly themes to develop imagination, invention, and collaboration. Students are divided into groups and sent off to devise brief scenes, to be performed at week's end before faculty and peers (Sherman 2010, 88–9). In this autonomous collective work, it is understood that leaders will emerge and shift. Students learn to function as cocreators in a process in which the role of the director is "to receive and to organize" everyone's contributions (Delpech 2004). The *auto-cours* not only demands invention and creative risk but forces students to repeatedly confront the complexities of cooperative group work. It is the engine that has driven the development of so many devising companies following students' graduation from the program (Delpech 2004).

The knowledge that they were "in the rare position of having a small organization that we were tending" back home gave special impetus to their studies. Rothenberg and Bauriedel "were, to put it mildly, eager to share everything we'd learned" (Bauriedel 2016, 357). Undeterred by geography, the company formalized their business structure via correspondence, incorporating long distance. Drawing upon both the Jeune Lune model and their *auto-cours* experience, they structured Pig Iron as a collective headed by three artistic directors, Rothenberg, Bauriedel, and van Reigersberg. From the outset, work was created collectively, with Rothenberg as principal stage director and Bauriedel directing on occasion.

Pig Iron regrouped in Philadelphia in the summer of 1996 for the creation of *Dig or Fly*—a synthesis of legends of excavation and flight: the vanishing of Amelia Earhart, Heinrich Schliemann's search for Troy, the mythical fliers Daedalus and Icarus. With this second production, Rothenberg and Bauriedel set to work implementing what they had learned from Lecoq. Central to their process was the *enquête* ("investigation"): a key phase in Lecoq training consisting of research aimed at developing a theatrical language specific to the story to be told (Bauriedel 2016, 357).

Introduced at the end of year one, the *enquête* is rooted in "concrete observation of life." Carlos García Estéves (associate artist with the Laboratory of Movement Study–École Jacques Lecoq) writes that "for every *enquête* you find a style or a way to tell a story that you did not know before, so a new theatre appears." To achieve this, "you must be able to see the world upside down. This is Lecoq's provocation: to see life with a different eye" (Estéves 2016, 167). Bauriedel, too, emphasizes that "Lecoq taught his students how to look very carefully … not as a scientist with clinical distance, but as an artist who is moved by what he/she sees" (Bauriedel 2016, 357). The *enquête* brings together deepened attention to observation with creation methods learned through the *auto-cours*. Students in the Paris school choose a theme related to the social milieu of the city, immerse themselves for several weeks in observation-based research, "then return to the school and transpose what we observed into a dramatic language and tell the story of this observation" (Estéves 2016, 167). At École Jacques Lecoq, the *enquête* is "the culmination of the theme of observation" (Bauriedel 2016, 359). For Bauriedel, it became an essential point of departure in work creation, "an endless source of artistic inspiration," and fundamental to Pig Iron's process (Bauriedel 2016, 357).

For *Dig or Fly*, the preliminary *enquête* consisted of a visit to an archaeological dig in Delaware, where the actors sat "in the hot sun," watching researchers "sift through piles of dirt outside a home … once owned by a signer of the Declaration of Independence." The archeologists' repetitive physical actions—"sifting dirt, discarding sifted dirt, piling up fresh dirt to be sifted"—generated a "vivid" gestural "picture of the action of digging," rendering cultural metaphors concrete: "uncovering the past, taking away layers of history, uncovering the dead." The field trip inaugurated the emergence of a shared set of company practices (Bauriedel 2016, 360).

In September, Bauriedel returned to Lecoq, while Rothenberg did a four-week *stage* with Ariane Mnouchkine's Théâtre du Soleil then returned to the United States to join van Reigersberg, commencing creation of a third original work, *Poet in New York*. A dance-theatre "biographical fantasia" based upon Federico Garcia Lorca's 1929 sojourn in Manhattan, *Poet* was a bilingual one-man show, featuring van Reigersberg in eleven roles that included Salvador Dali, blues singer Victoria Spivey, and the ghost of Walt Whitman (Rothenberg 2004). *Poet* garnered the company's first ripples of attention from New York critics, went on to win the UK's Total Theatre Award at the 2000 Edinburgh Festival, and remained in the company's repertoire into 2008.

By the time Bauriedel completed his second year at Lecoq, the young troupe had substantial training to draw upon, including significant encounters with the work of Théâtre du Soleil (Rothenberg) and Joseph Chaikin (Bauriedel and van Reigersberg), a year of observation and training with the Lecoq-based performers of Théâtre de la Jeune Lune (Bauriedel), one year and two years, respectively, of study at École Jacques Lecoq (Rothenberg and Bauriedel), and three years of Graham technique (van Reigersberg). Along the way they had formed new collaborative relationships that would soon bring new members.

And so, in the summer of 1997, Pig Iron deepened its commitment to company life and moved to Philadelphia (van Reigersberg 2019).

Philadelphia

If training gave the group its impetus and character, time and place made the company possible. Pig Iron settled in Philadelphia as the city was cresting toward its peak years as a mecca for young artists. Actor Geoff Sobelle, who joined Pig Iron in 2000, recalls Philadelphia in the early 2000s as a perfect storm of creative possibility:

> We could live cheaply—if you were paying more than $400 per month for rent, you were doing something wrong—and you had a really interesting DIY environment. And then there was the Fringe Festival, which was just coming up at the same time as Pig Iron—so there's a presenter who's at the same level you're shooting for. And there were other companies—Headlong Dance, New Paradise Laboratories … There was a cabaret, there was kind of a burlesque scene, there was a great music scene, great visual arts.
>
> (Sobelle 2017)

For Pig Iron, Philadelphia also meant the possibility of maintaining ties with Swarthmore (located just 20 miles from Philadelphia), which provided some transitional infrastructure and, later, teaching and residency opportunities. And then there was funding. "I'm not going to say that there was a ton of money," Sobelle continues, "but there was funding. In those days: the Philadelphia Theatre Initiative, and the Independence Foundation. And then other things started to emerge" (Sobelle 2017).

The growing presence of so many "little companies" made for "a healthy kind of competition" and "a lot of cross-pollination." And the city's multiple colleges and art schools meant a steady stream of young talent. On the other hand, there was minimal competition from commercial theatre. "It [wasn't] a theatre town. But it *is* a college and university town. You have an audience, and you have a lot of energy" (Sobelle 2017).

It is an assessment echoed by Philadelphia press in the period. In 2004, *Broad Street Review* ran an article on the extraordinary growth of local theatre, noting that, until the mid-1990s, Philadelphia had been New York's tryout town, with little theatre of its own. But

> the past ten-plus years have witnessed a burst of home-grown theatre companies—more than 75 in the Metropolitan area .... This growth in turn has produced a genuine community of actors, drawn here by a combination that few other cities can offer: steady work, affordable living costs, and even (at some Actors' Equity houses), that holy grail for actors, health benefits.
>
> (Rottenberg 2004)

On the other hand, Philadelphia had no film or television industry—a plus, in Sobelle's opinion, making Philadelphia a kind of artistic retreat.

> There was no hope ever of getting discovered, or going on a commercial audition. So anybody that was working in Philly had basically made the decision, whether they knew it or not, to not pursue fame and fortune. They were truly doing the work, in this other way.
>
> (Sobelle 2017)

And then there were Philadelphia's industrial roots, which meant "very interesting architecture, and interesting spaces." The Philadelphia Fringe would play a key role in negotiating nontraditional and disused space for theatre artists to develop and exhibit their work (Sobelle 2017). Pig Iron would come to make promenade, site-specific performance one of the several cornerstones of their work.

Above all, what lingers for Sobelle is a powerful impression of community. "In my experience, Philadelphia was filled with a lot of people who cared for one another, deeply, really, actually, really cared. All of that to me is ultimately why all of this was so successful" (Sobelle 2017).

Development: The Next Scariest Thing

By 1997 Pig Iron was creating a show a year, sometimes two or more. *Poet in New York* was followed by the premiere of *Cafeteria*—an "offbeat slice of tragicomic Americana"—created in collaboration with puppet-makers from the Jim Henson workshop. Pure physical theatre without recourse to spoken language, *Cafeteria* earned Pig Iron its first Barrymore (Philadelphia's award for excellence in theatre). It also brought in three new performers: Trey Lyford (who would work with Pig Iron intermittently until 2000), Suli Holum (who joined following graduation from Swarthmore), and James Sugg, an operatically trained singer, who would remain with the company until 2014. Sugg brought the kind of background that had come to typify Pig Iron actors: a strong undergraduate education (Oberlin), strong artistic technique, and energetic curiosity. Previously untrained in physical theatre, he took to it with enormous pleasure. "That first year, was like going to Lecoq for me—learning those skills: the comic stuff, body stuff, neutrality stuff, generating stuff …." (Sugg 2017). James Sugg's early work with Pig Iron combined sound design and some intermittent acting; he would go on to become one of the company's most acclaimed performers.

The year 1998 brought four premieres: *The Tragedy of Joan of Arc*, *Gentlemen Volunteers*, and two more Lorca plays, forming a trilogy with *Poet in New York: The Trip to the Moon*, about Lorca's traveling theatre, and *The Impossible Play*, about Lorca's life under Fascism. It also brought two new actors: Emmanuelle Delpech and Cassandra Friend, who, having met Bauriedel and van Reigersberg at Ecole Jacques Lecoq in 1995, traveled to Philadelphia to collaborate on *Joan of Arc* and stayed on as company members. Delpech, especially, brought an artistically rigorous background: a degree in classical acting from Paris' École Supérieure de l'art dramatique, workshops in *commedia dell'arte*, courses in clowning at the Académie Fratellini (Paris' professional circus school) and two years of postgraduate training at Lecoq.

Pig Iron was rapidly establishing itself as a collective committed to venturing repeatedly into new territories. In contrast with *Cafeteria, Joan of Arc*, conceived as a meeting of Greek chorus and red-nosed clown, was text-based. And *Gentlemen Volunteers* took the company into three new formal explorations: promenade staging, soundscape, and a scenic minimalism that called for the evocation of the environment through mime.

A "site-specific World War I melodrama," scripted by Suli Holum and the ensemble, *Gentlemen Volunteers* told a Hemingway-esque story of "Yalies"-turned-ambulance-drivers (Van Reigersberg and Bauriedel), falling in love with a French (Delpech) and British (Friend) nurse. *Volunteers* also featured James Sugg, as *L'Homme de l'Orchestre/One-Man Band*, employing Foley sound timed to mimed action: the "ping" of extracted shrapnel dropping into a basin, the creak of an imaginary window opening.

The show's force lay in its spare theatricality and the continual revelation of its own mechanics. Set in cavernous space (the premiere was held at Philadelphia's Christ Church Neighborhood House, an open, high-ceilinged, exposed brick venue, 2000-foot square), the action unfolded in shifting playing areas, with the five performers leading the audience through a succession of immersive transitions. Erin Mee, reviewing the show for *Theatre Journal*, recalled, "We get lost in the train station, we show up and are addressed at the nurses' meeting as if we too had volunteered, we walk to the bar with Vincent" (Mee 2007, 109). James Sugg's sound effects were created "in plain sight with the simplest of objects" (Zinman 2006), and the four principal actors controlled their own lighting from the stage (Cofta 2015). They played multiple roles in addition to the two pairs of lovers, evoking battle scenes and crowds in bars. And at key moments of pathos, one of the four would silently mime emotional subtext: a racing heartbeat, the trail of a tear down a cheek, the invisible line of a man's gaze into the eyes of his beloved. Critics were moved and startled by the company's precise physicality and the potential of mime to evoke deep emotion:

> All the predictable stuff happens—the pandemonium of battle (astonishingly created by only four actors plus sound effects), nursing the wounded, writing letters, getting drunk at the bar, falling in love and falling into bed. But it's rendered by gesture more than word, without props, makeup or sets, relying on the actors' expressive faces and supple, strong bodies to convey ideas and impact. If the scene requires a desk, draw one in the air. Draw a window. Open it. Papers blow off the desk.
>
> (Zinman 2006)

Gentleman Volunteers sold out its Edinburgh run, taking both the 1999 Spirit of the Fringe Award and the Total Theatre Award, and winning glowing reviews. Back home in Philadelphia, James Sugg took the 1999 Barrymore for Best Sound Design. The production toured New York, London, and across Europe.

This artistic ethos of seeking and ever-changing was, and would remain, a point of pride. In 2004, describing Pig Iron's choice of material, Rothenberg spoke of continually striving toward "the next scariest thing" (Syssoyeva 2008, 186); writing in 2016, Bauriedel was still emphasizing this impulse, which he felt they had absorbed from Lecoq.

Lecoq urged everyone to stay in motion, to cease being static. I ... was inspired by him to evolve, change, move .... Business as usual for us meant going in the opposite direction from the thing we just did.

(Bauriedel 2016, 359)

By 1999, the company had already experienced its first waves of institutional change, gaining some members and losing others; of the original Swarthmore seven, just four remained: Rothenberg, Bauriedel, van Reigersberg, and Holum. But overall, the years from 1998 to 2010 would be marked by a certain stability within the flow and flux of running a small company on a tight budget. As their operating budget grew, the company began running on what Alex Mermikides has called a "core and pool" structure: maintaining a small group of salaried employees to keep day-to-day operations going, and jobbing in performers on a show-by-show basis, drawn from a pool of part-time company members and frequent collaborators (Mermikides 2013, 57). Bauriedel recalls:

We felt like the company could never afford ten company members full time, and that there would be on times and off times, and that meant that people were simultaneously developing other projects and other parts of themselves. Sometimes it would just be ten weeks and then they would come back to Pig Iron. I think that everyone really felt like Pig Iron was substantial, meaningful, home, family. In retrospect I think we could probably look at a roughly 10-year period where there was largely the same group of people with some coming and going.

(Bauriedel 2017)

In 1999, the ensemble made its first foray into Shakespeare, with *Newborn Things*, three short experiments with the late plays: *Tempest* as dystopic clown-theatre set on Ellis Island; a movement-based investigation of *Winter's Tale*; and a contemporary dance response to *Cymbeline*. That year also saw the company's first institutional collaboration, with Philadelphia's Arden Shakespeare Company on a children's show with masks and puppets, based upon Hans Christian Anderson's *The Snow Queen*.

The year 2000 brought yet another Lecoq-trained actor, Geoff Sobelle, who joined for the development of *Mission to Mercury* (2000), "a cabaret-ballet inspired by the rock band Queen" (Pig Iron. n.d., "Mission to Mercury"). A new turning point, *Mission* was an investigation into the theatrical possibilities of music as inspiration and constraint. That constraint, in Sobelle's words, "was only to use the music of Queen. You'll never hear recorded music. We'll reinvent it. Just with what we have" (Sobelle 2017).

The result was a concert show, reimagining Queen's music. "Radio GaGa" became a spoken word duet for two women; "Good Old Fashioned Lover Boy," a punk number featuring Sobelle in dress, red wig, and sequined boa; "Under Pressure" was sung by Philadelphia actress Sarah Doherty, "suspended over the theater's permanent seats," to the accompaniment of James Sugg's accordion and Geoff Sobelle's flute (Robb 2006). The entire cast sang; several played instruments.

Pig Iron continued to develop *Mission* over the next six years. The 2006 production won the company two Barrymores: Best Ensemble in a Musical and Outstanding Sound Design. Philadelphia critics loved the show, which seemed to embody what they had come to expect of Pig Iron. *Philadelphia Weekly*'s J. Cooper Robb gushed: "In *Mission* we meet not only the ghost of Queen's legendary vocalist Freddie Mercury, but also the specters of Shakespeare, Pirandello and others. All together, they give a concert as eternal as a Greek tragedy and as original as the best of Pig Iron's work" (Robb 2006).

Mission served the company as a kind of protracted *enquête*; their music-based discoveries would inflect a broad range of future work, from the devised *Lucia Joyce Cabaret* (2003) to their text-faithful and music-driven *Twelfth Night* (2012). The show also launched a collaboration with choreographer David Brick, founder of Headlong Dance Theatre, who would go on to develop several works with Pig Iron, including *Love Unpunished* (2006), a meditation on 9/11, which Brick would cocreate.

The year 2000 also saw the commencement of a major new endeavor: *Shut Eye*, a collaboration with Joseph Chaikin. Codirected by Chaikin and Rothenberg, with a set by Hiroshi Iwasaki, music by James Sugg, and script by Deborah Stein and the ensemble, *Shut Eye* was a poetic-absurdist piece—visual, acrobatic, musical—about sleep, waking, love and its failure, boundaries and boundary-lessness. Chaikin's inspiration was his sister, who had suffered a coma. It was Joseph Chaikin's final theatre project before his death.

The collaboration seemed to the company a bit miraculous. Though Pig Iron had been in existence for five years, the ensemble was still very young. Rothenberg was just 26; playwright Deborah Stein was "fresh out of college." Fifteen years later, Rothenberg wrote, "I sort of can't believe it happened. Joe Chaikin was one of our heroes, and his book *Presence of the*

Actor was a kind of bible for me. His experimental group, The Open Theater (1963–1973), was one of the templates for Pig Iron" (Rothenberg 2016). By 2000, Chaikin was suffering from aphasia; in the 1980s, he had had a stroke, which damaged the regions of the brain that control syntax, and he had taught himself to speak again. He had not devised an original work in some fifteen years, preferring to work with existing texts by Chekhov, Beckett, and Shepard, which he found easier to follow. "But Allen Kuharski ... arranged a [meeting], and for reasons I cannot explain Joe agreed to make an original work with us" (Rothenberg 2016).

Devising with Chaikin "was kind of a liberation"; in place of concepts, the actors began their process with words. "Either because of his aphasia, or because of who he is, all we had to start from was a sort of a haiku: "Maybe office/Ordinary day/Then sleeping, sleeping/Asleep/Dreaming/ Extraordinary." Elaborating, Chaikin added only "Office regular. Night dreams" (Rothenberg 2004). "We spent weeks playing with "Ordinary ... Dreaming ... Extraordinary." We laughed a lot. "95 percent funny, he instructed us. We could get on board with that" (Rothenberg 2016).

Placing the question "what is ordinary?" at the center of their *enquête*, the ensemble used Open Canvas and other Chaikin exercises to develop "a very specific state which we started to call ordinary." A vocabulary of commonplace actions of working life emerged: the behaviors of an office staff, medical attendants, a cleaning woman—tempered by a sense of play and sensitivity to audience. "We continually asked one another, 'what is the right amount of time to ...?' We looked for the perfect number of mops. 'Where is the gaze and focus?' That establishes a musical rhythm" (Rothenberg 2004). The precise delineation of behaviors designated as ordinary and awake versus extraordinary and dreamt produced a work in which the boundary between wake and sleep gradually blurs. In *Shut Eye* the ordinary (the small talk, competition, and anxiety of office life; cell phones, static, the slap of a mop) invades and is invaded by dreams of love, desire, terror, symbiosis, separation, invasion, loss.

Shut Eye was slated to open at the Painted Bride in Philadelphia on September 12, 2001. The company spent September 11 gathered in the home of choreographer David Brick, processing the shock of the terror attacks. "We didn't know if it was appropriate to open this work of fiction the day after 9/11. Or if anyone would come out to see it. No one really knew what was the right thing to do that day, or that week. But we went ahead and performed it, and it felt strangely resonant, and comforting" (Rothenberg 2016).

The show toured Edinburgh, San Francisco, New York, Poland. For Rothenberg it was a turning point. "Pig Iron changed after Joe. We trusted ourselves more. The work became more personal" (Rothenberg 2016).

Method

The company had grown again, joined by Sarah Sanford, a Lecoq-trained Swarthmore graduate. Between 2001 and 2005, they premiered a half dozen new works in a broad range of forms: *Anodyne* (2001), a return to promenade environmental performance exploring questions of how art represents violence and how audiences perceive that representation; *She Who Makes the Moon the Moon* (2002), a "shadow puppet dessert theatre spectacle" inspired by Italo Calvino, performed at a local creperie and featuring "live music and a white chocolate surprise" (Pig Iron. n.d., "She Who Makes the Moon the Moon"); *Flop* (2002), an all-female clown show about the accidental destruction of time; *James Joyce Is Dead and So Is Paris: The Lucia Joyce Cabaret* (2003), a rock cabaret about Joyce's gifted schizophrenic daughter, set in a madhouse to an original score by James Sugg with lyrics by Deborah Stein; and the OBIE Award-winning *Hell Meets Henry Halfway* (2004), a reworking of Witold Gombrowicz's gothic mystery, *Possessed*, with a script by playwright Adriano Shaplin of the Riot Group.

The company had developed a rhythm of production, typically opening a workshop performance in Philadelphia, putting the work back into development for a substantial period, premiering it fully staged at the Fringe, and then taking their most successful productions on tour. Increasingly, however, Pig Iron—still with no permanent space—was finding development support around the country; *Hell Meets Henry Halfway*, for instance, was created with support in New York from SoHo Think Tank and the Polish Cultural Institute. And beginning around 2001, the company entered a period of intensive touring, performing at festivals and theatres in England, Scotland, Ireland, Poland, Lithuania, Italy, Romania, Ukraine, Russia, Japan, and Brazil.

A pattern of work creation had also developed. New projects sprang from varied sources: curiosity, formal dares, social concerns, interesting improvisations cut from prior work. Once a theme was outlined, the company would set to work on a loose improvisational assignment. Early rehearsals began with warm-ups, followed by open-ended improvisation structures such as Open Canvas—in Sarah Sanford's words, "a great way to get through the bad first ideas and get to nuggets." When the ensemble identified promising moments, the actors would go off, *autocour* fashion, and "make something based on that nugget," then return to the rehearsal room and share. "It's like a beast that starts growing other limbs—one exercise gives rise to a moment, or to an encounter between two people on stage, and there's something in there" (Sanford 2017). James Sugg recalls: "You learn that the mathematical equation is 1 in 3. 1 in 3 times I go on stage, 1 in 3 times we make a show, 1 in 3 times I cross the threshold—it's gonna be good. The other 2, maybe it's fine ... We get used to failure. And then you have a couple good days and you thrive on this" (Sugg 2017).

Creative meetings of the ensemble were held regularly to address fundamental questions: *where are we at? where are we aiming? what do we need to do?* Sarah Sanford describes this exploratory phase as more "workshop" than rehearsal, with multiple workshops over an extended period "before you actually say, we're gonna rehearse for this many weeks, and then we're gonna show it" (Sanford 2017). Then comes what the company likes to call "the painful hinge": Rothenberg's "yeses" and "noes" in response to the material generated, a process of beginning to "limit the palette" (Syssoyeva 2008, 188).

The ensemble was by now working regularly with a writer in the room. Typically Pig Iron writers rely heavily on video: transcribing, culling, and shaping at home after rehearsals. Sometimes the emerging script is little more than a transcript of the evolving process; sometimes playwrights engage in more active creation; but scripts are always rooted in the generative capacities of the actors. Performers, too, engage in shaping the work, sometimes employing improvisation to achieve dramaturgical clarity—for example, an exercise Pig Iron calls "Five Frames": creating a sequence of five defining images to clarify what is most essential. Pig Iron actors have always understood themselves as cowriters: "There is a sense of authorship in the way we work" (van Reigersberg 2004).

Casting comes late in the process. For some pieces, characters are created in workshop; for others, determined in advance. When characters are predetermined, all performers play all roles during the improvisational phase; when there is a text, everyone learns all of it. Emmanuelle Delpech suggests that this feeds interpretation and frees the actor from over-identification with the role: "*I* am not the character, I bring particular things *to* the character" (Delpech 2004).

As a draft script emerges, the writer brings it back to the actors, who read through twice, then re-improvise. The writer then takes this revised material and rescripts it. Writing credit is typically jointly ascribed to playwright and ensemble. The company has worked with multiple playwrights over the years, some of whom, like Suli Holum, were Pig Iron members, and others, like Deborah Stein or Adriano Shaplin, established dramatists.

In 2005/2006, the company celebrated its tenth anniversary with a five-show season: the premiere of Brick and Rothenberg's *Love Unpunished* and a reprise of *Poet in New York, Hell Meets Henry Halfway, Gentlemen Volunteers,* and *Mission to Mercury.* The love of the Philadelphia critics for "their" company hit an all-time high. *Philadelphia Magazine* and *The Philadelphia Weekly* both awarded Pig Iron "Company of the Year." J. Cooper Robb opened his 2006 review of *Mission to Mercury* by reminding readers of Pig Iron's creativity, productivity, and centrality to the Philadelphia experimental theatre scene. "No Philadelphia company has created more memorable works over the last decade than the 10-year-old Pig Iron Theatre Company" (Robb 2006).

Pig Iron was by now a ten-member company: artistic directors Rothenberg, Bauriedel, and van Reigersberg; a designer, Perry Fertig; and six actor-creators: Emmanuelle Delpech, Cassandra Friend, Suli Holum, Sarah Sanford, Geoff Sobelle, and James Sugg—all of whom doubled variously as sound designers, musicians, composers, choreographers, assistant directors, and dramaturgs. They were supported by a managing director and development associate. And they had a network of local collaborators to draw from: designers, playwrights, musicians, actors. The company had grown, consolidated, and honed its creation and production methods—and was reaping the benefits in deserved acclaim.

But in keeping with the natural life cycle of groups, a second wave of institutional change emerged in this same period. Company members, coming and going with the production season, were forming new collaborative partnerships between projects, and creating original demanding works of their own—often years in the making—that took them away from Pig Iron for ever-longer periods (Bauriedel 2017). And then there were marriages, and babies (Bauriedel had his first child in 2006), bringing the time demands of child-raising and a pressured sense of financial responsibility. The company that had formed when its members were between twenty-two and twenty-four were approaching their mid-thirties.

But the impact of all that change would be gradual, and the core ensemble that was Pig Iron still had much good work ahead of them.

Key Productions: Chekhov Lizardbrain

"I feel like something special happened between '07 and '09," Rothenberg says: "a kind of culmination: this piece called *Chekhov Lizardbrain*. That piece was really detailed, it was tightly written, and the formal experiments were still baked into a character driven point of view" (Rothenberg 2017).

The four-man *Chekhov Lizardbrain*, cocreated and performed by Sobelle, Bauriedel, van Reigersberg, and James under the Rothenberg's direction, with a script by Robert Quillen Camp and design by Anna Kirly, was an astounding exploration of seemingly disparate elements: the loneliness of thought, the theatrical impulse, Temple Grandin's concepts of human versus animal perception, Chekhov's *Three Sisters*, autism, and Paul D. MacLean's theory of the "triune" human brain—three brain layers functioning independently of one another, each representing a phase of evolutionary development, including, deep in the brain stem, the "lizard brain," controlling emotion, and territorial behavior (Hagwood 2012). Comedic and clown-based, *Chekhov Lizardbrain* seemed nonetheless to take the company to new emotional and intellectual depths.

An absurdist "monodrama" in the sense intended by Russian avant-garde director, Nikolai Evreinov—expressing the perspective of a single character—*Chekhov Lizardbrain* "takes place in a mind that is falling apart, with fragments of memory and fragments of fantasy" (Rothenberg cited in Hagwood 2012). The plot, such as it is, is simple: Botanist Dimitri purchases a house in Oswego, New York, from three childhood friends, brothers Pyotr, Nikolai, and Sascha, whose mother has died and bequeathed them the property. Simplicity ends there. Every character is doubled, even tripled. Nikolai has an alter-ego: the eponymous Chekhov Lizardbrain, the play's master of ceremonies (both roles played by James Sugg, for which he won an Obie Award). And Pyotr, Nikolai, and Sascha appear sometimes as unremarkable brothers from upstate New York squabbling over inheritance, sometimes as indistinguishable Chekhovian men out of some bad regional production and, occasionally, as lizards. The story, to quote critic Charles Isherwood, "unfolds as a series of odd, seriocomic vignettes, in which Dmitry revisits again and again his interactions with the brothers" (Isherwood 2008). At the heart of his obsessive recollections seems to lie a traumatic memory of childhood fear and sense of betrayal. Or maybe not—because we cannot tell what is memory and what is fantasy, a drama concocted by a lonely brain to explain itself to itself.

Set on a circular stage surrounded by a red velvet rope, and making use of blocking patterns suggestive of the parade entry of circus performers, *Chekhov Lizardbrain* evokes an impression of the mind as circus: thoughts (embodied as characters) prancing in literal circles, returning again and again to the same incomplete plots, half recalled memories, and plaguing themes. Simultaneously, the dialogue, with its dreamlike digressions into questions of dramatic structure and the nature of memory, seems to propose a theory of mind in which the poetics of theatre and those of thought appear interrelated, perhaps mutually constitutive: drama as a play of memory and the construction of our memories as the making of a monodrama whose scenic space is circumferenced by the skull.

The production was a masterpiece of shifting tone. Opening in a mood of surreal buffoonery and vaudeville, some twenty minutes in, *Chekhov Lizardbrain* veers sharply into unexpected sorrow—about the human condition, loneliness, alienation. It is a brief detour—buffoonery reasserts itself—but once introduced, a consciousness of grief lingers. Critics were quick to compare its depths to Chekhov's and to muse upon how peculiarly moving the play proved to be—best summed up, perhaps, by the closing line of Isherwood's review: "Dmitri's personal obsessions are very much his own, but the insular world he inhabits resembles the interior of anybody's mind, that close, sweaty place where we're all inescapably alone" (Isherwood 2008).

It was a year of highs, bringing, in addition, the premiere of *Isabella*, Pig Iron's first full-length foray into Shakespeare. Based upon *Measure for Measure*, *Isabella* was a comic-grotesque meditation on desire and sexual hypocrisy, manipulation, power, the public performance of self, the terror of death—idiosyncratic, complex, and innovative.

Taking death as its central metaphor, the action was set in a morgue, with all characters except for the Duke, in varying degrees, "dead." The actors performed the seventy-five-minute show naked, their bodies grotesquely lit by a clinical light. Environment and action were dreamlike, poised between clown and tragedy, underscoring Shakespeare's language, thoughts, and relational structures. Though its montage structure and metaphorical physicality were typical of Pig Iron's sensibility, the project was in other ways atypical: it was the company's first time working with preexisting text and with classical language, and it was far more director-driven than their previous work. Despite its wildly imaginative idiosyncrasies, *Isabella* paved the way for what would be Pig Iron's most "traditional" production to date: 2011's *Twelfth Night, or What You Will*.

Twelfth Night

With multiple works in development and on tour, between *Isabella* and *Twelfth Night* the company premiered just three new shows, of which the most critically successful was *Welcome to Yuba City* (2009), a satire of the many myths of the American West (script by Deborah Stein and ensemble), staged in a stadium-sized performance space, with a hyperrealist set by Mimi Lien featuring pickup trucks, a diner, and car chases. Lien (best known for her Tony Award-winning designs for *Natasha, Pierre and the Great Comet of 1812*) had begun collaborating with Pig Iron in 2006, creating an enormous evacuation staircase for *Love Unpunished*. That collaboration marked the beginning of a new phase for Pig Iron, with design playing an increasingly active role in performance creation.

Twelfth Night brought together this growing interest in design with the company's love of music-driven performance and their investigations of Shakespeare. Their fourth Shakespeare, *Twelfth Night*, was Pig Iron's first to use the entirety of the text. For Rothenberg, this was a formal dare: to stage Shakespeare as Shakespeare, on Pig Iron's terms (Rothenberg 2017). The result was a fluid blend of narrative drama and Pig Iron invention: musically driven, clown-based, physically unbound, and yet continually alluding to a neo-Elizabethan presentational style (the stage was broad and shallow, and the actors frequently played complex text at the forestage, directly to the house). The seventeen-member cast, a mix of company members and local actors and musicians, worked seamlessly together on stage, achieving a unified style. Raucously energetic, the performance was nonetheless marked by a lucidity of thought, deriving in part from expressive physicality, in part from tempo: lines were delivered with an easy pacing unusual in Shakespeare productions, breaking apart the phrasing to reveal the thoughts and balancing the rhythmic demands of the poetry with the rhythms of a modern syntax.

Taking their cue from "Illyria" (a Greco-Roman term for a territory loosely corresponding to the Western Balkans), Rothenberg and designer Maiko Matsushima set *Twelfth Night* in a sort of anteroom (which managed simultaneously to evoke a street) of a Yugoslav home circa 1960—gray cement, peeling floral wallpaper in muted tones, and doors whose wooden moldings seemed to hail from some earlier era—a device which in turn justified the use of a five-piece Balkan Gypsy-Jazz band that seem to have wandered off the set of a Kusterica film and lurched happily into *Twelfth Night*. From its first absurdist entrance (building comically to Orsino's much anticipated "If music be the food of love, play on"—that line withheld so long by van Reigersberg's white-suited, urbane Orsino that the audience became giddy with anticipation), the band set the tone for every shift of atmosphere, from exuberant bouffonade, to violently drunken clown, to hopeless yearning. As the plot progressed, so did the music, increasingly driving and scoring the action, sculpting transitions, lifting and sustaining audience mood.

Like the Balkan band, Matsushima's remarkable set was only nominally justified by this unifying "Illyria" logic. At core it was an expression of energy and a playground for the dynamic bodies of Pig Iron actors: stage left, a wide flight of stairs; upstage, a pair of chipped and peeling neo-Victorian double doors; stage right, a steeply curving ramp suggestive of a skateboarder's quarter pipe, with a door in its side, and topped by a balcony. Stairs and doors and ramp facilitated fantastical entrances and exits, unexpected tempo shifts, and dream-like transitions. Bodies rolled slow motion down the stairs or shot down the ramp; actors scrambled upward, chasing one another to the balcony and sliding back helplessly; props tumbled onto the set; doors opened revealing the band when least expected. The show, which ran nearly three and a half hours, sped by, driven by rapid mood shifts, an exhilarating score, and a carefully crafted play of imagery, tempo, and atmosphere in the transitions, hearkening back to Pig Iron's pure physical theatre roots.

Twelfth Night was a culmination—and a moment of transition. By 2012, several of the original company members—including Emanuelle, Friend, Holum, and Sobelle—had wandered off into new companies, independent work, and/or family life. Bauriedel, who had children, and had begun doing more and more teaching, largely ceased performing after *Chekhov Lizardbrain*. Several associate performers, too, left in this period, having either founded companies of their own or ceased to make theatre. Those who remained were feeling the strain of a fifteen-year working relationship begun when they were fresh out of college.

The *Twelfth Night* ensemble would continue to tour the show into 2014, but the tour was a tiring one, with its cast of seventeen and "monstrous" set. Sanford did her last show with Pig Iron—*99 Breakups*, an immersive, environmental work—in 2014; now married to James Sugg and pregnant with their first child, she was experiencing both physical strain and emotional ambivalence. As to Sugg, he was becoming tired of the theatre altogether—tired of composing under pressure, tired of performing (which had begun to cause him stage fright), tired of juggling competing contractual demands and exhausting schedules—and increasingly interested in having the sort of a life that a career in the theatre would never buy. He gave a last performance in 2015 as Chekhov Lizardbrain, became a real estate agent, and didn't look back (Sugg 2017).

For Rothenberg, the loss of core company members was particularly painful and hard to comprehend; he did not have a child of his own until 2015, and until he did, could not quite grasp how the changing lives of his colleagues were altering their relationship to theatre.

> My perspective has changed so much since I had a baby two years ago ….The way I want to be a parent, the way I want to spend my free time, the way I want to make my art, the things I'm interested in as a creator, all those things have shifted. And since I think I was late to the game, I think I was somewhat ungenerous with my colleagues who were starting that process sooner.
>
> (Rothenberg 2017)

In 2012, the company was reconfigured: formally disbanded and reestablished with van Reigersberg and Rothenberg as the new founders, Rothenberg and Bauriedel as co-artistic directors, and van Reigersberg as "co-artistic director emeritus."

But despite these upheavals, Pig Iron continued to do what it has always done best: transform itself.

The Pig Iron School

In 2008, Bauriedel had begun to lay the foundations for the Pig Iron School for Advanced Performance Training, a postgraduate certificate program in physical theatre and devised performance. At the time, Rothenberg regarded the project with ambivalence, fearful that it would siphon energy away from production. Bauriedel, however, was enthusiastic, and the school moved ahead, opening its doors in 2011, with Bauriedel at the helm. In 2015, in partnership with Philadelphia's University of the Arts, the Pig Iron School began offering an MFA in devised physical theatre.

The school drew former company members back into the fold. Current faculty include Bauriedel, Delpech, Sanford, Rothenberg, van Reigersberg, and Allen Kuharski (who teaches History, Theory, & Practice of Ensemble Physical Theatre); for a time, Geoff Sobelle was listed on the faculty as well, but his touring schedule has since made that impossible. The current faculty also includes two teachers of voice, an Alexander Technique specialist, and several physical theatre artists who have become associated with Pig Iron's recent work, including Aram Alan Aghazarian (who teaches *jeu* and the absurd), a graduate of the LISPA Lecoq program in London; Nichole Canuso (dance-theatre), a member of Headlong Dance Theatre; and Nick Gillette (acrobatics), a graduate of the Pig Iron School whose own company, Almanac, specializes in Dance-Circus-Theatre.

The foundational components of the program are Movement (acrobatics, dance-theatre, core training, improvisation, composition), Improvisation (daily investigations in response to themes), and Ensemble Creation (*auto-cours*). There is strong emphasis on mask (neutral, larval, and character) and bouffon. And though rooted in Lecoq pedagogy, the program features elements unique to Pig Iron's method and the particular talents of its faculty. Van Reigersberg teaches courses in cabaret creation and Open Canvas; Sara teaches "Performance Dares"; Bauriedel offers a course called "Thinking Like a Producer"; Rothenberg leads investigations of Shakespeare.

For Bauriedel, the school was a logical outgrowth of the sixteen years of company work that preceded it.

> A school was just giving a name to the nature and quality of our rehearsal process. We posed questions and sought answers in performance. We came to a project like we aspire to come to education—to research and uncover what we don't know, what is hidden, what is impossible to talk about. ... We aspire with the school to continually evolve what theatre is and what it can mean to us as a society.
>
> (Bauriedel 2016, 359)

Community as Collaborator

As of 2018, Pig Iron was operating with three artistic directors, five company members (Rothenberg, van Reigersberg, Mimi Lien, Jennifer Kidwell, and Mel Krodman), six associate artists (Bauriedel, Sanford, Sobelle, Sugg, and Alex Torra), seven full-time administrative staff, and a fifteen-member board of directors. Since 2012, Pig Iron has premiered seven new works, continuing to push the boundaries of theme and form. And since 2013, the company has opened a significant new path of exploration: community collaboration.

Pig Iron's thirty-third production, *A Period of Animate Existence* (2017), cocreated by Dan Rothenbenberg, designer Mimi Lien, composer Troy Herion, and the ensemble, is a non-narrative, intermedial performance exploring the Sixth Extinction: our own "perilous" era, "in which we foresee the loss of 20 percent to 50 percent of all species on earth." *How do we contemplate the future in such a moment?* is the production's underlying question (Pig Iron n.d., "A Period of Animate Existence").

Structured in five "movements," *Animate Existence* is monumental in scope. Formally, it explores the possibilities and limits of intermediality, engaging a contemporary chamber choir, a 22-piece new music ensemble, two children's choirs, a professional chorale, solo instrumentalists, professional actors and movement artists, non-professional community performers including children and the elderly, performing machines, and transforming set pieces. The structuring principles for the work were the nineteenth-century symphony and "hallucinatory visions" (Pig Iron n.d., "A Period of Animate Existence"). Four years in the making (2013 to 2017), the production was made possible by a broad network of support in the form of funding and residencies.

This bold and labor-intensive experiment premiered at Philadelphia's Annenberg Center during the 2017 Fringe Festival to mixed reviews. Critics were polarized: variously swept away, bewildered, angry (Hughes 2017; Kind 2017; Rosenfield 2017; Shapiro 2017; Zinman 2017). At issue was the cost of production.

Pig Iron, Rothenberg, and Philadelphia's arts funding community took media heat for the show—which "infamously" cost $400,000 in foundation grants (Stearns 2017)—on the grounds of what might best be termed a perceived failure of messaging value ("there must be more effective and creative ways of communicating the direness of our global situation") and of funders to give their support to diverse and emerging artists (Rosenfield 2017). Lost in the media brouhaha was the fact that the show had done precisely that: given voice, visibility, and a theatrical frame to dozens of new artists, of a highly diverse sort, if "diversity" may be understood to encompass not only ethnicity but also age, abledness, and the amateur/professional spectrum. Lost too was the nature of the performance experiment, seen by at least one unhappy critic as obscenely wasteful: "This would all be fine if Philadelphia's grantors weren't hurling money at Pig Iron, a company with no background in environmental issues, so they could spend four fiscal years tackling the subject" (Rosenfield 2017).

Pig Iron, of course, has never had a background in any subject the company has taken on; the principles of the *enquête*—to investigate, to observe, to give form—drive their creativity. But at core the subject of *A Period of Animate Existence* may be less the state of the environment than the state of ourselves: the nature of groups, the nature of communication, the way we make and unmake the world together, and the place of theatre in our groupness and of our groups within the theatre. The question of community was at the heart of the company's four-year process, the reason for its unusual production costs, and its central artistic challenge. Critic Wendy Rosenfield provides Dan Rothenberg's perspective in her otherwise critical article:

> Rothenberg bristled at a Philadelphia *Inquirer* article featuring the show's price tag, $400,000, in its headline. He said in an email he'd prefer to see that number in more context, and some of the context he cited was this: "Each movement [there were five] had its own creation and rehearsal process. We had three cadres of volunteers: the elder choir, the children's choir, and the community choir." These groups received travel stipends, and the professional actors and various choirs, adult performers, and musicians negotiated separate payments.
>
> (Rosenfield 2017)

The production might be best understood as an experiment in the process of working with multiple community performance groups, at a scale large enough to accommodate them all. The very epic scope of the performance grew, at least in part, from the desire to hold the space for so many community members—and offered them a platform (the Fringe) and a frame (the aesthetic construct of the show) which would validate their time, energy, and effort and render them socially visible in a way usually reserved for professional artists.

In 2016, Pig Iron established a residency program for an interim associate artistic director, opening the way for new artists to direct and facilitate work creation. At the time of writing, that position is held by Nell Bang-Jensen (assistant to Rothenberg on the creation of *Animate Existence*), who has taken Pig Iron further into the realm of community-centered art making with *The Caregivers*, introducing the notion of "citizen-artists" into the company's lexicon, and drawing community members more fully into the creation process. Covering the production for the *Broad Street Review*, critic Alix Rosenfeld rewrites the media narrative surrounding *A Period of Animate Existence*, now framed as a step along the path toward vigorous community collaboration: "Pig Iron has incorporated community members into its work before … as in *Period of Animate Existence*" (Rosenfeld 2018). Rosenfeld's article focuses on questions of process and purpose, distinguishing between "civic practice" (which she defines as made for the community by *either* professionals *or* community members) and "social practice" (collaborative creation engaging *both* professional creators *and* community creators). She places this new work squarely in the latter category: "*Caregivers* is perhaps the first time for the company that citizen artists were given the creative genesis of all scripted text, with Bang-Jensen and other artists shaping the outcome." (Rosenfeld 2018).

Tendrils, Offshoots, Seeds

I first encountered the Pig Iron company in 2004, when the young ensemble toured *Shut Eye* to San Francisco's Z Space. Finding their work remarkable, I wrote a chapter about the company for a volume of essays on collective creation, a project which entailed multiple interviews with the founders, and rehearsal and performance observations. Returning some twelve years later to observe current work and conduct fresh interviews, I have been struck above all by the sense that, step by step, and in ways perhaps unrecognized by the company, Pig Iron has seeded change in the landscape of American theatre.

As I alluded earlier, many of Pig Iron's founding and early members and collaborators (among them Cassandra Friend, Emmanuelle Delpech, Suli Holeman, Dito van Reigersberg, Sarah Sanford, Geoff Sobelle, and Trey Lyford) went on to forge significant careers of their own, both as creators of original work and as teachers of devising. Through their performances, their teaching, their collaborations, and their companies, Pig Iron artists have made devised practice normative for an ever-expanding network of young theatre artists.

And while it would be going too far to suggest that we can trace a Pig Iron "influence" in the independent work of all those former company members, Geoff Sobelle, for one, acknowledges that there are guiding principles which inevitably linger from their years of collaborating. With regard to his own work, he cites the focus on creating "a kind of culture, and a language, and a cosmology," for each show, the "marriage of strict rigor and play," and the centrality of the warm-up, research, and Open Canvas: "Group warm-up is physical—and it's an important bonding thing, and then it leads into the research. It leads into Open Canvases."

With its current work in community collaboration, the company continues to widen its impact. And then there is the school. The dominant impulse of graduates, according to Bauriedel, is "to go out and form companies, and develop original projects" (Bauriedel 2017). And then there are the many graduates (Rothenberg estimates a hundred by now) who are working actors in Philadelphia, bringing an ethos of collaborative physical theatre to companies like the Wilma, Arden Shakespeare, the Interact, and Theatre Exile.

Like its model, École internationale de théâtre Jacques Lecoq—the generator of so many contemporary devising companies around the globe— the Pig Iron School has begun seeding new forms and new ensembles. And through its school, its collaborators, and its community, Pig Iron is extending its reach, generating artistic outcomes far beyond its control.

CHAPTER 5
RUDE MECHS
Jane Baldwin

Prologue: 2017 Austin

The year 2017 should have been a banner year for the Rude Mechs, the celebration of their twentieth anniversary as Austin, Texas, leading experimental ensemble theatre. Instead, they lost the Off Center, their performing, rehearsal, teaching, and office space, which they had operated since 1999. It was there that they had developed their ideas, techniques, and styles. As the *Austin Chronicle* critic Robert Faires reminds us, "The Rudes entered the Off Center as a young troupe making bold original work in Austin and left it as a company that theatre makers across the globe looked to for innovation and inspiration" (Faires 2017).

Austin's fast-growing economy, along with its increase in population and concomitant rise in real estate prices, was responsible for the Rude Mechs' dispossession. As early as 2012, the University of Texas at Austin acquired the property and raised the rent to market rates, which ultimately became unaffordable. Undeterred, the Rude Mechs began looking for a new space while continuing to rework *Field Guide*, a piece loosely based on Dostoevsky's *The Brothers Karamazov*, commissioned by Yale Repertory Theatre in 2014 to be premiered in January 2018.

Unable to find a theatre, the resourceful company established a plan for their upcoming, twenty-first season, titled "Crushing Austin." Despite the title's vengeful tone, the Rude Mechs defined their goal as the desire "to insert creativity into every nook and cranny of Austin with the very best new independent cultural productions" (Rude Mechs Website 2017a). They drew up a list of ten multifarious shows, each to be given in one of the city's ten council districts in a variety of venues: bars, clubs, restaurants, even people's homes. Some were sketches; others were plays, works-in-progress, comedy workshops, even discussions. Using this method, they anticipated bringing about greater intimacy between the city and themselves while raising money to prepare for the future, a future they hoped would be spent in Austin in their own theatre.

Origins: Shakespeare at Winedale

Of the seven founders of the company that became the Rude Mechs, six emerged from a demanding summer program run by the English department of the University of Texas at Austin: Shakespeare at Winedale. The program had begun in 1970 as the brainchild of Dr. James Ayres, an English professor. The concept was (and still is) for the students to develop a depth of understanding of Shakespeare's works through practical and creative means: acting, designing, building, sewing, stage managing, doing whatever was needed to bring a play to life. Three productions per summer was the norm, presented in a barn that served as the theatre. Given that Winedale is in the countryside roughly 75 miles from Austin, the students spend a little over two immersive summer months living and working together seven days a week, isolated from their everyday lives.[1] It is the kind of creative experience that forms strong bonds.

Few students enter Winedale with prior theatre experience. As Rude Mechs cofounder Lana Lesley recalls: "Many were academics or just curious (that was me) or interested in spending their summer out of town, or they craved a group experience. It's a liberating environment for study because you are not expected to deliver fantastic performances; you are there to learn" (Faires 2004). And learn they did under Professor Ayres, whose first theatrical endeavor had been in the English literature classroom, where he encouraged students to enact scenes from Shakespeare's plays, an exercise he continued throughout his teaching. Through their self-directed stagings, his students discovered that each play contained many possible interpretations. Ayres or "Doc," as the students called him, saw the Winedale program as an extension of this coursework. He believed that the actor's imagination and talent could supersede the director's creative role in a production. He cast the plays, but neither blocked nor rehearsed them. Instead, students explored and developed ideas on their own and, at a given point, held a showing for Ayres, who critiqued their work. This cyclical process continued until the play was on its feet.

Shawn Sides attended in 1986, 1987, and 1988. Lana Lesley was in the 1991 and the 1993 programs. In 1993 she worked closely with future Mechs Kirk Lynn and Madge Darlington. Lesley was cast as Winedale's first female Hamlet, with Darlington playing Horatio and Lynn, Hamlet's dead father.

New York City

Shortly after the 1993 season ended, Lana Lesley and Kirk Lynn took off to New York City. New York was a long-standing dream of Lesley's, though she was not yet tempted by a life in the theatre. Both worked hard to survive in the expensive city: Lesley labored sixty-five hours a week at an immigration law firm; Lynn was employed by Zagat and wrote during his off-hours. For Lesley, the turning point was meeting Shawn Sides—another former Winedale student, though their years there had not coincided.

Sides had arrived in New York a year or so earlier to enter a master's program at NYU that allowed her to divide her studies between the Department of Performance Studies, where she took most of her theoretical/academic courses with Richard Schechner, and the Gallatin School where students designed their programs with the assistance of faculty advisers. Consequently, Sides was free to pursue acting outside of NYU with teachers of her choosing. Although she gained much from all her acting classes, Anne Bogart and SITI Company, with their emphasis on devised imagistic theatre techniques, were the most influential in her development (Sides 2017a, 2017b).

As often as financially possible, Sides attended experimental downtown theatre. Among the groups she followed was Big Dance, headed by choreographer Annie-B Parson and actor-director Paul Lazar. Their productions, generated over a long period, combine dance, acting, and song and draw on a wide range of literature for source material. And of course, she frequented SITI's productions, some of which were devised and other based on classical works. At the Ontological-Hysteric Theatre, Richard Foreman was creating a new theatrical paradigm that Sides, like many aspiring theatre-makers, found interesting. Foreman's productions consisted of his own plays based on his philosophical ideas and views of art. Ellen Stewart's legendary La MaMa and the Neo-Futurists drew her in as well. The Wooster Group, directed by Elizabeth LeCompte, another source of inspiration, devised many of their productions from existing literary sources, often spending years on their development. The Rude Mechs follow a similar but not identical model. That so many New York avant-garde companies were led by women, some feminists, like Anne Bogart and Elizabeth LeCompte, were surely an inspiration for Sides.

Her opportunities to further her own talents during this time were limited. She participated in several "terrible student projects" and served as assistant director to Schechner for the program's production of *Three Sisters* (Sides 2017a). At roughly the same period, Kirk Lynn wrote *Lust Supper*, a four-hander that he and Lana Lesley decided to self-produce. Lesley and Sides were both in it; Lynn directed. Sides remembers it "as the best thing I got to act in" during the New York period (Sides 2017a). Audiences for *Lust Supper* were sparse and the show closed quickly, leaving Lesley and Lynn in difficult financial straits. Nevertheless, that experience turned Lesley into a theatre convert whose desire was to make art with her two best friends. She and Lynn decided to return to Austin, where they joined up with old friends at Winedale's 1995 reunion; Shawn Sides went with them.

One consequence of that reunion was the formation of a group called the Boxtree Players. The Boxtrees planned to perform *The Two Gentlemen of Verona*. The production was never realized, mainly because the women wanted to name the company the Rude Mechanicals after the would-be actors in *A Midsummer's Night Dream*. A vote was taken, which the men "rigged," and when the women in the group—Kathy Blackbird, Kirsten Kern, Sarah Richardson, Lana Lesley, Shawn Sides, and Madge Darlington—discovered they had been deceived, they walked out (Lynn 2017). It was of course not the name that was at issue but deeper questions: how a collective makes decisions and the role of gender in that process. The experience proved galvanizing. Just a few months later, the ex-Boxtree women, along with Kirk Lynn, founded the Rude Mechanicals.

Building a Feminist Ensemble, Austin Style

The Rude Mechanicals was established as a nonhierarchical feminist collective. With this goal in mind, the team formed an administration of seven Co-Producing Artistic Directors—or "COPADs"—consisting of six women and one man. Unlike most feminist collectives, the Rude Mechanicals did not opt for a company that would consist of women and produce plays that dealt only with women's circumstances. For them, a feminist is a person who practices gender equity.

As a nonhierarchical ensemble, their decisions are reached by consensus, sometimes a contentious process but one that is adhered to. Originally, the COPADs wanted the freedom to investigate different aspects of theatre-making rather than being assigned a position such as director or actor. They soon realized that each person had a specific area of strength and concentrated on that skill. Sides directs most of the shows and Lesley almost always acts. However, they have kept their initial impulse and from time to time, they experiment with a different undertaking. Lesley has directed and written; Darlington, the technical and production supervisor, has staged productions; director Sides has acted, and playwright Lynn has directed and acted. The Winedale practice of sharing tasks has been retained with actors functioning as designers and technicians and vice versa.

At the outset, the collective was uncertain about the direction of its repertoire. Initially, according to Madge Darlington, the group assumed they would concentrate on Shakespeare as they had done at Winedale and had planned to do with the Boxtrees (Darlington 2017). Nonetheless, they debuted in October of 1996 at the Auditorium on Waller Creek with an original play, Kirk Lynn's *Pale Idiot*, directed by Kirsten Kern. Lynn, influenced by absurdist theatre, wrote it in that mode. It revolves around a town whose residents feel threatened by the presence of an "idiot." A health inspector is called in to remove the danger of possible infection by testing the population for imbecility, posing questions no one is able to answer. Both comical and political in spirit,[2] *Pale Idiot* was in tune with the mood of Austin's emerging theatrical scene.

From 1995 to 1996—just as the Rude Mechanicals were preparing to launch their first season—Austin seemed to lose more small theatre than it was gaining. An article by the Austin critic Robert Faires proclaimed that "Austin's theatre refuses to fade," before going on to paint a portrait of theatrical apocalypse: "The past twelve months saw some of Austin's brightest theatrical talents leave us," including artistic director Mark Ramont of the Capital City Playhouse, the "physically daring" Troupe Texas, a much-loved performance space, Chicago House, and "theatre artists Norman Miller and T.J. Goudet" who had both just passed away. That same year also saw the US Senate's attacks on arts funding, threatening the growth of alternative theatre everywhere (Faires 1998). Nonetheless, the *Chronicle*'s optimism proved justified. Within just a few years, a new wave of Austin theatre-makers would emerge. Fringe theatre was on the rise with up-and-coming playwrights such as Ruth Margraff, Daniel Alexander Jones, Dan Dietz, and Lisa D'Amour creating work for the new small theatres; and the Rude Mechanicals would soon find themselves at the center of that ferment. Though their own productions were "more populist and slapsticky," they felt a strong bond with these experimental theatre-makers (Lynn 2017).

In that first year, life in Austin was good, though they were unable to support themselves making theatre. Playhouses, often renovated warehouses or storefronts, had limited seating between 50 and 90 and runs averaged two weeks. Theatre tickets were inexpensive; audiences small but growing. The Rude Mechanicals had day jobs, and rehearsals were often held in the evening. Shawn Sides and Lana Lesley dubbed films and did voice-overs. Additionally, Sides served as the troupe's bookkeeper, Lesley as business manager, and Sarah Richardson as marketing director.

In the summer of 1997, Shawn Sides left New York and accepted Lynn and Lesley's invitation to live at their house, where she would complete her master's thesis, a process that took longer than she anticipated. Her degree, like the program she followed at NYU, had two components: theory and practice. Sides's thesis examined the ways in which experimental theatre companies of the time interwove multiple texts to create a single new work, as for example, SITI's 1995 production of *Small Lives/Big Dreams* based on Chekhov's major plays. Plus, she proposed a theory of audience reaction to these multi-textual works, which argued that "a discourse was taking place between the makers and the spectators" (Sides 2018a). This theory would be incorporated into the Rude Mechs' works in which interaction between actors and audience has an important role.

First Collaborative Creation

To fulfill the second part of her degree requirements, Sides directed *curst & Shrewd: The Taming of the Shrew Unhinged*, a collaborative creation that deconstructed the original work. It is ironic that after her long period of studying and working on Shakespeare's plays at Winedale, this devised piece would be the only "Shakespearean" work she would direct for the Rude Mechs. Disturbed by *The Taming of the Shrew*'s misogyny, Sides had been mulling over the play for years. The productions she had seen overlooked this aspect, preferring to emphasize the couple's sexual attraction and downplay Petruchio's cruelty to Kate. Moreover, she had been upset by the snide attitude of a professor with whom she studied in 1988. After lecturing on *The Taming of the Shrew*, he responded to her question about its sexism with "What sexism? I don't know what you are talking about" (Martini 1997a). *curst and Shrewd* can be viewed as the company's answer to his question.

This devised production, Sides's first directing experience, made use of her New York background as a student and theatregoer and was surely unlike anything Austin had seen before. The concept was hers while much of the text was put together by the cast and Kirk Lynn. It would be a metatheatrical piece, as are several of Shakespeare's plays. Of the six women cast, five played Kate. Initially, the five characters (who use their own first names) all want to be Kate, but as the piece progresses, the part becomes less appealing to them. The male actors play existing roles taken from *Taming of the Shrew*. Dr. Narrator, who began each scene, was created for Lana Lesley. The wry comic role, which she played microphone in hand, included trying to keep the characters in line, explaining the play's action to the audience, singing Marlene Dietrich's part of "Dot's Nice-Donna Fight" (recorded with Rosemary Clooney, a 1950s hit) and referencing societal ideas of the time. Interspersed with *curst & Shrewd*'s new material are scenes from *Taming of the Shrew*.

Devising a script was a novel experience for all. The eleven actors familiarized themselves with Shakespeare's text. In addition, they researched women's issues: gender bias, unequal pay, violence against women, and unwanted sexual advances. They were encouraged to share documents, poems, stories, letters, or whatever appealed to them (Lynn and Sides 2003, 1). The cast turned in more than two hundred pages. Sides shared with Lynn the task of paring down all that material to fit a seventy-five-minute show. The company rehearsed for three months and opened in September of 1997.

Sections of Shakespeare's play are dropped, the rest restructured. Kate's final speech is heard at the opening as a voice-over. As this plays, the five Kates enter each quoting short sections of literary criticism about the relationship between Kate and Petruchio, some of it anti-Kate. From behind her podium, Dr. Narrator lectures on the scold's bridle, a medieval torture instrument used to punish women who spoke out of turn. Jason A. Phillip recounts a personal narrative, "Retard," which he performs as a young child, holding a teddy bear. The thirteen scenes called movements in *curst & Shrewd* are taken from *Taming of the Shrew*.

Sides drew on Viewpoints and collage to guide *curst & Shrewd*'s shape, using Anne Bogart's training technique that concentrates on an awareness of space and time. Although only Sides had experience with Viewpoints, its emphasis on the physical was absorbed by the actors who were young, willing, disciplined, experienced in playing Shakespeare, and used to working collectively. Collage in theatre-making is similar in approach to its function in the visual arts, where it consists of using various materials that are arranged and attached to a surface. Here the collage begins with *Taming of the Shrew*, the base of and the *raison d'être* for the project.

Movements are occasionally all male (called "guyness") or female ("galness"). In Movement 2, the five women divide up the lines in *Taming of the Shrew* where Bianca begs her sister Kate to untie her hands. Stereotypical "rules" for how women should behave to attract men are given, followed by Kate and Petruchio's meeting in Movement 3, "Wooing," in which Kate breaks all the rules. "Wooing" is ostensibly the end of Shakespeare's Act 2, Scene 1, where Petruchio begins his taming in the guise of a suitor. Some dialogue is changed and a line of Kate's is lifted from *Romeo and Juliet*. In *Taming of the Shrew*, Kate slaps Petruchio while in *curst & Shrewd* the two hit each other. Twice Petruchio responds to her using Stanley Kowalski's lines in *A Streetcar Named Desire*.

After Kate's father Baptista agrees to the marriage and a substantial dowry for Kate, a slide show begins featuring the "Women of Sonora," an online dating site. As the audience watches, cows replace women as a dating option. Kathy Blackbird has a monologue about consistently attending weddings where she has to keep smiling and participate in the rite of being a single woman in a crowd of single women who wait for the bride's bouquet to be thrown.

In Movement 6, Kate's wedding day, Petruchio arrives late and in this adaptation the guests ignore his presence and chat among themselves. Carried away by their growing discomfort, Kathy, Amy, José, Kirsten, Gavin, Kristin, Ehren, Sarah recount tales of dreadful weddings they suffered through. Petruchio gives his "She is my goods, my chattels" speech, in a somewhat altered form, and he and Kate leave with Petruchio's servant. As he talks, the women sit to watch a stylized swordfight performed by the young men. Part I ends.

Early in Part II, José Hernandez has a personal narrative "be white? a work in progresso?" reminiscent of Jason A. Phillips's earlier childhood narrative. The part follows Petruchio's mistreatment of Kate, although now Shakespeare's lines are coarsened more than previously. For instance, Kate's "Belike you mean to make a puppet of me" becomes "Belike you mean to make a whore of me." In the midst of Kate's conversion into an obedient wife, a television game show, "Name that Shrew," is played with applause and music in the background. The Narrator is the host and the women the contestants, who largely get the answers wrong. Suddenly, excerpts from "Ain't I a Woman?" Sojourner Truth's famous argument for women's rights is heard.

All is resolved and a luau party complete with Hawaiian drums and "violent hulas" is held to celebrate. After a lighting change, the actors rearrange themselves in the same positions they had when the piece began. Kate's final speech is heard and the women, including the Narrator, repeat their opening speeches.

The process used in *curst & Shrewd* in which a literary work was the starting point for a devised production with comic, even farcical, elements—an emphasis on physicality, intense theatricality, and an interest in contemporary ideas—laid the foundation for the Rude Mechanical's future. *curst & Shrewd* initiated their interaction with the audience, a technique related to immersive theatre. Just before *curst & Shrewd* began, audience members were handed papers with numbered quotations taken from the writings of celebrated authors. When a number was called, the quotation was read. Handheld microphones, videos, and voice-overs would continue to be used in many of their productions.

Very importantly, *curst & Shrewd: The Taming of the Shrew Unhinged* gave Kirk Lynn new insights. "I didn't know what I was doing yet. I really think *curst & Shrewd* was the first piece that had a real Rude Mechs' feel to it because Shawn brought an outside influence that had to do with integrating movement-based theatre" (Lynn 2017).

Critic Robert Faires, in the only review I found, described it as a performance piece that resembled a passionate conversation at a party where discussion sometimes gets out of hand. He was impressed with its inventiveness, taken aback by its seeming randomness, and noted the actors' commitment to the work (Faires n.d.). *curst & Shrewd* was performed at Hyde Park Theatre, a fifty-seat house.

Finding Their Way

The following season the Rude Mechanicals presented a November revival of Lynn's *Lust Supper*, staged with an emphasis on movement. Sarah Richardson directed it ably according to reviewer Adrienne Martini, who commented on her "sculpting furious fits of movement" (Martini 1997b). Madge Darlington designed the simple but effective set. None of the actors had appeared in their earlier productions. The Rude Mechanicals still maintained their original structure of the COPADs working with local actors. Several years would pass before they took in company members. Critical appreciation of their style, ideas, playfulness, and performance skills came quickly. By 1997, three of their productions—*Too Much Light Makes the Baby Go Blind* (written by the Neo-Futurists), *curst & Shrewd*, and *Ubu Roi*—were placed among the top ten shows of the year by the *Austin Chronicle*. Twenty years after their debut they would number thirty-three members, including five Co-Producing Artistic Directors.

In April of 1998, Madge Darlington directed the world première of Percy Shelley's dramatic poem *Prometheus Unbound*, first published in 1820. The impetus was Shelley scholar Michael Simpson's request. Even though Darlington was dubious about its playability, she took on the challenge since she "felt sure that the text didn't exist that my colleagues in Rude Mechanicals couldn't perform and perform well" (Rude Mechs Website 2018b). Scholars and critics are divided about Shelley's intention. Some believe he wrote it as a closet drama, while others believe its stage directions denote an interest in performance.

The unusual play had an unusual production. Each of the three acts was presented in a different location on the Austin campus over the three-day Easter weekend so that the audience would experience a journey that would end at the time and place of Prometheus's unbinding. In order to handle the drama and the production's complexities, Darlington collaborated with several Rude Mechanicals, one for each segment. Another of her interesting choices was using distinctive stage conventions in every act. Early on, the choral aspect was prominent. By the third act, contemporary theatre practices such as video had been incorporated into the nineteenth-century work (Morton 2006, 83). Darlington's production is respected in the world of Shelly scholarship and remains the sole theatre performance of his *Prometheus Unbound* (Rude Mechs Website 2018b).

Their next piece was Kirk Lynn's *Crucks*, to be directed by Shawn Sides. At about the same time several COPADs and three actors who worked with the Rude Mechanicals (Shawn Sides, Kathy Blackbird, Lana Lesley, Sarah Richardson, Katie Glynn, Amy Miley, and Gavin Mundy) decided to take a three-week intensive summer workshop with SITI (Saratoga International Theatre Institute) in Saratoga Springs, New York, prompted by Side's enthusiasm for the training. Then as now, there was a demand for places in the workshop. In 1998, fifty-five was the limit so the seven Rude Mechanicals were delighted when they were accepted. While waiting for a response, they had started rehearsing *Crucks*.

Anne Bogart founded SITI with acclaimed Japanese director and movement teacher Tadashi Suzuki (see the chapter by Scott T. Cummings in the first volume). The training involves both the Suzuki and Bogart (Viewpoints) techniques taught separately. Each day the Mechs had ninety minutes of Suzuki and ninety minutes of Viewpoints. Suzuki is physically challenging, as those Rude Mechanicals new to the practice discovered on day one when they began class by stomping on the floor as hard as they could for several minutes. (The aim behind the exercise is to reconnect actors to the earth.) Viewpoints, while not as physically intense as Suzuki, requires a great deal of concentration on the moment and the development of "kinesthetic awareness," that is, the ability to be affected by and react spontaneously to what is happening in the space. In addition, they took a daily Movement Lab as well as a Play Lab, where SITI performance methods were the class topic. They also had assigned "Compositions," which were miniature performance pieces that they developed collaboratively to show Bogart the following week. The actors felt that it was an invaluable learning experience but were unsure how they were going to use it (Faires 1998).

On returning to Austin, they resolved to adhere to the SITI procedure of ongoing practice and spent a year trying to impose it on all their actors. Weekly training programs were held and actors were also required to use SITI style warm-ups, but they proved unsuccessful. A number of performers had experienced different types of training that worked well for them without damaging either the result or the collective. Ultimately the company abandoned the practice of imposing a unified method of warm-up and training. In Lana Lesley's words, "all the different things that people bring to the room, their training and their thoughts about how they do their work are so varied that they just add to the pile" (Graves et al. 2017).

Meanwhile, Sides and her actors went back to rehearsing *Crucks*, the second play of the *Faminly Trilogy* that began with *Lust Supper*. "Faminly" is Lynn's neologism that combines famine and family. The trio of plays takes place around a table and involves a bottle of wine. Other than that, they have little in common except that the style resembles that of the absurdists, particularly Ionesco. Little information is available about *Crucks* beyond a short description and a shortened review in the *Austin Chronicle*. Sarah Hopola found it "darkly amusing and disquieting," albeit "winningly performed" (Rude Mechs Website 2018a). *Crucks* was nominated for an Austin Table Award, an annual event to celebrate local artists. Kirk Lynn, pleased with Side's directing, commented: "She made of *Crucks* what wasn't on the page, what I couldn't put on the page" (Polgar 1998). *Crucks* played at the Public Domain Theatre July 16 to August 8, 1998. Since the Public Domain Theatre has neither a stage nor formal seating, reconfiguring it to fit a play is not a difficult task.

The 1998 season ended with *Salivation*, the last of Lynn's trilogy, directed by Gavin Mundy. *Salivation* is, according to its author, "a twisted, raucous folk tale celebrating birth and creation" (Rude Mechs Website 2018c). Robi Polgar of the *Austin Chronicle* described it as "an ever-increasing mess of double crosses, double entendres, and seeing double. *Salivation* pours out all over the stage (and theatre) like a bubbly intoxicant" (Rude Mechs Website 2018c). Jamie Smith Cantara of the *Austin American-Statesman* wrote: "Although celebratory and cartoonish compared with his darker, earlier plays, fans of Lynn will see the same intelligence and absurdity at work" (Rude Mechs Website 2018c).

Finding a Space

The year 1999 brought big changes. Lana Lesley had adapted Donald Barthelme's postmodernist and sexualized version of *Snow White* that she planned to direct. Her production manager found a much-needed venue which was under the control of a group of visual artists who allowed the Rude Mechanicals to use the facility. In April, the company presented *don b's snow white: Lost Among the Dwarves*, their first work in this space. Sarah Hopola of the *Austin Chronicle* enjoyed Lesley's "solid production" and its "high-energy performances" especially "Shawn Sides' vampy stepmonster figure" (Hopala 1999). She complimented Lesley's blocking and "well-crafted moments of theatre" (Hopala 1999).

The former warehouse, where they performed, was to become the Off Center—their rehearsal and performance space for the next eighteen years. During the summer the visual artists relinquished their lease to the Rude Mechanicals, who took their first steps in renovating the venue. The production manager's father donated an old HVAC unit that supplied heat and air conditioning (it was still working when the venue closed). In November, upon the company's return from a workshop, they signed a lease with a real estate investor who ousted the artists and rented the rest of the building as a warehouse. When money was available the company continued to make improvements doing the work themselves. In 2007 when they acquired the Off Shoot, which was also formerly part of the warehouse, a group of architects donated "their sweat and their smarts" to convert it to a classroom and rehearsal space (Lesley 2018). Over the years other planned expansions were frustrated by several ownership changes and broken promises that led eventually to the Rude Mechs being forced out.

Grrl Action

1999 was also the year the feminist collective introduced Grrl Action, a summer training program in autobiographical writing and performance for adolescent girls, headed by Madge Darlington. The impetus was concern about low self-esteem in girls. Thus, the program's aim was to give them a voice through which they would learn that their stories and consequently their lives were of value. Diversity, both socioeconomic and racial, was a significant aspect of the class. Students were divided between wealthy young girls, often daughters of the company's patrons, and girls who lived in a group home. Free to say whatever they wanted, the girls discovered they were not alone in their angry feelings and painful experiences. Sharing brought them closer and freed them to use those aspects of their lives to create art. In the early years of Grrl Action, the Rude Mechs brought in feminist artists such as Deb Margolin, Peggy Shaw, and Terry Galloway to perform one-woman shows in the Off Center and to serve as an influence for the students.[3] At the end of the course, the students presented their own devised solo shows to an audience. Subsequently, the training program brought in boys as well as girls since the COPADs realized that "high school students and middle school students these days don't have the same concept of gender that we grew up with so we expanded it to include all genders" (Darlington 2017). The era of transfeminism had begun. To commemorate it, the name Grrl Action was changed to Off Center Teens.

Significant Productions: Lipstick Traces

Lipstick Traces: A Secret History of the Twentieth Century (2000), the company's second collaborative creation, would open doors for the newly renamed Rude Mechs.[4] (When the COPADs chose to call their company the Rude Mechanicals, they were unaware that the name is widely used by Shakespeare troupes). Shawn Sides and Kirk Lynn had read rock critic Greil Marcus's 1989 book independently, and both were enthusiastic about turning it into a devised piece. The 500-page text is a sociological and cultural analysis of twentieth-century avant-garde anti-art and nihilist movements that focuses principally on Dada, the Lettrists, the Situationists, and the British punk rock band the Sex Pistols. Greil Marcus gave the company the rights to the book, stipulating only they not insert him into the play as a character nor consult him. He was curious "to see what they came up with" (Moser 1999).

In their adaptation the Rude Mechs animated this intellectual tome through the creation of characters, movement, sound, dialogue, and comedy. Dr. Narrator (Lana Lesley) was revived and revised to serve the play as its historian. Malcolm McLaren, the Sex Pistols' former manager and ex-Situationist, appears as an egocentric raconteur. Guy Debord, the founder of the Situationist International, expounds on his beliefs. Although there are three Dadaists, the emphasis is on Richard Huelsenbeck, a performer at the Cabaret Voltaire in Zurich. Johnny Rotten (né Lydon) shows a side of himself unknown to the public. A medieval precursor, John of Leyden, a radical Anabaptist who took over the city of Münster, introduces the play. Under his rule polygamy was introduced, money abolished, private property prohibited, and work repudiated. A religious war ensued and John of Leyden was captured, tortured, and executed.

The company adopted the *curst & Shrewd* model to create the piece. Sides directed and Lynn was credited as the writer while ten actors, of whom only six were in the cast, contributed to the script. To cover the historical eras, they broke into small research groups. In all, the groups produced 600 pages. To assess the scenes and cut the material to playable size, Sides worked with the actors. No textual changes were made without the agreement of the author. Everyone in the rehearsal room could question or comment. As with *curst & Shrewd*, Lynn produced the final script and he and Sides worked together structuring it, sometimes amicably, sometimes not. The two found that disagreement often helped them achieve better results. Lynn estimates that "about seventy percent came straight from the book" (Calhoun 2000). Nonetheless, the play is considerably shorter because its visual values often replace text.

The Rude Mechs had committed to taking the developing piece to New York for the August 1999 Soho Think Tank's Festival of fringe theatre held at the Ohio Theatre's black box. The actors were Lana Lesley, Ehren Conner Christian, Jason Liebrecht, Michael T. Mergen, Gavin Mundy, and Robert Pierson. In its first iteration, *Lipstick Traces* was forty-minutes long. Despite pre-opening disasters such as the light cues disappearing, the show went well. Unbeknownst to the Rude Mechs, Marcus's friend John Rockwell, the editor of the *New York Times* "Arts and Leisure" section, was in the audience. Sides received a backstage call from Marcus saying he had spoken to Rockwell, who was "ecstatic" about the Rude Mechs' work.

They returned to Austin and premiered their seventy-five-minute version at the Off Center in September. It was a hit with audiences and local reviewers. Marcus came to see it and was thrilled, as was Sides when he told her that "she had staged the book [he] wanted to write" (Salamon 2001). The Austin Theatre Critics Table named it the Outstanding Comedy of the year and Sides received a directing prize. Riding on their success, the Rude Mechs revived *Lipstick Traces* in 2000 and invited several producers to fly to Austin to see it. Melanie Joseph, the artistic director of the Foundry Theatre, decided to give it a full production at the Ohio in July 2001 and tour it. The play was reworked and New York actors David Greenspan, James Urbaniak, and T. Ryder Smith assumed the roles of Malcolm McClaren, Guy Debord, and Richard Huelsenbeck. A few reviews were less than laudatory. Academics Martin Puchner and Patricia Ybarra each wrote an interesting, yet largely unfavorable essay of the Rude Mechs' play.[5] While they enjoyed the acting, both writers felt that the play's theatricality detracted from the ideas underlying the work and were particularly disturbed by the lack of any analysis of the avant-garde.

Lipstick Traces: The New York Performance

Before the lights come up Johnny Rotten (Jason Liebrecht) in a voice-over complains, "Ever get the feeling you've been cheated?" A recording of "*Quearens me*" from Berlioz's *Requiem* fades in. Strip lights on the floor revealed the heretic John of Leyden dressed as a monk in a brown robe, a rope tied around his waist. As the music plays softly, he slowly moves downstage preaching that the only sin is to "abstain from your innermost desire" and kneels. His last words are "who has killed mankind?"

Offstage a man utters, "Who killed Bambi?" (the title of a Sex Pistols' song) and Malcolm McLaren enters in a purple jacket, striped shirt, and a purple tie and lights a cigarette. The stage lighting matched his colors and would continue to do so for all his scenes. The character is dapper, pretentious, and blasé. The actor playing John of Leyden scrambles to his feet and exits as McLaren says "thank you Ean"; an obvious laugh line, but also a device typical of the Rude Mechs' non-realist style, in which the actor does not fully identify with the character. McLaren, the Sex Pistols' erstwhile manager, resumes his long speech on his importance in the world of youth culture. We learn that Johnny Rotten was renamed by Malcolm McLaren because of his decaying teeth and to brand him as tough. McLaren was behind the Sex Pistols' first and last studio produced album, *Never Mind the Bollocks, Here's the Sex Pistols*, found offensive by many, exactly the reaction they coveted. *Épater les bourgeois* might have been the Pistols' motto had they been French and born in the nineteenth century.

The stage darkens and the noise of a screeching microphone is heard. When the lights come up, a skittish Lana Lesley, dressed in black leather, is behind her mic. She announces she has a Ph.D. in narration and that while "non-fiction," she is not real. Her presence causes the tempo to speed up.

McLaren brings on a chalkboard that has the history of rebellious anti-art movements scribbled on it. Dr. Narrator whips through the chronology beginning with the Dadaists. At the scene's end, actors perform an intricate set change where every prop is placed in a circle of light while punk music plays. One actor jumps up and down throughout the song in a manner reminiscent of both Suzuki training and the Pogo.

Dadaists Hugo Ball, Tristan Tzara, and Richard Huelsenbeck perform a nonsense Dada poem in three languages simultaneously, becoming violent and hitting each other as they move around the stage. Various noisemakers add to the pandemonium: Huelsenbeck beats his notorious drum and questions whether language can express human doubt. Evidently not, because he loses his speech and makes terrifying sounds for the remainder of the scene. John Leydon's audition for Malcolm follows. The heretic John of Leyden reappears. Dada Death wearing a skull wanders on with a jukebox and a shabby Johnny makes his entrance wearing his signature safety pins. Dr. Narrator is tremulous. John of Leyden and his namesake embrace.

Guy Debord, the founder of the Situationists, enters. The Situationists, disgusted by modern life and capitalism, attempted to change society by dropping out of it and inspiring others to do so. Although he detested spectacle, Debord wrote and made films. They were anti-spectacle in that they showed a blank screen and used voice-overs to explicate his ideas. Debord was an influential force behind the French insurrectionary events of May 1968, likely the highlight of his life since students and workers were taking action.

In the second half of the play, death has an even stronger role. Dada Death seats himself in a chair. Huelsenbeck, now a psychiatrist, puts a bag over his head and shoots at the audience with a bogus gun. In return Dada Death shoots him. For a long moment Huelsenbeck's mouth bleeds as he continues to talk and then exits. Upset, the narrator explains it never happened, that the play will return to nonfiction.

A slide announces "Notre Dame Easter Sunday 1950" and Michel Mourre, a Lettrist, in the Heretic's garb, enters pulling a rope the length of the playing area and accuses the Catholic Church of infecting the world with its funereal mortality. Dada Death comes on pulling a platform with Huelsenbeck wearing Hugo Ball's famous Magical Bishop costume and describes Mourre's fate.

John Lydon takes over for his other self and recounts that Johnny Rotten is a fiction he created, influenced by Lawrence Olivier's portrayal of

Richard III. He attacks Malcolm as "the master of deception" and before leaving informs the audience that "chaos is my philosophy." In the last four minutes and thirty seconds of the play the narrator rushes through the history of the twentieth century, using three easels, the chalkboard, and a map stand that are brought on by actors.

Johnny, Debord, and Huelsenbeck pick up their easels and exit. Malcolm wants the parting shot, which is "And what is history anyway?" Dr. Narrator keeps talking until she is cut off by a blackout. Her final words are "Because a life infused with surprise is better …"

The cast is excellent. T. Ryder Smith's imaginative performance as Huelsenbeck is magnetizing and frightening, particularly in the second half of the play. Jason Liebrecht is angry and frenetic when he appears as Johnny Rotten, but tempered and thoughtful when he speaks as John Lydon. David Greenspan's Malcolm McLaren is flamboyant, conceited, and all-knowing as he waves a cigarette around. Lana Lesley achieves the not quite real quality the character mentions while remaining funny, excited, scared.

Shawn Sides's direction is admirable. The production's rhythm and moods are constantly changing. The blocking is varied, making good use of the entire stage. The extraordinary lighting is the work of Heather Carson, also known in the art world for her "sculpted light." Almost every scene has a predominant color and most are evocative of a punk rock concert. Darrell L. West's sound scheme that utilizes screeching, crashing noises, a variety of background music, low irritating sounds as, for example, the humming vibration under Debord's film suits the play perfectly.

Lipstick Traces had a long touring life. In January and February of 2002, the company went to Columbus, Ohio; Minneapolis, Minnesota; Cedar Rapids, Iowa; and Houston, Texas. September and October of the same year found them in Seattle, Washington, and Los Angeles, California. In July 2003, the company made its first trip abroad when it toured to Salzburg, Austria. Throughout *Lipstick Traces*' years on the road, the Rude Mechs continued to develop work, at least one piece per year, some like the biographical *Requiem for Tesla* (2001 and 2003), highly experimental. The play explores Tesla's brilliant inventions, his competition with Thomas Edison, and his madness. Technically, the high point was shooting off a Tesla coil in the Off Center, a choice that prevented the show from touring. The work is also notable for inaugurating the Rude Mechs' long-term relationship with composer Graham Reynolds, now a company member.

Company Changes

Over time the company accepted new members, some of whom had different training and came from other areas of the country. Thomas Graves arrived in Austin in 2004 as part of a journey to explore small independent theatres in the United States. As a boy in Louisville, Kentucky, he studied acting at Walden Theatre, whose realistic and psychological training and choice of repertory were not satisfying to Graves. He dropped theatre when he entered college and majored in sociology and anthropology. Two experiences reawakened his interest in performance. He read Anne Bogart's *A Director Prepares* and stumbled on old copies of *The Drama Review* in the library's basement. Editor Richard Schechner's linking of performance and anthropology aligned with Grave's experience. Upon graduating, he took classes with Anne Bogart and the SITI Company, his first contact with devising. A SITI member suggested Graves get in touch with the Rude Mechs on his way cross country.

He was greatly impressed by the company and remained as a volunteer. That same summer the Rudes held auditions—an unusual event—for *Cherrywood: The Modern Comparable*, and Graves was cast. He lent a hand wherever it was needed and soon became an intern, then a company member, and in 2008 the Rude Mechs offered him the position of COPAD, his "dream job" (Graves 2018). Not only does he share the Rude Mechs' aesthetic but their leftist politics and feminist perspective as well. Graves believes they "brought [him] on because they had found themselves in a difficult place interpersonally and needed to shake things up and have some new energy" (Graves 2018). As a COPAD he continues to act, direct, create, design and often serves as technical director. When the Rude Mechs were still at the Off Center, he was the venue manager, responsible for its maintenance and renovations. He longs to have a space again.

Hannah Kennah came to Austin in 2008 with a strong training background (Kenah 2018). As an undergraduate at Dartmouth she majored in literature and theatre. Acting classes were traditional, which was not the case at the Dell'Arte School of Physical Theatre in Blue Lake, California, where she studied for a year. Dell'Arte's broad curriculum includes mask, clown, and commedia dell'arte work along with improvisation and devising. She, too, took the summer intensive with the SITI Company. Although performing has been the major aspect of her theatrical career, writing has always appealed to her. Devising gave her the opportunity to serve as a writer as well as an actor. Local companies in Austin have produced her plays. At the time of writing she is an MFA candidate in playwriting at the Michener Center at the University of Texas at Austin.

She began working with the Rude Mechs in 2008, her first year in Austin when they engaged her as a member of the dance team for *I've Never Been so Happy* (Kenah 2018). That same year she acted in *The Method Gun*. In 2009, she performed in the Rude Mechs' reconstruction of *Dionysus in 69* and was invited to join the company. Kenah volunteered to generate text for the 2014 *Now Now Oh Now*, since Kirk Lynn was not working on it. The company followed its customary method in that everyone involved contributed ideas and text, which Kenah ultimately cut and pulled together. *Now Now Oh Now* took the Rudes' belief in giving the audience an interactive experience further than before. Attendees were limited to thirty people who all participated as both players and observers. The play toured to Duke University, Philadelphia, Miami, and Yale. She authored *Field Guide* in a similar fashion.

New Venues and Collaborations

In 2005, the Rude Mechs workshopped *Get Your War On*, an anti-Bush, anti-war on terror play, adapted from a book of the same name by David Rees which began life as an online satirical comic strip whose characters sit around the office talking and arguing about the Iraq war, drinking coffee, all the while spouting obscene expletives. It was popular with people disillusioned and upset by the war. The Rude Mechs fit into that category as did their appreciative Austin audiences.

In 2006 and 2007, the company presented this very funny new work in two Texas cities—Houston and Marfa—and then moved onto New York, Washington, DC, and Philadelphia before going to the Irish Galway Arts Festival and then to Edinburgh to participate in the Festival Fringe. To their joy and surprise, the Rudes won the Total Theatre Award for Best Original Work by a Collective/Ensemble. In all probability it was a meaningful experience for the Fringe audience to see these talented Americans express their political stance through comedy. They went back to the United States to perform it in Seattle and returned to Europe to give their last performances of *Get Your War On* at the Kiasma Festival in Helsinki, Finland, in October 2007. *Get Your War On* was directed by Shawn Sides and played by Lana Lesley, Sarah Richardson, Jason Liebrecht, Ron Berry, and Kirk Lynn.

During the summer of 2007, the Rude Mechs participated in the Orchard Project, a new residency designed for theatre ensembles to create pioneering works in a collaborative setting. A former resort located in the Catskills outside the small town of Hunter, it provided calm, beauty, and the opportunity to mingle with peers. At about the same time, the company received a Creative Capital Grant. *Lipstick Traces* and *Get Your War On* had moved the Rude Mechs to a new level, allowing them to slow down and devote their time to developing one new piece per year. That summer they undertook *The Method Gun* and met Radiohole, a company similar to the Rude Mechs in that they were collectively run, had their own theatre, and made their own plays (Dyer 2013). When the Rude Mechs returned to the Orchard Project in 2009, it was to bring their Texas musical *I've Never Been So Happy* to a new level. Directed by Thomas Graves and Lana Lesley with music and lyrics by Peter Stopschinski, it was very successful, especially in their home state. Their last sojourn at the Orchard Project, which limits companies to three residencies, was in 2012 when they became friendly with the Philadelphia-based devising company Pig Iron, which also shares much in common with the Rude Mechs. While there, the two ensembles created short pieces together.

The Method Gun

The Rude Mechs, with the support of a grant from the National Endowment for the Arts, started working on *The Method Gun* in 2007 and gave its first performance at the Off Center in 2008. A second production took place in Austin the next year. Its world premiere took place at the 34th Annual Humana Festival of New American Plays in 2010, an acknowledgment of the Rude Mechs' growing importance in the theatre world. *Method Gun's* final performance was held at Midtown Arts and Theatre Center in Houston on May 28, 2016.

While the COPADs view it as their most finished production (since its six years of touring gave them the freedom to rework it multiple times), it has the same movement-based, immersive, anti-establishment, irreverent "slap-sticky" style as found in their other shows and they developed it using their customary inclusive consensual devising process.

Unlike *curst & Shrewd* and *Lipstick Traces*, the source of *The Method Gun* is not obvious, although it seems to point to the Chekhovian gun and Lee Strasberg. Kirk Lynn asserts that Chekhov's *Uncle Vanya* is the root of *The Method Gun*. The title character spent long years on the family estate working for and aiding his former brother-in-law, Professor Serebryakov. When Vanya discovers the professor is not the intellectual force he believed and that Serebryakov is planning to sell the estate, he becomes enraged and tries to shoot him. In *The Method Gun*, Shawn Sides, playing herself, proposes the company cancel the show they are working on and sell all the equipment and invest the money, thereby infuriating her colleagues. Thomas is so impassioned that he finds a gun and, like Uncle Vanya, fails to kill his former guru who is now his enemy.

Both Shawn Sides and Kirk Lynn say that they were "intrigued by the idea of a fictional acting guru more than anything else. We'd all had various 'guru'-like teachers who deployed a kind of pedagogy of personal charisma, and that's what we all were interested in digging into" (Sides 2018b). Company members felt a personal connection to the piece that allowed them to both honor and mock their own authority figures. Seventeen Rude Mechs participated in developing the original script.

Of the five actors in *The Method Gun*, only two had any exposure to Method-based acting whereas four had experienced SITI training. Lesley and Sides commented that its physical discipline, which requires putting one's center of gravity in stress, allows the SITI actor to experience a state similar to that experienced by actors who employ emotional memory (Graves et al. 2017).

Method Gun: The Performance

The play works on multiple levels and focuses on the fears, yearnings, feelings of inadequacy, and vulnerabilities of actors and, ultimately, their courage. Its expository opening takes the form of a pre-show chat with the audience in which Thomas playing himself explains that Stella Burden, an acting teacher and director in the 1960s and 1970s, deserted her company and disappeared into South America. The players, lost without their guru, continued to practice her exercises, rehearsed the show they worked on for nine years, and ultimately played it once. Hannah, also playing herself, reveals that it was *A Streetcar Named Desire* performed without Stanley, Stella, Blanche, and Mitch, the principal characters. As characters in *The Method Gun*, the Rude Mechs are in possession of an unopened letter written by Stella, some of her exercises, her gun, and a soap statue of a tiger. These materials allow them to reenact the original. In this play within a play within a play, at times the Rude Mechs portray themselves; at others they embody Stella Burden's company as Connie, Carl, Robert, Koko, and Elizabeth Johns, as well as performing Tennessee Williams's minor characters. Early on, one of the characters remarks, "I think Stella intended to confuse observers from time to time," which may have been the Rude Mechs' aim (Rude Mechs 2010).

Stella Burden's teaching technique, called the Approach, parodies Lee Strasberg's psychologically based Method, particularly his affective memory exercise in which actors call forth and relive a personal emotional experience internally step by step so they can eventually access it and perform the feeling. In *Method Gun*, the actors work on Stella Burden's crying practice, during which they set a timer for three minutes and sob, tears running down their cheeks, until the timer goes off and the scene ends. Further into the play, they do another exercise quite different from Stella's emotionally packed work entitled "kissing practice," a lesson in how to give the impression of the act without doing it, borrowed from Robert D. Taylor's *Theatre: Art in Action*, a text for young beginners.

A sixth character, the Tiger, is played by alternating actors in a tiger suit, his voice supplied by an actor off to the side speaking into a microphone. The Tiger (who holds a mic) mainly addresses the audience and is both funny and threatening with his vanity, self-importance, and ability to kill. He appears on three occasions. Danger and humiliation are prominent elements in the play. In one scene, Thomas and Jason (Liebrecht) cross the stage naked except for balloons attached to their penises, a moment that literalizes acting as exposure. A monologue follows in which Shawn berates herself for her voice, her appearance, and her onstage conduct.

The wordless scene that demonstrates the actors' courage as well as their skills occurs at the play's end after Shawn (as Elizabeth Johns) in a burst of rage tells the company that she is quitting, that "Stella is never coming back," that "the Approach is bullshit," and everything they have done "is nothing." At that moment the lights go down, the ambiance changes, and the stage turns blue as the actors move to their places to begin their silent performance of Stella Burden's *A Streetcar Named Desire*. Lamps on pendulums drop down and begin swinging at a constant speed while the actors play their roles, incorporating the lights into their movement with no sign of fear. There is a balletic quality to their precision and grace, which fully engages the spectators. In scenes where there are only one or two actors, the others push the pendulums to maintain their speed. All the actors except Shawn move upstage right and sit, while she goes to unlock the box to read the letter Stella left. Fog appears upstage left, and the tiger comes through it in his third entrance saying she has to leave with him. Stella's letter instructs Elizabeth Johns to go to San Francisco, start an acting school, and become a guru. She and the tiger depart together.

The character of Stella Burden is drawn in part from the former actress Stella Adler, remembered for her teaching and her most famous student, Marlon Brando, the star of *A Streetcar Named Desire*. In the process of developing the play, the Rude Mechs studied videos of Adler's teaching and describe her as "mean" (Graves et al. 2017). Though Stella Burden does not appear onstage, she is a strong presence like Adler. In actuality, Adler rejected Strasberg's Method and used her own technique, which drew on Stanislavski's training. The other influence on the character was performance artist Chris Burden, reputed for inviting a friend to shoot him (Graves et al. 2017).

Audiences enjoyed the play; on the whole reviews were good; they met other theatre makers, were interviewed on NPR, had a wonderful time, and toured to Boston's Arts Emerson and Ohio State University's Wexner Center for the Arts before returning to Austin. In 2011, Joan Anderman, in a review for the *New York Times*, identified the Rude Mechs as one of the four most experimental companies in the country (Anderman 2011). Over the next few years, they appeared at Yale's Boundaries Festival, New York's Live Arts, The Radar Los Angeles Festival, Philadelphia Live Arts Festival, and the Portland Institute for Contemporary Art TBA Festival where a video of *The Method Gun* was recorded.[6] In 2012, they participated in the Brisbane Power House Festival in Australia. In the last few years of touring *Method Gun*, other productions were developed at the Off Center that would also tour.

Conclusion

Productions discussed in this chapter have concentrated primarily on several collective collaborations that toured widely and treat a variety of topics. In fewer than twenty-one years, the Rude Mechs created and produced thirty original works.[7] They also initiated a series called Contemporary Classics whose purpose was to recreate productions by companies that had influenced them. Ultimately, only two were completed because of insufficient documentation of the original productions. They were the Performance Group's *Dionysus in 69* (1968) and Mabou Mines's *B. Beaver Animation* (1974), both directed by Shawn Sides and Madge Darlington. Kirk Lynn instituted a series modernizing Shakespeare's infrequently played works through updating the language to contemporary English. At this point, three have been played: *Fixin' Timon of Athens*, *Fixin' King John*, and *Fixin' Troilus and Cressida*. "Second stage" productions were launched in 2003 to give less experienced company members the opportunity to develop work at low expense since they had a venue, materials, light, and sound gear. During its existence, twelve new works were created. However, the participants did not make sufficient use of the opportunity to consider it programming. As a result, it was replaced by Rude Fusion, a program that allowed the Rude Mechs to exercise part of their mission to "build a home for Austin artists," meaning that other companies were able to present their own work at the Off Center at reasonable rental fees and/or sometimes performed with the Rude Mechs (Graves et al. 2017). Thus, the death of the Off Center in 2017 undermined the experimental theatre at large in Austin.

However, due to their indomitable desire to make art, the Rude Mechs have continued to create and plan for the future while discovering new approaches to existing circumstances. *Field Guide*'s world premiere on January 26, 2018, at the Yale Repertory Theatre was the Rude Mechs' last major production whose beginnings predated the loss of the Off Center. The 2018 version was its third iteration. *Not Every Mountain*, the first episode of a trilogy begun in the spring of 2017, opened at the Chicago Pivot Festival in early June of 2018 followed by a week of performances at the Guthrie Theatre in Minneapolis. Thomas Graves conceived, designed, and directed it, while Kirk Lynn is responsible for the text, and Peter Stopschinski composed the music and sound design. It has a cast of ten (Dembin 2017). *Grageriart*, a comical musical collaboration between Stopschinski and Lana Lesley, appeared at Austin's prestigious Fusebox Festival in 2018. Renamed "Design for Everyone," it is currently being developed into a play directed by Paul Soileau and has received NEA funding. *High Crimes: The Impeachment of the Worst President in US History*, Thomas Graves's work on Andrew Johnson, was workshopped in November 2018. Shakespeare's *Henry VIII* had been intended to be "fixed" by Kirk Lynn and given a reading in March 2019, before the COVID crisis intervened. April would have seen the world première of Thomas Graves's and Jennifer Kidwell's performance piece, *Table Workshop*. The season was meant to close with an interactive installation workshop for *Design for Everyone* in May.

At their February 2018 retreat, the COPADs decided to consolidate their personal assets in order to buy a lot and then raise money to build a venue. Their intention was to diversify by bringing young people, people of color, differently abled, and trans people into this truly feminist company.

CHAPTER 6
RADIOHOLE
Steve Luber

Of the Gravity of the Radiohole, and Why It Does Not Prevent Them from Often Doing Inconsiderate Things, a.k.a. the Introduction[1]

The program for Radiohole's first performance, *Bender*, featured the following program note:

> Leading experts now estimate that the music business is currently 90 percent hype and 10 percent bullshit. Radiohole, bless their hearts, have gone far beyond that. Their music needs no hype. It transcends the very essence of the bullshit for which the public pays millions each year. Do not be fooled by gossip and idle rumors. In a world of sham, Radiohole are truly the genuine article.

The note reads as off-kilter, funny, and pompous all in one. It is exemplary of a company that, for the past twenty years, has been making work that attempts to escape the hype-bullshit machine of contemporary art and remain faithful to an aesthetic and ideological performance process. In that time, Radiohole has maintained their egalitarian working style, their rebellious, uproarious reputation, and the hedonistic excess of their work.

Excess would be the most succinct theme of Radiohole's work. They are excessively committed to an egalitarian organization, one they admit is doomed to fail; they are excessive in the physical and social lengths they go to create and perform; most notably, their performances are Bacchanalia fueled by sexual, culinary, violent, alcoholic excess. It's not only a method but a lifestyle, with "free beer" as a staple of every Radiohole performance. Radiohole audiences are undoubtedly more responsive and rowdier than a typical art-house crowd, and performances are punctuated by the rhythmic snapping of beer cans opening.

The anything-goes feel of excess translates to the content of the work, which has been called "a sort of mashup of ideas and concepts plumbing the depths of the American collective imagination" and "a sort of torrential museum of 21st-century American madness" (Grote 2006; Barker 2017, 177), with the only through-line being "a sort of"—that is to say, that Radiohole gives audiences and critics a difficult time in pinning down what they do and why they're doing it. Indeed, I long ago grew tired of the "disappointingly reductive" discourse surrounding the company as "out there" or as an "ain't it wild, gang?" novelty (see Luber 2007, 157). While the excess of Radiohole can appear flip, off-putting, or even self-defeating on the surface, underneath is now a sustained, marathon-like critique of the United States—its economy, its arts scenes, its citizens—in all its absurd, abject hilarity and horror.

Radiohole has become the paradigm of artmakers under US democracy, much in the way Alexis de Tocqueville described democratic tendencies almost 200 years ago—as indulgent, secular, physical, crude, if admirable; Radiohole, as Tocqueville described people living in democratic times, attempt to form new modes of knowledge "that they cultivate [science, literature, and the arts] after their own fashion and bring to the task their own peculiar qualifications and deficiencies" (1972 [1945], 40). That cultivation has led to some very messy experiments in process, content, and reception. Despite working with an ideology rooted in a utopian political system, Radiohole produces some of the most outlandish, grotesque, and sardonic performances. How are we to compromise the egalitarian spirit with the hyperreal performance of excess? Through a set of interviews, correspondences, and performance case studies, I will argue that the unique work of Radiohole, because of its performance of excess and referentiality, is necessary to the maintenance of democracy: Radiohole may, in fact, be saving us all.

Of Some Sources of Poetry among Radiohole Performances, a.k.a. Genealogy

Radiohole is made up of Erin Douglass, Eric Dyer, Scott Halvorsen Gillette, and Maggie Hoffman. Over the company's twenty-year life span, they have collaborated with a rotating roster of "Associated Holes," including Ilan Bachrach, Amanda Bender, Jim Findlay and Iver Findlay (both in their capacity as the company Collapsable Giraffe and as individual artists),

Jason Grote, Romanie Harper, Ryan Holsopple (31 Down), So Yong Kim, Catherine McRae, Joseph Silovsky, and Kristin Worrall. The story of their formation illustrates their limbs of the Experimental Performance Family Tree.

The group coalesced slowly throughout the 1990s. Dyer and Silovsky met at Bard as undergraduates. Silovsky then worked with Hoffman and Halvorsen Gillette while studying at the Art Institute of Chicago. When Hoffman, Silovsky, and their collaborator Regi Metcalf came to New York in 1996 to perform at the Ontological-Hysterical, the home of Richard Foreman, the pair stayed with Dyer. Eventually, employment brought them all to New York: Dyer was an associate and technician for the Wooster Group, Hoffman continued to perform downtown with artists such as Elevator Repair Service and the Foundry, and Halvorsen Gillette had been brought to the city in 1995 by John Jesurun and Mike Taylor and worked for the Wooster Group, Foreman, and others. After a series of such intersections, they came together to create *Bender* (1998) and *The History of Heen: Not Francis E. Dec, Esq.* (1999), presented at the Wooster Group's home, the Performing Garage. While working on *Heen*, Douglass, an intern for the Group, was assigned to help Radiohole. They asked her to direct. She was clearly attuned to the Group's process and aesthetic, and became the fourth member for their next project, *Rodan: A Jive Hummer.*

Downtown giants loom large here—the Wooster Group, Foreman, Jesurun. Like the progeny of icons, Radiohole is unavoidably influenced by these predecessors, while constantly trying to escape those influences and conventions. A number of important tropes and commonalities are clear; the first is the downtown New York scene of the 1970s, each part of which Bonnie Marranca wrote about as the "Theatre of Images" (1977). While not devoid of dialogue as Marranca sets down, it still shuns most notions of conventional dramatic forms, and "Actors do not create 'roles.' They function instead as media through which the playwright expresses his [*sic*] ideas; they serve as icons and images. Text is merely a pretext—a scenario" (1977, x–xi). And while each of these early influences upon the company belong to a generalized late twentieth-century aesthetic, they also each had profoundly unique styles and foci in their process and performances. At base, I bring these elements up to display how members of Radiohole are influenced by these companies, but more importantly, how they react against them.

From Foreman, the members of Radiohole developed a strong, almost obsessive sense of imagery and place. A Radiohole performance has a similar aesthetic of controlled chaos, a silly dreamscape. Playwright, critic, and eventual collaborator Jason Grote grounded their designs in seventeenth-century "wonder cabinets" or collections of curios (2006). But unlike Foreman's sets, which seem more a Victorian dystopia, Radiohole's owe more to early twentieth-century lowbrow forms such as vaudeville or Max Fleischer cartoons or more recent punk/zine/DIY culture of the 1990s.

From Jesurun and Taylor, the company likely has developed a keen sense of media and tinkering. The company has always embraced a certain "trash aesthetic," partly thanks to funding restrictions, but have incorporated complex design and tech elements into all their performances. Like the work of Jesurun, the technology is necessary, not an ornament; sometimes the technology is even used against itself to further the atmosphere or messaging. Televisions are too small to see; sound has been mixed to dissonance. And while their pieces have never been as grandiose or explicitly tech-heavy like the Builders Association, Ex Machina, or Laurie Anderson, they have concocted some lavish technical experiments, played with new tech toys, and relied on software, apps, and good old-fashioned engineering to maintain their onstage control. The trash aesthetic can appear deceptively simple and adds to the feeling of excessive clutter.

It is to the company's credit that this has gone under-discussed by scholars and performance critics when imagining the Radiohole canon; they have incorporated these technologies almost seamlessly or, more to the point, in a contemporary frame for creating and reading performance. This can be credited to the immense collective experience of the group in design, engineering, technology, and performance; the group focuses these skills into their complex but exacting kinetic stage pictures. In addition, Radiohole has come of age in the era of cell phones—later smartphones—and more accessible programming capabilities, all of which they have mobilized. They have engineered set pieces to see how much weight they could handle during the action of performance; as Dyer put it in an interview: "And I think part of it was an engineering thing. How far we can push structural integrity with this stuff by putting mass on it in *Fluke*, say, where people climb on it. Or in *Heen* or *Rodan*, we built these edifices that were these performing machines that were like jungle gyms; we pushed that material to its maximum" (Barker 2017, 185). They have also used more explicit "advanced tech," like "audio spotlights" to mess with the minds of audience members, and most cues are triggered these days by the performers' cell phones (see Luber 2007). This is all in addition to some innovative lighting and sound work the group has put together. But perhaps what has been most significant and subtle is how they develop their live tech deployment in performance. Once run from samplers and mixers, mobile and software technologies have allowed the group to control and/or sabotage performances with increasingly flexible and dynamic tools.

The strongest legacy, though, comes from the Wooster Group. Indeed, the resonances are myriad: both employ mobile media-set-pieces; mine artistic, historical, and literary source texts in the service of mashing up, dissociating, and subverting a sense of historical and performance narrative; blur lines between performer and character, performance and the present moment; convey a holistic and virtuosic sense of precision, even in moments of apparent chaos; have developed an aesthetic that is unmistakable, equally confounding and exciting, frustrating and illuminating, obtuse and simplistic. The biographical work of Spalding Gray and the Wooster Group's *Rhode Island Trilogy* plays out in the company's continuing confessional texts peppered throughout their performances. The uniquely engineered set elements that are almost cyborgian, like those of *House/Lights* or *To You, the Birdie!* are echoed in Radiohole pieces like *Bender, Whatever, Heaven Allows* (2010), and *Inflatable Frankenstein* (2013). Finally, the collective generation of a performance text is most crucial to Radiohole, who have taken this element that the Wooster Group had refined so well, and found its borderline-absurd extreme. The equal-participant model is one such extension foundational to the ideology of the company. Much like the Wooster Group, Radiohole uses a number of source texts for both quotation and derivation in each piece; they both use these texts, as David Savran eloquently posited, as an offering for sacrifice, each reference "becoming merely one morsel to be devoured by a text that remains radically plural and irreducible, a text that defies a single reading" (Savran 1988, 52).[2] Unlike the Wooster Group, however, the text is not a subsidiary of the action, nor is it treated that way in the generation of performance.

All of these companies are or were led by strong—some might say authoritarian—auteurs (Foreman, LeCompte, Jesurun), with members developing skills that supplemented performance—graphic design, lighting, welding, electrical work. And each of these influences embraced quite a dense, high-art aesthetic. Notably, Radiohole has consistently generated work as a collective—no set roles in production, no central writer or director—an egalitarian ethic of creation. This makes Radiohole stand out, even among other twenty-first-century experimental companies. Members of Radiohole continued or continue to work with the Wooster Group in particular, as well as collaborate with many other limbs off this Downtown family tree. But they have cultivated an aesthetic that they only accomplish together as Radiohole. The radical democracy fosters such a strong commitment to form, resulting in a unique performance alchemy. Their commitment to this ideology vastly influences their process, reception, and visibility in the field, and somewhat paradoxically situates them as one of the most unique and yet overlooked companies at work in the United States today. I can only speculate as to why: their embrace of lowbrow jokes and innuendo, of the pop within the experimental, less frequent and lower-profile presentations of their work. Sometimes sometimes such a strong voice makes trouble for fostering a vocabulary for discourse at all; and even when recognized for the work, their institutional critique fosters a mistrust of financial supporters— an aversion to selling out to a corporate artscape or selling short of their work made under sponsored conditions. How is a radical performance company meant to function, in both creation and influence, in a neoliberal system? Somewhat paradoxically, Radiohole's greatest powers and difficulties derive from the same radical democratic work ethic.

In What Spirit Radiohole Cultivates the Arts, a.k.a. Process

Many elements, styles, and processes of the people and groups mentioned above have indeed filtered into the Radiohole process: the density of the sets and text, the disposal of literary traditions, the use and misuse of source texts, and the nuanced incorporation of technologies. But there are a number of facets of the Radiohole process that set it apart from predecessors, namely in their avowal of an egalitarian collective, contributing to a unique aesthetic and dysfunctional functioning, as described below. Whether elements or whole-cloth performances succeed or fail, the process is radical in its form and political implications.

While the term "collective" can define all kinds of working relationships and an array of processes, Radiohole builds their shows together—everyone has a say in the writing, everyone has a say in the design and deployment of stagecraft, everyone shapes the aesthetic of each piece. Their work is reminiscent of the compulsion Tocqueville points out in a democratic state: "In democratic communities the imagination is compressed when men [sic] consider themselves; it expands indefinitely when they think of the state. Hence it is that the same men [sic] who live on a small scale in cramped dwellings frequently aspire to gigantic splendor in the erection of their public monuments" (1972 [1945], 53). What is the Radiohole performer if not living on a "small scale in cramped dwellings"? What is the Radiohole performance if not a public monument to the excess and curiosities of this democratic culture? Each member is indefinitely bolstered by the work with others.

And while each member has their own strengths and even concentrations, the pieces are ultimately created, written, designed, directed, and run by "Radiohole." This guiding principle has a profound effect on the work. The most immediate effect is the stunning inefficiency of this all-hands-on-deck approach to labor. Without compartmentalization, each element must be tested, altered, and retested at least four times.

At least.

In order to better understand how Radiohole works, I interviewed them in Dyer's apartment in 2017 after months of email conversations and information-gathering. It seemed only fair to conduct an interview with all of them in the same room—the myth of Radiohole should be built collaboratively as their work is. History should be written and contested live, and each should have an equal voice in this chronicle. This, of course, means there is an excess of history, multiple narratives overlaid on an attempt to secure one story. When all write the stories, no one will be definitive, or, when generated together, all that attributable. A conversation about what Radiohole is and how they work, therefore, is a collective performance, of which this chapter, in large part, is an artifact, and as such should be considered expert and counterfactual, excessive and incomplete—not to mention that it is all put through an academic meatgrinder in the form of my own narrative and research, the eyes of multiple editors, all of whom have worked to generate material for (an admittedly minor) academic market and labor force. It is something of an exercise in futility to convey the spirit of Radiohole within these parameters.[3]

Ultimately, all parties must be happy with the way a particular moment, look, or text comes across, which leads to heated conversation, arguments, walkouts, and occasional parting-of-ways. Indeed the early Radiohole rehearsals were infamous and included many shouting contests and thrown beer bottles. Writing for *The Brooklyn Rail*, Grote observed, "Radiohole operates more like a sort of anarchist affinity group. They work by consensus (which really means by fighting until they're all exhausted enough to agree on something), but they're small enough, and know each other so well, that this type of creation-by-radical-democracy seems to be working" (2006). Of course, Grote never exactly defines what it means for Radiohole to "work" for a group whose output blurs the line between function and dysfunction, precision, and chaos. In conversation, Hoffman claims that the "struggle gets easier," as they have learned over the course of two decades how to work better together, and, arguably, as they have personally grown comfortable in their own lives, with side-hustles, relocations, and families.

But this is also a part of a discussion about how to communicate a Radiohole process for an academic essay, which proved just as obtuse as ever: "We don't understand. The four of us have no idea where we come from. We're just here. And it's completely inchoate," says Halvorsen Gillette.

"No, we don't come in completely inchoate!" Dyer jumps in. When I explain I'm trying to convey a sense of process, Halvorsen Gillette smiles genuinely and retorts, "I don't even feel like that's a fucking thing." And thusly I'm given a significant glimpse into the Radiohole process.

A sizeable percentage of Radiohole performance can be categorized as misinformation or anti-knowledge-making as well. One need only consider their fragmented and warped revisionist history of literature, history, or pop culture, not to mention their elision on questions of process and politics or their refusal to land on a singular history of almost anything with regard to themselves as a collective. Indeed, even the name of the company is offered as, at best, layered, if not a series of counterfactuals derived from the Bible, science, and/or theoretical physics.[4] But in conversation, the group's form belies the content. While we discuss the contingencies involved in making work—how much time and money is available, who brings a current obsession to investigate, and whatever other "personal shit" is being brought to the table—I'm privy to the debates and conversations and processes that go into the creation of a Radiohole narrative or some approximation thereof. And while the result is quite dissonant and ultimately unresolved, the system of checks and balances, of testing ideas, of contesting definitions (the room argues over the definition and mobilization of "irony" for an extended period of time, as they do "ensemble" and "political correctness"), is clear; the interdependence of personalities and tastes reveals itself.

Ideas are presented, competing ideas arise, debate abounds—sometimes tactful and caring, sometimes aggressive. Deadlocks are possible for sure and sometimes indicative of where the idea will live—outside Radiohole-land. And to be clear, these heated discussions and arguments, though sometimes romanticized or idealized in discourse, can have significant repercussions. Sometimes obstacles are circumstantial, such as when Halvorsen Gillette moved to Vermont in 2004, slowing the group's creative process, which consequently left Halvorsen Gillette out on occasion. Rehearsal periods are interrupted by the need for tempers to cool; side projects (particularly those that pay) take priority.

But Radiohole has continued to make work at an impressive clip, proving that compromise, and their own unique brand of compromise, is necessary for creation, in every nook and cranny of performance, as Douglass draws one of the (very few) conclusions: "It's the little compromises that make it so good."

The equal exchange of ideas translates to the productions themselves, where all members are responsible for all aspects of production—sets and props, marketing, fund-raising, and of course, running the shows, which they all do mostly onstage. They also take turns running the box office, which has led to some missing cues, and, for *Fluke*, a telematic ticket-taker in the form of Halvorsen Gillette, who appeared on a monitor above a fishbowl-cashbox live on video chat from Vermont, in one of the most faithful gestures I have seen any company extend to its audience (see Luber 2007, 156). While much of the performance magic is not necessarily revealed, the labor most certainly is. Performers are not simply performing action and text within the world of the performance; they create the world as they go, which can lead to madcap ballets and feats of athleticism, punctuated by moments of almost imperceptible shifts in sound, light, and movement.

And the goal, the endgame of these considerations, remains almost entirely insular to the group, which leads to a second important component of Radiohole's ethic: the shunning of corporate structures in the running and creative processes of the organization. Much of this is a disdain for the influence of capitalist systems, but there is also a deeper tendency toward freedom; a citizen of democracy as described by Tocqueville "will soonest conceive and most highly value that government whose head he has himself [*sic*] elected and whose administration he [*sic*] may control" (287). Radiohole is radical democracy in this sense, trimming all mediators and depending upon the work of themselves alone.

This is difficult to sell, then, to cultural organizations and grant-dispensing institutions. Radiohole is mostly funded by small contributions from supporters and friends. They are consistently awarded grants by New York State and City cultural offices and have been presented by a variety of performance venues in the United States and abroad.[5] Ultimately, though, the lack of ostensible hierarchy creates a series of challenges in a marketplace of performance that still speaks a language of strict disciplinarity and bureaucratic silos. Discussing the egalitarian approach in 2012, Dyer has said, "the *process*, the back end of what we do, is very political. It comes out of a direct reaction to the way most theater is structured which basically mimics the structure of a corporate hierarchy" (Browning 2012, 43). But does the ideology stem from the process, or is it the other way 'round?

Either way, Radiohole has experienced a number of limitations as a result: there have been grants that they cannot apply for because the application requires a single name or recipient: "You can never credit anyone entirely for anything in ensemble work," Halvorsen Gillette states proudly, and capitalism rewards singular genius. There is also a bias in the market for figureheads or leaders as vehicle for demystifying process or meaning. This makes their narrative in the critical and artistic discourse unconventional, somewhat less accessible, and removed. Radiohole is not PR friendly. They do not have a rise-to-stardom or rise-to-notoriety story; many of their performance documents cannot be printed in mainstream publications; indeed, their website stubbornly maintains its gloriously turn-of-the-twenty-first-century look.

It all adds up to apparent defiance in the face of trends toward homogeneity of the International Performance Festival Circuit or Off-Off-Broadway as stepladders to commercial success. Halvorsen Gillette mentions something quite revealing while discussing process: "I think we're obsessed with our own loser-dom." The reflexivity is important: the company's marginalization is a quality they embrace politically and mine aesthetically, but are also bound to judge after nearly twenty years of work together. Their commitment to ideology has served them well in the work, poorly in the market. Halvorsen Gillette adds firmly "Because we've insisted on being egalitarian, we've failed in the marketplace of the art world; we make work that fails aesthetically."

"But what's failure, though?" asks Douglass, stating that this may be a non-issue, or at least a distraction.

"It's a beef!" Dyer calls out.

"Well …" interjects Hoffman, "I feel like a lot of times there are roles given—that one person is more the writer, is more the director. That with ensembles, it's not like—I don't know anybody who works exactly the way we do." In other words, some of these systems exist because they can work even for other companies that label themselves "ensembles" or "collectives." This is one significant method of contribution to the Radiohole debates, as challenge-via-temperance. Hoffman steps up to clarify how the group defines failure and their relationship to the market. And they continue to argue the merits of their radical democratic work and the need/definition of success, and a chicken-and-the-egg conundrum of playing the corporate-institutional game to get funding.

The process of defining process, too, is a moving target. But of course, this is a process, only one that Radiohole works out piece by piece and certainly not in conversation. As Dyer has stated in the past, "Yes, we choose a different subject or a different theme or a different book, but it's almost incidental to working together—the way that we relate to each other and have evolved over the years is one ongoing working process" (Browning 2012, 42). The sets of compromises, the arguments, the walkouts are all part of this process, and the egalitarian spirit ensures that not one of them sees it the same way as any of the others; the result is a layered, referential, often manic performance style, as is evident in taking a closer look at specific pieces. The two presented here are somewhat less documented than others, and I think present quite dynamic contrasts over the trajectory of the artists' careers and how the group has maintained its special blend of profanity and integrity in the face of shifting political, economic, and artistic landscapes.

Why the Americans have never been so eager as the French for General Ideas in Political Affairs, a.k.a. *Radiohole Is Still My Name*

Radiohole was quite prolific after the first production, *Bender* (1998). They produced six shows in as many years: *A History of Heen: Not Francis E. Dec, Esq.* (1999), *Rodan: a jive hummer* (1999–2000), *Bend Your Mind Off* (1999–2000), *Wurst (take it and eat it!) (I mean, take it and keep it)* (2001), *None of It: More or Less Hudson's Bay, Again* (2002), and *Radiohole Is Still My Name* (2004). In this time, the group received a fervent, if small, critical and artistic following, as they continued to mine the obscure and epic for their aesthetic goulash of performances. They took apart historical figures such as the schizophrenic conspiracy theorist Dec, French philosophers like Jean Baudrillard, the atomic bomb, the *Nibelungenlied*, the Germanic myth behind the Ring Cycle and Siegfried, and arctic exploration.

By 2004, they had reached a new quantum of existence: they had earned some critical and institutional support (*None of It* was the first to be presented, in this case by P.S. 122), found a rhythm in the creation and production of work, and begun to come to terms with no longer being early-career artists. Combine this with the upheaval of Halvorsen Gillette's relocation to

Vermont, and the group was primed for professional reckoning. The result was *Radiohole Is Still My Name* (colloquially referred to by the company as *Name*), one of their most resonant and memorable performances.

Rooted in fascinations with the plays of the Situationist International (S.I.), a radical anti-capitalist art collective from France in the 1950s to 1960s, and spaghetti westerns, for *Name* Radiohole built their own Through-the-Looking-Glass vision of the United States. Indeed both *The Society of the Spectacle* (1967, the most enduring manifesto from the S.I.) and spaghetti westerns are warped, European interpretations of the US democratic project, albeit from very different vantages. To quote Debord, in this environment of spectacle, "Images detach from life; spectacle is a concrete inversion of life, the autonomous movement of non-life" (1994, 12). It is a fantasy of the glory of the westward expansion, a story of images to affirm our current lifestyles of passivity, of western non-expansion. Radiohole's Wild West is dominated by excesses of sex, food, violence, and manifest destiny; it is cheap and superficial, much like the monuments raised in Tocqueville. Moments of ruthless self-deprecation are dotted with almost messianic pride. A dream of the good life, a just life, is overtaken by a fast-food franchise named Norton's Disco Chicken Lickin' Haven.

To open, associate Joe Silovsky sets up a paper scroll the width of the stage that features a crudely drawn Western landscape, as he manipulates a small family car driving along. Dyer narrates with genre clichés, peppered with Situationist Marxism:

> The American West. A strange land, beautiful and savage—buzzards, flies, diseased livestock, thunder, lightning, locusts—and the systematic production of all the diversions and works of a society. The American West: where a man with nothing to lose can lose still more. Where a man can search his whole life for justice, and find only the smoking end of a gun.
>
> (Radiohole 2004)

Upon the car's arrival, the paper falls away and a bright light shines at the audience (the blistering desert sun? an icon of cool, cinematic entrances?), where Hoffman, Dyer, and Douglass are silhouetted, epic Western soundtrack music blaring. They set up TV dinner trays and stools stored within briefcases full of cash, and proceed to perform a strange dance that involves Hoffman sensually rubbing her posterior with a fried chicken drumstick, Dyer using a salt shaker on a stick to season his penis, and Douglass playing with her exposed breast. They all seem nonchalant, routine in this dance, even when they begin to interact, salting or jiggling each other's private parts.

They have entered the Wild West and are looking for a spot to call home but remain unimpressed. Silovsky, on a child's tricycle, defends it: "It's such a lovely town! It just needs a 7-11. AM/PM Mini Mart—no, those are out of business—and it'd be just like America!" (ibid.). A series of Western scenes play out, including a love triangle and a shoot-out between Douglass and Hoffman. Everyone gets shot (represented by confetti poppers that the cast wear affixed to their costumes), and Dyer takes advantage of the quiet to dispense with the "cowboy stuff" and monologue a bit about the Situationist International and what the art collective means to him. When he veers into personal territory, he is laughed offstage, and Hoffman introduces Douglass as the company member tasked with solving Radiohole's funding issues, which have been depleted due to war and recession. Douglass makes the stakes clear:

> By making the right choices, we can make the right choice for our future. If Radiohole goes to sleep, the rest of the world is in trouble. If we blink, the rest of the world will close their eyes. So we're not blinking, and we're not going to sleep. Our strategy at Radiohole will require us not to go to sleep. This will require new resources.
>
> (ibid.)

But this too is interrupted by Silovsky bringing gifts of food, and a conversation that ends with warnings of poverty and demoralization give way to the entire company sitting at a short table and proceeding to gorge on baskets of fried chicken and biscuits, cans of green beans, and forties of Budweiser for a full six minutes. The company barely speaks the entire time, as though they are competing to eat the most. (Buckets were kept by either end of the table in case of a gastrointestinal emergency.) The display is by turns disgusting, hilarious, mesmerizing, and downright impressive.

It makes for a visceral performative counterpoint to the intellectual, Marxist-inflected theories of the Situationists, which lamented how power and spectacle alienate and divide contemporary citizens from themselves and others. Spectacle is "*capital* accumulated to the point where it becomes image" (Debord 1994, 24, original emphasis), and excess represented the false consciousness of freedom and choice. In order for Radiohole's West to become the American West, it needs a 7-11. It needs to incorporate the iconography, the representation of the United States. With their artists' banquet, Radiohole is making a satirical comment on art as excess, akin to the US-brand democratic excess of fast food and cheap booze enabled by the whims of state funding and its fluctuating coffers due to wartime and the United States' global manifest destiny. Artists are as victimized as any other citizen, and the inherently tainted reach of capital makes slaves of us all for the system's consumption.

The banquet stands as the most visceral and direct commentary on what is expected of artists, how they are expected to work and placate the citizenry, and the ugliness in the dissonance of a society's romantic, spectacular ideations of the artist and the stark reality of living as an artist in the twenty-first-century United States. Of course, this is just as true of the Wild West; the West of John Wayne and John Ford are similar fantasies to both cover up the arduousness of the Manifest Destiny, but more importantly to sanitize history and to reaffirm American morality, justice, and honor of an era that often dispensed with these qualities entirely, especially when mandated by the republic. This is why the West in Radiohole's world seems more cinema, more montage (to return to the Marxist inflection) than place. This is why the tumbleweeds "roll" across the stage atop RC cars. The impression has overtaken the reality; we like the iconography better. It is awash in romanticism, heroism, and adventure, as opposed to disease, oppression, and genocide. Radiohole is amplifying these tendencies, not satirizing so much as exploding them enough to expose the fantasy and the absurd desires that undergird our collective, pop-influenced memory of the American West.

The ideology of hierarchical mistrust and belief in the evils of capitalism is shared by the Situationists, the radically individual cowboys of cinema, and Radiohole itself. Toward the completion of the piece, Douglass recounts a bad dream that looms over the entirety of the performance: "I done dreamed we got ambushed by music hating, reg'lar crust loving, chicken salters." The acceptance of the spectacle, the surrender, seemed to be antithetical to the Radiohole project.

But this is the cultural and sociological moment that the group was facing, and the feared "chicken salters" indeed took over and further gentrified the Collapsable Hole's Williamsburg neighborhood, and Radiohole had to return west in *Tarzana*. If *Name* was playing up the melodrama of the Wild West, *Tarzana* aimed to flatten it, to accentuate the two-dimensionality of living the artistic life in the Great American Cities.

How Quality Suggests to the Americans the Idea of the Indefinite Perfectibility of Man, a.k.a. *Tarzana*

After *Name*, the company began to experiment more with their form. The visions got more ambitious, sprawling—their environments became more grandiose. *Fluke (The Solemn Mysteries of the Ancient Deep) or Dick Dick Dick* (2006) took on *Moby Dick* as a metaphor for the American experiment; ANGER/NATION (2008) featured a lush den of sensuality in a mashup of the films of Kenneth Anger and writings of the nineteenth-century hatchet-wielding temperance crusader, Carrie A. Nation; *Whatever, Heaven Allows* (2010) took on a similar virtue-sin dichotomy with Douglas Sirk's 1950s cinematic melodramas and Milton's *Paradise Lost*; and *Inflatable Frankenstein* (2013) was inspired by, well, Mary Shelley's *Frankenstein*.

Acknowledging the company's sustained excellence, the company was awarded the P.S. 122 Spalding Gray Award in 2009, given to fund new work by established artists; meanwhile, in the largest coup against the company, the Collapsable Hole, their home space that they had shared with the Collapsable Giraffe in Brooklyn since 2000, closed in 2013 with a characteristically Dionysian funeral that took over the streets of Williamsburg (for an account, see Barker 2017).

The lack of home turf complicated already hectic and demanding schedules. As a potential remedy for this new set of circumstances, the group accepted a challenge that was entirely new to them as Radiohole: a play. La MaMa was paying tribute to Tom Murrin, a longtime resident performer in the downtown scene (best known to many as "The Alien Comic"), who had passed away the year before. Radiohole agreed to take on Murrin's play *Myth (or Maybe Meth)* (1969) but was given license to give it the Radiohole treatment. The result was *Myth or Meth (or Maybe Moscow?)*. Even with creative liberties, the group admits that it was an awkward first experience with any sort of responsibility to an outside force. To make matters more difficult, neither Douglass nor Hoffman had the time to rehearse given new professional and personal demands. Murrin's text made up much of the performance, as did Radiohole's explicit and implicit referentiality to the bygone downtown scene and Murrin's signature meta-comedy. But in process, personnel, and performance, *Myth or Meth* seems the least "Radiohole" performance to date.

Despite its obstacles and somewhat mismatched styles, *Myth or Meth* made room for the company to reconsider its working process, and so they offered their first commission to playwright and sometime conspirator, Jason Grote. Grote had been a downtown fixture as a playwright and critic, with a noted performance blog and plays such as *Maria/Stuart* (2008), and had recently gone west to make a career as a screenwriter for television shows such as *Smash, Mad Men,* and *Hannibal.* This unique blend of avant-garde and pop sensibilities in many ways makes Grote as ideal a fit as possible for the inaugural Radiohole commission.[6] According to the group and Grote, he was given no parameters, no requests, and Radiohole was to take total control once the piece had been written. In one striking example, the group decided to draw character names at random at the first rehearsal. In other words, these were two parties who felt trusting enough to surrender to each other.

Grote presented the group with *Tarzana*, a meditation on cities as space and place via Kandor (the capital city from Superman's home planet of Krypton that was shrunk and saved in a bottle by supervillain Brainiac), Robespierre's political theory, and a dash of the late 1970s NYC punk scene.[7] Grote and Radiohole also credit filmmakers David Lynch and Alejandro Jodorowsky as influences, though I would be hard-pressed to name a Radiohole performance that did *not* feature that combination of humor, grotesque, and surrealism.

Kandor, of course, does not exist, but the performance takes on this notion of spaces that are dreamed as much as realized. Despite the fictional setting of the play, the title indicates an actual place that is also not a place. Tarzana is now a suburb of Los Angeles in the San Fernando Valley and was once the 540-acre estate of Edgar Wright Burroughs, writer of the Tarzan books, the land for which he purchased in 1919. He planned to preserve it, but eventually developed it as a suburb and began to sell it off, mobilizing the language of colonization: "Let me tell you of the sort of colony I'd like to see grow up around my home—a colony of self-respecting people who wish to live and let live—who will respect the rights and privileges of their neighbors, and mind each his own affairs." Of course, the fine print contained a stipulation that "said premises or any part thereof shall not be leased, sold, or conveyed to or occupied by any person not of the Caucasian race" (Jurca 2001, 42). An environment marketed as a libertarian dream is, in fact, subject to the same oppressive projects of colonialism, themes reflected in the very premise of Burroughs's popular novels of the same name. The deceptive promises that place provides is at the heart of *Tarzana*.

The most striking element of the performance is its set: all in black and white, cartoonish if not comic bookish, and flat. This is quite a departure from the typically colorful, cluttered sets of previous performances. A cardboard sofa is center stage, flanked on either side by cardboard phone booths. A cardboard chandelier hangs from the rafters. All is dwarfed by a giant cardboard TV upstage (this is where newscasts will be made and karaoke will be sung). Indeed, most every object and decoration onstage is fashioned out of cardboard. The pristine material makes for a stark medium, as the stage is systematically defiled in splatters and pools of milk, blood, and urine. While cheap, the entire set has to be remade for each performance.

The opening episode begins quiet and slow: Hoffman, as Robespierre, is dressed in eighteenth-century-ish attire and slumps in a chair whispering ardently into a microphone (made of cardboard); Douglass and Dyer, as "2 Non Blondes," sit in robes on the couch, chattering to themselves and smoking (cardboard) cigarettes, while associates Amanda Bender works a cardboard hotdog cart, writing down notes with a comically oversized pencil (also cardboard), and Ryan Holsopple, dressed as an unkempt Superman (with cardboard "S" insignia hanging from his chest), paces back and forth from phone booth to phone booth, drinking down two half gallons of milk (upsettingly, not cardboard) as he strips off his cape and tights, throws them out, and dons a new, identical set. Somewhere in the middle, Halvorsen Gillette enters dressed in an identical super-costume and stares at the rest of the stage, fists on hips, in disapproval. Finally, Holsopple makes himself a sandwich, cuts off the crust with a pair of scissors, then rolls and squishes the sandwich into a phallic cylinder and stuffs it in his red briefs. In response, Halvorsen Gillette reaches under his own briefs and pulls out his testicles, where they remain for the rest of the performance; he returns his fists to his hips.

"Welcome!" Holsopple smiles genuinely, "to the bottle city of Kandor!"

Throughout, Superman refrains, "I want to talk about cities," and indeed, this seems to be the main meditation of the piece, supplemented by tropes involving guillotines, hot dogs, guns, impotence, and vampires. All of the characters vacillate between self-involvement and self-doubt. Most characters are killed or kill themselves multiple times. Robespierre stops her paranoid monologuing enough to hump the hotdog vendor. Superman mows a vinyl lawn and waxes philosophical as would a bourgeois-bohemian suburbanite, trying to understand "my alienated relationship with my present world." He is nostalgic for a time that never was and still hopes for "the utopian city of the future." He is simultaneously entranced and saddened by the world he and his kind have engendered.

Robespierre often reads tracts from cardboard books, delineating recipes for a Reign of Terror: "Virtue without terror is disastrous [...] The thought of the self gives rise to all these vampires." She, too, expresses profound doubt in her deeds. She expresses the derailing of her championing the rights of the bourgeoisie and poor in Radiohole-speak: "All I wanted to do was buy the kids a tube steak!" and proceeds to the inherently clumsy task of trying to hang herself from a cardboard chandelier with a rope attached to a cardboard noose. After failing at this, she makes numerous other attempts with pills, alcohol, razor blades, and electrical sockets—all cardboard—and finally succeeds with a gun. Superman pours red paint on her head.

These oddly parallel characters intersect at the heart of the performance in which Hoffman-Robespierre shares a memory of the wonder and confusion of creating art in Brooklyn in her mid-twenties—that special comingling of thrill and existential dread that is common to the age, of both the person and bohemian neighborhood. As she relates her memories, special guest performers go-go dance upstage as vampire cupcakes, while Superman runs and dies with a bang center stage over and over again. With each collapse, Hoffman has to stop her monologue, put down her book, and dump fresh blood on him. Becoming more and more frenetic, she eventually runs out of blood and finds some milk to dump on him. Without blood or milk, she squats and urinates on Superman through her tights. It's an astonishing feat, and a reminder of the extremes that Radiohole is still willing to go through, the mind-numbing repetition of the creative cycle, and the frustrations and relief that come from the process. The repetition and obscene crescendo resonates with the banquet of *Name*, a glorious moment where the political and moral failures of these situations defy words, and we are only left with the violence and madness of consumption, excess, and waste.

The whole episode is an emotional and physical mess, which leads to the lengthy dénouement—a New-Orleans-style funeral for Radiohole itself. Hoffman returns to deliver a brief and angry eulogy, as weeping mourners lean over a coffin-shaped piece of cardboard covered in dirt: "Let us take heart. This is the sanctity of truth. Here lie the founders of Radiohole. The avengers of humanity and destroyers of Art Crust," Hoffman shouts, "the avengers of humanity and the destroyers of our trust." The coffin is carried away, as a trailing cardboard-playing band plays Dixieland jazz upon exeunt.

Superman delivers one final matter-of-fact monologue while snacking on a hot dog on the couch: "I've died a couple of times already. The worst consequence was that I came back exactly as who I was before." He tells us "they" are outside the theatre, being taken away in a police car, not able to distinguish between the sirens "they" are whooping and the thing itself.

Why stage one's own funeral, then? Is it to signify the end of a company that had a home, who only had time and energy and passion to dedicate to artmaking, who existed specifically in a time and place that no longer is? Is it a joke about the complacency of growing older? (Back in *Name*, Dyer was already lamenting that he was getting too old for all the "dumpster diving and ramen noodles.") It could just be a reenactment of the end of the Collapsable Hole. Or a statement about what Radiohole might be in the future.

What each of these elements in *Tarzana* has in common is the world in which they live—Robespierre's France, Superman's Kandor, the punks' downtown NYC, Burroughs's Tarzana, and Radiohole's Williamsburg—is an ideation. It is a vision for a utopia-adjacent world of fertile creation and justice. And, as with all utopias, these could never be and never quite were. The purity of the idea, the pristine white cardboard, is shown to be inevitably destroyed, besmirched, and awash with blood, sweat, and piss. But art, even art in a utopian regime, cannot exist without blood, sweat, and piss.

This also connects to *Name* in that both performances by a Brooklyn-based collective take on various times and spaces of the false consciousness of American imperialism, not to mention the constant return to excess characteristic of most Radiohole performances. The grandiosity of both ideas, the need to expand and exploit and take, seems to offend the sensibilities of a radically democratic ideology and thus translate to the grotesquerie toward which Radiohole is drawn. This allies itself with the company members' experiences as working artists and the expectations placed upon them in the face of proportionally laughable resources. Give us money, the Radiohole dares, and we can make you a set of cardboard—then pee on it.

How the Taste for Physical Gratification Is United in Radiohole to Love of Freedom and Attention to Public Affairs, a.k.a. the Conclusion

Returning to that first Radiohole program, I remember how mystified and excited I was before *Bender*, reading the note over: "Leading experts now estimate that the music business is currently 90 percent hype and 10 percent bullshit. Radiohole, bless their hearts, have gone far beyond that. […] In a world of sham, Radiohole are truly the genuine article."

It was unruly, it was funny, it was brilliant. It was also plagiarized. The note for *Bender* was taken almost word for word from the liner notes and review by T.M. Christian for a 1969 self-titled album by the Masked Marauders. To continue the dizzying spiral of referentiality, neither T.M. Christian nor the Masked Marauders were real. The review of the album was a satirical take on a fake supergroup (rumored to be made up by Bob Dylan, Paul McCartney, John Lennon, and Mick Jagger) for an album that didn't exist, written by Greil Marcus under the pseudonym of Christian. But the piece garnered so much attention that the joke was extended by *Rolling Stone* editors: they helped record a real album with a group of ghost musicians and vocal impersonators. The album was remarkably successful for what was, at base, an indictment of the capitalist structures driving the music industry. It was a simulacrum of a hoax, written by a fake rock critic, all of which appeared as the uncredited take on a downtown New York performance in 1998. (One of the tracks on the Masked Marauders album, "More or Less Hudson's Bay Again," became the subtitle for Radiohole's subsequent performance, *None of It.*)

There is something dazzlingly illustrative in this citationality of the Radiohole program note, one that goes a long way to describe the Radiohole aesthetic and place among performance collectives of the twenty-first century. Marcus's work of journalism is indeed facetious—meant to annoy, upset, and mock art criticism and the art market it serves, but it is also beautifully incisive, reflexive, and grounded in its satire. Moreover, it is an effusive piece about a super-group, a band that is predicated on excess and the need to push high heights higher. The review is ultimately coming from a place of grave concern for the field, a breadth of knowledge as to why one should be concerned, as well as one that is well placed to change it, to shift the conversation by upending convention (or, in this case, the existence) of how art is made in a supercharged capitalist society. A fake review by a fake critic of a nonexistent band reveals the Emperor has no clothes on; indeed, the momentary success of the real-fake band exemplifies the power of this exercise and the sad truth of a public's willingness to consume the hoax despite seeing the hoaxiness of it all. This theme has remained painfully relevant moment to moment in the United States and its shared upbringing of Radiohole over the past twenty years. If anything, the chaos of Radiohole's worlds has come to seem more a premonition than a satire.

In a way, though, Radiohole is the Masked Marauders: a group of talented artists who work under the veil of a larger critique of the culture from which they had been forged. The way through is to mine the depths of their individuality as artists and as a collective of outsiders. Consider the affinities they express in their references: Debord, Baudrillard, Dec, visionaries behind the spaghetti westerns—all of these are outsiders looking in at US democracy, politics, and art-making in various ways. The egalitarian spirit that represents all that is right and all that is wrong with the sphere of artistic production in the country led me to depend upon Tocqueville as my guide through the works of Radiohole. They are all theorists of worlds that cannot be—utopias, in many cases, and all of them work in opposition to the forces of accepted reality. Radiohole cannot work in a utopia, and so they stage the contradictions, joys, and errors of their work and lives under late capitalism. In a rare moment of explanation, Dyer admits of *Tarzana*: "I think what those characters have in common is literally us [...] I think it's really about Radiohole as an ensemble being together—our performance style, our approach to the work, and our ability to take disparate elements and make them coexist onstage, with a little more than a relationship of textures and maybe themes" (Tran 2015). Radiohole, as an entity, is the subject of its own process, performance, and modes of inquiry. They exemplify the glories and failures of radical democracy.

Radiohole's excess can thus be represented by the idea of another French theorist and critic, Georges Bataille; in many ways, Radiohole is the excess energy of the general economy. In *The Accursed Share*, Bataille theorizes that certain energies need to be expended beyond those necessary for an economy to function; if these excesses are not released, they are mobilized for destructive forces—namely, war. Excess in gratification, such as that discussed by Tocqueville, mitigates the violent tendencies of capitalist regimes. Bataille writes, "independently of our consciousness, sexual reproduction is, together with eating and death, one of the great luxurious detours that ensure the intense consumption of energy" (1988, 35). What are these factors if not the ties that bind all Radiohole performances: sex, eating, death?

When I wrote about *Fluke* in 2006, I described Radiohole's work as hyperreal. But with hindsight and from the despair I feel in 2020, I understand that the hyperreal—beyond, supplanting the real—is not quite right, and I return to the visceral, political, and violent implications of excess. Excess itself is a type of beyond, but it connotes more important and grave repercussions with regard to waste, value, and shared resources; it is at once about the body and about late capitalism, performance, and institutional violence. The hyperreal is an important theoretical critique; excess is the very real work of shit and spreadsheets.

In staging these impulses, in giving creative voice to the rawness of experience in the face of an oppressive set of political forces, Radiohole exposes basest needs, instincts, and fantasies of contemporary culture. These fantasies of excess create exciting, hilarious, and deeply affecting performances and by maintaining an ideal in process in which all voices are heard—no one reference, no one perspective is privileged in the work. Excess reveals the forms of liberation and oppression in democratic culture, and, by extension, artmaking. So when Douglass, in *Radiohole Is Still My Name*, bombastically claims, "If Radiohole goes to sleep, the rest of the world is in trouble. If we blink, the rest of the world will close their eyes. So we're not blinking, and we're not going to sleep. Our strategy at Radiohole will require us not to go to sleep," what she is really letting us know is that Radiohole is the only force keeping this powder keg of a culture from exploding.

CHAPTER 7
THE CIVILIANS
Sara Freeman

Origins, Key Influences, Legacy

Critics and scholars initially positioned the Civilians as a theatre company that makes non-narrative performances based on interviews. Initially called a "documentary cabaret theatre" (Estvanik 2004, 24), it is really the combination of the objective and the subjective in storytelling that defines the group's wide range of work, rather than a strict approach to documentary theatre. Founded in 2001 by Steve Cosson,[1] the group took inspiration in part from the methods of Britain's Joint Stock Theatre Company, melded with a desire to fully integrate music and a cabaret sensibility with ethnographic immersion and author-led devising. Cosson (or playwrights like Anne Washburn and Neal Bell) and composer-lyricist Michael Friedman scripted the resulting material into theatrical form that combined scenes, direct address in the mode of both personal statement and information-driven lecture-demonstration, stylized movement, and songs. Sarah Kozinn writes that this process produced performances that are "plot-free, like a series of vignettes strung together by common themes. The shows create an open-ended journey rather than a conclusive story with a beginning, a climatic middle, and resolution" (2010, 192).

After its first two shows, the company seemed to feel the need to prep audiences to receive a "plot-free" cabaret enacted by artists who alternate between presenting themselves as performers (often using their own names) and embodying an interview subject. The opening of *(I am) Nobody's Lunch* addresses those characteristics as features, not bugs, of their aesthetic. The show begins with a performer delivering a type of prologue directly to the audience in their "self" persona. The speech greets the audience in a way that seems unscriptedly casual ("Oh hi, gosh wow, hi everyone") and briefly describes the ensemble's method ("we interviewed people and asked them how they know what they know"). The prologue then targets two issues: confusion and genre expectations. "Look here's the thing," says the Performer. "We did some focus groups and some of our previous audience members expressed a feeling that .... that our show was well, confusing. So—that is NOT what we want to do to you, is that clear?" At the end of the prologue, having de-confused the audience by setting the scene about political events in 2003 that informed the interviews, the Performer declares, "Also! Last thing. This is a *cabaret*, ok? So there's no plot. No. Plot. As in story" (Cosson 2009, 75).

The Civilians approach differs from the two basic streams of interview-based theatre that had roughly settled out in the early twenty-first century: there's a British-based verbatim stream, where theatrical events are assembled from texts like judicial inquiries, government reports, and interviews conducted by the performers or writers typified by Johnathan Kent and Richard Norton-Taylor in the tribunal plays created for the Tricycle Theatre.[2] The other stream might be called the US-based Anna Deveare Smith school of documentary theatre, where the recreation of interview subjects' behavior and intonation by an actor holds the seeds to assembling a multi-voiced theatrical representation of a community or event. Just as groups such as Moisès Kaufman's Tectonic Theater Project or Alecky Blythe's Recorded Delivery continue to renegotiate documentary theatre techniques, the Civilians' work activates an Anglo-American heritage while consistently reinventing what it means to research, interview, or reproduce sources *and for what ends*. As of 2011, the company describes itself as "America's Center for Investigative Theatre," a loose designation wherein the investigation can, and does, take many forms, especially in the Research and Development (R&D) series for emerging artists the company has run since 2010.

Early Civilians shows are made of many little stories, and they are structured with strong attention to holistic rising and falling trajectories of the cumulative effects of the stories. Songs interrupt the individual narratives but also confirm and extend the show's themes and the patterns. By the second decade of the company's work, shows like *The Great Immensity* and *Pretty Filthy* have become fully plotted; and some employ fully enacted characters and performers making no reference to the performer-self. It is not right, however, to suggest that later Civilians, work is traditionally dramatic, especially if that implies that the dramatic is more mature artistically than cabaret, which is a mature form in its own right. The Civilians' work constantly redraws the line between play and cabaret, the dramatic and the deconstructive, with both dialogue and lyrics always incorporating direct language from interviews.

Cosson is highly aware of the Civilians' aesthetic debts, including those to Brecht and Weil, as well as Joint Stock, and its formal in-between-ness in relationship to new writing, devising, verbatim theatre, collective creation, and musical theatre. The Civilians has grown into more of a new writing theatre than many experimental American ensembles, and its style is less deconstructive than lightning-rod companies of both the generation before and after it, like the Wooster Group or Nature Theatre of Oklahoma. But the company also finds the usual structures of new play development to be a hard fit because new play models can be too focused on the literary experience of a play script. Similarly, while songs are central to Civilians' performances, the role music plays can be alternately close to and quite far away from book-musical structures. Likewise, there is clearly a queer through-line to the company's work and it exhibited early and admirable sensitivity to dynamics of race and casting, but it has never organized itself around queer identity or activism related to gender, sexuality, and race.

The company straddles waves of aesthetic experimentation among New York theatres and combines organizational structures in ways that differ from mainstream American theatre companies (Peterson 2012, 2–5). In the critical frames provided by scholarship from Rachel Anderson-Rabern, Katherine Syssoyeva, and Scott Proudfit, they are a third-wave, post-utopian ensemble with a strong leader, driven by the desire to encounter something in the world through research, interviews, and immersion, and render those materials or pretexts into a socially compelling theatrical format. They started with a loose collective identity but professional consolidation points at a future focused on becoming a sustainable institutional structure for investigative theatrical experiments. The tagline about being a "Center" for investigative theatre signals that growing institutional trajectory.

Between 2001 and 2008, the company's associate artists held relatively close together, generating ideas, doing workshop processes while working other day jobs, self-producing a show, and taking it on tour. Cosson and Washburn were the primary writers, Friedman was the only composer, Cosson and Anne Kauffman were the only two to direct. The company successfully brought its work to London and Edinburgh in its first two years and won an OBIE in 2004. This early recognition marked them as an ensemble with a mission and a distinctive role to play in Off-Broadway theatre in reimagining musical and documentary theatre.

Part of the Civilians' inbuilt post-utopian, third-wave identity is that the company was not set up with a vision of a permanent ensemble nor the expectations of a communitarian, leader-less process. All the associate artists, including Cosson and especially Friedman, continued to pursue projects in other venues, and new artists were incorporated into the

Civilians fold such that now there are some associate artists who have never met each other or worked on a project together.[3] The company-centric period gave way into a phase of diversifying and opening up between 2008 and 2015. These years saw the Civilians entering partnerships and residencies with major regional theatres, arts labs, and universities as a way of underwriting, developing, and circulating their work and addressing frustrating limits of self-production and tours where the finances barely broke even. Cosson notes that the way the company traverses categories makes grant applications hard with both private foundations and government programs: the group is either "too much or not enough" because there is a "relentless pressure to fit into a narrowly defined niche" (Cosson 2018a). Cosson became the ensemble's paid artistic director in 2004 and the company began hiring full-time producing directors (later called executive directors or managing directors) in 2005, adding part-time staff like bookkeepers and literary associates in 2006 and 2007. In its second phase, it earned some large-scale grants, started an education program, made its first strategic plan, released a cast recording of *Gone Missing*, and published a collection of six of its plays.

During these years, the Civilians looked to diversify their creative platform, using cabaret one-off events as a workshop space and making a presence for their live theatre in digital media. Projects were seeded with composers and writers other than Cosson, Washburn, and Friedman— José Rivera wrote *Another Word for Beauty* and Hector Buitrago composed its music, Bess Wohl wrote *Pretty Filthy*, Jill Sobule composed *Times Square*, Jordan Harrison wrote *Maple and Vine*. The company created the Extended Play blog as a forum for analysis and reflection; hosted trial run and retrospective cabaret evenings at Joe's Pub and the Public Theatre Lab; curated the Let Me Ascertain You (LMAY) podcast; and pioneered the structure of an annual Research and Development group to encourage new cohorts of artists to work in the Civilians mode and remake the processes of investigation and music composition to suit their topics and visions.

During this phase, the Civilians were at their most community-specific and locally involved, invested in Brooklyn, its neighborhoods, and its local government processes with shows like *In the Footprint: The Battle over Atlantic Yards*. At the same time, professionalization and institutionalization brought with it expanded staff and organizational structures and the company celebrated its tenth anniversary season. A strong jolt of financial support came in the form of a 2010 $700,000 National Science Foundation grant to fund the *Great Immensity* process. In 2014 *The Great Immensity* opened in New York. Though the pace of full production slowed after that, in other areas momentum carried across into 2016. The company workshopped Washburn's *Mr. Burns: A Post Electric Play*, which premiered at Woolly Mammoth Theatre in Washington, DC, and has been produced all over the country. Meanwhile, the R&D groups tried out specific material in the cabaret and on podcasts and new commissions were pursued, like a residency at the Metropolitan Museum of Art and a partnership with Minneapolis Children's Theatre for a show about ice hockey and kids sports culture in Minnesota, *The Abominables* (2017).

In September 2017, Michael Friedman's sudden and shocking death, of complications from HIV-AIDS, decisively altered what was coalescing as the third phase in the company's development. Friedman was diagnosed only nine weeks before his death, apparently after years of not being tested for the disease. As an extended, posthumous *New York Times* profile on Friedman observes, his death "rattled the theater world, both because he was seen as among the brightest lights of his generation and because it shocked those who had come to see H.I.V. infection as a chronic but manageable condition, at least for those with health care" (Butler 2018). Oskar Eustis, artistic director of the Public Theatre and significant supporter of both the Civilians and all of Friedman's projects, is quoted as saying that Friedman's death was "a real warning shot across the bow for anybody who thinks this disease isn't deadly anymore. It just killed one of the most brilliant and promising people in the American theater" (Paulson 2017, AR1).

The Abominables is the last Civilians show Friedman composed. The company experienced a pause as it sought a post-Friedman manifestation. Personal grief and changes in funding models and administrative staff defined 2018, since the NSF grant ended and staff turnover meant the hiring of both a new managing director and a new literary associate. In 2018, the Civilians was a company in transition; Friedman's death created a rupture but not an obliteration. As Isaac Butler wrote in *Artforum* reporting on "The Song Makes a Space" benefit the Civilians hosted to raise money for a Michael Friedman Legacy Fund in June 2018, "In a way, we gathered at Joe's Pub in part to witness our own transformation through the alchemy of his songs. One of the questions raised by his passing is what exactly The Civilians will be without him" (Butler 2018). Cosson reported being in the midst of a new phase of strategic planning and reflected on being surprised about "how hard it continues to be" to stabilize funding: "It doesn't always feel like there is a way forward for theatre companies like mine" (Cosson 2018b).[4]

Starting in 2019, the company began to find some new trajectories. On the one hand, the organization was still in flux after losing Friedman. On the other hand, the company's reputation continues to consolidate. If the initiative to create the Legacy Fund reaches its goal, the Civilians will superintend an endowment for younger artists. Likewise, there was an *Encores Off Center* performance of *Gone Missing* in July 2018. Just prior to his death, Friedman had taken a new post as artistic director for the summer program at New York City Center, which is a series of concert revivals of Off-Broadway musicals using the same format as the larger *Encores* series that revisits musical theatre's forgotten gems. The programming of *Gone Missing* both honors Friedman's legacy and cements the breakthrough Civilians show as a twenty-first-century experimental musical touchstone.

The Civilians is now a small-scale theatre institution, and its R&D series continues to support startling new rounds of exploration as the company also launches its first major post-Friedman shows. In early 2020, the Civilians coproduced the successful New York premiere of Lucas Hnath's play *Dana H.*, which uses recording of Hnath's mother recounting extraordinary and violent event in her life as its dialogue to which the actress ventriloquizing the role essentially lip synchs, again pushing the boundaries for how it supports interview-based experiments with theatre. The company was set to open new musical about the wake of the Second World War and Japanese internment called *Whisper House* (Kyle Jarrow book, Duncan Sheik lyrics, Cosson director) as the COVID-19 pandemic closed all the theatres in New York City. *Whisper House* was postponed, and it remains unclear when theatres will re-open and if the show will be able to be remounted in 2021 or 2022.

History and Development of Methods

The notion of starting anew with each project is part of the company's sense of mission and technique. "We don't know the answer before we do a project," said Cosson. He contends that the Civilians get talked about as if they are a young company still, and that they are stymied by the critical desire to talk about "young downtown theatre troupes." "We're not a young company," he asserted. "I wasn't young even when we started." In critical discourse, when it is not about actual chronological age, youth as a concept seems to be a stand-in for a new aesthetic or an avant-garde disregard of form or tradition. But the search for the new in and of itself is not the Civilians' value. What their work holds in focus and what defines their methods is an investigation of the experience of being an insider or an outsider to specific subcultures, communities, or experiences.

The interview process that grounds the company's artistic methods grew out of an urge to "look outside, go on the street, pay attention," said Cosson. A motivating notion of "turning outward" and "learning something before making something" indexes the group's civic and political impulses. Their work is both ethnography and civics. This is part of the double resonance of the company's name. Cosson chose the name because theatre professionals, echoing people in the armed forces, often refer to people not in the business as "civilians": people who haven't laid down their life for the set of principles that drives the artist or the warrior, people who don't wear the uniform. But who are the civilians in the company's name? Is it that the company members strive to be like civilians in their approach to the world, not like theatre professionals? Or is it that civilians are their subject? They are theatre professionals who immerse themselves in different aspects of civilian life in order to recreate and interrogate it. There's a resonance with notions of the public sphere in this concept of "civilians": civilians are the public. Civilians are citizens, the subjects of the public sphere, and the company is part of that body politic. They are the Civilians.

As guiding principles, the values in the Civilians' method boil down to risk, civics, and interrogation, and these values underwrite their techniques. The type of risk the Civilians value isn't about pushing the physical limits of the performers or transgressing social norms. The key to a Civilians project is that they don't know the answer to what they are investigating before they start. Cosson defines this in-built risk as "the proposition is somehow unknown." The second value returns to the notion of civics, blended with a drive that parallels both investigative journalism and cultural criticism. An ideal Civilians project should be something that "feels like someone should be doing it, but nobody is. There is a need to the subject." The topic should reflect a need of society, or a community or locale, to understand or know or see itself. But also, it should be somewhere theatre hasn't gone before and "we don't know how to make a play about it yet." This value underscores the relationship between form and content in the Civilians' work. Part of the job of the investigation is to figure out how to make a play about the topic: the form follows the content.

The third Civilians value, interrogation, is the second face of investigation. Investigation means information-and experience-gathering and interrogation demands testing and measuring what is gathered, with particular attention to the way human beings create stories to explain or authorize things. When the Civilians interrogate a story, part of what they are asking is not just, Cosson said, "is this true" but also "how do people use narrative to explain experience and what does that narrative allow, occlude, or oppress?" This is a fundamental postmodern urge, but the Civilians negotiate it with explicit reproduction of direct language and other documentary struggles with concrete experience as aspects of truth and fact. The Civilians are well aware that that their story will not be neutral or objective, and Cosson stressed that in testing a story, the company values finding "a resolution to the storytelling process that produces an acceptance of greater complexity and confusion," while also providing a type of aesthetic coherence, if not narrative closure. That may be why many Civilians productions end in a space of both nostalgia and wonder: the world is so big and so small, everything is connected but we can't always grasp hold of it, so there is satisfaction in the beauty of the impossibility in the final stage moment but also a sense of how much is unresolved.

The way the Civilians conduct interviews is the part of their methods most directly drawn from the company's genealogical connection to Joint Stock, the London-based theatre company which from 1974 until 1989 worked in mode of sociological and socialist theatre, using a method of author-led devising and workshops based on interviews and immersion in communities. Because Cosson earned an MFA in directing at UC San Diego in 1999, he took classes from Les Waters, who joined the faculty there in 1995. With Joint Stock, Waters was assistant director to Max Stafford-Clark for *Cloud Nine* and directed *Fen*, *Fire in the Lake*, and *Mouthful of Birds*; at San Diego Waters introduced his students to Joint Stock's repertoire and taught interviewing methodology. The four rules Cosson distilled from Waters and which he now teaches to actors are: avoid value statements; let people talk about what they want to talk about; get them to talk about what is most interesting to them; and get people to talk past their practiced conversational scripts. Joint Stock interviews were conducted without tape recorders, with the re-play of the interview from memory by the actor-interviewer serving as the embodied documentation and living text to be worked with in rehearsal. Civilians' processes initially relied only on the Joint Stock mode of playback, but also now use tape recorders, and the collaborating playwright uses both the performances and the transcripts to splice together material (Kozinn and Cosson 2010, 190).

The model Joint Stock's method provided to the Civilians is definitional. But it is also easy to overemphasize the early framing the company put forth and miss the way a company evolves as it approaches two decades in existence. Cosson's graduate school experience and continued professional relationship with Waters created a sense of contact with British alternative and political theatre techniques. It provided Cosson with a model from which to elaborate his own political, directorial, authorial, and collaborative urges, in dialogue with his love of music and the absolutely compelling necessity for him of working with Friedman. Joint Stock provided a guiding ideal. From Joint Stock's repertoire, Civilians shows are more like *The Speakers*, Joint Stock's breakthrough piece that wowed critics because of its promenade staging and atmospheric recreation of Speaker's Corner in Hyde Park, or the one-off Dionysic cabaret *Doomducker's Ball*. It is also interesting that Civilians shows share structural elements with Joan Littlewood and Theatre Workshop's *Oh! What a Lovely War* and Monstrous Regiment's *Scum* (also about the Paris Commune).

The key creative strategies apparent in Civilians texts and librettos are the use of overlapping narratives matched by simultaneous speaking in performance (columns of text running parallel to each other on a page, meant to be spoken aloud in continuous counterpoint); and the exploration of distancing techniques that sit in tension with the high sense of witness produced when actors reproduce the tone, cadence, and intonation of their interview subjects. The Civilians' production techniques center on the use of different musical styles and genres; quotations of daily speech; abstract or stylized movement; strong juxtapositions often made with lack of transitions; and actors playing multiple characters. Whereas Joint Stock's shows, at their best, created a sense of multiple objective viewpoints being combined, the Civilians swirl together objective and subjective modes of perception, direct scene enactment, allusion or fantasy, and extended jokes. This may account for the way Joint Stock shows were often described as powerful for their distanced social critique, and the Civilians are more often identified by their whimsy, their pastiche, and the surprise of the cumulative social insight that arises from their assemblages.

Like Joint Stock, the Civilians also consistently begin investigations out of a hunch or personal interest only to discover that by the time they are actually making the show that topic is at the center of current events. Kozinn notes that in the case of a developmental reading *The Great Immensity*, the company "could not have predicted that the reading would coincide" with an environmentally devastating oil spill that was in the news. "It was a coincidence, and in many ways the art of the coincidence has defined the company's methodology," which was a signature of Joint

Stock as well (Kozinn and Cosson 2010, 189).[5] This strong cultural currency frames the political impact of the otherwise abstract or whimsical aspects of their dramaturgy. However, the Civilians' embrace of cabaret is not just playful; it indexes the company's understanding of variety forms as demotic, transgressive spaces in the same way that drew early twentieth-century avant-garde groups like the Dadaists, Futurists, Expressionists to music hall and cabaret. The Civilians' cabaret mode also cradles the gay and queer identities that are absolutely part of the Civilians sensibility. Cosson and Friedman both acknowledge themselves as gay artists for whom the sense of being interested in outsider perspective relates to the experience of marginalized sexual or gender identities.

The sense of queerness in the Civilians' work is most visible in aspects like the running, pointed, knowing jokes about Tom Cruise in *Nobody's Lunch*; the sense of pan-directional love, longing, and loss in *Gone Missing*; the investigation of masculinity in *Shadow of Himself*; the interest in and figuration of Arthur Rimbaud in *Rimbaud in New York*; the role of the Ted Haggard scandal in *This Beautiful City* and the show's illustration of conflict around evangelical political activism in relation to gender and sexuality, as well as its engagement with transgender identity and spirituality; the sex positivity and investigation of the porn industry in *Pretty Filthy*; the embrace of female and femme gender performativity in *Another Word for Beauty*; and many of the topics in the Let Me Ascertain You podcasts including the episodes devoted to Holy Matrimony, Sex Variants 1941, and Porn. Overall, form and content for the Civilians aims to be always already inclusive of the queer—and to move in objective-subjective oscillation in the civic realm from a place where queerness already factors in.

The Great Immensity, the third show closely analyzed below, is the outlier in this sense. Among the Civilians' shows, it focuses more than usual on a heterosexual couple, questions of reproduction, and children. The imagistic and thematic world of the play parallels the survival of the planet and all its species to the question of whether a marriage can endure when the partners have wanted to produce children and cannot do so together in the end. *The Great Immensity* is also the least self-documentary in the reflexive way of Civilians' plays, and the characters are characters, not performers.[6] The play is still interview-based, but its central story is invented whole cloth. The plot about a cameraman's activist quest and his wife's search for him after he disappears employs dialogue that synthesizes interviews and conversations the company had on location at research stations at the Barro Colorado Island in Panama and Churchill, Canada, but is not always based on direct recreation of specific interview subjects. In this way, *The Great Immensity* is a limit case about the way the Civilians practice documentary theatre, as developed below in thick descriptions of their three most pivotal shows, which are united mainly in that they treat the company's great and perpetual themes of memory and community.

Before turning to the productions in detail, it is helpful to give an example of the development process the company goes through the course of residencies, workshops, multiple readings, and extended iterations of performance. For instance, *This Beautiful City* was supported by both the Sundance Theatre Lab and the Humana Festival of New American Plays at the Actors Theatre Louisville, among many other institutions. The process started with an investigative trip to Colorado Springs in the fall of 2006 that put company members there as the Ted Haggard scandal erupted, overlapping the November elections.

Then, from January 8 to February 14, 2007, artists Emily Ackerman, Marsha Stephanie Blake, Brad Heberlee, Stephen Plunkett, Alison Weller, along with Cosson, Friedman, and cowriter Jim Lewis went into residency at Colorado College in Colorado Springs. With a group of thirteen students, they conducted more interviews. In the summer of 2007, Lewis, Cosson, and Friedman worked on the show at the Sundance Theatre Lab, presenting a draft version of it. On October 1, 2007, the company did a reading of the show at the Abingdon Theatre Company in New York, a theatre that focuses on new play development. The credits in the published script also thank Z-Space Studio in San Francisco for providing developmental support, which suggests workshops or readings there (Hansel and Wegener 2009, 57).[7] In early 2008, the company went into its finalization stage and rehearsal at Actors Theatre Louisville. *This Beautiful City* premiered at the Humana Festival on March 5, 2008. In June of 2008, it performed at the Studio Theatre in Washington, DC, which coproduced the premiere under the aegis of its Opening Our Doors initiative. In October, the show was at the Center Theatre Group in Los Angeles with a somewhat revised script, which is the one published in the *Humana Festival 2008: Complete Plays* volume. After a further tour, college performances, an appearance at the Aspen Ideas Festival, and more in 2009 the show closed out its production run at the Vineyard Theatre in New York. A long and varied development process like this outlines the amount of time and space needed by a group of collaborators to engage in an investigative process, assess what they've found, conceive a show, work the text and score, rehearse it, revise it, and let it mature in performance.

Key Productions and Projects

Gone Missing, *This Beautiful City*, and *The Great Immensity* constitute, in consecutive order, the company's breakthrough in the New York theatre scene, their first major commission and wide circulation across the whole country, and their largest scale and highest funded project-to-date. In the world of ideas, Civilians shows move from the concrete to the abstract. *Gone Missing* began with bounded questions about the experience of losing things, but the show could not help becoming about the abstract experience of loss, longing, nostalgia, and memory. *This Beautiful City* wanted to pin down the dynamics of evangelical Christianity in the United States, getting concrete about religious freedom, anti-LGBT politics, and the contested terrain of the self in religious spaces. In investigating that territory, the play turns out to be about transcendence, ecstasy, and community. *The Great Immensity* anchors itself to science about receding glaciers and species extinction while also documenting human political initiatives related to climate change. The heart of the play, though, is about sacrifice, love, and reorienting the self in the scope of the universe. In the Civilians' oeuvre, there is a strain of work that wonders if all human beings can focus on is, bluntly, the elemental human purposes of "fucking and dying" (the name of one of the LMAY series of podcasts). But while that deeply naughty, joyously sex-and-death obsessed side to the Civilians' work shows up in many of the company's cabarets and shows, these three major works reveal the Civilians above all as good citizens, emphasizing how across their work they are concerned with how to be a human, how to be American, and how to be part of nature.

Gone Missing

Gone Missing begins with the sound of bubbles, as if something lost were sinking under the surface of the water. The performance begins with a sound, then a collage of voices, then three brisk monologues, and then arrives at its first song, the titular song, which has a pop-punk jangle to it and reflects on loss at different phases of life. Accompanied by piano, bass, and drums, the six-person ensemble, all clad in identical gray business suits, hair slicked close to their head, looking masculine androgynous with a type of 1980s new wave irony, each stand at the microphone and sing a verse, joining in the chorus and then driving into a longer monologue about a scarf and the introduction of a saga about a lost shoe.

In performance, the sound of underwater bubbles repeats at transitions, conjuring the sense of sinking underwater foreshadows the imagery related to the Sargasso Sea, the Bermuda Triangle, and the lost continent of Atlantis that develop in a sequence of fabulated scenes of public radio interviews with a fictional expert on loss named Dr. Palinurus (the name of a character from Virgil's *Aeneid*). Across the seventy-five-minute piece, here are all the missing items named: a dog, backpack, bird, teeth, ring, wallet, body, picture, toothbrush, sweater, socks, scarf, shoe, kitten, pearl ring, silver ring, sapphire ring, phone, another dog, doll, palm pilot, head, fingers, ID badge, and a platinum necklace. So many of these objects are stand-ins for the self (ID, teeth, phones), for family and romantic relationships (rings, necklaces), or objects of affection in their own right (dogs, kittens, and dolls) that it soon becomes clear that anything lost is a form of lost self or lost love. Indeed, while the company had asked interview subjects about possessions, the speakers keep bringing up the loss of other, less tangible things like their mind, or "my sense of humor, the plot, any sense of self-worth, the will to live," or things like language, security, and trust (Cosson 2009, 35–68).[8]

Patterns linking the different stories of loss include the experience of digging through muck to find lost things, the work of trying to get someone to return something you lost that they found, and the situations where the realization of loss is delayed versus ones where the knowledge is immediate. Among the figures who speak more than once is the woman who doggedly attempts to get her friend to interface with the manager of small theatre space and to send her back the shoe she is sure she lost when changing clothes there. Her quest and the Dr. Palinurus scenes are the structure around which all the other songs and stories are woven. As a through-line, the lost shoe is about distance and displacement, because, in the end, the woman finds her shoe when it spills out onto the floor of a cab while she is in Brazil because it had been tucked in the hidden pocket of her suitcase. For a split second, she doesn't realize about the compartment, and so when her shoe is just there, on the floor, her sense of the uncanny is profound. It's magical despite a very concrete explanation. Her shoe has come back to her in the most unlikely way; it was also never lost, but she couldn't know that. The mystery of object permanence is not just for toddlers in *Gone Missing* and proving that is one of the jobs of the Dr. Palinurus scenes: it turns out that Freud's first job as a researcher, before his turn to psychology, was to "find the testes of eels," which led him to the Bermuda Triangle, also known as the Sargasso Sea, where all eels go to mate. The play posits that the eel's homecoming for mating, the lost and found of the Sargasso Sea, resonates with how Freud understands the relationship of pleasure and pain in loss, with the problem of nostalgia, that is the pain of homecoming.

Shoes and eels provide one kind of through-line to the piece; the songs provide the other. The nine songs constellate around the issue of love and the problem of losing people, as seen particularly in "The Only Thing Missing Is You." In the interviews for the piece, Civilians artists did not allow the interviewees to talk about losing people. This was not an avoidance of death or love as topics, since both topics figure hugely in the play, but rather it was a formal boundary that forced the interviewees to talk in concrete terms and instead allowed the artists to elaborate the love at the heart of every loss in the songs and the arrangement of material.

This tension between the formal prompt to interview people about lost *things* and the motivating need to address the loss of human beings creates the space for the way *Gone Missing* folds in a meta-address of the interviewing process. At three points the text includes the "character" addressing the company member interviewing them, saying they want to talk about losing a person or asking if they are telling the type of story the interviewer wants. In performance, the actor who is speaking those lines is both channeling the interviewee and indexing the presence of themselves or another company member as the interviewer.

The gray suits worn by the ensemble lend the performance a sense of clinical distance and gender fluidity in the investigation that redoubles the purposely angular choreography. Different interview subjects are heard from more than once and are not always embodied by the same performer. An older woman, Dr. Palinurus, and the New York cop, among others, speak at regular intervals in the show and are played by different male and female actors in each of those moments. As a production, *Gone Missing* posits that human beings are united in our experience of losing things and of seeking something bigger: individuals lose specific things, but we all seek community, and we all lose track of the details in our memory.

In 2018, in a recording of self-documentation interviews made for the Lobby Project of the *Encores* revival of the show, members of the first cast of *Gone Missing* described it as "the most important play I've ever done" because the themes of community and memory forged a bond for artists and audience alike (Brown 2018). The revival concert provoked a strong fit of nostalgia for critic Alexis Soloski, who wrote in the *New York Times*: "I remembered every single song though I hadn't heard them in more than a decade," and continued:

That said, the songs don't sound the same. We're all 15 years older (those of us who got to grow older, anyway), and the points of impact have shifted. Hearing them, I felt a happy-sad nostalgia, not only for the composer himself but also for the theater scene that birthed him—those theaters in the East Village and the Lower East Side and those post-show bars, many of them now gone.

In the Lobby Project one of the most moving refrains is "I don't remember why the grey suits; I wish I could remember why the grey suits." Whose idea was it? How did they get here? After Friedman's death, *Gone Missing* is indeed the Civilians' Atlantis.

This Beautiful City

The Civilians set themselves down in Colorado Springs during a presidential election year and discovered that residents of Colorado Springs across the political and religious spectrum think of it as a place that is special because of its relationship to nature and God. The text of the play is prefaced with an epigraph from the book of Jeremiah in the Bible: "Work for the well-being of the city where I have sent you, and pray to the Lord for this. For if it is well in the city you live in, it will be well with you." Colorado Springs is a city in the mountains, full of people working toward what they believe is the highest calling for its well-being. The notion of the city on the hill, or the delectable mountains and the celestial city, echoes throughout white American national literature and political speeches, from *The Pilgrim's Progress* to Ronald Reagan's campaign and presidential speeches. Colorado Springs is both "this beautiful city" in a local way and the city on a hill, standing in for America as a Christian dream of that city-paradise.

If *Gone Missing* is a play about how to be human by coming to terms with loss, *This Beautiful City* is a play about what we're searching for when we ourselves are lost. Using a convention somewhat like what Paula Vogel does with the Greek chorus who delivers driving instructions in *How I Learned to Drive* (1997), *This Beautiful City* inserts interludes with a Trails Guide who is narrating how to hike in the Colorado wilderness around Pikes Peak. The Trails Guide ostensibly describes how to orienteer, practice good hiking techniques, and respect nature. But this documentary reflection of the importance of outdoor pursuits in experience of the area also provides symbolic commentary on the work of navigating the self in community. The subject of the Civilians' investigation was evangelical Christianity and its role in American politics. Embedded in that subject is the problem of how people get lost on the way to paradise. Says the Trails Guide, prophetically, "Do not panic. Virtually all people who get lost are eventually found, either alive or dead, so the idea is to stay alive no matter how long you have to stay lost" (Hansel and Wegner 2009, 103).

In the show, the urge to seek a paradise, in a place, or community, or a connection, rubs up against the need for a city to be a civic space that hosts divergent viewpoints. The dynamics of insider and outsider experiences in ecstatic groups, alternative communities, the military, and large religious structures meant that the show portrays a wide range of representative interview subjects and costuming that replicated the dressed-down outdoors wear favored in the mountain west. The artists performed their words with a disarming earnestness and relative deemphasis of abstract choreography, instead employing physicality of worship practices from sites like the mainline mega church, New Life; the radical communitarian group the Revolution House of Prayer (RHOP); and the Black church Emmanuel Baptist. In performance, one of the repeated gestures of the performers was for them to reach up toward the sky or out to each other as they recreated people who were witnessing, singing praise songs, or testifying. Hands turned in or out, swaying, or even jumping up and down, it was a gesture of celebrating, surrendering, praying, protesting, a gesture that underwrites group movement during the praise songs, especially the most vulnerable song from the show, "Take Me There."

The play is structured through a series of parallels and dialectical contrasts. It begins with a collage of community voices which like those in *Gone Missing* provide inbuilt acknowledgment of the Civilians' presence and method as interviewers. The second scene sets up two coffee shops, one where the associate pastor of the New Life church is being interviewed, the other where a writer for an alternative weekly holds forth. Act I goes back often to this type of contrast between the viewpoints of those who experience themselves to be saved and those who find the dominance of an evangelical mindset to be stifling the city. Parallel plots develop: alongside the story of Ted Haggard stepping down from his leadership of New Life after he was exposed for sleeping with a male escort and taking drugs runs the story of the pastor of Emmanuel Baptist slowly coming out as gay and therefore losing his leadership of his congregation. Meanwhile, there are subplots about conflicts around evangelical practice within the Air Force Academy, which is also located in Colorado Springs, and about a transwoman's quest to live fully as a sexual and spiritual person.

The play's second act continues the parallelism, tracking what happens in the two church communities as they each lose their leader, but it also does something a bit harder: it tries to capture what happens when community structures splinter, especially under pressure from online commentary in a globalized, digitized world. In the middle of the second act, the electric Scene Five recreates a fiery sermon from the new pastor at Emmanuel Baptist on the theme of freedom. The new Emmanuel pastor exhorts the congregation to let go of despair and remember that they've felt the presence of God: "Who the Son has set free is free indeed. So stop looking to other folks to validate you. Stop it. If your phone doesn't ring, CALL YOSELF! STOP IT! If don't nobody lay hands on you, put your hands on your own head. BLESS YOSELF!" The text's rendition of Black vernacular English matters to documenting the African American congregation, contrasting its arc of religious prejudice and inclusion to those pursued by the white hippies at RHOP and the largely white conservatives at New Life. *This Beautiful City* is not the Civilians' only engagement with race, but it is the first to include a Black community on a large scale. The treatment demonstrates their commitment to interviewing across racial demographics and embodying the words directly. The Civilians may perform interview subjects fluidly across gender, but when they perform racialized identities, they cast in a color conscious way, so this male pastor was played by Marsha Stephanie Blake, herself a Black actress.

Alongside the representation of Emmanuel Baptist, *This Beautiful City* makes an important move by focusing on a pivotal concluding speech and song to the character T-GIRL CHRISTIAN. T-Girl's speeches come from interviews conducted in 2006 and 2007, and in the intervening decade in the United States there has been a revolution in wider consciousness about trans identity and the language used by trans people and about trans experience. While the play uses terms like transsexual and girl in a way it might not now, it is clear that the language comes directly from the interview subject and that T-Girl's role in the show is to anchor the religious groups' actions about gender, sexuality, and sin to a lived experience of transgender identity. T-Girl's dignity is enormous and her compassion extremely moving. In fact, it is her song that elaborates the play's title and imagery about cities and paradise. T-Girl describes that before her transition she was an urban planner. In the song "Urban Planning," which recounts her thoughts but is sung by a different performer as it interweaves with T-Girl speaking, the lyrics say:

> You design a neighborhood
> One year later there it is.
> (…)
> It's paradise.
> Yes It's paradise.
> It's a paradise that you've made.

But the problem with the urban planning paradise she made, T-Girl realizes, is that it didn't factor in the people. "I had never thought of the people. They move, they get in the way." Without people, it's almost a paradise; but people are necessary, as is their freedom. As her monologue concludes, T-Girl says, "Now I see the people. And this is a beautiful city (…) I like seeing Pikes Peak out my front door" (Hansel and Wegener 2009, 66–7).[9]

T-Girl's speech gives way to the play's final monologue and song. The last speech records Marcus Haggard's sermon to the New Life congregation after his father stepped down. The song commemorates Katherine Lee Bates, the lyricist who wrote "America the Beautiful" after a trip where she saw Pikes Peak. Marcus Haggard's sermon urges his father's shell-shocked congregation to embrace genuine love in the wake of his father's disgrace and face their fear of being exposed. The song calls to the weary traveler: "Are you still up there on that mountain? Were you seduced by all the beauty?" Haggard ends by raising a prayer: "Stop hiding. Be vulnerable (…) Let God show us how to be completely exposed." *The Great Immensity* takes up this same problem of vulnerability and loss, this time expanding the company's previous explorations of psychology and spirituality to include activism.

The Great Immensity

Metaphorically, the Civilians' three major works chart a course from Atlantis, to the city on the hill, to Noah's ark. With this play, the Civilians' position as documentarians who are really American eschatologists becomes clear. *The Great Immensity* turns to the end of things, the final destiny of human beings, and judgment, perhaps not rendered by a divine force but rather by the inexorable processes of biology and entropy. The company's concerns with memory and community drive this investigation of how to convince the earth's population to save their own habitat; the play asks how to save the world when you've lost faith in humanity. It concludes that the answer may be by sacrificing yourself.

The ark in the play is a Chinese container vessel named the Great Immensity, and the plot forms around plans to hijack the ship and use it to disappear a group of teenage "Earth Ambassadors," one from every nation of the world, who are en route to the United Nations Climate Summit. The disappearance aims to symbolize the fate of human beings on a decaying planet and form a protest that demands united action. But that's where the play ends; the play begins with Karl, a TV producer, and unfolds as he joins the secret mission by jumping back and forth in time between Karl's steps toward engineering the disappearance and his wife's quest to find him. Phyllis's pursuit of her husband takes her from Panama to Manitoba, from the tropics to the tundra, and the contrast of hot and cold illustrates the extremes that pressurize the plot and characters, as well as the world.[10]

In performance, video scenography aided the time jumps and the movement in locations in performance: the show had a strong, frontal design with a large video screen topping a wide, shallow, horizontal performance space divided up by different panels of corrugated metal that could be rearranged to create different rooms or locales. The video screen showed both live stream and prerecorded material. One of the songs, "We Are Legion," echoing the language of the Anonymous hacker collective and representing the power of specialized online networks for activism, was performed entirely on the screen. Scenes seamlessly integrated the video, using it when the characters are involved in live chat with other characters or using it for transitions and as backgrounds to songs. Occasionally, the videos provided a hard cut, an abrupt transition from one moment to another, or projected a scene title and information about time, date, or place. The effect was Brechtian but also like life in the twenty-first century, where things happen live and online simultaneously, images and text all the time across distance and in our closest intimacies. *The Great Immensity* has no group choreography to speak of, and stylistically, it is as if video replaced dance in the Civilians' vocabulary.

The status of *The Great Immensity* as more of a type of theatrical realism (fiction observed from life) rather than documentary (direct reproduction of life) and a play-with-music rather than a cabaret demarcates it from *Gone Missing*. Yet, there are echoes of all of the Civilians' repertoire of techniques and topics throughout the show: one fleet-footed song sequence featuring all the performers in gray suits summarizes every United Nations Climate Accord since the 1970s and the relative lack of resulting action. The performers wear *Gone Missing*-esque suits for this number, wryly comment on the history they are conveying, presenting a pan-national, language-roving, gender-fluid rundown on the intractable problems of collective action in relation to the climate. Likewise, interludes of cabaret wit include a straw-hatted number about the last living animal in a species that's gone extinct looking for love and a torch song dedicated to the performer's passion for "charismatic megafauna" like pandas and polar bears.

The repeating image of the play is boats, big and small, creating a pattern of associations about individuals as boats versus boats as ecosystems that house complex networks of life forms, establishing tension between Noah's ark and "the last living man all alone on a boat with no hope and no plan," as the lyrics to the play's final song put it. The Great Immensity itself, the cargo ship, gets personified by a performer and sings its own song, melding the objective and subjective. In this song, and others, Friedman repeats the lyrics "oh, the world is wide, and oh, the world is so small," setting it to a haunting run of notes that is both melancholic and hopeful. Every character in *The Great Immensity* struggles with the knowledge that climate change is a disaster mainly for humans: long term, the world itself will survive, plants and animals will adapt, and bacteria will thrive. "There will be a world when this world is only memories," sings the ship spotter. The themes of community and memory that link the Civilians' work are here both an elegy and a challenge to audiences.

Critical Reception

It is notable that the press reviews for *The Great Immensity* don't mark the show out as something special, in the way critics did immediately with *Gone Missing* and *This Beautiful City*. Reviews acknowledge the huge impact of the Civilians' "research dramaturgy" as a model and praise the group's "frisky and inventive" ways across their body of work but damn the show with faint praise: "thoughtful but strained" said Joe Dziemianowicz in the *New York Daily News*. In the *New York Times*, Charles Isherwood judged that the "narrative through-line feels like a flimsy pretext for the show's lengthy lesson plan," while appreciating that "many passages are written with an enlivening humor." Adam Feldman in *Time Out* summed up reactions as: "It's not easy preaching green" (Dziemianowicz 2014; Feldman 2014; Isherwood 2014). Political and documentary work often meets with the idea that it is "propagandistic, didactic, or a drag," in the words of Scott Brown at *Vulture*. Most reception of the Civilians doesn't follow this vein, and Brown argues that is because the Civilians are "excellent guerrilla journalists" who get "extraordinary candor from deceptively ordinary interviewees" (Brown 2013). But with environmental activism as the subject, charges of didacticism bubble up. Paradoxically, the treatment of environmental precarity in Washburn's *Mr. Burns* accomplishes what *The Great Immensity* might have wanted to by being deconstructive of *The Simpsons* and other pop icons, formally disorienting, and tragic rather than earnest, and therefore Washburn's show received far more critical praise. *Pretty Filthy* also sidestepped reception focused on its didacticism, perhaps because it has the salacious fun of being about the porn industry—though it is really a documentation about labor conditions—and because it nakedly avoids the need to encourage any reform on the part of the audience.

The Civilians may not frame themselves as a political theatre company, nor do their plays move from documentation to direct activism; still their projects consistently focus on class, economics, power, real estate, and the environment, particularly after 2008. There is proportionally more reporting about *The Great Immensity* than any of their shows because of the furor it caused among Right-wing media outlets for receiving government research funding (Tran 2017). *The Great Immensity* is also is the subject of extended treatment in *Resilience: A Journal of the Environmental Humanities*, which did a special section on the show and provided a suite of reviews of the show by humanities scholars, who read the show quite differently than the New York critics, finding it both moving and a "memorable intervention" in cultural dialogue about climate change. Nicole M. Merola specifically praises the way the production leaves "dangling narrative threads" and even features an "incomplete sentence for its last lyric" and "an unresolved melodic line as its last sound" because that is discomfiting state humanity itself in relationship to the environment (Lioi 2014; Merola 2014, 135–9). The Civilians may not be a non-narrative company, but they continue to confound narrative expectations for the sake of their content.

Within theatre-focused publications, the magazine *American Theatre* included the Civilians in its strong package of articles "On the Real" about US documentary theatres in 2017 (Parenteau 2017). The scholarly journal *TDR* published a special section about American avant-garde theatre in New York City in 2010, including Sarah Kozinn's overview of the company and interview with Cosson. In their introduction to the *TDR* special section, editors Mariellen R. Sandford and T. Nikki Cesare identify that the relationship of the avant-garde to the mainstream of society is no longer contentious, so that instead of attempting to shock or offend, experimental theatres of the twenty-first century now tend to startle and defend: that is, use theatre to defend against the political outrages of the moment and to startle audiences "into remembering that theatre once had the capacity to rouse" awareness, an experience that "has the potential to build a relationship between artist and audiences, to help both to understand (…) and change" (Cesare and Sandford 2010, 9). The Civilians fit into the framework because of their resistance to what Cosson calls the "theatre of assurance," which aims to soothe an audience. As Cosson says, the company takes a stand "that we are interested in seeing ourselves and thinking about ourselves and reflecting upon ourselves as players and as members of the body politic. We are responsible to that, and influenced by that, and shaped by that, and maybe determined by that in some ways, and maybe sometimes trying to liberate ourselves from that in other times."

Perhaps the most straightforward assessment of the Civilians comes from Eustis, who has championed the company since its inception. "I sometimes think the Civilians are the only necessary ensemble in New York," he wrote:

> Their work is both of the New York downtown scene, with all the sophistication and hipness that implies, and of a much older American tradition of telling the stories of the people. They are in the world, and of it. Their theatre embodies what is best about the form: connection to community and the highest artfulness, playfulness and seriousness side-by-side.
>
> (Eustis 2009, v)

Like the Eustis and the Public Theatre, the Civilians exert their influence not only through their fully produced shows but also in the way their initiatives foster successive generations of artists. It is not fully possible to survey the reception of the Civilians yet or place them in their full artistic context, because so much of their recent work has been in residency with students in university theatre programs and supporting the R&D group.[11] The reach of the R&D group is already wide: writers and directors like Jason Grote, Jackie Sibbles Drury, Mia Rovegno, Heidi Schreck, Lila Neugebauer, Mary Kathryn Nagle, Lauren Yee, Matthew Paul Olmos, and many others have spent time incubating projects there. There may be many inheritors to their propagation of investigative theatre, who rework methods as the Civilians did with Joint Stock, renewing documentary theatre, cabaret, and avant-gardism as they go.

Productions

Canard, Canard, Goose
Gone Missing
The Ladies
(I am) Nobody's Lunch
Shadow of Himself
This Beautiful City
Paris Commune
You Better Sit Down: Tales from My Parents Divorce
In the Footprint: The Battle over Atlantic Yards
Maple and Vine
Mr. Burns
The Great Immensity
Be the Death of Me
Pretty Filthy
Rimbaud in New York
Another Word for Beauty
The Undertaking
Times Square
The Abominables
Paul Swan Is Dead and Gone
Dana H
Whisper House

For detailed and ongoing production chronology, as well as material about the LMAY Cabarets and Podcasts, the R&D group performances since 2010, the company residency at the Metropolitan Museum of Art 2014–2015, and Friedman's *State of the Union* Songbook project, see the company website http://thecivilians.org/.

CHAPTER 8
600 HIGHWAYMEN
Rachel Anderson-Rabern

We know that this is a lie.
And that's okay.

(Browde and Silverstone, The Fever 2017)

The Collective Contagion of 600 HIGHWAYMEN

600 HIGHWAYMEN is a moniker, an invitation, and an expression of play and possibility that designates the performance work of Abigail Browde and Michael Silverstone. The two, spouses and cocreators, met during their undergraduate studies at New York University and then took separate artistic paths before beginning intentionally collaborative work together in 2009. Before working with Silverstone via 600 HIGHWAYMEN, Browde developed her practice by performing in her own projects while also working with New York downtown artists and companies, including Witness Relocation and John Jesurun. Simultaneously, Silverstone expanded his directing experience, devoting substantial focus to new play development, directing plays in Sing Sing and Fishkill correctional facilities, and assistant directing *Three Days of Rain* on Broadway in 2006 (Browde, Email Correspondence 2018). While sharing some common educational roots, Browde and Silverstone also contribute distinct sensibilities, aesthetics, and professional experience to their creative unity. The partnership called 600 HIGHWAYMEN has created, as of 2020, twelve original works while developing two more, *The Total People* and *The Following Evening*, which are currently in process. They have developed and toured work through the United States and Europe, including three inclusions in the Public Theatre's Under the Radar Festival: *The Record* in 2014, *Employee of the Year* in 2016, and *The Fever* in 2017. Notably, the partnership received an OBIE grant award in 2014 in support of their ongoing practice, and *The Fever* was nominated for a Bessie Award for Outstanding Production in 2019. Based in Brooklyn, much of the possibility and play generated by 600 HIGHWAYMEN stems from ways in which Browde and Silverstone's processes and performances forge

imperatives to reshape and redefine boundaries: boundaries among cultures, among genres, among artistic mediums, and between self and others. This last emerges most urgently through risky performance moments, instances that stage collaboration as active presence among audience members and performing artists.

Routes and Roots

Anchoring 600 HIGHWAYMEN to a historicized trajectory of influences and terminology is an uneasy venture, given Browde and Silverstone's avoidance of siloed artistic identity that might implicitly accompany aesthetic labels and categories. Browde describes this as an almost physical act of creative fluidity: "We feel most comfortable when we can hop between boundaries" (Browde and Silverstone, Interview 2018). Some of these boundaries include those tacitly imposed by classifying performance-making projects as experimental, for example. The two note that the gulf between the performance-making community of downtown New York and the more textually driven arena of Broadway and Off-Broadway can be vast. This poses particular challenges for a team like 600 HIGHWAYMEN, with both facility and interest in moving among performance-making approaches that may or may not utilize preexisting dramatic texts. That is, while they develop original pieces, Browde and Silverstone also have training, aesthetic interests, and artistic voices they might levy toward staging plays within the context of a new millennium (Browde and Silverstone, Interview 2018). In terms of the development and ongoing influence of 600 HIGHWAYMEN in the United States in particular, this creates a series of conundrums that might be familiar to several groups included in this volume: when we consider ensemble theatre practice, or collective creation, separately from mainstream theatre-making practices, is there a danger that we reinforce divisions within fields of artistic practice? When a team or group has grown from nascent beginnings toward an international reputation, yet retains a commitment to radical process and practice, what happens next? In the absence of a concrete theatrical home, where and how does a group creating original performance produce when they have reached a certain level of recognition? If 600 HIGHWAYMEN have been featured at the Public's Under the Radar Festival three times, how long can audiences perceive the group as "under the radar" and what steps beyond the fringe might be available to them? Must the work continue to inhabit spaces edged into the margins outside mainstream theatre-making?

These questions provoke vital echoes that are relevant for collectively and collaboratively motivated performance-making generally but take on unique contours when applied to a creative team. To create in concert with others, to seek out new modes and models of interrelation and power-sharing is itself a radical and humane act. For a twosome, the action of partnership becomes the locus of the process, and ensemble-making extends from that foundation. As a couple that creates together, Browde and Silverstone entwine with ongoing histories of partnerships that bridge the personal and the aesthetic. Other US American touchstones include spouses and cofounders Julian Beck and Judith Malina of the Living Theatre, Lin Hixson and Matthew Goulish of Goat Island and subsequently Every House Has a Door, Annie-B Parson and Paul Lazar of Big Dance Theatre, and Kelly Copper and Pavol Liska of Nature Theatre of Oklahoma. Of course, for each of these partnerships, the organization of corresponding companies, and the methodologies that shape specific projects, is unique. The charismatic leadership, genealogical significance, and utopian aspirations of the Living Theatre, for example, are well-documented. In contrast, Browde stresses, "We don't truly think of ourselves as a 'theatre company' as I think neither of us was particularly attracted to the idea of a company like a collective. Sometimes I think of 600 HWM much more as a moniker for the two of us, than anything else" (Browde, Email Correspondence 2018). Browde's rejection of "collective" models emphasizes ways in which the ensemble ethos of 600 HIGHWAYMEN develops and grows from a clearly articulated dyad, in contrast to group-centric ideals that motivated so much US American collective creation practice of the 1960s and 1970s. In place of those ideals, 600 HIGHWAYMEN's partnership puts down roots that enable new forms of ensemble to take shape.

Browde and Silverstone's creative partnership presses against the boundary of its own twosome from the moment audiences read or utter the name. 600 HIGHWAYMEN conjures images that exceed two minds, two bodies. Imagining six hundred, the inner eye expands to make room for crowds, for multitudes (Browde, Email Correspondence 2018). While Browde and Silverstone are two individuals, 600 HIGHWAYMEN expands and contracts to accommodate exactly that number as well as many more. Almost like a Poppins magic carpet bag, the name gestures toward the near-infinite capacity of groupness: a crowd, a mob, a party, a threat, a body. Among its other qualities, then, the name is a kind of phenomenological joke that reminds us that even within the intimacy of a partnership, one is always within a wider world peopled with both crowds and solitude. The juxtaposition of lawlessness, play, and isolation is fitting, given the source material. Of the process of arriving at their name, Browde writes:

> 600 HIGHWAYMEN comes from, strangely enough, *Waiting for Godot*. Two random words in Lucky's long monologue. In 2011, when we were in the throes of making our second piece "Empire City," we knew we wanted a name that wasn't just our names together, as we had been doing. We wanted the idea that when we plus whomever we were collaborating with, came together it was this other thing. And we wanted a name that indicated a sense of scale and also mystery. And also, perhaps, a little mischief. We got really lost in the naming process—there's a funny googledoc somewhere with the list of outtakes. In general, we found that we really like band names more than theatre company names—they tend to be more inventive.
>
> (Browde, Email Correspondence 2018)

As Browde and Silverstone began collaborating in 2009 and did not arrive at 600 HIGHWAYMEN until 2011, for two years they primarily utilized designations that did not—Browde indicates—leave enough space for others. The values and inspirations Browde describes here inflect ways in which collective creation functions for this group. The emphasis on play and irreverence is clear; mischief, curiosity, and delight all contribute to the environments Browde and Silverstone construct. Mischief, a toothless and joyful companion to rule-breaking, suggests that 600 HIGHWAYMEN move toward the unity of pleasure and productivity. When one makes mischief, for example, one creates something that previously wasn't there. Mischief is also a form of making that relies on audience and witness: one produces, one anticipates another's response, and one perhaps observes another's encounter with one's mischief. In a way, moving toward mischief ushers in a doubled theatricality: the maker creates the circumstances for, and then perhaps initiates or observes, encounter.

Encounter as expression of ensemble practice is one way 600 HIGHWAYMEN's work resists the terminological container of the word. The "other thing" that is more than Browde and Silverstone, the "thing" that needed a name that was more than the sum of their two parts, is a dynamic conceptualization of collaboration and human connection that retains the freedom to shift and restructure itself from project to project. Both artists are, significantly, widely generous and very clear in their acknowledgment of the collaborating artists who have contributed heavily to particular projects. For example, Eric Southern, Brendon Wolcott, Emil Abramyan, and David Cale are four collaborators, designers, and musicians/performers, whose artistic voices thread through 600 HIGHWAYMEN's pieces. Wolcott and Abramyan composed music for *The Fever*, for example, that exceeded what was used in the show by a scale of whole albums. Browde and Silverstone credit them, along with Southern, with creative contributions that bring dramaturgy together with musical composition and design. 600 HIGHWAYMEN is more than two; Browde and Silverstone do not work in isolation through the entirety of their performance-making processes. Yet, their partnership is the condition from which multiplicities of collaboration emerge.

600 HIGHWAYMEN evokes Samuel Beckett and the stakes and substance of both partnership and encounter when Browde indicates that she and Silverstone borrowed from Lucky's monologue in *Waiting for Godot*. Lucky's speech, a flurry of half-thoughts, a parade of shattered images spoken aloud into a barren landscape, flows from a body that is both human and inhuman within the context of the play. Pozzo, Lucky's master, abuses him, cracks his whip, and erases Lucky's body and presence through language. Pozzo rests in the company of Vladimir and Estragon, as Lucky waits on the end of a rope, listening to Pozzo describe relief at coming upon two humans. "Yes, the road seems long when one journeys all alone [...]" (Beckett [1954] 1982) Pozzo and Lucky are both two and not two, partnered onstage in this scene with Vladimir and Estragon. These two respective partnerships orbit one another, provoking by turns the violence, need, and inevitability of relationality. *Waiting for Godot* opens with this image: Estragon waits alone. He pulls at his boot, and Vladimir enters; with Vladimir's entrance comes the first line. A return, a reunion adds one and one. When two emerges, this result generates the spoken language of the play. In "The Writing of the Generic" in *On Beckett*, Alain Badiou engages the concept of Two in relation to Beckett's work, a becoming that generates encounter and, through encounter, love. He writes, "[...] love begins in a pure encounter, which is neither destined nor predestined, except by the chance crossing of two trajectories" (Badiou 2003, 27). Further, he claims that "the encounter is the founding instance of the Two as such" (Badiou 2003, 28). Perhaps, in these opening moments of *Waiting for Godot*, the enactment of two trajectories crossing in the forms of Vladimir and Estragon gives rise to encounter, and encounter, in turn, gives rise to speech. Following Badiou, that instance of crossing constitutes "the founding instance of the Two as such" (Badiou 2003, 28). That founding, the folding of one into Two is encounter, and encounter is that from which love begins.

The love Badiou invokes is, perhaps, devoid of both sentimentality and sexuality; it is a state made possible by the instant of relationality. What happens if, regarding 600 HIGHWAYMEN, part of what the team borrows from Beckett is an investigation of relationality that starts from two in order to find further trajectories, an evocation of love as encounter rather than utopian expression?

While the romantic sentiment is clear, Eliza Bent's 2015 article "in honor of Saint Valentine's Day" profiling five theatre couples, including Browde and Silverstone, offers further language for situating love as encounter. Bent summarizes the couple's movement toward creative partnership, writing, "The idea to work together built up gradually, and the year the two got married they decided to give it a try" (Bent 2015). In an interview for the article, Silverstone speaks to the complexity of and motivations for making performance with a spouse, saying, "It's [...] important to figure out why you're working together and be clear and literal about what that thing is. For me, it was falling in love with the things Abby can do that I can't do" (Bent 2015). This language resists an intersubjective reading of partner process and instead sketches process as a conjunction of abilities, a crossing of two trajectories. Notably, it frames love in the rehearsal space, in service of creative processes, as a consequence of *doing*. Silverstone's love language around "things Abby can do that I can't do" suggests a renewing recognition, a seeing of the doing of the Other: a continuous investment in encounter. Encounter may ontologically reside in Two, but as collaborators and their trajectories multiply, it becomes contagious.

"In the year of their Lord …": Organizing Processes[1]

Lucky's monologue from *Waiting for Godot* is, in part, an explosive attempt to organize what cannot be rendered logically, somewhat akin perhaps to the chaotic nature of ordering process into performance-making. When words pour out of Lucky's mouth during his speech in *Waiting for Godot*, the onslaught of fragmentation is almost too much for the listeners to bear, an excess at once caught up in familiar minutiae and unyoked from sense. In one sliver of speech captured by 600 HIGHWAYMEN, Lucky numbers the year "six hundred and something" with the imprecision of a tattered memory or tattered mind. Yet, the evident inertia of his attempt creates its own form of action, engaging disorder almost violently through the void of Lucky's open mouth. Chaos, scarcity, excess—these all thread through the performance-making processes of 600 HIGHWAYMEN even as they gravitate toward work that investigates the nature of risk and relationality.

Money and time are persistent points of scarcity for the team, as with so many other performance-making entities. Browde describes *The Fever* (2017) as the first piece for which they had "adequate funding for the creation of the show" and *Employee of the Year* (2014) as 600 HIGHWAYMEN's first commissioned piece (Browde, Email Correspondence 2018). *Employee of the Year* was co-commissioned by Mount Tremper Arts and New York City's French Institute Alliance Française's Crossing the Line Festival, whereas *The Fever* was commissioned by the Public Theatre's Under the Radar Festival and funded by the New England Foundation for the Arts' National Theatre Project, the Andrew W. Mellon Foundation, and the Jerome Foundation. Colleges and universities have also aided in providing space and time for processes of development. *The Fever*, for example, was developed over the course of two years and involved residencies at Arizona State University in Tempe, the University of Colorado at Colorado Springs, and On the Boards in Seattle. Artist residencies at colleges and universities often involve some measure of teaching responsibilities; situating 600 HIGHWAYMEN as artists also involves acknowledging Browde and Silverstone's relationships with academia and institutions of higher education. In a panoramic snapshot, a circle completed when the group toured *The Fever* to Stanford University in 2018. Browde and Silverstone met during a seminar on Avant-Garde performance at New York University, taught by Branislav Jakovljevic, a scholar who subsequently became Professor (and for a time, Chair) of Theatre and Performance Studies at Stanford University.

Touring is a vibrant and, of late, perpetual state of being and working for 600 HIGHWAYMEN. It's also a financial necessity, especially in the United States, where the market for innovative, original theatrical work is so dispersed. Silverstone likens touring to a nomadic lifestyle where one is always trying to find an audience or a market: "It's like being a traveling salesmen, because not one single city in the country can sustain us" (Browde and Silverstone, Interview 2018). Since *The Fever* premiered in early 2017 at the Under the Radar Festival in New York, 600 HIGHWAYMEN have toured the show to dozens of venues inside and outside the country, including the Wexner Center for the Arts (Columbus, Ohio), American Repertory Theatre (Boston, Massachusetts), Museum of Contemporary Art (Chicago, Illinois), FringeArts (Philadelphia, Pennsylvania), Walker Art Center (Minneapolis,

Minnesota), Sibiu Fest (Sibiu, Romania), Zürcher Theatre Spektakel (Zürich, Switzerland), MESS Festival (Sarajevo, Bosnia), and many more. As they travel, in and out of suitcases, cities, and countries, the team continues to invest in developing future projects. Browde writes,

> *The Fever* was made while we were actively touring *Employee* and *The Record*. And currently we're building some new projects while the *Fever* still has an active tour life. It can be disorienting, to work in starts and stops and to search for newness while revisiting something old. (Michael once very accurately described touring a show as "kissing an old lover"—you can feel *why* you were attracted to them, why you used to do this, but it's no longer the current thing.)
>
> (Browde, Email Correspondence 2018)

Browde's description of touring as a collapse of new and old, of nostalgia and innovation, suggests an environment that resists a cohesive narrative structure. Chronologically, the team experiences their own work in substantially different ways than an audience would, perhaps more akin to a time web than a timeline. Processes of touring, then, become engagements with history in the midst of present encounters and plans for the future. Within this threefold moment, the team invests in strategies for avoiding sameness, for moving forward with radical process. Browde observes that the "process of us *discovering* the process seems to be some central spine. It's like we almost keep ourselves as amateurs of our own projects. I think Michael and I both fear the pull—now that we've made several works—of a 'rinse and repeat' mentality" (Browde, Email Correspondence 2018). Repeated contact with former work creates grooves of familiarity, a sensation the team seeks to move away from when discovering the "central spine" of a new work's new process. Both Browde and Silverstone's articulations of their performance works are anatomical, as though each set of processes and each resulting performance is its own new body: a spine, a lover. Attempts to keep themselves as "amateurs," non-professionals enmeshed in worlds of professional performance-making, render the team uniquely equipped to greet and retreat from their performance works relationally. Sometimes they kiss an old lover, sometimes they move toward the untested encounter of a new process, a new risk. One consequence of touring, at least for groups that experience touring and creating as coexisting endeavors, is the discursive relationship between new and old that emerges—a relationship that creates a kind of order out of chaos in the form of the "central spine" of discovery.

Risk and Contagion: Key Productions

The risky moments and experiments that comprise the processes and concepts for 600 HIGHWAYMEN's work emerge from performance structures that investigate the potentiality of encounter: to provoke violence or caretaking, to meet love or death, to discover togetherness or isolation, to experience the crises of utter joy or crippling failure. The team's productions eschew utopian ideals of encounter by contending with risky performance elements that can be both uncontrollable and unpredictable.

For example, *This Great Country* (2012) springboards from Arthur Miller's *Death of a Salesman* into performance that challenges the very nature of the canon of American realism. Utilizing seventeen actors, 600 HIGHWAYMEN pulls apart the cohesion of character through bodies, age, race, gender, and ethnicity. They strip the work to lines that impart narrative essentials, paring the text into an approximately one-hundred-minute performance. Within the extracted arc of *Death of a Salesman*, they infuse the piece with dance, movement, and the beautiful starkness of performed aesthetics that invest in presence. Writing in *The New Yorker*, Hilton Als remarks on the team's casting strategies, "They conduct casting calls in a variety of ways—newspaper ads, the Internet—and audition whoever turns up" (Als 2013). Even before the process begins in the rehearsal room, Browde and Silverstone set up methods that celebrate both egalitarianism and randomness. Whatever ideals might softshoe into performance spaces for audience consumption, there are clear and often troubling power dynamics built into the infrastructure of performance making in the contemporary United States. Miller's *Death of a Salesman* is exemplary of many of these power dynamics, as an irrefutably canonical dramatic text that, well into the twenty-first century, continues to manifest the authority of whiteness and maleness as the epicenter of American storytelling. In many ways, the industry of performance-making substantiates these signifiers of authority. Professionalism and training, commodities that many aspiring actors seek to acquire as stepping stones into an unstable industry, come at a very real economic cost. What demographics might fall through the sieve of artistic experience, if resources are scarce and socioeconomic status disadvantaged? How might theatre training itself substantiate whiteness as "neutral" on American stages?

The casting for *This Great Country* implicitly evokes these questions by putting unexpected bodies in relation to one another and to Miller's text. These bodies then, alongside one another, perform difference precisely because of how they resist, aesthetically and performatively, the neutrality of bias prompted by either the expectations of performing arts industry, Miller's text, or both. For example, Browde notes the tendency of writers and interviewers to refer to some of the performers from *This Great Country* in particular as untrained performers, amateur performers, or even as nonperformers. While the backgrounds of the performing artists can and do vary, she emphasizes that they are all performers. They self-identify as performers and actors; they answered a casting call and began the process of working in a rehearsal room together (Browde, Interview 2019).

Within that rehearsal room for *This Great Country*, Browde and Silverstone worked with the ensemble in order to open up Miller's text as a kind of lyrical object as well as a narrative. Rather than moving through the lens of American realism, they adopted a relationship to the text that was intended to excavate its internal rhythms—breaking it down into a complex set of paced beats, perhaps closer to musical notation than to the "beats" an actor might perform following Stanislavsky's teachings on crafting character. Their initial cast of seventeen, assembled in Austin in preparation for the Fusebox Festival in 2012, began by repeatedly reading aloud from pared-down text in order to experiment with different character/actor combinations. The precise casting within the group emerged from these experiments. The characters of Linda, Biff, and Happy Loman were generally anchored to individual actors: Lana Dieterich, Derek Kolluri, and Matthew Scott Butterfield, respectively. A total of six actors played the role of Willy Loman, representing a range of ages, genders, races, and ethnicities. Browde describes this process as one of posing questions to a canonical text and then listening carefully. "You can transform to whomever, and the story will hold you. Isn't there so much more poetry in being able to read the story from whatever identities and bodies these actors have?" (Browde, Interview 2019). There is something to this query that is more than rhetorical, which invites audiences to simultaneously recognize and accept the specificity of bodies that signify, together with an invitation to broaden our witnessing toward recognizing the poetry of humanness.

Allowing and guiding performers to simply be, comprises a deeply meaningful set of values Browde and Silverstone apply in their performance projects. This is, perhaps, one reason audiences and critics seize upon performers' relationship to character in *This Great Country* as indicative of amateurism or unprofessionalism. Mistaking the aesthetic says more, perhaps, about an audience's horizon of expectations than it does about the virtuosity of performers and performance. Lana Dieterich, who played Linda Loman in Austin in 2012 as well as in Manhattan in 2013, is an Equity actor who has enjoyed a long career on stage as well as in television and film. In *This Great Country* she was, as she is, very much a professional performer. Her ability and virtuosity, however, were uniquely directed for this production. Browde describes the process of moving away from psychological realism and toward a different mode of presentation while working with Dieterich: "The way she was asked to perform for the show was more about asking her to be bare and seen, rather than asking her to transform for a character. She's being asked to be Linda Loman, but she's always asked to be a human being" (Browde, Interview 2019). One can conceptualize this as a clear relationship to theatricality, to moving toward a poetic theatre that invests in exposure rather than illusion. The design of the production, credited to Eric Southern, Gavin Price, and Asta Bennie Hostetter, supports this. In 2012 in Austin, a large bingo hall situates the action, in 2013, the group trades this container for an abandoned storefront—both lit with fluorescent overhead lights that provide literal mirroring opportunities for performers to be "bare and seen" throughout these different iterations of the production (Browde, Interview 2019). This unadorned aesthetic, this bareness of seeing and being seen, is one way in which *This Great Country* welcomes audience engagement in a cocreative process.

In the absence of the comfortable contours of American realism, 600 HIGHWAYMEN proposes a relationship between performer and audience that is mutually active. Browde describes the process of working with actors as one that carefully engages the gaze, the position of the eyes, as a central apparatus for meaning-making. Other modes of meaning-making that actors might associate with individual transformation toward character development, they deliberately work away from. In conversation, Browde uses Matthew Butterfield, the actor who played Happy in the Austin and New York productions, as an example. She says, "You have no burden to convince me that these are your thoughts. What if you, Matthew Butterfield, standing in this room at this time, is enough? What if you don't have to manipulate the words, to manipulate me, to convince me of anything?" (Browde, Interview 2019). This becomes a process of asking the actors to do less. When actors do less, creating greater distance between the word and the individual body that speaks the word, audience members must do more. It becomes, as Browde describes it, a kind of investigative puzzle. "Can there be space between the words I'm saying and who you are looking at, and can you the audience put it together?" (Browde, Interview 2019). The group's intervention with *Death of a Salesman* is more about this puzzle, crafted through relationship to the text, than it is about dismantling the text itself. As the piece progresses, that gap between word and character decreases. Perhaps this is not a function of the actors gradually trying harder to convince the audience by representing and displaying emotions but is a function of the audience accepting and internalizing the emotional power of actors who acknowledge being seen.

For example, some scenes achieve a horrifying resonance because of who the audience sees and the dynamic that emerges without any adornment of "convincing" whatsoever. In one such example, the text offers a dialogue between Willy Loman and his boss, Howard. It's a desperate scene, in which Willy is ultimately fired. In *This Great Country*, the casting and the presence of the actors brings vast meaning-making to the moment. The performer playing Willy speaks through a clear material obstacle—his command of English is uneasy, uncomfortable. He desperately seeks respite and support from Howard, while quite literally lacking the ability to pull the phrases he needs out into the air with confidence and clarity. Meanwhile, Howard is played by a child, Will Johnson, who is distracted by his smartphone. There are multiple layers of encounter at stake here, framed by the text: Miller's time period collides with the present, language collides with language, culture with culture. The power dynamics of Miller's scene slip into sharp relief as the audience watches an adult who presents as East Asian, for whom English is very evidently not the first language, prostrate himself before a white child.

It is vividly evident that many of those on stage would not traditionally align with the casting requirements of a *Death of a Salesman* production; neither of the actors mentioned above would be cast as Howard or Willy. Yet the presentation of a diverse ensemble that shutters Miller's characters into many voices and ushers in many differences allows 600 HIGHWAYMEN to explore the multiplicities of community imbedded into any comprehensive exploration of American capitalism: race, ethnicity, class, ability, gender, age. That is, ways in which 600 HIGHWAYMEN challenge and press against historical representations of Miller's text, in turn, reveal dynamic explorations of the core concerns the script proposes. The resistance of a heavy accent and a child's presence to the symbolic space of performance itself is equally prescient and is perhaps the beating heart of 600 HIGHWAYMEN's aesthetic questioning. Can the realness of encounter, experienced in a performance space, reorient its excess toward the surrounding world? What realities reveal themselves when a community that should never exist, together in this place with this text, suddenly and simply does? What dreamscapes does this conjure, and what latent hierarchies does this expose?

Inclusive ensembles that upend audience expectation, and that trouble relationships between actor and onlooker, reoccur in various configurations throughout 600 HIGHWAYMEN's pieces. *The Record* (2013), for example, rehearses forty-five strangers separately and then brings them together in performance. In *Employee of the Year* (2014), five girls, who were nine years old when the show premiered and twelve when it closed, comprise the entirety of the cast. The unrehearsed, the unexpected, the unmarked, these are the qualities that infuse the performance environments 600 HIGHWAYMEN construct, all of which set the conditions for very present encounters to take place in theatrical spaces. That simple fact of assembly matters, as Silverstone and Browde acknowledge and explore. Silverstone names the power dynamics and possibility inherent in existing in a space together, "We want our shows to be messing with the dials and the hierarchies. I want there to be a lot at stake in the way we assemble people" (Gansky 2015). In *This Great Country*, audiences confront the jarring differences among bodies we expect to see outside and inside the theatre. Browde describes performing for and with others as connection to basic human instinct, "Humans perform for one another. We look at one another. It's what we've always done. Staring at each other—whether it's on the subway, in the grocery store, or onstage—feels like second nature, like eating, breathing, talking, and so on" (Gansky 2015). The performers of *This Great Country* do not look and sound like the performers who are authority figures in the "dials and hierarchies" of theatrical representation, nor do they look and sound like the representatives who comprise the upper echelons of US national governance, for that matter. They do, however, look and sound very much like a cross-section of a New York City subway. While staging a shortened version of Miller's text, such an ensemble, so unapologetically distinct, cannot avoid the deep resonance of its own multiple identities. Some resonances create new links with the play, some dismantle power dynamics that saturate theatre production industries. Some construct offers for audiences, experiences and representations of emotionally rich presence and encounter. Hilton Als describes the performance of Ashley Kaye Johnson, who appears in *This Great Country* as a dancer and as young Linda, as unusually arresting, "sure and unself-conscious, steady in its joy" (Als 2013). While Johnson, a young adolescent, shines out of the production for Als, her remarkable performance bears the hallmarks of the values that 600 HIGHWAYMEN advances throughout the entirety of the ensemble. Joy and inclusion, sometimes experienced through awkwardness and always enabled through risk, comprise some of 600 HIGHWAYMEN's most powerful provocations.

While the cast of *This Great Country* contributes to a narrative concerning difference and wholeness, *The Fever*, first produced at the Public Theatre's Under the Radar Festival in 2017, places the audience at the center of the performance event while leaving gritty, everyday group-centered exploration intact. Upon entering the space, audience members see a configuration of chairs arranged in a rectangle around a deeply reddish floor. There is one row only; everyone has a front seat to the open space in front of them. The arrangement is intimate, the two short sides of the rectangle contain only about a dozen seats, while the longer sides contain less than two dozen. The four corners of the rectangle remain open, which rescues the environment from claustrophobia. Individuals are close to one another, even rubbing elbows, but no one is trapped. This is a space in which audience members watch one another, sit together, anticipate together, expose themselves together. Suddenly, a movement of hands begins along one bank of the audience; it travels through each of the four banks until all (who choose to) perform the similar gesture together. Within the first few moments of performance, audience members receive and respond to multiple offers from the performance ensemble. Each audience member must decide whether to adopt the physical gesture as it passes like a wave through or across each seat. This is a clear cue to everyone in the room, the performance has begun and it relies on communal action. When the collective gesture subsides, a spoken line comes from a woman, someone who looks like any other audience member, someone who entered with the rest of us, didn't she? In most locations, most audience members are unlikely to recognize Abigail Browde. Slowly and clearly, she offers an image: "Picture a town. That's where we'll start. Picture a town." To the person next to her, she asks, "Would you raise your hand? This is a woman. She is here just like this" (Browde and Silverstone, *The Fever* 2017). The audience member sitting next to Browde must decide, when asked, whether or not to raise a hand. As these and other modest negotiations play out, a room of witnesses watches one another's choice points. Yet 600 HIGHWAYMEN build in subtle reminders that these are offers, proposals, rather than audience interaction demands.

The power dynamics that separate prepared performance member and audience member flatten out through structural configurations that fracture inculcated expectations of performance conventions. Upon entering, everyone sits together; there are no physical boundaries between actor and witness. As the piece progresses, other boundaries begin to break down as well, a little at a time. For example, where is the line between waiting and beginning? When the wave gesture becomes apparent and travels from one pair of hands to another, it is a surprise. Is the performance starting? Has it already begun? Further, how can audience members identify themselves in relation to the piece's performers? Where is the line between performer and observer? Who has control of this script? Quickly and gently, the performance destabilizes spectators and any expectation of unchallenged passivity.

Through successive performance moments, 600 HIGHWAYMEN provide an occasionally unsettling juxtaposition of performance structure and individual agency. Originally, 600 HIGHWAYMEN began their development of the piece in response to *Rite of Spring*. This early inspiration veered somewhat throughout development, as midway through the process Browde described the relationship to *Rite of Spring* as "'loosely inspired by' at the moment. I think we're in a 'breaking up' period with *Rite of Spring* as a source. We need to see other people" (Gansky 2015). The ritual echoes of *Rite of Spring* remain, however. The group's performers offer clear patterns and directives to audience members, yet so much relies on audience response that each performance has the potential to be fundamentally different. Not in overall structure, perhaps, but moment to moment, tone by tone; human agency is on display. First, the piece gives the audience an imaginary community, a springboard for a subtly developing narrative. Browde and Silverstone's text starts as a story full of shadowy memories, fragments of emotion, and collective action. There is a town, full of inhabitants. There is a woman named Marianne, there is a party. There are neighbors, children, memories. There is a stranger. One by one, the group's performers, initially invisibly blended with each new audience, emerge as such: they ask audience members to represent characters, to stand, to perform gestures, to perform actions, to lift, to hold, to assist, to touch, to move together. Sometimes these requests posit a single body in the space; sometimes requests situate two or more bodies in relation to one another. Sometimes the group's performers invite the whole audience to involve themselves. At every stage, *The Fever* walks a delicate track that places audience response and interaction, never entirely predictable, within a container of choreography and performance structure. Remarkably, individual choice remains at the center of that structure, much of which is folded into *The Fever*'s text. Members of 600 HIGHWAYMEN request audience assistance neutrally, and politely. "Will you," they often ask, "will someone," "would you?" The politeness, the unadorned and simple expression of respect that infuses each request, is strangely high stakes. It is less like a participatory performance and more like a participatory event. The difference, it seems, is the absence of character. Audience members and performers are, it seems, stripping down the dressings of character into real encounters among real people.

In one section, a performer, originally played by Marchánt Davis, asks an audience member to touch him intimately, on his face. "Will you bring your fingertips to my face? And your whole hand onto my cheek? And the other one, bring it there too" (Gansky 2015). Marchánt tempers the imperative with a quick opportunity for departure or escape. "If you don't want to be here anymore, you can go sit down" (Gansky 2015). Moments like this fill the performance with an array of invisible doorways; audience members can step in and recede at will. Accordingly, individuals primarily self-select, a phenomenon the group inspires by often articulating requests to the whole room. This strategy increases as the performance unfolds, after Browde and Silverstone, both of whom join the banks of witnesses/performers, prime the audience by inviting particular individuals to partake in early moments. When audience members self-select, and thereby take ownership over particular moments, other witnesses perceive those choice points as part of the unfolding narrative enacted by the specificity of the people in the room. For example, in one moment of performance, a performer—originally played by Tommer Peterson, asks the room, "Will the strongest person stand up?" (Gansky 2015). During the evening performance on January 14, 2017, at the Under the Radar Festival, there was a long silence before anyone identified themselves as "the strongest person." That choice, negotiated by each individual in the room, was in that moment a shared experience of self-reflection and self-perception. After several beats, a young, slight woman stood, and the room erupted in laughter and applause.

The collegial and empathetic tone of *The Fever* tempts positivist readings of ways individual and group agency manifest in the stage space. In his review for *The New York Times*, Charles Isherwood calls the piece "a lovely, haunting meditation on human connection, and disconnection" that ultimately "plays upon the idea of friendly interaction among comparative strangers" (Isherwood 2017). Isherwood calls the friendliness, the desire to help and the revelatory nature of our own implicit dependence upon one another, contagious. Moments in the piece support this: an older performer, originally played by Tommer Peterson, falls repeatedly and asks audience members for help. Later, another performer, originally played by Marchánt Davis, does the same. Yet another performer, originally played by Jax Jackson, places his physical safety in the literal hands of audience members, as they lift him over their heads and carry him across the stage space. These snapshots of helplessness, even consciously staged helplessness, elicit visible instincts on the part of audience members to provide aid. As a group, it seems, the audience cannot let a lone individual lay, uncomfortable, on the ground before them. As a group, it seems, the audience cannot resist requests for assistance, opportunities to play part of the story. The story is, after all, comfortably serene in its evocation of nostalgia, its universality that is general enough to keep any one individual from identifying too personally, too urgently. Fortunately, for those in the audience who typically avoid audience participation with great enthusiasm, there is just enough distance, just enough choice, and little enough asked, that the moments of most obvious witnessing will be those moments when someone opts in. Those moments, strung like beads as the minutes of the performance tick by, stage the beauty of collectivity in encounters that are, at first glance, a possible utopia of intimacy and kindness. As the performance progresses, we the audience see one another more clearly, or at least differently and with greater specificity, as the seventy minutes of engagement unfold. As a critic and witness, Isherwood views this phenomenon with surprised optimism, hearkening evidence of hope in the theatre. Others, perhaps due to matters of taste or perhaps attending performances whose audiences veered too far toward sentimentality and compliance, find these encounters saccharine. Helen Shaw of *Time Out* describes the piece as "claustrophobically sweet" and "a touch too gentle" (Shaw 2017). Max McGuinness, who reviews *The Fever* in *The Financial Times*, sees no core risks establishing high stakes of performance, "No one is going to object to being asked to do nice things to each other. What's missing in *The Fever* is a bit of vinegar to set off all that sweetness. True drama needs conflict so it's too bad the happy fever never breaks here" (McGuinness 2017). While their critical perspectives vary, Isherwood, Shaw, and McGuiness share vocabulary that renders the piece almost innocuous: sweet, gentle, happy, friendly. *The Fever*, as 600 HIGHWAYMEN describe it, "tests the limit of individual and collective responsibility, and our willingness to be there for one another" (HIGHWAYMEN n.d.). The positivist interpretations extracted by these three critics, whether complimentary or cynical, obscure ways in which *The Fever* examines these principles through a lens that is far more nuanced than utopian, far more dangerous than it appears on the surface.

The title, *The Fever*, suggests a viral offering in accordance with Charles Isherwood's descriptor: contagious. But what does the piece transmit, as it infectiously makes its way into the lived experience of those who share these encounters? Might it be something more than, or even something in tension with, friendliness? Browde and Silverstone both note the extreme difficulty of creating the piece, in part because of its reliance on the audience, with all the ethical questions and vulnerabilities that entails. Silverstone notes that the demands of the project shifted lines among actor and onlookers in profound ways, for *The Fever* "could no longer be about one group of people looking at another" (Browde and Silverstone, Interview 2018). Instead, Silverstone and Browde describe the piece as engaged with the materiality of interpersonal, and even political, encounter. Silverstone describes the questions guiding development as "political, but I wouldn't have named them that [...] why is it we're so afraid of other people? [...] What does it feel like to be touching each other? [...] How do we be the truest sense of ourselves when we're 73 people in a room, which is clumsy, awkward?" (Browde and Silverstone, Interview 2018). McGuiness of *The Financial Times* asserts, "No one is going to object to being asked to do nice things to each other" (McGuinness 2017). However, that's not quite the task 600 HIGHWAYMEN advance throughout *The Fever*. While the immediate requests of and invitations to audience members are generally supportive ones, the textual framework for audience action and interaction provides a doubled perspective regarding community building. Audience members might acquiesce, might stand when asked, touch when asked, and assist when asked, but why? Does that very willingness, generally expressed by *The Fever*'s attending audience groups across the United States as well as in Romania, Germany, Bosnia, and so on, expose a kind of infectious mob mentality that can be oriented toward violence as easily as "nice things"?

Even as *The Fever*'s initial narrative of a woman and a party casts audience members in the role of a cohesive community, the group establishes that community as a site of othering, of threat. One performer, played by Michael Silverstone, continues speaking the story of a party that ends, a woman named Marianne who sees a stranger outside the window and feels afraid. Michael invites audience members to stand as he continues the story:

(Now there are many people standing on the perimeter)
And something is rising in us.
And more of us are there. *(more people stand)*

And more. *(more people stand)*
And more of us. *(more people stand)*
Something is rising.
And now all of us. *(everyone stands)*
We are all there.
And this is a feeling of-
being together.
All of here,
In the darkness
Watching this person who doesn't belong.
Coming together around them.
What did we do?
We are on the verge of something.
What did we do?

(Browde and Silverstone, *The Fever* 2017)

In this segment of the piece, the audience is invited, for the first time, to stand together as a single body. The energy of all these bodies standing in a small, single space is heavy; the volume of a soundscape intensifies and helps to gather tension. Given the text that Silverstone speaks as the bodies stand and take up more vertical space, one of the group's guiding questions comes into sharp focus: Why is it we're so afraid of other people? Fear and "other" are the operative concepts in the question, uncomfortably hand in hand with the feeling of belonging that *The Fever* simultaneously invokes in this moment, "[…] this is a feeling of- being together" (Browde and Silverstone, *The Fever* 2017). Being together is a feeling or a phenomenon, it seems, that emerges only when there is an other that is isolated, apart from the group. The other, in this story, is identifiable only as someone "who doesn't belong" (Browde and Silverstone, *The Fever* 2017). What happens next, when the group feels fear and identifies one who is other, who doesn't belong? The group, as the performance text shapes it, surrounds the other, encloses them. The group threatens, subsumes, and rejects. And then what? *The Fever* doesn't answer this question but leaves it lingering in audience member's imaginations. "What did we do?" asks Michael, "We are on the verge of something. What did we do?" (Browde and Silverstone, *The Fever* 2017). The stakes are high, the promise violent, though the inflection of the query gives nothing away. Audience members, all of whom may well be standing in this moment, are implicated one by one as part of the "we." Yet, there is also a joy in the power of standing as one. What do we make of our own collective identity in that instant, how do we square our pleasure with the implicit threat that accompanies our groupness, our community making?

Contagion and *infection*—these terms sit heavily throughout our context of the global COVID-19 pandemic, a time when liveness and contact are replaced with social distance. It is fitting, perhaps, that contagion and infection connote both invisibility and speed. When levied toward emotional response, these connotations quickly usher in dangerous possibility. In *Viral Performance: Contagious Theatres from Modernism to the Digital Age*, Miriam Felton-Dansky writes: "In the cultural imagination of the dawning twenty-first century, the most virulently viral emotions included anxiety, paranoia, and terror" (Felton-Dansky 2018). In *The Fever*, audiences encounter proposals that extend these "virulently viral emotions" into the context of the twenty-first century's second decade, a moment when the political stage of the United States increasingly floods with discourses around otherness and othering. Browde and Silverstone both note the extreme difficulty they experienced when moving through the two-year creation process of *The Fever*. Browde describes the process as "an unsustainable level of difficulty," while Silverstone remembers the development as "dirty" and even "really violent" (Browde and Silverstone, Interview 2018). Given the reliance on audience members, and the vulnerability of sharing emotion, space, and touch with others, such a vigorous struggle is perhaps unavoidable. As Browde says, the development process required them to "fail with others" (Browde and Silverstone, Interview 2018). Risking with others, even with friends and collaborators, is enormously exposing. Failing, then, is even more so. One can imagine the missteps, the collapsed possibility, the rejection by audiences, the anger and dismay of audience members, and so on, as stepping stones marking the shifting shape of the show through its many incarnations into what it became. Audiences, as with any group, can coalesce or sever. *The Fever* relies on a particular mode of agreement from the audience, an esprit that prompts audience members to become part of an "us." Finding the necessary structure and tone would, doubtless, come after a wave of experiments—with audiences in the room—that were more or less effective. For a show like *The Fever*, a less effective experiment might prompt little emotional response in audience members. Worse, it might prompt refusal or even trauma.

Participation can look, as *The Fever* reminds audiences, passive as well as active. As events and encounters unfold in the stage space, audience members function either as proactive participants or as bystanders. To be a bystander suggests a watching, a witnessing while bearing tacit responsibility. This is just one marker of the cultural context of the show's development and performance. 600 HIGHWAYMEN began working on the project in the time period leading up to the 2016 US presidential election, finished developing the piece post-election, and premiered it just weeks before Donald Trump's inauguration. Within a sharply polarized political climate, then, *The Fever* parallels renewed viral emotions, "anxiety, paranoia, and terror" (Felton-Dansky 2018). Through pre- and post-election political rhetoric, polemics seeking to feed extreme nationalism play out in a global arena, as America's executive branch lobbies for (nearly) closed borders and decreased federal protections for protected classes. The "us" and "them" paradigm seeps through discourse focused on national and international interests, and fraying civil rights, an insidious infection that *The Fever* signifies more than once. When Tommer Peterson, a white man past middle age, asks the audience "Will you leave me," how does that compare with the later moment when Marchánt Davis, a young Black man, asks someone else "Will you leave me?" Is there hesitation in one moment but not for another? How is seeing a young Black body, motionless on the ground, different from seeing an older white body? When are audience members more or less complicit as bystanders, and why do we agree to abandon these bodies in the first place? In this contagion, perhaps we are the germs. This possibility shudders similarly in the moment when the audience hears themselves in Silverstone's narrative, "Watching this person who doesn't belong. Coming together around them. What did we do?" (Browde and Silverstone, *The Fever* 2017). In order to create a feeling of belonging, must we exclude the other? If a group can be an expression of utopic community, it can also be a dangerous mob that exists to exclude. It can embody, and perhaps even tends toward, violence.

The Fever is just one microcosm of 600 HIGHWAYMEN's ongoing, evolving project that asks people to see one other, to experience the curiosity, joy, and sometimes terror that human connection can engender. When audience members see themselves as bystanders, as lovers, as players, as humanitarians, as instruments of nostalgia, as community participants, as purveyors of violent threat, these are possible identities 600 HIGHWAYMEN summons into a consciously performative space. The reality of the event is not important, the everyday specifics of Marianne and her party are not important, though the moods these specifics elicit certainly are. The safety is in the very framework of performance, which is the framework that enables audiences to risk just enough but not too much. Throughout the performance, as prompts and invitations unfold, the audience is secure in the fact that "we know this is a lie. And that's okay" (Browde and Silverstone, *The Fever* 2017). This safety is both true and untrue. 600 HIGHWAYMEN tests the degree to which the stage functions as a semiotic space and the degree to which the theatrical arena can and does prompt real encounters. The risk of *The Fever* is twofold: these encounters might reveal the dirtiness, the violence that underlies the optimistic, collectivity of groupness. Or, perhaps just as dangerous, audiences might—even when facing one another—choose bystander status. As bystanders, audience members might decline aid or might decline to play. Even if individuals don't explicitly withdraw, they can withhold; each individual can decline help another. Each can decline to see themselves.

NOTES

Preface

1   See the statement at https://www.weseeyouwat.com/

Chapter 2

1   In addition to the volumes edited by Syssoyeva and Proudfit (2013a, 2013b, 2016), which combine broad overviews with essays by contributors on individual companies (not all from the Unites States), two collections on the special topic of US-devised theatre have appeared: *Theatre Topics* (15.1, 2005); and *The Drama Review* (54.4, 2010). Scores of essays on individual companies, devising pedagogy, and related subjects have been published in these journals and others. More recently (2019), Jeffry Mosser has developed the podcast "From the Ground Up," featuring interviews with US ensemble leaders and artists.

2   Katheryn Mederos Syssoyeva (2008) suggests two models of collective creation, one mostly political that descends from protest theatres of the Global South and informs the 1960s collectives in the United States, and another rooted in European modernism that is largely aestheticist and apolitical. She notes that in the US context, these paths are "sometimes parallel, sometimes convergent," the latter constellation combining the political and the aesthetic (183). I see these convergences becoming more robust under the aegis of neoliberalism, establishing one trajectory into the social turn that characterizes contemporary ensemble creation.

3   One of the strongest statements has been posted by Rachel Chavkin on the company website for the TEAM, entitled "15 commitments on our responsibilities and accountability to racial equity and justice." See http://theteamplays.org/.

4   The year 2019 also saw a museum exhibition featuring the Group's work at the Carriage Trade in New York, casting a retrospective shade over their corpus.

5   http://thewoostergroup.org/since-i-can-remember.

6   From the NET "Manifesto" at https://www.ensembletheaters.net/about/manifesto: "Some ensembles create original work; others work interpretively or with adaptations. Some ensembles are rooted in the community, whether that community is geographic, intellectual, aesthetic, or ethnic. Other ensembles

consciously stand apart from community in order to critique and provoke. All of us create theater that is meaningful to each member and to our diverse audiences."

7 One of the first widespread uses of the term "devised" appeared in the special issue devoted to devising in *Theatre Topics* (15.1, 2005), which featured mostly applied theatre practices but included essays by Mary Zimmerman (Lookingglass), Joan Schirle (Dell' Arte), Moises Kauffamn (Tectonic), and Stacy Klein (Double Edge).

8 https://www.dramatistsguild.com/advocacy/industry-contracts/devised-theatre

9 Alex Mermikides expresses these concerns while addressing the specific case of the National Theatre and Katie Mitchell. See Mermikides (2013).

10 Strangely, all links to the post are now dead: see http://www.tcgcircle.org/2011/08/what-if-devised-theatre-moved-to-the-mainstream-of-theatre-making/.

11 Ensembles feel the AEA Showcase Code, among other problems, limits performance runs (currently at twenty-four performances) and rehearsal schedules (set at six weeks), treating collaborative theatre-makers as if their goal is to transfer work to Broadway or Off-Broadway. They have unsuccessfully sought waivers (like the one granted to Los Angeles-area 99-seat theatres) and continue to push the issue of allowing producers to pay into actors' pension and welfare funds in lieu of salary. See Sobeck (2010) and Louloudes (2012).

12 For ensemble theatre and the UK creative industries, see Mermikides (2013) and Tomlin (2015a).

13 Neoliberalism's effects on communities of color and low wage earners, where social mobility is idealized while at the same time held back by virtue of predatory lending practices, lack of affordable housing and access to federal housing loans, mass incarceration, and other obstacles, are detailed by Jacob Hacker (2019), David Theo Goldberg (2009), and Darrick Hamilton (2019), among others.

14 For a partial list, see http://www.critical-stages.org/12/international-theatre-and-performing-arts-festival-guide/. Another interactive map can be found at http://performap.com/.

15 See the Association's website at https://www.usaff.org/. Another curated listing of US fringe live art festivals can be seen at https://theprojectartist.com/fringe-performing-arts-festivals-in-us/. The social network Contemporary Performance maintains an international list at https://contemporaryperformance.com/festivals/.

16 https://conservativefestivaloh.com/.

17 Paige McGinley (2010) and Rachel Anderson-Rabern (2020, 21–2) provide extensive lists of such university-based affiliations to which many more are being added every year.

18 See Nicholson (2014) and Hughes and Nicholson (2016) for distinctions.

Chapter 3

1 This genealogical perception is restated by Weems in 2006, with the added assertion that "the Performing Garage and the Living Theatre were frequently ideologically opposed to media and based their work on physical ritual and the sanctity or at least the undeniable presence of the performer" (Marranca 2008, 204).

2 The titles of productions are capitalized by the company.

3 *SUPER VISION* played at the Royal Court (Liverpool) as part of the European Capital of Culture programme. Company members led workshops (which I participated in and helped to coordinate) with budding, multimedia artists.

4 In recent years, these workshops have been branched into "Introductory" and "Advanced" sessions.

Chapter 4

1 *The Serpent* (1968), collectively created by the Open Theatre (1963–1973) under the direction of Joseph Chaikin and Roberta Sklar, script by Jean-Claude van Itallie; *Terminal* (1971), collectively created by the Open Theatre under the direction of Sklar and Chaikin, script by Susan Yankowitz.

Chapter 5

1 The program has grown much larger and more elaborate since Rude Mechs attended in the late 1980s.

2 In the early years the Rudes were uninterested in building an archive. As a result valuable material has been lost.

3 Deb Margolin was one of Shawn Sides's acting teachers in New York.

4 I was given a copy of the unpublished script and granted permission to view the company's archived video.

5 See Puchner (2004) and Ybarra (2005).

6 I used this video as a source for this chapter.

7 To find the current list of Rude Mechs productions, go to https://rudemechs.com/thework/thelist/.

Chapter 6

1 I thank the late Alexis de Tocqueville for his section headings of *Democracy in America*, which I've adapted as my own.

2 The specific "offering" Savran discusses in this passage is T.S. Eliot's *The Cocktail Party* within the Wooster Group's *Nayatt School* (1978).

3 All quotations below are drawn from that conversation on August 12, 2017, unless otherwise noted.

4 See Barker (2017, 175).

5 According to the group: Radiohole has been funded by the New York State Council on the Arts and the NYC Department of Cultural Affairs, as well as the Edith Lutyens and Norman Bel Geddes Fund (2008, 2005), Creative Capital (2008–2009), the Altria Group (2006), Rockefeller Multi-Arts Production Fund (2004), Katherine Dalglish Foundation (2005), Edward T. Cone Foundation (2005), The Nancy Quinn Fund (2009, 2005), Foundation for Contemporary Performance Art (2004). Presenting organizations include, in NYC, P.S.122 (now Performance Space New York), the Kitchen, the Performing Garage, La MaMa; in the United States at the Walker Arts Center, the Andy Warhol Museum, EMPAC (Experimental Media and Performing Arts Center), On the Boards, Mass Live Arts; in Europe at Copenhagen's PSK Festival, Dublin Fringe Festival, Brussel's Kaaitheater, Gronigen's Noorderzon Festival, Austria's Donau Festival, Denmark's Teater Katapult; and in Norway at Black Box, BIT Teatergarasjen, Teaterhuset Avant Garden, Tou Scene (Douglass 2018).

6 "The Crash," the *Mad Men* episode Grote is best known for, is notably the series' strangest and one of the most engaging. Many of the characters are high on the same drug (speed) for the duration of the action, which is told in a disorienting, nonlinear fashion. The resonance with Radiohole's aesthetic is evident.

7 For more on Kandor, see *Action Comics* #242, July 1958 to start.

Chapter 7

1 With a founding board of directors including Michael Friedman Jennifer Morris, and Anne Kauffman.

2 Renamed the Kiln Theatre in 2018, the Tricycle Theatre was part of a pioneering arts in Kilburn High Road, London.

3 The most consistently involved artists across the company's eighteen years, besides Friedman, Cosson, Washburn, and Kauffman, are Jennifer Morris, Emily Ackerman, Colleen Werthman, Stephan Plunkett, Damian Baldett, Quincy Bernstine, Aysan Celik, and Trey Lyford.

4   The company experimented with funding projects using Kickstarter and
    Indiegogo around 2013 and 2014, when those crowdsourcing technologies felt
    freshest, but that is not a long-term solution. The company has seen its annual
    budget top $400,000, yet it still struggles with being securely funded year to
    year. All subsequent quotes from Cosson are from this interview.

5   See Ritchie (1989) for an overview of how this often happened for Joint Stock.

6   The Civilians' most usual mode when names are used is that the "character"
    name is that of the artist who originally did the interview or developed the part
    in workshop. This is how *Mr. Burns* works, for instance.

7   Credits for development are acknowledged in the play text: Steve Cosson, Jim
    Lewis, and Michael Friedman. This description is also based on the tabulations
    in the Civilians MASTERLIST file of company activities from 2001 to the
    present.

8   All quotations from the script come from the version in the Civilians
    Anthology. The play text credits "Interview with Dr. Palinurus" to Peter Morris.
    Observations of the performance come from the archival video held by the
    Civilians on their Vimeo site, accessed by the author between April and July
    2018.

9   Descriptions of the performance are based on the author's viewing of the show
    at the Humana Festival, in the Pamela Brown auditorium, Actors Theatre
    Louisville, March 2008.

10 Unpublished manuscript of *The Great Immensity*, shared with the author by
    Cosson and Moll; observations of the performance come from the archival
    video of the performance at the Public Theatre, held by the Civilians on their
    Vimeo site, accessed by the author between April and July 2018.

11 Jenny Morris, C.A. Johnson, and Cosson were in residence at NYU in
    partnership with Playwrights Horizons during 2017, doing workshops
    with students for a play Johnson composed about the rising appetite for
    authoritarian leadership. The play had workshop production with student
    performers in December 2017.

Chapter 8

1   Beckett ([1954] 1982), 51.

BIBLIOGRAPHY

Als, Hilton. (2013). "The Theatre: 'This Great Country.'" *New Yorker*, July 15. https://www.newyorker.com/culture/culture-desk/the-theatre-this-great-country (accessed October 1, 2018).

Alston, Adam. (2013). "Audience Participation and Neoliberal Value: Risk, Agency and Responsibility in Immersive Theatre." *Performance Research* 18(2): 128–38.

Anderman, Joan. (2011). "Many Methods to Collaborative Madness." *New York Times*, February 22.

Anderson-Rabern, Rachel. (2020). *Staging Process: The Aesthetic Politics of Collective Performance*. Evanston: Northwestern University Press.

Aronson, Arnold. (2000). *American Avant-Garde Theatre: A History*. London and New York: Routledge.

Auslander, Philip. (1994). *Presence and Resistance: Postmodernism and Cultural Politics in Contemporary American Performance*. Ann Arbor: University of Michigan Press.

Auslander, Philip. (2004). "Postmodernism and Performance." In *The Cambridge Companion to Postmodernism*, Steven Connor, ed. Cambridge: Cambridge University Press: 97–115.

Badiou, Alain. (2003). *On Beckett*. Edited by Alberto Toscano and Nina Power. Manchester: Clinamen Press.

Bailes, Sara Jane. (2011). *Performance Theatre and the Poetics of Failure: Forced Entertainment, Goat Island, Elevator Repair Service*. London and New York: Routledge.

Baldwin, Jane. (2008). "Collective Creation's Migration from the Côte d'Or to the Golden Hills of California." In *Vies et morts de la création collective/Lives and Death of Collective Creation*, Jane Baldwin, Jean-Marc Larrue and Christiane Page, eds. Boston: Vox Theatri: 31–51.

Baldwin, Jane. (2016). "Raising the Curtain on Suzanne Bing's Life in the Theatre." In *Women, Collective Creation, and Devised Performance*, Kathryn Mederos Syssoyeva and Scott Proudfit, eds. London: Palgrave Macmillan: 29–50.

Baldwin, Jane, Jean-Marc Larrue, and Christiane Page, eds. (2008). *Vies et morts de la creation collective/Lives and Deaths of Collective Creative*. Boston: Vox Theatri.

Banes, Sally. (2000). "Institutionalizing Avant-Garde Performance: A Hidden History of University Patronage in the United States." In *Contours of the Theatrical Avant-Garde: Performance and Textuality*, James Harding, ed. Ann Arbor: University of Michigan Press: 217–38.

Banks, Daniel (2016). "Hip Hop as Pedagogy: The Hip Hop Theatre Initiative." In *Theatre and Cultural Politics for a New World*, Chinua Thelwell, ed. London and New York: Routledge: 147–63.

Barker, Jeremy. (2017). "Radiohole's *Tarzana*." Photography by Maria Baranova. *Chance Magazine* 1 and 2: 173–98.

Bataille, Georges. (1988). *The Accursed Share: An Essay on General Economy, Volume 1: Consumption*. New York: Zone Books.

Bauriedel, Quinn. (2004). Correspondence with the author, March 23.

Bauriedel, Quinn. (2016). "Disponibilité and Observation." In *The Routledge Companion to Jacques Lecoq*, Mark Evans and Rick Kemp, eds. Oxford: Routledge Press: 356–62.

Bauriedel, Quinn. (2017). Interview with the author.

Bauriedel, Quinn. (2019). Correspondence with the author, January 21.

Beckett, Samuel. ([1954] 1982). *Waiting for Godot*. New York: Grove Press.

Benevente, Javiera. (2019). "The Promise of the Commons." October 10. https://howlround.com/promise-commons (accessed January 2, 2020).

Bennethan, Joss. (2014). *Making Theatre: The Frazzled Drama Teacher's Guide to Devising*. New York: Nick Hern Books.

Bent, Eliza. (2015). "5 Theatre Couples Who Work Together to Stay Together." *American Theatre Magazine*, January 30. https://www.americantheatre.org/2015/01/30/5-theatre-couples-who-work-together-to-stay-together/ (accessed June 15, 2018).

The Berkeley Rep Magazine. (2008–2009). *The Arabian Nights* (program), issue 3.

Berlant, Lauren. (2011). *Cruel Optimism*. Durham: Duke University Press.

Bîcat, Tina and Chris Baldwin, eds. (2002). *Devised and Collaborative Theatre: A Practical Guide*. Ramsbury, Marlborough and Wiltshire: Crowood Press.

Bielby, Liz. (2014). "Each Project's Like a New Album: How a Band Model Works for Us." *HowlRound*, November 14. https://howlround.com/each-projects-album (accessed December 11, 2019).

Billington, Michael, Mireia Aragay and Pilar Zozaya. (2004). "The State of British Theatre Now: An Interview with Michael Billington." *Atlantis* (June): 89–100.

Biner, Pierre (1972). *The Living Theatre*. New York: Horizon Press.

Bishop, Claire. (2004). "Antagonism and Relational Aesthetics." *October*: 51–79.

Bishop, Claire. (2005). "The Social Turn: Collaboration and Its Discontents." *Artforum* 44(6): 178–83.

Bishop, Claire. (2012). *Artificial Hells: Participatory Art and the Politics of Spectatorship*. New York: Verso Books.

Boal, Augusto. (2019). *Theatre of the Oppressed*. London: Pluto Press.

Bogart, Anne. (2001). *A Director Prepares*. London and New York: Routledge.

Bogart, Anne. (2007). *And Then, You Act: Making Art in an Unpredictable World*. London and New York: Routledge.

Bogart, Anne and Tina Landau. (2005). *The Viewpoints Book: A Practical Guide to Viewpoints and Composition*. New York: Theatre Communications Book.

Bonczek, Rose Burnett and David Storck. (2013). *Ensemble Theatre Making: A Practical Guide*. London and New York: Routledge.

Bottoms, Stephen J. and Matthew Goulish. (2013). *Small Acts of Repair: Performance, Ecology and Goat Island*. London and New York: Routledge.

Bottoms, Stephen J. (2006). *Playing Underground: A Critical History of the 1960s Off-Off-Broadway Movement*. Ann Arbor: University of Michigan Press.

Bibliography

Bourriaud, Nicolas, Simon Pleasance, Fronza Woods and Mathieu Copeland. (2002). *Relational Aesthetics*. Dijon: Les presses du réel.

Boudreaux, Frank. (2014). "Aggressive Inefficency: From Page to Stage with Rachel Chavkin and Alec Duffy." *The Brooklyn Rail*, https://brooklynrail.org/2014/12/theater/aggressive-inefficiency-from-stage-to-page-frank-boudreaux-with-rachel-chavkin-and-alec-duffy (accessed October 1, 2019).

Britton, John, ed. (2013). *Encountering Ensemble*. London: Bloomsbury.

Browde, Abigail. (2018). Interview by Rachel Anderson-Rabern, September 17.

Browde, Abigail and Michael Silverstone. (2017). "The Fever." New York, January 4.

Browde, Abigail and Michael Silverstone. (2018). Interview by Rachel Anderson-Rabern, September 28.

Brown, Kylie. (2018). "What We Made—*Gone Missing*, Encores! Off-Center, the Lobby Project." n.d. https://soundcloud.com/thecivilians/what-we-made-gone-missing-encores-off-center-the-lobby-project?mc_cid=336eb230dc&mc_eid=%5BUNIQID%5D

Brown, Scott. (2013). "The Civilians' Steve Cosson Likes His Theater Dead." *Vulture*, June 28. http://www.vulture.com/2013/06/steve-cosson-likes-his-theater-dead (accessed June 1, 2018).

Browning, Barbara. (2012). "Radiohole." *Bomb* 118 (Winter): 40–6.

Bruin, David (2017). "The New York City Performance Space-Time Continuum." *Theater* 47(2): 1–7.

Builders Association, company website: buildersassociation.org.

Builders Association. (n.d.). "Productions: *ELEMENTS OF OZ*." https://www.thebuildersassociation.org/prod_oz (accessed January 8, 2019).

Bull, John, and Graham Saunders. (2016). *British Theatre Companies: 1965-1979*. London; New York: Bloomsbury Publishing.

Butler, Isaac. (2018). "Attention Deficit." *Artforum*, July 3. https://www.artforum.com/diary/isaac-butler-at-a-benefit-for-the-michael-friedman-legacy-fund-75844.

Butler, Judith. (2016). *Frames of War: When Is Life Grievable?* New York: Verso Books.

Calhoun, Ada. (2000). "Everything Is Possible … Again." *The Austin Chronicle*, September 1, 2.

Callens, Johan, ed. (2004). *The Wooster Group and Its Traditions* (Vol. 13). Brussels: Peter Lang.

Callery, Dymphna. (2001). *Through the Body: A Practical Guide to Physical Theatre*. London and New York: Routledge.

Calvino, Italo. (1997). *Invisible Cities*. Translated by William Weaver. London: Vintage Books.

Canning, Charlotte. (1996). *Feminist Theaters in the USA: Staging Women's Experience*. London and New York: Routledge.

Carlson, Marvin. (2001). "Theatre and Performance at a Time of Shifting Disciplines." *Theatre Research International* 26(2): 137–44.

Carr, Tessa. (2015). "Devised Theatre: Drive Creativity by Inviting All to Help Steer a Play from Idea to Stage." *Southern Theatre* 56(2) (Spring): 6–15.

Castells, Manuel. (2013). *Communication Power*. Oxford: Oxford University Press.

Center for Disease Control and Prevention. (2020). "Covid-19 in Racial and Ethnic Minority Groups." https://www.cdc.gov/coronavirus/2019-ncov/need-extra-precautions/racial-ethnic-minorities.html

Cesare, T. Nikki and Mariellen R. Sandford. (2010). "To Avant or Not to Avant: Questioning the Experimental, the New and the Potential to Shock in the New Garde." *TDR: The Drama Review* 54(4): 7–10.

Chalmers, Jessica, ed. (1999). "A Conversation about *JET LAG*." *Performance Research* 4(2): 57–60.

Chavkin, Rachel. (2011). "What If … Devised Theatre Moved to the Mainstream of Theatre Making?" In Virginia P. Louloudes (2012), *Theatres for the 21st-Century* (Alliance of Resident Theatres). https://www.art-newyork.org/assets/documents/theatres-for-the-21st-century.pdf (accessed December 11, 2018).

Coen, Stephanie. (1995). "The Body Is the Source: Four Actors Explore the Rigors of Working with Master Teachers Anne Bogart and Tadashi Suzuki." *American Theatre* 12(1) (January): 30–4, 70–6.

Cofta, Mark. (2015). "*Gentlemen Volunteers.*" *Broad Street Review*, December 15. https://www.broadstreetreview.com/theater/pig-irons-gentlemen-volunteers.

Cohen, Jordan. (2017). "An Oz for Us All." *PAJ: Performing Arts Journal* 39(2): 75–8.

Cohen, Robert. (2010). *Working Together in Theatre: Collaboration and Leadership*. New York: Macmillan International Higher Education.

Cohen-Cruz, Jan. (2015). *Remapping Performance: Common Ground, Uncommon Partners*. New York: Palgrave Macmillan.

Collins, John. (2013). "Elevator Repair Service and the Wooster Group: Ensembles Surviving Themselves." In *Encountering Ensemble*, John Britton, ed. London: Bloomsbury: 234–49.

Collins-Hughes, Laura. (2018). "*STRANGE WINDOW: THE TURN OF THE SCREW*; Henry James for the Gig Economy." *New York Times*, December 13. https://www.nytimes.com/2018/12/13/theater/strange-window-the-turn-of-the-screw-review.

Cornish, Matt. (2019). "*Everything*" *and Other Performance Texts from Germany*. Calcutta: Seagull Press.

Cosson, Steve, ed. (2009). *The Civilians: An Anthology of Six Plays*. New York: Playscripts, Inc.

Cosson, Steve. (2018a). Interview with Sara Freeman, April 23. Civilians Offices in Green Point, Brooklyn, digital recording.

Cosson, Steve. (2018b). Video Interview with Sara Freeman, June 11. Digital audio recorded.

Cummings, Scott T. (2006). *Remaking American Theatre: Charles Mee, Anne Bogart and the SITI Company*. Cambridge: Cambridge University Press.

Cvejić, Bojana and Ana Vujanović, eds. (2010). *Exhausting Immaterial Labor in Performance*. Belgrade and Aubervilliers: TkH and Les Laboratories d'Aubervilliers.

Darlington, Madge. (2017). Author's interview, December 4.

Davis, Mike. (2006). *Planet of Slums*. New York: Verso Books.

Debord, Guy. (1994). *The Society of the Spectacle*. Translated by Donald Nicholson-Smith. New York: Zone Books.

Bibliography

De Peuter, Greig. (2014). "Beyond the Model Worker: Surveying a Creative Precariat." *Culture Unbound: Journal of Current Cultural Research* 6(1): 263–84.

Delpech, Emmanuelle. (2004). Interview with the author.

Del Vecchio, Jennifer. (2012). "*SONTAG: REBORN* and *You, My Mother*" (review). *Theatre Journal* 64(4): 592–5.

Dembin, Russel M. (2017). "Building a Mountain to Scale." *American Theatre* 34(6) (July/August): 30–3, 69.

Diamond, Elin, Denise Varney, and Candice Amich, eds. (2017). *Performance, Feminism and Affect in Neoliberal Times*. London: Palgrave Macmillan.

Dixon, Steve. (2005). "Theatre, Technology, and Time." *International Journal of Performance Arts and Digital Media* 1(1): 11–29.

Dixon, Steve. (2010). "The Philosophy and Psychology of the Scenographic House in Multimedia Theatre." *International Journal of Performance Arts and Digital Media* 6(1): 7–24.

Douglass, Erin. (2018). Email to the author, July 14.

Durham, Leslie Atkins. (2009). "Found Images and Networked Americas in The Builders Association's *ALLADEEN*." *Theatre Journal* 61(4): 521–38.

Dyer, Eric. (2013). "Rude Mechanicals." *Bomb* 122 (Winter): 42–9.

Dziemianowicz, Joe. (2014). "Review of *The Great Immensity*." *New York Daily News*, April 25. http://www.nydailynews.com/entertainment/music-arts/great-immensity-theater-review-article-1.1768260.

Estéves, Carlos García. (2016). "Auto-cours, enquêtes, commandes." In *The Routledge Companion to Jacques Lecoq*, Mark Evans and Rick Kemp, eds. Oxford: Routledge Press: 165–78.

Estvanik, Nicole. (2004). "The Civilians." *American Theatre* 21(10): 24.

Eustis, Oskar. (2009). "Forward." In *The Civilians: An Anthology of Six Plays*, Steve Cosson, ed. New York: Playscripts, Inc:v.

Faires, Robert. (1998). "Austin's Rude Mechanicals Get Inspired Training at SITI." *The Austin Chronicle*, July 31.

Faires, Robert. (2004). "More Words from Winedale: Additional Life Lessons and Meditations from Winedale." *The Austin Chronicle*, July 23, 2004.

Faires, Robert. (2017). "The Secret History of the Off Center." *The Austin Chronicle*, June 30.

Faires, Robert. (n.d.). "Curst & Shrewd: An Invigorating Chat." *Austin Chronicle*.

Favorini, Attilio. (2013). "Collective Creation in Documentary Theatre." In *A History of Collective Creation*, Kathryn Mederos Syssoyeva and Scott Proudfit, eds. New York: Palgrave Macmillan: 97–114.

Feldman, Adam. (2014). Review of *The Great Immensity*, *Time Out*, April 25. https://www.timeout.com/newyork/theater/the-great-immensity.

Felton-Dansky, Miriam. (2018). *Viral Performance: Contagious Theaters from Modernism to the Digital Age*. Chicago: Northwestern University Press.

Firestone, Lonnie. (2014). "Change by Degree." *American Theatre*. n.d. https://www.americantheatre.org/2014/12/11/change-by-degrees/

Fischer, Iris Smith. (2011). *Mabou Mines: Making Avant-Garde Theater in the 1970s*. Ann Arbor: University of Michigan Press.

Florida, Richard. (2002). *The Rise of the Creative Class*. New York: Basic Books.

Forsgren, La Donna L. (2018). "From 'Poemplays' to Ritualistic Revivals: The Experimental Works of Women Dramatists of the Black Arts Movement." In *The Routledge Companion to African American Theatre and Performance*, Kathy Perkins et al. eds. London and New York: Routledge: 250–6.

Fragkou, Marissia. (2018). *Ecologies of Precarity in Twenty-First Century Theatre: Politics, Affect, Responsibility*. London: Bloomsbury.

Fraser, Nancy. (2017). *The Old Is Dying and the New Cannot Be Born: From Progressive Neoliberalism to Trump and Beyond*. New York: Verso Books.

Freeman, John. (2007). *New Performance/New Writing*. New York: Macmillan International Higher Education.

Freire, Paolo. (1970). *Pedagogy of the Oppressed*. New York: Penguin.

Fryer, Nic. (2010). "From Reproduction to Creativity and the Aesthetic: Towards an Ontological Approach to the Assessment of Devised Performance." *The Journal of Applied Theatre and Performance* 15(4): 547–62.

Gallagher-Ross, Jacob. (2018). *Theaters of the Everyday: Aesthetic Democracy on the American Stage*. Evanston: Northwestern University Press.

Gansky, Ben. (2015). "600 Highwaymen." *BOMB*, April 30. https://bombmagazine. org/articles/600-highwaymen/ (accessed October 1, 2018).

Gener, Randy. (2008). "Electronic Campfires: The Builders Association Signals through the Flames with Messages for a Hyper-Mediated World." *American Theatre* 25(10): 28–31, 84–7.

George-Graves, Nadine, ed. (2015). *The Oxford Handbook of Dance and Theater*. USA: Oxford University Press.

Giesekam, Greg. (2007). *Staging the Screen: The Use of Film and Video in Theatre*. Basingstoke and New York: Palgrave Macmillan.

Giroux, Henry A. (2014). *Neoliberalism's War on Higher Education*. Chicago: Haymarket Books.

Goat Island. (1995). *Goat Island*, Newsletter March.

Goat Island. (2000). *School Book 2*, Goat Island.

Goldberg, David T. (2009). *The Threat of Race: Reflections on Racial Neoliberalism*. New York: John Wiley & Sons.

Gordon, David. (2020). "The Forty-Year Rehearsal: The Wooster Group's Endless Work in Progress." *Harper's Magazine*, January. https://harpers.org/ archive/2020/01/the-forty-year-rehearsal-wooster-group-elizabeth-lecompte/ (accessed January 19, 2019).

Goulish, Matthew. (2002). *39 Microlectures: In Proximity of Performance*. London; New York: Routledge.

Govan, Emma and Helen Nicholson and Katie Normington. (2007). *Making a Performance: Devising Histories and Contemporary Practices*. London and New York: Routledge.

Graves, Thomas. (2018). Email to author, April 26.

Graves, Thomas, Lana Lesley and Shawn Sides. (2017). Author's interview, May 28.

The Great Immensity, unpublished manuscript, Civilians office files.

Greenfield, Adam. (n.d.). Artist's interview with Kirk Lynn. Playwrights Horizons. (accessed June 13, 2017).

Bibliography

Grote, Jason. (2006). "The Only Hole That Matters: Radiohole's *Fluke* at the Collapsable Hole." December 8. https://brooklynrail.org/2006/12/theater/the-only-hole-that (accessed June 30, 2017).

Hacker, Jacob S. (2019). *The Great Risk Shift: The New Economic Insecurity and the Decline of the American Dream*. Oxford: Oxford University Press.

Hagwood, Rod Stafford. (2012). "This Is Your Brain on Pig Iron." *South Florida Sun Sentinel*, March 19. https://www.sun-sentinel.com/entertainment/events/fl-xpm-2012-03-19-fl-sh-pig-iron-chekhov-lizardbrain-031612-20120319-story.html.

Hamilton, Darrick. (2019). "Neoliberalism and Race." *Democracy Journal*, 53. https://democracyjournal.org/magazine/53/neoliberalism-and-race/.

Hancock, Alan (1995). "Chaos in Drama: The Metaphors of Chaos Theory as a Way of Understanding Drama Process." *NADIE Journal* 19(1): 15.

Hansel, Adrien-Alice and Amy Wegener, eds. (2009). *Humana Festival 2008: The Complete Plays*. New York: Playscripts, Inc.

Harding, James, ed. (2000). *Contours of the Theatrical Avant-Garde: Performance and Textuality*. Ann Arbor: University of Michigan Press.

Harding, James, ed. (2015). *The Ghosts of the Avant-Garde(s): Exorcising Experimental Theater and Performance*. Ann Arbor: University of Michigan Press.

Harvey, David. (2005). *A Brief History of Neoliberalism*. Oxford: Oxford University Press.

Harvie Jen. (2005). *Staging the UK*. Manchester: Manchester University Press.

Harvie, Jen. (2013). *Fair Play: Art, Performance and Neoliberalism*. London: Palgrave.

Harvie, Jen and Andy Lavender. (2010). *Making Contemporary Theatre: International Rehearsal Processes*. Manchester: Manchester University Press.

Haskell, John and Annie-B Parson. (2007). "Big Dance Theater." *BOMB* 101(Fall): 42–7. http://www.jstor.org/stable/40428144 (accessed August 11, 2017).

Hautyunyan, Angela, ed. (2012). *Intersections: Practices of Curating, Education and Theory*. Bristol, UK: Intellect Books.

Heddon, Deirdre and Jane Milling. (2006). *Devising Performance: A Critical History*. New York: Palgrave Macmillan.

Herrington, Joan. (2000). "Directing with the Viewpoints." *Theatre Topics* 10(2) (September): 155–68.

Hilfinger-Pardo, Paz. (2013). "Building Chartres in the Desert: The TEAM. Collective Intelligence and the Failure of Ideals." In *Encountering Ensemble*, John Britton, ed. London: Bloomsbury: 222–33.

Hopala, Sarah. (1999). "Don B's Snow White: Lost among the Dwarves." *The Austin Chronicle*, April 16.

Horwitz, Andy. (2012, 2013). "The Politics of Cultural Production (or, Devise This!), Parts I and 3." https://www.culturebot.org/2012/11/15219/the-politics-of-cultural-production-in-theater-or-devise-this-part-i/, https://www.culturebot.org/2013/02/15952/the-politics-of-cultural-production-in-theater-or-devise-this-part-iii/ (accessed August 5, 2018).

Horwitz, Simi. (2017). "Enter Stage Right." *American Theatre*, October 24. https://www.americantheatre.org/2017/10/24/enter-stage-right/ (accessed October 11, 2019).

Hughes, Jenny and Helen Nicholson, eds. (2016). *Critical Perspectives on Applied Theatre*. Cambridge and New York: Cambridge University Press.

Hughes, Laura Collins. (2017). "A Cast of 87 Sounds a Climate Change Alarm." *The New York Times*, September 24. https://www.nytimes.com/2017/09/24/theater/annenberg-center-pig-iron-theater-fringe-festival.html.

Hunka, George. (2010). "The Booking of the Play." *Theater* 40(2): 19–41.

Isherwood, Charles. (2014). Review of *The Great Immensity*, *The New York Times*, April 24. https://www.nytimes.com/2014/04/25/theater/the-great-immensity-gives-environmentalism-its-own-lyrics.html.

Isherwood, Charles. (2017). "'The Fever' Finds That Friendliness Can Be Contagious." *New York Times*, January 5. https://www.nytimes.com/2017/01/05/theater/the-fever-review-under-the-radar.html (accessed October 1, 2018).

Isherwood, Charles. (2008). "For a Solitary Soul, Memories Are Raucous Company." *The New York Times*, October 11. https://www.nytimes.com/2008/10/11/theater/reviews/11liza.html?action=click&module=RelatedCoverage&pgtype=Article&region=Footer.

Israel, Baba. (2009). *Remixing the Ritual: Hip-Hop Theatre Aesthetics and Practice*. Baba Israel: Self-published.

Jackson, Shannon. (2004). *Professing Performance: Theatre in the Academy from Philology to Performativity*. Cambridge: Cambridge University Press.

Jackson, Shannon. (2011). *Social Works: Performing Art, Supporting Publics*. London and New York: Routledge.

Jackson, Shannon. (2012). "Just-in-Time: Performance and the Aesthetics of Precarity." *TDR/The Drama Review* 56(4): 10–31.

Jackson, Shannon and Marianne Weems. (2015). *The Builders Association: Performance and Media in Contemporary Theater*. Cambridge and London: MIT Press.

Janiak, Lily. (2014). "New Plays in New Ways: Redeveloping the New Play Development Model." *Theatre Bay Area*, June 16. https://www.theatrebayarea.org/news/177885/New-Plays-in-New-Ways-Redeveloping-the-New-Play-Development-Model.htm (accessed January 3, 2019).

Jannarone, Kimberly, ed. (2015). *Vanguard Performance beyond Left and Right*. Ann Arbor: University of Michigan Press.

Jones, Seth G., Catrina Doxsee and Nicholas Harrington. (2020). "The Escalating Terrorism Problem in the United States." https://www.csis.org/analysis/escalating-terrorism-problem-united-states.

Johnston, Chloe and Coya Paz Brownrigg, eds. (2018). *Ensemble-Made Chicago: A Guide to Devised Theater*. Evanston: Northwestern University Press.

Jones, Omi Osun Joni L. (2015). *Theatrical Jazz: Performance, Àṣẹ, and the Power of the Present Moment*. Columbus: Ohio State University Press.

Jones, Omi Osun Joni L., Lisa L. Moore and Shannon Bridgforth. (2010). *Experiments in a Jazz Aesthetic: Art, Activism, Academia, and the Austin Project* (Vol. 23). Austin: University of Texas Press.

Jurca, Catherine. (2001). *White Diaspora: The Suburb and the Twentieth-Century American Novel*. Princeton, NJ: Princeton University Press.

Bibliography

Kakutani, Michiko. (2019). "The 2010s Were the End of Normal: A Decade of Distrust." *New York Times*, December 27. https://www.nytimes.com/interactive/2019/12/27/opinion/sunday/2010s-america-trump.html (accessed March 17, 2020).

Kaye, Nick. (1994). *Postmodern Performance*. Basingstoke: Macmillan.

Kaye, Nick. (2007). "Screening Presence: The Builders Association and dbox, *SUPER VISION* (2005)." *Contemporary Theatre Review* 17(4): 557–77.

Kemp, Rick. (2018). "Devising—Embodied Creativity in Distributed Systems." In *The Routledge Companion to Theatre, Performance and Cognitive Science*, Rick Kemp and Bruce McConachie, eds. London and New York: Routledge: 48–57.

Kenah, Hannah. (2018). Email to author, March 6.

Kerrigan, Sheila. (2001). *The Performer's Guide to the Collaborative Process: A Practical Guide*. Portsmouth, NH: Heinemann.

Kershaw, Baz. (1992). *The Politics of Performance: Radical Theatre and Cultural Intervention*. London and New York: Routledge.

Kershaw, Baz. (2016). "Towards a Historiography of the Absent: On the Late Pasts of Applied Theatre and Community Performance." *Critical Perspectives on Applied Theatre*: 15–39.

Kind, Lily. (2017). "A Period of Animate Existence (Pig Iron): Creating an Environment for Thought." *Phindie*, October 6. http://phindie.com/16245-pig-irons-a-period-of-inanimate-existence/.

Kolin, Philip. (2010). "Sampling and Remixing: Hip Hop and Parks's History Plays." In *Suzan-Lori Parks: Essays on the Plays and Other Works*, Philip Kolin, ed. Jefferson, NC: McFarland & Company: 65–79.

Kotsko, Adam. (2018). *Neoliberalism's Demons: On the Political Theology of Late Capital*. Palo Alto: Stanford University Press.

Kozinn, Sarah and Steve Cosson. (2010). "Discovering What We Don't Know: An Interview with Steve Cosson of the Civilians." *TDR: The Drama Review* 54(4): 188–205.

Krumholz, Brad. (2013). "Locating the Ensemble: NACL Theatre and the Ethics of Collaboration." In *Encountering Ensemble*, John Britton, ed. London: Bloomsbury: 212–21.

Laermans, Rudi. (2012). "'Being in Common': Theorizing Artistic Collaboration." *Performance Research* 17(6): 94–102.

Lavender, Andy. (2016). *Performance in the Twenty-First Century: Theatres of Engagement*. London and New York: Routledge.

Lee, Young Jean. (2009). "Nature Theatre of Oklahoma." *BOMB*, July 1. https://bombmagazine.org/articles/nature-theater-of-oklahoma-1/ (accessed June 3, 2017).

Lehmann, Hans-Thies. (2006). *Postdramatic Theatre*. London and New York: Routledge.

Lemke, Sieglinde. (2016). *Inequality, Poverty and Precarity in Contemporary American Culture*. New York: Palgrave Macmillan.

Lesley, Lana. (2018). Email to author, April 6.

Lewis, Ferdinand. (2005). *Ensemble Works: An Anthology*. New York: Theatre Communications Group.

Linder, Evan. (2016). "The New Colony." *Theatre Topics* 26(2): E-19–E-22. doi: 10.1353/tt.2016.0045.

Lindsey, Chad and Carrie Heitman. (2014). "It All Comes Back to the Hook." *HowlRound*, November 20. https://howlround.com/it-all-comes-back-hook (accessed July 3, 2019).

Lioi, Andrew. (2014). "Introduction." *Resilience: A Journal of the Environmental Humanities* 2: 1.

Listengarten, Julia and Cindy Rosenthal, eds. (2018). *Modern American Drama: Playwriting 2000–2009.* London; New York: Bloomsbury Publishing.

Littlefield, Henry. (1964). "*The Wizard of Oz*: Parable on Populism." *American Quarterly* 16(1): 47–58.

London, Todd, Ben Pesner and Zannie Giraud Voss. (2009). *Outrageous Fortune: The Life and Times of the New American Play.* New York: Theatre Development Fund.

Lorey, Isabelle. (2015). *State of Insecurity: Government of the Precarious.* New York: Verso Books.

Louloudes, Virginia P. (2012). *Theatres for the 21st Century: A Report on Sustainable Models for New York City's Off and Off Off Broadway Theatres.* New York: Alliance of Resident Theatres. https://www.art-newyork.org/assets/documents/ theatres-for-the-21st-century.pdf.

Luber, Steve. (2007). "Dicking around with Radiohole: Toward Hyperreal Performance and Criticism." *TDR* 51(4) (Winter): 156–62.

Luber, Steve. (2017). Interview with Radiohole: Erin Douglass, Eric Dyer, Scott Halvorsen Gillette, and Maggie Hoffman. August 12.

Lynn, Kirk and Shawn Sides. (2003). "Dramaturgy: A Co-consideration of the Dramaturgical Role in Collaborative Creation." *Theatre Topics* 13(1) (March): 111–15.

Mann, Paul. (1991). *The Theory-Death of the Avant-Garde.* Bloomington: Indiana University Press.

Marcus, Greil. (1989). *Lipstick Traces: A Secret History of the Twentieth Century.* Cambridge, MA: Harvard University Press.

Marranca, Bonnie. (1977). *The Theatre of Images.* New York: Drama Book Specialists.

Marranca, Bonnie, ed. (2008). "Mediaturgy: A Conversation with Marianne Weems." In *Performance Histories.* New York: PAJ Publications: 189–206.

Martin, Emily. (1994). *Flexible Bodies: Tracking Immunity in American Culture from the Days of Polio to the Age of AIDS.* Boston: Beacon Press.

Martini, Adrienne. (1997a). "Lust Supper: Delivering Fresh Blood." *The Austin Chronicle*, November 14. https://www.austinchronicle.com/arts/1997-11-14/518871/ (accessed July 14, 2018).

Martini, Adrienne. (1997b). "Ripping the Shrew: The Rude Mechanicals Tear into Shakespeare." *The Austin Chronicle*, August 15. https://www.austinchronicle. com/arts/1997-08-15/529415/ (accessed July 14, 2018).

McGinley, Paige. (2010). "Next Up Downtown: A New Generation of Ensemble Performance." *TDR/The Drama Review* 54(4): 11–38.

McGrath, John. (2004). *Loving Big Brother: Surveillance Culture and Performance Space.* London and New York: Routledge.

McGuinness, Max. (2017). "The Fever, Public Theater, New York—'A Warm, Fuzzy Glow.'" *Financial Times*, January 9. https://www.ft.com/content/11fdff4e-d657-11e6-944b-e7eb37a6aa8e (accessed October 18, 2018).

Bibliography

McKenzie, Jon. (2002). *Perform or Else: From Discipline to Performance*. London and New York: Routledge.

McLeod, Kembrew. (2019). *Downtown Pop Underground: New York City and the Literary Punks, Renegade Artists, DIY Filmmakers, Mad Playwrights, and Rock 'n' Roll Glitter Queens Who Revolutionized Culture*. New York: Abrams Press.

Mee, Erin. (2007). "Review: Gentlemen Volunteers by Dan Rothenberg; Mission to Mercury by Dan Rothenberg; Love Unpunished by Dan Rothenberg and David Brick." *Theatre Journal* 59(1) (March): 106–10.

Mermikides, Alex. (2013). "Collective Creation and the 'Creative Industries': The British Context." In *Collective Creation in Contemporary Performance*, Kathryn Mederos Syssoyeva and Scott Proudfit, eds. London: Palgrave Macmillan: 51–70.

Mermikides, Alex and Jackie Smart, eds. (2010). *Devising in Process*. London: Palgrave.

Merola, Nicole M. (2014). "Review of *The Great Immensity*." *Resilience: A Journal of the Environmental Humanities* 2(1) (Winter): 135–9.

Miller, Heidi R. (2007). "*SUPER VISION*" (review). *Theatre Journal* 59(4): 658–60.

Miller, Hillary. (2016). *Drop Dead: Performance in Crisis, 1970s New York*. Evanston: Northwestern University Press.

Monks, Aoife. (2005). "'Genuine Negroes and Real Bloodhounds': Cross-Dressing, Eugene O'Neill, the Wooster Group, and The Emperor Jones." *Modern Drama* 48(3): 540–64.

Morris, Stephen Leigh. (2013). "Group Think." *American Theatre*, 3.1 (March). https://www.americantheatre.org/2013/03/01/group-think/ (accessed October 14, 2017).

Morton, Timothy, ed. (2006). *The Cambridge Companion to Shelley*. New York: Cambridge University Press.

Moser, Margaret. (1999). "Greil Marcus and the Mad Parade." *The Austin Chronicle*, September 10. https://www.austinchronicle.com/arts/1999-09-10/73749/ (accessed July 14, 2018).

Mosser, Jeffry. (2019). "From the Ground Up" (podcast). https://howlround.com/series/ground-podcast.

Newfield, Christopher. (2008). *Unmaking the Public University: The Forty-year Assault on the Middle Class*. New Haven: Harvard University Press.

Nicholson, Helen. (2014). *Applied Drama: The Gift of Theatre*. New York: Macmillan International Higher Education.

Nielsen, Lara D. and Patricia Ybarra, eds. (2012). *Neoliberalism and Global Theatres: Performance Permutations*. New York: Palgrave Macmillan.

Oddey, Alison.(1994). *Devising Theatre: A Practical and Theoretical Handbook*. London and New York: Routledge.

Osumare, Halifu. (2015). "Hip-Hop Theatre." In *The Oxford Handbook of Dance and Theatre*, George-Graves, N., ed. Oxford: Oxford University Press: 604–23.

Osumare, Halifu. (2016). *The Africanist Aesthetic in Global Hip-Hop: Power Moves*. New York: Palgrave Macmillan.

Overlie, Mary. (2016). *Standing in Space: The Six Viewpoints Theory and Practice*. Self-published.

Ozgun, Aras. (2012). "Post-Fordism, Neoliberalism and Cultural Production." In *Intersections: Practices of Curating, Education and Theory*, Angela Hautyunyan, ed. Bristol, UK: Intellect Books: 36–45.

Parenteau, Amelia et al. (2017). "On the Real: Documentary Theatre." *American Theatre*, August 22. https://www.americantheatre.org/category/special-section/on-the-real-documentary-theatre/.

Parker-Starbuck, Jennifer. (2004). "Global Friends: The Builders Association at BAM." *PAJ: Performing Arts Journal* 26(2): 96–102.

Pasolli, Robert. (1972). *A Book on the Open Theatre*. New York: Avon.

Paulson, Michael. (2017). "Brilliant, 41, and Lost to AIDS: The Theater World Asks Why." *New York Times* (Late Edition), October 15: AR 1.

Perry, Mia. (2011). "Theatre and Knowing: Considering the Pedagogical Spaces in Devised Theatre." *Youth Theatre Journal* 25(1): 63–74.

Persley, Nicole Hodges. (2015). "Hip-Hop Theater and Performance." In *The Cambridge Companion to Hip-Hop*, Justin A. Williams, ed. Cambridge: Cambridge University Press: 85–98.

Perucci, Tony. (2018). "'The New Thing': Three Axes for Devised Theatre." *Theatre Topics* 28(3): 203–16.

Pesner, Ben. (2006). "Where Are We Now?" *American Theatre*, 23 (July/August): 36–45. https://www.ddcf.org/globalassets/doris_duke_files/download_files/TCG2006ConversationsintheField.pdf (accessed July 28, 2018).

Peters, Michael Adrian and Petar Jandrić. (2018). "Peer Production and Collective Intelligence as the Basis for the Public Digital University." *Educational Philosophy and Theory* 50(13): 1271–84.

Peterson, Kimberley Suzanne. (2012). "A Versatile Group of Investigative Theatre Practitioners: An Examination and Analysis of The Civilians." Master of Arts Thesis, San Jose State University.

Phillips-Fein, Kim. (2017). *Fear City: New York's Fiscal Crisis and the Rise of the Age of Austerity*. New York: Metropolitan Books.

Pig Iron. (n.d. a). "A Period of Animate Existence." https://www.pigiron.org/productions/period-of-animate-existence (accessed October 12, 2018).

Pig Iron. (n.d. b). "Mission to Mercury." https://www.pigiron.org/productions/mission-mercury (accessed November 30, 2018).

Pig Iron. (n.d. c). "Pig Iron School." https://pigironschool.org/mfa- (accessed January 4, 2019).

Pig Iron. (n.d. d). "She Who Makes the Moon the Moon." https://www.pigiron.org/productions/she-who-makes-moon-moon (accessed August 22, 2018).

Pogrebin, Robin. (2008). "The Lords of Dumbo Make Room for the Arts, At Least for the Moment." *New York Times*, March 6. https://www.nytimes.com/2008/03/06/arts/design/06dumb.html (accessed February 18, 2018).

Polgar, Robi. (1998). "Young Guns and Typewriters." *The Austin Chronicle*, September 18.

Puar, Jasbir, ed. (2012). "Precarity Talk: A Virtual Roundtable with Lauren Berlant, Judith Butler, Bojana Cvejić, Isabell Lorey, Jasbir Puar, and Ana Vujanović." *TDR/The Drama Review* 56(4): 163–77.

Bibliography

Puchner, Martin. (2004). "Society of the Counter-Spectacle: Debord and the Theatre of the Situationists." *Theatre Research International* 29(1): 4–15.

Radiohole. (2004). "Radiohole Is Still My Name." http://radiohole.com/read/show-name.html (accessed September 1, 2020).

Radosavljević, Duška. (2013a). *The Contemporary Ensemble: Interviews with Theatre-Makers*. London and New York: Routledge.

Radosavljević, Duška. (2013b). *Theatre-Making: Interplay between Text and Performance in the 21st Century*. New York: Palgrave Macmillan.

Rancière, Jacques. (2007). *The Emancipated Spectator*. New York: Verso.

Ridout, Nicholas and Rebecca Schneider. (2012). "Precarity and Performance: An Introduction." *TDR/The Drama Review* 56(4): 5–9.

van Reigersberg, Dito. (2004). Interview with the author.

van Reigersberg, Dito. (2017). Interview with the author.

van Reigersberg, Dito. (2019). Correspondence with the author. January 22.

Ritchie, Rob. (1989). *The Joint Stock Book*. London: Methuen.

Robb, J. Cooper. (2006). "Mercury Rising: Pig Iron's Production Reinterprets Classic Queen Songs as Spoken Word, Punk and Jazz." *Philadelphia Weekly*, February 22. http://www.philadelphiaweekly.com/arts/mercury-rising/article_9014a3f1-94e0-50cb-af50-a4855d7c051a.html.

Rodriguez, Diane. (2012). "Ownership Morphing into Investment." *HowlRound*, October 17. https://howlround.com/ownership-morphing-investment (accessed May 2, 2018).

Rosenfeld, Alix. (2018). "Pig Iron Spotlights Caregivers in Its Latest Social-practice Piece." *BroadStreetReview.com*, May 21. https://www.broadstreetreview.com/wnwn/pig-iron-spotlights-caregivers-in-its-latest-social

Rosenfield, Wendy. (2017). "Pig Iron at the Trough." *BroadStreetReview.com*, October 3. https://www.broadstreetreview.com/editors-corner/philly-fringe-2017-a-postmortem.

Rottenberg, Dan. (2004). "Guide to Philadelphia Theater Troupes." *Broad Street Review*, November 1.

Rothenberg, Dan. (2004). Interview with author.

Rothenberg, Dan. (2016). "A Reading of Shut Eye." In Pig Iron, "Le Pig Blog." May 25. https://www.pigiron.org/blog/reading-shut-eye.

Rothenberg, Dan. (2017). Interview with the author.

Rothenberg, Dan. (2019). Correspondence with the author, January 21.

Rothenberg, Dan, Dito van Reigersberg and Quinn Bauriedel. (2004). Interview with the author.

Royster, Francesca T. (2014). "Experiments in a Jazz Aesthetic: Art, Activism, Academia, and the Austin Project." *Text and Performance Quarterly* 34(4): 431–3.

Rude Mechs. (1997). Script, *Curst & Shrewd: The Taming of the Shrew Unhinged*.

Rude Mechs. (2001). Script, *Lipstick Traces*, 2001.

Rude Mechs. (2007). Script, *Get Your War On*, May 1.

Rude Mechs. (2010). Script, *The Method Gun*, February 23.

Rude Mechs. (n.d.). "Get Your War On" (video)

Rude Mechs. (n.d. a). "Lipstick Traces" (video).

Rude Mechs. (n.d. b). "The Method Gun" (video).

Rude Mechs Website. (2017). "Twenty Rude Years—We Made It!" https://
rudemechs.com/twenty-rude-years-made/ (accessed July 13, 2017).

Rude Mechs Website. (2018a). "Crucks." https://rudemechs.com/shows/crucks.html
(accessed July 14, 2018).

Rude Mechs Website. (2018b). "Prometheus Unbound." https://rudemechs.com/
shows/prometheusunbound.html/ (accessed July 14, 2018).

Rude Mechs Website. (2018c). "Salivation: Press." https://rudemechs.com/shows/
salivation.html/ (accessed July 14, 2018).

Rushdie, Salman. (2012). *The Wizard of Oz* (BFI Film Classics). London: British
Film Institute.

Salamon, Jeff. (2001). "Lipstick Traces: An Unruly Ode to Punk as History's Nay
Vote." *New York Times*, May 6. https://www.nytimes.com/2001/05/06/college/
lipstick-traces-an-unruly-ode-to-punk-as-historys-nay-vote.html.

Sanford, Sarah. (2017). Interview with the author.

Saunders, Graham. (2015). *British Theatre Companies 1980–1994*. London:
Bloomsbury.

Savran, David. (1988). *Breaking the Rules: The Wooster Group*. New York: Theatre
Communications Group.

Savran, David. (2004). "Obeying the Rules." In *The Wooster Group and Its
Traditions*, Johan Callens, ed. Brussels: Peter Lang: 63–70.

Savran, David. (2005). "The Death of the Avant-garde." *TDR/The Drama Review*
49(3): 10–42.

Savran, David. (2010). "Liberté, Fraternité, Corbusier!: An Interview with Alex
Timbers." *TDR/The Drama Review* 54(4): 39–53.

Schechner, Richard. (1981). "The Decline and Fall of the (American) Avant-Garde:
Why It Happened and What We Can Do about It." *Performing Arts Journal*:
48–63.

Schechner, Richard. (2010). "The Conservative Avant-Garde." *New Literary History*
41(4): 895–913.

Schechner, Richard. (2012). "Building the Builders Association: A Conversation
with Marianne Weems, James Gibbs, and Moe Angelos." *TDR/The Drama
Review* 56: 36–57.

Schechner, Richard, Jerry Rojo and Brooks McNamara. (1975). *Theatres, Spaces,
Environments: Eighteen Projects*. New York: Drama Book Specialists.

Schiller, Robert J. (2012). "Spend, Spend, Spend. It's the American Way." *New York
Times*, January 14. https://www.nytimes.com/2012/01/15/business/consumer-
spending-as-an-american-virtue.html (accessed May 30, 2019).

Schmor, John B. (2004). "Devising New Theatre for College Programs." *Theatre
Topics* 14(1): 259–73.

Seabrook, John. (2000). *Nobrow: The Culture of Marketing, the Marketing of Culture*.
New York: Vintage Books.

Shank, Theodore. (2002). *Beyond the Boundaries: American Alternative Theatre*.
Ann Arbor: University of Michigan Press.

Shapiro, Howard. (2017). "Philly Fringe Review: 'A Period of Animate Existence.'"
WHYY, September 23. https://whyy.org/articles/philly-fringe-review-a-period-
of-animate-existence/.

Bibliography

Shaw, Helen. (2017). "January Theater Festivals Roundup: Under the Radar Edition." *TimeOut New York*, January 7. https://www.timeout.com/newyork/blog/january-theater-festivals-roundup-under-the-radar-edition-010617 (accessed October 1, 2018).

Sherman, Jon Foley. (2010). "The Practice of Astonishment: Devising, Phenomenology, and Jacques Lecoq." *Theatre Topics* 20(2): 88–99.

Shillinger, Liesl. (2004). "A Little Taste of Hell." *New York Times*, November 9. https://www.nytimes.com/2004/11/09/theater/reviews/a-little-taste-of-hell.html?_r=0.

Sholette, Gregory. (2011). *Dark Matter: Art and Politics in the Age of Enterprise Culture*. London: Pluto Press.

Sides, Shawn. (2017a). Email to author, July 14.

Sides, Shawn. (2017b). Email to author, September 25.

Sides, Shawn. (2018a). Email to author, March 23.

Sides, Shawn. (2018b). Email to author, April 19.

600 HIGHWAYMEN. (n.d.). *The Fever*. http://www.600highwaymen.org/the-fever/ (accessed September 2, 2018).

Sobeck, Janine. (2010). "Theater Outside the Box: Devised Work." Davis Performing Arts Center, Georgetown University, Washington DC, February 19–20. https://howlround.com/sites/default/files/wp-content/uploads/2012/01/Devised-final-report.pdf (accessed March 8, 2019).

Sobelle, Geoff. (2017). Interview with the author.

Stearns, David Patrick. (2017). "Pig Iron's Fringe Show Comes with a $400,000 Price Tag and a Cast of 87." *Philadelphia Inquirer*, September 18. https://www.philly.com/philly/entertainment/arts/pig-irons-

Stevenson, Seth. (2013). "Mad Men 'The Crash' Recap: Speed Episode, Reviewed." *Slate*, May 20. https://slate.com/culture/2013/05/mad-men-the-crash-recap-speed-episode-reviewed.html (accessed August 4, 2017).

Sugg, James. (2017). Interview with the author.

Sussman, Mark J. (2004). "*ALLADEEN*" (review). *Theatre Journal* 56(4): 695–7.

Svich, Caridad. (2003). "Weaving the 'Live' and the 'Mediated': Conversation with Marianne Weems." In *Trans-Global Readings: Crossing Theatrical Boundaries*, Caridad Svich, ed. Manchester: Manchester University Press: 50–6.

Syssoyeva, Kathryn Mederos. (2008). "Pig Iron: A Case Study in Contemporary Collective Practice." In *Vies et morts de la création collective/Lives and Death of Collective Creation*, Jane Baldwin, Jean-Marc Larrue and Christiane Page, eds. Boston: Vox Theatri: 31–51.

Syssoyeva, Kathryn Mederos and Scott Proudfit, eds. (2013a). *A History of Collective Creation*. New York: Palgrave Macmillan.

Syssoyeva, Kathryn Mederos and Scott Proudfit, eds. (2013b). *Collective Creation in Contemporary Performance*. London: Palgrave Macmillan.

Syssoyeva, Kathryn Mederos and Scott Proudfit, eds. (2016). *Women, Collective Creation, and Devised Performance: The Rise of Women Theatre Artists in the Twentieth and Twenty-First Centuries*. New York: Palgrave Macmillan.

Taintor, Meg. (2014). "Attending My Own Wake." November 19. https://howlround.com/attending-my-own-wake (accessed August 4, 2017).

Thompson, James. (2012). *Applied Theatre: Bewilderment and Beyond*. Frankfurt: Peter Lang.

Thompson, Susan Wright. (2007). "*Tout ensemble*: The Actor-Creator and the Influence of the Pedagogy of Jacques Lecoq on American Ensembles." PhD diss., Tufts University.

Tomlin, Liz. (2015a). "The Academy and the Marketplace: Avant-Garde Performance in Neoliberal Times." In *Vanguard Performance beyond Left and Right, Kimberly Jannarone*, ed. Ann Arbor: University of Michigan Press: 264–82.

Tomlin, Liz, ed. (2015b). *British Theatre Companies: 1995–2004*. London and New York: Bloomsbury.

Toqueville, Alexis de. (1972 [1945]). *Democracy in America, Volume 2*. Translated by Henry Reeve and edited by Phillips Bradley. New York: Vintage Books.

Tran, Diep. (2015). "Radiohole Returns to Gooey Form with *Tarzana*." *American Theatre*, July 21. https://www.americantheatre.org/2015/07/21/radiohole-returns-to-gooey-form-with-tarzana (accessed July 1, 2018).

Tran, Diep. (2017). "How a 'Climate-Change Musical' Became a Right-Wing Punching Bag." *American Theatre*, June 5. https://www.americantheatre.org/2017/06/05/how-a-climate-change-musical-became-a-right-wing-punching-bag/ (accessed March 25, 2019).

Uno, Roberta. (2004). "The 5th Element: Hip-Hop Culture Confronts Theatre and Asks, 'Where to Go beyond the Borders of Outreach and Audience Development?'" *American Theatre* 21(4): 26–31.

Vanden Heuvel, Michael. (1993). *Performing Drama/Dramatizing Performance: Alternative Theatre and the Dramatic Text*. Ann Arbor: University of Michigan Press.

Van Dijk, Bert. (2011). *Devised Theatre: A Practical Guide to the Devising Process*. Plimmerton, NZ: Bert van Dijk.

Virilio, Paul. (1988). "The Third Window: An Interview with Paul Virilio." In *Global Television*, Cynthia Schneider and Brian Wallis, eds. Cambridge, MA: MIT Press: 185–97.

Walsh, Fintan and Matthew Causey, eds. (2013). *Performance, Identity, and the Neo-Political Subject*. London and New York: Routledge.

Wandor, Michelene. (1984). "The Impact of Feminism on the Theatre." *Feminist Review* 18 (Winter): 76–92.

Wang, Meiyin. (2011). "The Theatre of the Future." *HowlRound*, February 9. https://howlround.com/theatre-future (accessed February 1, 2018).

Weems, Marianne. (2016). "Art Work: An Evening with Marianne Weems." The New School, New York City, June 7. www.youtube.com/watch?v=MnZtnmOSpwk.

Wehle, Philippa. (1998). "Overlapping Worlds: The Builders Association and *JUMP CUT (Faust)*." *Theatre Forum* 14: 4–9.

Wehle, Philippa. (2002). "Live Performance and Technology: The Example of *JET LAG*." *PAJ: Performing Arts Journal* 24(1): 133–9.

Weinberg, Mark S. (1992). *Challenging the Hierarchy: Collective Theatre in the United States*. New York: Greenwood Press.

Bibliography

Wickstrom, Maurya. (2006). *Performing Consumers: Global Capital and Its Theatrical Seductions*. London and New York: Routledge.

Wickstrom, Maurya. (2012). *Performance in the Blockades of Neoliberalism: Thinking the Political Anew*. London: Palgrave Macmillan.

Williams, Justin A., ed. (2015). *The Cambridge Companion to Hip-Hop*. Cambridge: Cambridge University Press.

Wiles, Timothy J. (1980). *The Theater Event: Modern Theories of Performance*. Chicago: University of Chicago Press.

Wilson, James Andrew. (2012). "When Is a Performance? Temporality in the Social Turn." *Performance Research* 17(5): 110–18.

Ybarra, Patrick. (2005). "The Whole Thing Is over by Nine O'Clock: The Rude Mechs Adaptation of Greil Marcus's Lipstick Traces." *Journal of Dramatic Theory and Criticism* 19(2): 7–30

Ybarra, Patricia. (2017). *Latinx Theatre in the Times of Neoliberalism*. Evanston: Northwestern University Press.

Ybarra, Patricia. (2018). "Neoliberalism, Professionalization, Debt, and the MFA." *Journal of Dramatic Theory and Criticism* 32(2): 151–9.

Zazzali, Peter and Jeanne Klein. (2015). "Toward Revising Undergraduate Theatre Education." *Theatre Topics* 25(3): 261–76.

Zenenga, Praise. (2015). "The Total Theater Aesthetic Paradigm in African Theater." In *The Oxford Handbook of Dance and Theater*, George-Graves, ed. Oxford: Oxford University Press: 236–51.

Ziegler, Julian E. (2020). *Burning Down the House: Newt Gingrich, the Fall of a Speaker, and the Rise of the New Republican Party*. New York: Random House.

Zinman, Toby. (2006). "Gentlemen Volunteers." *Variety*, January 9. https://variety.com/2006/legit/reviews/gentlemen-volunteers-1200519405/.

Zinman, Toby. (2017). "Hello Earthlings; Also, Goodbye." *Broad Street Review*, September 23. https://www.broadstreetreview.com/theater/philly-fringe-2016-pig-iron-theatre-companys-a-period-of-animate-existence.

Zinoman, Jason. (2008). "Pulling the Plug on Digital Bonding." *New York Times*, November 21. www.nytimes.com/2008/11/21/theater/reviews.

INDEX

Abdoh, Auteur Reza 96
The Hip-hop Waltz of Eurydice 91
Abingdon Theatre Company 203
Abramyan, Emil 221
Abrons Art Center 68
Académie Fratellini 129
Ackerman, Emily 203
Actor's Equity Association (AEA) 55, 93,
    240 n.11
Actors Theatre of Louisville 52, 203
Adelaide Fringe 67
Adler, Stella 169
Afghanistan 8–9
AIDS crisis 42
Almeida Theatre 69
al-Qaeda 6–9
Als, Hilton 225, 229
alternative theatre 53, 66–7, 69–70, 77, 79,
    151, 201
Amazon 13
American Association of Community
    Theatres 67
American Realness 68
American Repertory Theatre 69, 223
America Online (AOL) 5
AmericUS company 92
Amoralists 81
anarcho-pacifism 40, 55
Anderman, Joan 169
Andersen, Arthur 7
Anderson, Hans Christian 131
Anderson, Laurie 96, 174
Andrew W. Mellon Foundation 223
Android system 12
Angelos, Moe 100, 102–3, 106, 109, 115,
    117–18
Anna Deveare Smith school of
    documentary theatre 194
Annenberg Center 143
Antenna Theatre 40
applied theatre 36–41, 43–4, 51, 74–5, 82,
    88, 90, 240 n.7

Approach teaching technique 168
Arab Spring revolts, 2011 32
Arden Shakespeare Company 131, 146
Argelander, Ron 73
Artaud, Antonin 41, 51
artisanal crafting process 99
Aspen Ideas Festival 203
Association of Performing Arts Presenters 68
The Austin Project 89
Austin Theatre Critics Table 160
Australia 36, 67, 95, 169
avant-garde 35, 38, 40, 42, 46–8, 53, 71, 74,
    80, 149, 213
Ayres, James 148

baby boomers 71
Bachrach, Ilan 172
Badiou, Alain 221–2
Baer, Martha 96, 101
Bailes, Sara Jane, *Performance Theatre and
    the Poetics of Failure* 85
Bailiwick Theatre 69
Ball, Hugo 162
Banes, Sally, liminoid space 71, 77
Bang-Jensen, Nell 144–5
banks/banking 6–7, 12
    collapse of 2, 10
Banks, Robert 91
Barba, Eugenio 36
Barbagallo, Jess 118
Bataille, Georges, *The Accursed Share: An
    Essay on General Economy, Volume
    1: Consumption* 191
Bates, Katherine Lee, "America the
    Beautiful" 210
Baudrillard, Jean 181, 191
Baum, L. Frank 109
Bauriedel, Quinn 121–7, 129–31, 136–7,
    141–2, 146
Bausch, Pina 96
Beau Geste company 44
Bechtel, Roger 83

Index

Beckett, Samuel 221
Beck, Julian, *The Life of the Theatre* 72
Bent, Eliza 222
Berkeley, Busby 111, 115
Berlant, Lauren 64
Biden, Joe 11, 18
Bielby, Liza 50
Big Art Group 81
Big Dance Theatre company 58, 149, 219
Bing, Suzanne 123
BIPOC (Black, Indigenous, People of Color)
    killing of 19–20, 24
    -led companies 88–9
Bishop, Claire 42–3
Black Arts Movement 92
Blackbird, Kathy 150, 154, 156
Black Lives Matter (BLM) movement 4,
    20, 45
Black Monday market crash of 1987 5
Black Power Movement 40
Black vernacular oral culture 92
Blake, Marsha Stephanie 203, 209
Blau, Herbert 40
Blessed Unrest company 77
Blouin, Cara 69
Boal, Augusto 42
    Theatre of the Oppressed 39–40
Boccaccio, Giovanni, *Decameron* 117–18
Bogart, Anne 149, 153, 156, 164
    Anne Bogart: Viewpoints 73
Bonney, Jo 92
Boudreaux, Frank 85
Bourdieu, Pierre 64–5
Bourriaud, Nicholas 42–3
Boxtree Players group 150–1
Brandt, Susanna Margaretha 98
Brater, Jessica Silsby 53
Breuer, Lee 53, 77
Brick, David 132–3, 136
Bridgforth, Sharon 88–9
broad remit companies 37–9, 41, 49, 56,
    81–3, 87–8, 90
Broadway model 53, 56, 60–1, 111, 218
Brooklyn Academy of Music (BAM) 67,
    95–6
Brooklyn College Community
    Partnership 108
Brook, Peter 53
Browde, Abigail 217–24, 226–7, 229–32,
    234–6

Brownrigg, Coya Paz, *Ensemble-Made
    Chicago: A Guide to Devised
    Theatre* 82
Brown, Scott 212
Builders Association company 42, 44,
    49–50, 53, 66–7, 95, 98–9, 174
    Alladeen 81, 104–6, 114, 116–17
    CONTINUOUS CITY 100, 108, 114,
    116–18
    critical reception 116–17
    Decameron 110, 117–19
    ELEMENTS OF OZ 109–14, 116
    foundations 96–8
    House/Divided 81, 100, 113, 116
    IMPERIAL MOTEL (FAUST) 97–8, 114
    INVISIBLE CITIES 108
    JET LAG 101–4, 113, 116
    JUMP CUT (FAUST) 97–8
    MASTER BUILDER 96–7, 100, 113–15
    methodology 98–102
    SONTAG:REBORN 115
    SUPER VISION 81, 99, 101, 106–8, 113,
    118, 241 n.3
    themes and aesthetics 112–16
    21st Century Storytelling workshops 99
    XTRAVAGANZA 111–12, 114–15
Buitrago, Hector 196
Burden, Chris 169
Burden, Stella 167
    A Streetcar Named Desire 168–9
Burroughs, Edgar Wright 47
Bush, George H. W. 7, 21, 28
Bush, George W. 4–9, 31, 75
    invasion against Iraq 6, 8, 11
    "Mission Accomplished" 8
    "War on Terror" 8
Business Roundtable 26
Butler, Isaac, *Artforum* 197
Butler, Judith 65
Butterfield, Matthew Scott 226–7

CalArts 77
Cale, David 221
Calvino, Italo 108, 134
Camp, Robert Quillen 137
Cantara, Jamie Smith 158
Capital City Playhouse 151
capitalism 41, 43, 53, 56, 64–6, 112, 162,
    180, 184, 191, 228
Carlos, Laurie 88

Carnegie-Mellon MFA in Video and Media
    Design for Performance 77
Carriage Trade 239 n.4
Castells, Manuel 114
Center Theatre Group 53, 55, 203
Cesare, T. Nikki 213
Chaikin, Joseph 122, 126
    illness 133
    "Open Canvas" 122–3, 133
    The Presence of the Actor 72, 132–3
Chalmers, Jessica 96, 101, 103
Chambers, Colt 69
Chavkin, Rachel 54–5, 239 n.3
    Natasha, Pierre, & the Great Comet of
        1812 56
Chicago House 151
Chicago Pivot Festival 170
Children's Theatre of Minneapolis 44
China 15, 21–2, 27
Chong, Ping 40, 77
Christian, Ehren Conner 160
Christian, T. M. 190
Churchill, Caryl, Fen 73
Cincinnati Playhouse company 92
Citizen's United v. Federal Election
        Commission 9
Civilians theatre company 52, 58, 66–7, 73,
        195–6, 243 n.4, 243 n.6
    The Abominables 197
    "America's Center for Investigative
        Theatre" 194
    Another Word for Beauty 196, 202
    Artforum 197
    This Beautiful City 81, 202–4,
        207–10, 212
    Cloud Nine 200
    critical reception 212–15
    Doomducker's Ball 201
    Encores Off Center 198
    Extended Play blog 196
    Fen 200
    Fire in the Lake 200
    In the Footprint: The Battle over Atlantic
        Yards 196
    Gone Missing 196, 198, 202, 204–8, 211
    The Great Immensity 81, 194, 196–7,
        201–4, 210–13, 243 n.10
    history and development 198–203
    Let Me Ascertain You (LMAY) 196, 202,
        204, 215

    Lobby Project 206–7
    Mouthful of Birds 200
    (I am) Nobody's Lunch 193, 202
    Oh! What a Lovely War 201
    Pretty Filthy 194, 196, 202, 213
    production techniques 201
    Research and Development (R&D)
        group 194, 196–8, 214–15
    Resilience: A Journal of the
        Environmental Humanities 213
    Scum 201
    Shadow of Himself 202
    The Speakers 201
    Time Out 212, 233
    values 199
    Vulture 212
    Whisper House 198
civil rights movement 1, 20
Clark, Brian, Group Theatre 72
Clarke, Martha 40
classical liberalism 25–6, 31
Cleater, John 97
climate change 20–2, 29. See also
        environmental movements
Clinton, Bill 4–5, 7, 14, 21, 28–30
    "Don't Ask, Don't Tell" policy 5–6, 12
    impeachment against 4
Clinton, Hillary 11, 13
    vs. Trump (votes) 14
Cohen, Robert 50
collaboration/collaborative creation 35, 37,
        39–40, 43–4, 48–51, 56, 58, 61, 63, 71,
        74, 80, 82–5, 88–9, 91, 98, 102–3, 105,
        108, 114, 122, 125, 129, 132, 136, 139,
        142–6, 152–5, 159, 165–70, 218–22
Collapsable Giraffe company 64, 172, 185
Collapsable Hole 64, 184–5, 189
Collective Consciousness Theatre 91
collective theatrical creation 3, 25, 35–6,
        38–41, 44–5, 47, 51, 53–5, 58, 72–3,
        74, 77–8, 80, 84, 87, 89, 93, 121–3,
        145, 218–20, 220, 239 n.2
Collins, John 83
commodity/commodification 30–1, 53, 59,
        66, 77–9, 86, 225
community-directed theatres 37, 39, 41–2,
        44–5, 49, 88, 91
Compass Players 72
conservatives/conservatism 1, 4–5, 11,
        14–17, 22, 26–8, 69, 75, 93, 111, 209

Index

Conservative Theatre Festival 69
constituency-directed companies 36,
    39–40, 44
contemporary ensembles 48–9, 77, 81,
    87, 156
Contract with America 1, 4
Cooperman, Robert 69
Copeau, Jacques 36, 123
Cornerstone Theatre company 44
    *Cornerstone Community Collaboration
    Handbook* 60
Cornish, Matthew 72
Cosson, Steve 52, 73, 193–203, 213–14
counterculture 1, 26, 32, 35–7
COVID-19 pandemic 3, 18, 55–6, 70, 170,
    198, 236
    economic crisis 5, 15, 22–4
Cramer, Erin 96
creative economy 31
crimes. *See also* police brutality
    gun violence 18–20
    hate-crime violence 17
    murder of George Floyd 4, 22, 24
    school shootings 6, 19
    sexual abuse by Harvey Weinstein 16
    shooting of Michael Brown 20
    shooting of Trayvon Martin 12, 20
Crossing the Line Festival 223
Crowhurst, Donald 102–4
Cultural Odyssey company 88
Cummings, Scott T. 73, 156
Curious Theatre 92
Cvejić, Bojana 57, 65

Dada/Dadaists 159–60, 162, 202
Dafoe, Willem 46–7
    The Last Temptation of Christ 46
    Platoon 46
D'Amour, Lisa 151
dance-clown-theatre collective. *See* Pig Iron
    Theatre company
Dar-a-Luz Company 91
Darlington, Madge 148, 150–1, 155–6, 159,
    169
Dasté, Jean 123
Davis, Eisa 90
Davis, Marchánt 232–3, 237
Davis, Mike, *Planet of Slums* 108
Davis, R. G. 123
Davis, Ronnie 72

dbox 106, 114
Debord, Guy 160–3, 182, 191
Decroux, Etienne 123
de Jong, Constance 101
de Leon, Aya 90
Dell'Arte Company 67, 164
Delpech, Emmanuelle 129, 135–6, 141, 145
Del Vecchio, Jessica 115
democracy 32, 40, 86, 172, 176–7, 179, 191
Democratic Party 28
de Peuter, Greig 64
devised theatre 24–5, 37, 41–2, 45, 52–3, 76,
    79, 99, 240 n.7
    in higher education 77
    rise within neoliberalism 57–65
Devised Theatre Working Group 68
devising ensembles 31, 36–7, 45, 49–50, 52,
    55, 67, 69, 74–5, 91
Dieterich, Lana 226–7
Dietz, Dan 151
Digital Theatre 78
Digital Theatre+ 78
Diller, Liz. *See* Diller + Scofidio
Diller + Scofidio 102–3, 112, 114
Dionisio, Gabriel "Kwikstep" 90–1
Director's Guild of Great Britain 55
Dixon, Steve 113
DIY culture 62, 174
Dobson, Dan 97, 99–100, 110
documentary cabaret theatre. *See* Civilians
    theatre company
Dole, Robert 4
Donovan, Sean 109, 118
Doris Duke Foundation 51
Dostoevsky, Fyodor, *The Brothers
    Karamazov* 147
dotcom bubble, collapse of 5, 12, 31
Douglas, Paulette, *The TEAM Makes a
    Play* 81
Douglass, Erin 172–3, 179–80, 182–3, 185,
    187, 192
Dow Jones Industrial Average 5
Downtown ensembles/theatre 55, 63
Dramatists Guild, *Devised Theatre: A
    Resource Guide* 52
drug epidemic 2
Durham, Leslie Atkins 105, 117
Dyer, Eric 172–4, 178–83, 187, 189, 191
Dylan, Bob 190
Dziemianowicz, Joe 212

École internationale de théâtre Jacques
Lecoq 123–4, 127, 129–30, 146
auto-cours ("self-course") 125–6
enquête ("investigation") 125–6
École Supérieure de l'art dramatique 129
economy
creative 31
e-commerce 5
economic crises of 2020 (COVID-19
pandemic) 3, 5, 15, 22–4
economic policy 3, 15, 28, 32
experience 43
global 57
neoliberalism 24–34, 57–65
post-Fordist 30
precarity 65
recession 5, 31
Edinburgh Fringe Festival 66
Edmonton International Fringe Festival 67
education 71, 74–5, 112, 196
arts 71, 75
devised theatre in higher 77
educational policy 75–6
higher education 57, 75–7, 79
K-12 75
post-secondary 76
STEM (science, technology, engineering
and mathematics)-related fields 76
student debt crisis 76
egalitarian company structures 35, 49, 59
egbé 88
election(s) 10, 15, 33
1996 4
2000 20–1
2016 13, 15
2020 1, 18, 23–4
Clinton *vs.* Trump 14–15
Elevator Repair Service theatre group 56, 58,
83, 85–6, 173
El Teatro Campesino (ETC) company 35
Emerging America Festival 69
En Garde Arts company 96
Enron scandal, 2001 7
ensemble-created theatre 22, 25, 29, 31,
33–4, 37, 39–40, 43, 45, 48, 51,
56, 58–9, 61, 64–5, 70, 74, 78–9,
87–8, 93
second-generation/second-wave 35–6,
53–4, 73–4, 87
third-wave/-weave 36, 53–4, 57–9, 74, 86

ensemble creation 22, 39, 41–3, 45–6, 51,
54–5, 57–8, 61, 63, 78, 85–7, 93
diversifying 87–92
ensemble theatres 70, 76, 78, 80, 82
collaboration in 83–4
enterprise culture 62–4, 79
environmental movements 20–2
equal-participant model 175
Ernst 47
Estéves, Carlos García 125–6
Etchell, Tim, *Certain Fragments* 78
ethnic-based ensemble theatre techniques 92
EuroMayDay events, 2001 32
European Festival Association 67
European Union (EU) 10, 32, 65
state-sponsored theatres in 66
Eustis, Oskar 197, 214
Evreinov, Nikolai 137
Ex Machina company 174
experimental theatre 46, 48, 75, 95, 99–100,
122, 136, 151–2, 170, 213
Experimental Theatre Wing at NYU 73
Ex. Pgirl theatre group 58
Expressionists 202

Facebook 3, 13, 108
Faires, Robert 147, 151, 155
Falwell, Jerry, Moral Majority 27–8
Feldenkrais, Moshé, *Awareness through
Movement* 72
Feldman, Adam, *Time Out* 212
Felton-Dansky, Miriam 236
feminism/feminist 1, 28, 39, 42, 69, 88, 96,
115, 149–52, 159, 170
Ferguson Unrest, 2014 4
Festival d'Automne 67
Festival of fringe theatre 160
Festivals of American Community Theatre 67
Findlay, Iver 172
Findlay, Jim 172
Florida, Richard, *The Rise of the Creative
Class* 62
Floyd, George, murder of (2020) 4, 22, 24
FoolsFURY Festival 68
Forbes, Kamilah 68, 90
Forced Entertainment 78, 85
Ford Foundation "Future Aesthetics"
conference 91
Ford, John 184
The Grapes of Wrath 100

Index

Forearmed Productions 69
Foreman, Richard 40, 96, 149, 173–4
formalist theatre 42–4, 77, 86
Forum Theatre techniques 39
Fox, Jonathan 90
The Frantic Assembly Book of Devising Theatre 78
Fraser, Andrea 96
Fraser, Nancy 33
freelance model 57
freie Szene (free-scene) movement, German 37
Friedman, Michael 193, 195–6, 198, 201–3
   death of 197, 207
   State of the Union Songbook project 215
Friend, Cassandra 129, 136, 140, 145
FringeArts, Philadelphia 223
Fringe BYOV (Bring Your Own Venue) 68
fringe festivals 58, 66–71, 92, 143. *See also specific fringe festivals*
fringe theatre 44, 151, 160
Full Circle Souljahs company 90
Fuller, Loie 111
FURY Factory Festival of Ensemble and Devised Theatre 68
Fusebox Festival 226
Futurists 202

Gallagher-Ross, Jacob, *Theatres of Everyday Life* 86
Gallatin School 149
Galloway, Terry 159
Garay-English, Olga 51
Garcia, Ana "Rockafella" 90–1
Gener, Randy 100
gentrification 64
Ghost Road Company 40, 42, 44
Gibbs, James 103, 106, 108
Giesekam, Greg 115–16
Giessen Institute for Applied Theatre Studies 72
Gillette, Halvorsen 173, 178–81, 187
Gingrich, Newt, *Contract with America* 1, 4
Global Climate Coalition 21
globalism 3, 27
global warming 20–1
Glynn, Katie 156
Goat Island company 42–3, 56, 58, 70, 85–6, 219

It's an Earthquake in My Heart 78
Small Acts of Repair 78
Gob Squad company 72
Goethe's *Faust* 97–8
Goldberg, David Theo 240 n.13
Gombrowicz, Witold, *Possessed* 134
Gomez-Peña, Guillermo 91
Goodman Theatre 92
Google 3, 5, 13
Gore, Al 7, 20–1
Graves, Thomas 164, 170
Gray, Spalding 47, 175
   Impossible Vacation 46
Great Depression 3, 25, 100, 109
Great Recession 2, 10, 30, 54–5, 64–5, 76, 85, 87
Greenspan, David 161, 163
Greer 47
Grote, Jason 173–4, 177, 186, 214, 242 n.6
Grotowski, Jerzy 41, 47, 53, 122
Grundgens, Gustaf 98
gun violence 18–20

Hacker, Jacob 240 n.13
Haggard, Marcus 210
Hallereau, Claire 118
Halprin, Anna, *Taking Part: A Workshop Approach to Collective Creativity* 72
Halvorsen Gillette, Scott 172
Hamilton, Darrick 240 n.13
The Hangers company 40
Happenings 72
Harper, Romanie 173
Harrison, Jordan, *Maple and Vine* 196
Harris, Rennie 90
   Facing Mekka 90
Harvie, Jen 51
   Fair Play 38, 41
Headlong Dance Theatre company 42
Heberlee, Brad 203
Heddon, Deirdre, *Devising Performance: A Critical History* 36. See also Milling, Jane
Heller, Hannah 109
Herion, Troy 143
Hi-Arts Hip-Hop Theatre Festival 68
Hinds, Rickerby 90
Hinterlands band 50
hip-hop culture 89–92
Hip Hop Theatre Initiative 91

Hixson, Lin 40, 42, 219
Hnath, Lucas, *Dana H.* 198
Hoch, Danny 68, 90
Hoffman, Maggie 172–3, 178, 180, 182–3, 185, 187–8
Holeman, Suli 145
Holsopple, Ryan 173, 187
Holum, Suli 121, 129, 131, 136, 140
"site-specific World War I melodrama" 129
Holzer, Jenny 96
Hook & Eye Theater of Brooklyn 50
Hopola, Sarah 157–8
Hostetter, Asta Bennie 227
HowlRound Theatre Commons, Emerson College 78
Huelsenbeck, Richard 160–3
Humana Festival 53, 73, 92, 203, 243 n.9
Human Genome Project 12
Hurricane Katrina 9, 21
Hussein, Saddam 8–9
Hyde Park Theatre 155, 201

Ibsen, Henrik, *Hedda Gabler* 97
Ice Factory company 68
Iizuka, Naomi 54
immersive theatre 38, 68, 155
Independence Foundation 127
Instagram 13
instrumentalization of insecurity 33
Interact company 146
interdisciplinary practices 88
intermedia 93, 95, 98, 143
international fringe festivals. *See* fringe festivals
International Monetary Fund (IMF) 10, 32
International Performance Festival Circuit 180
iOS operating system 12
iPad/iPod 12–13
iPhone/smartphones 12
Iraq, invasion of 6, 8–9, 11
ill-treatment of Iraqi prisoners 9
Isherwood, Charles 232–3
Islamic State of Iraq and Syria (ISIS) 8
Israel, Baba 90

Jackson, Jax 233
Jackson, Shannon 30, 53, 63–4, 70, 85, 101, 116
Jafferis, Aaron, *Shakespeare: The Remix* 91

Jagger, Mick 190
Jakovljevic, Branislav 223
jazz 88–9, 92, 124, 188
Jerome Foundation 223
Jesurun, John 98, 101, 173–4, 217
Johnston, Chloe, *Ensemble-Made Chicago: A Guide to Devised Theatre* 82
Johnstone, Keith, *Impro!* 72
Joint Stock Theatre Company 73, 193, 200–2, 214
Jones, Bill T. 90
Jones, Omi Osum Joni 88
and Bridgforth 89
Jazz Performance 88
Searching for Osun 88
sista docta 88
Jones, Rhodessa 74
The Medea Project 88
Joseph, Marc Bamuthi 90, 91
Joseph, Melanie 161
Judson Dance Theatre 72
just-in-time production 60, 86

Kanopy streaming video platform 78
Kansas City Repertory Theatre 44, 53
Kantor, Tadeusz 47, 122
Kauffman, Anne 195
Kaye, Nick 115–16
Keaton, Buster 116
K-12 education 75
Kenah, Hannah 164–5
Kennedy, Adrienne 54
Kennedy Center American College Theatre Festival 77, 90
Kern, Kirsten 150
Kerry, John 8–9, 11
Kershaw, Baz 74
Kester, Grant 42
Kidwell, Jennifer 142, 170
Kim, So Yong 173
King, Martin Luther 12
Kirk Douglas Theatre 53
Kolluri, Derek 226
Kondek, Chris 97, 106
Kozinn, Sarah 193, 201, 213
Kraken company 40
Krasnoff, Sarah 102–4
Krodman, Mel 142
Kruger, Barbara 96
Krumholz, Brad 82–3
Kuharski, Allen 122–3, 133, 141

Index

Kushner, Tony, *Angels in America, Part I: Millennium Approaches* 28

Laing, Stewart 106, 108, 119
La Jolla Playhouse theatre company 53, 67
La MaMa ETC troupe 66, 149, 185
Landau, Tina, *The Viewpoints Book* 73
LANE (Leveraging a Network for Equity) 88
Lavender, Andy 43
Lazar, Paul 149, 219
Lazzarato, Maurizio 85
LeCompte, Elizabeth 149
    The Emperor Jones 46–7
    The Hairy Ape 46
    The Temptation of St. Anthony 46
Lecoq, Jacques 40, 123, 125–6
Lee, Young Jean 54, 83
Lehmann, Hans-Thies 43, 101
Lennon, John 190
Lerman, Liz 74
Lesley, Lana 148–52, 156–8, 160–1, 167
Lessac, Arthur, *Body Wisdom* 72
Lewis, Ferdinand 37, 60, 62
Lewis, Jim 203
liberal arts 80
Liebrecht, Jason 160–1, 163
Lien, Mimi 139, 142–3
Liska, Pavol 83, 219
LISPA Lecoq program 142
Literary Managers and Dramaturgs of America (LAMDA) 73
Littlefield, Henry, *The Wizard of Oz* 109
Living Theatre company 35, 40, 55, 66, 72, 90, 219, 241 n.1 (Chapter 3)
Local Programs network 88
London, Todd 52
Lookingglass Theatre company 42, 52, 56, 58–9
Lorca, Federico Garcia 126, 129
Lorey, Isabell
    precarization 33
    "State of insecurity" 57
Lori-Parks, Suzan 54
Lydon, John 162–3
Lyford, Trey 129, 145
Lynn, Kirk 148–9, 151–2, 158–60, 166–7, 169–70
    Crucks 156–7
    Faminly Trilogy 157
    Lust Supper 150, 155, 157

    Pale Idiot 151
    Salivation 157
Lyon, David 107
Lyons, Robert 68

Mabou Mines theatre company 2, 35, 44, 56, 59, 77, 96, 169
MacKaye, Steele 111
Mad River Festival 67
mainstream theatre 44, 51, 91, 93, 218
Mamet, David, *The Anarchist* 69
management systems 60–1
Manifest Destiny 81, 184
Marcus, Greil 159–60, 190
Margolin, Deb 159, 241 n.3 (Chapter 5)
Margraff, Ruth 151
market-based reforms 79
Mark Taper Forum 53, 92
Marlowe, Christoph, *Faust* 98
Marranca, Bonnie 116
    "Theatre of Images" 173
Martini, Adrienne 155
The Masked Marauders 190
Matsushima, Maiko 139–40
Matta-Clark, Gordon 97
McCain, John 11
McCartney, Paul 190
McGinley, Paige 240 n.17
    "Next Up Downtown" 93
McGrath, John, *Loving Big Brother: Surveillance Culture and Performance Space* 108
McGuinness, Max 233–4
McIsaac, Paul 90
McKenzie, John 60–1
McLaren, Malcolm 159, 161–3
McRae, Catherine 173
Mee, Erin 130
Meisner technique 123–5
Mercury, Freddie 132
Meredith Monk company 96
Mergen, Michael T. 160
Mermikides, Alex 131, 240 n.9
Merola, Nicole M. 213
MESS Festival 224
#MeToo movement, 2017 16
Metropolitan Museum of Art 197, 215
MFA programs 71, 73–4, 77
Michael Friedman Legacy Fund 197–8
Mickery Theatre company 66

Microsoft 5
MIDI triggers 97, 108
Miley, Amy 156
Miller, Arthur 96, 224, 226, 228–9
Milling, Jane, *Devising Performance: A Critical History. See also* Heddon, Deirdre
Minneapolis Children's Theatre 197
Miranda, Lin-Manuel, *Hamilton* 17, 91
Mirza, Rizwan 102, 106–8, 116
mixed media/multimedia 96, 98
Mixing Texts workshop 91
Mnouchkine, Ariane 36, 123
    Théâtre du Soleil 122, 126
modernism 44, 239 n.2. *See also* postmodern/postmodernism
Molette, Barbara 54
Mondo Bizarro 58
Montclair State University (New Jersey) 77
Moreno, Jacob
    psychodrama 72, 90
    theatre-as-therapy 72
    The Theatre of Spontaneity 72
Morris, Peter 243 n.8
Morris, Steven Leigh 48
mortgage crash/crisis 7, 9–10, 32, 81
Mosser, Jeffry 239 n.1
Mount Tremper Arts 223
Mourre, Michel 162
Movement Theatre Company 90
MPAACT Theatre 90
multiculturalism 28, 88
Mundy, Gavin 156–7, 160
Murrin, Tom 185
Museum of Contemporary Art 223
MySpace 16, 108

NACL (North American Cultural Laboratory) 82
National Association of Manufacturers 26
National Endowment for the Arts 166
nationalism 14–16, 28, 237
National Performance Network (NPN) 45, 51, 88
National Science Foundation 196
National Theatre of Scotland, *Architecting* 69
National Theatre of the United States of America (NTUSA) 50, 81
National Theatre Project 223

Nature Theatre of Oklahoma 58, 69, 83, 86, 195, 219
Neighborhood Playhouse 123–4
neo-avantgarde 71
Neo-Futurists 149, 155
neoliberalism 24–34, 41, 45, 47, 57–66, 75, 79–80, 84–7, 93, 239 n.2, 240 n.13
Network of Ensemble Theatres (NET) 49
Neumarket Theatre 97
New Colony Theatre 52
New Democrats 1, 4, 9, 11, 13, 15, 21, 24, 28–9
New Labour 62, 76
New Left protest theatre 123
New Ohio Theatre 68
New Paradise Laboratories 44, 53
new play development 51–2, 54
New Public Management (NPM) 60
"New Work, New Ways" event 51
New World Theatre (NWT) 91–2
New York International Fringe 68
New York Theatre Workshop 92
New York University (NYU) 73, 149, 152, 223
Next Wave Festival 67
Niche festivals 67
Nixon, Richard 2
    impeachment against 1
Nobrow 47, 93
nongovernmental organizations (NGOs) 26
nonhierarchical company structure 35, 42, 49, 59
nonprofit theatre sector 37, 39, 45, 49, 52, 55, 59, 90, 92
North American Free Trade Agreement 15
NYC: Up Close Festival 68

Obama, Barack 2–3, 11–14, 21, 30, 76
Obergefell v. Hodges 12
Occupy Movement, 2011 32–4
Off-Broadway theatre 195, 218
The Off Center 64, 147, 158–9, 163–4, 169–70
Ohio Theatre 68, 160
On the Boards company 67
OntheBoards.tv 78
Ontological-Hysteric Theatre company 149
open-access festival 68
Open Model 79
Open Theater company 35, 42, 72, 133
    The Serpent 122, 241 n.1 (Chapter 4)
    Terminal 122, 241 n.1 (Chapter 4)

Index

Operaiso school 85
operating systems 5. *See also specific operating systems*
Oregon Shakespeare Festival 53, 91–2
Orlando International Fringe Theatre Festival 67
Osumare, Halifu 89–90
Out of Hand company 44
Overlie, Mary, "the Six Viewpoints" 73
Ozgun, Aras 63

Paik, Nam June 96
Palin, Sarah 11
Parker-Starbuck, Jennifer 117
Parson, Annie-B 149, 219
Pence, David 97, 101–2, 110, 117–18
Performance Group 35, 42, 73, 169
Performing Garage 46, 48, 241 n.1 (Chapter 3)
Peterson, Tommer 232, 237
Philadelphia Theatre Initiative 127
Phillips, Heaven 106
physical theatre 36, 68, 77, 121, 123, 129, 140–2, 146
Pierson, Robert 160
Pig Iron School for Advanced Performance Training 141–2, 146
Pig Iron Theatre company 42, 53, 66, 74, 121
  Anodyne 134
  awards 130, 136
  Cafeteria 129
  The Caregivers 144–5
  Chehov Lizardbrain 137–8, 140
  collaborations 142–5
  Cymbeline 131
  development 145–6
  Dig or Fly 125–6
  enquête ("investigation") 125
  "Five Frames" 135
  Flop 134
  foundations 121–7
  Gentlemen Volunteers 129–30, 136
  Hell Meets Henry Halfway 134, 136
  The Impossible Play 129
  Isabella 138–9
  James Joyce Is Dead and So Is Paris: The Lucia Joyce Cabaret 134
  Joan of Arc 129
  Love Unpunished 132, 136, 139
  Lucia Joyce Cabaret 132
  methodology 134–41
  Mission to Mercury 131–2, 136
  Newborn Things 131
  99 Breakups 140
  The Odyssey 124
  Open Canvas 145–6
  A Period of Animate Existence 143–5
  in Philadelphia 127–34
  Poet in New York: The Trip to the Moon 126, 128–9, 136
  She Who Makes the Moon the Moon 134
  Shut Eye 81, 132–3, 145
  The Snow Queen 131
  Tempest 131
  The Tragedy of Joan of Arc 129
  Twelfth Night 132, 139–41
  Welcome to Yuba City 139
  Winter's Tale 131
PigPen Theatre 38
Ping Chong/Fiji Company 35
Playback Theatre 90
Playwrights Horizons 243 n.11
Plunkett, Stephen 203
The Point arts agency 92
Polgar, Robi 157
police brutality. *See also* crimes
  Ferguson Unrest 4, 20
  killing of BIPOC citizens 19–20, 24
  murder of George Floyd 4, 22, 24
political theatre 43, 201, 213
polyculturalism 92
populism 2, 15, 81
  liberal-based 33
  populist 11, 13–17, 69
pop-up event festival 68
Portland Center Stage company 53
Portland Time-Based Art Festival 67
postdramatic theatre 37, 43, 101
post-Fordist economy 30, 61–2
postmodern/postmodernism 38, 40–4, 47. *See also* modernism
  postmodernist performance 36, 40, 42–3
post-racial America 2, 12
Power, Will 90
precarity 25, 30, 32–4, 42–3, 57, 64–5, 76, 80–2, 88, 112, 213
Presence Project 116
Price, Gavin 227
professional theatre 37, 48, 55–6, 59, 63

Proudfit, Scott 71
    *Collective Creation and Contemporary
        Performance* 45
    A History of Collective Creation 36
Public Domain Theatre 157
Public Theatre 48, 51, 53, 68, 73, 197, 214,
    217, 223, 230, 243 n.10
Puchner, Academics Martin 161

Queen (band)
    "Good Old Fashioned Lover Boy" 132
    "Radio GaGa" 132

race/racism 3, 12, 18–19
    killing of BIPOC citizens 19–20, 24
    murder of George Floyd 4, 22, 24
    racial violence by police 4 (*see also*
        police brutality)
    shooting of Trayvon Martin 12
Radar Festival 68
Radiohole 38, 49, 64, 73, 81, 85, 171, 242
    n.5, 243 n.4
    ANGER/NATION 185
    and arts 176–81
    "Associated Holes" 172
    Bender 171, 173, 175, 181, 190
    Bend Your Mind Off 181
    The Brooklyn Rail 177
    Fluke 174, 179, 185, 191
    Frankenstein 185
    history 172–6
    *The History of Heen: Not Francis E. Dec,
        Esq.* 173–4, 181
    Inflatable Frankenstein 175, 185
    Myth or Meth (or Maybe Moscow?) 185
    *None of It: More or Less Hudson's Bay,
        Again* 181, 190
    Paradise Lost 185
    Radiohole Is Still My Name 181–4,
        188–9, 192
    Rodan: A Jive Hummer 173–4, 181
    The Society of the Spectacle 182
    Tarzana 184–9, 191
    Whatever, Heaven Allows 175, 185
    *Wurst (take it and eat it!) (I mean, take
        it and keep it)* 181
Rae, Paul 117
Rainer, Yvonne 73
rain pan 34 company 58
Ramont, Mark 151

Rand, Ayn 111
Read, Nate 121
Reagan, Ronald 5–6, 26, 28, 58
Recorded Delivery 194
REDCAT company 67–8
regional theatres 44, 48–9, 51–3, 55, 57, 59,
    68–9, 196
relational art 43
Republican Party 3–4, 11, 15
Republican Theatre Festival 69
resident theatre 39, 55, 93
Rhoderick, Jay 121
Richardson, Sarah 150, 152, 155–6
rich theatre 53
Ridout, Nicholas 63
Rimini Protokoll 53, 72
Riot Group 69–70, 134
Rites and Reason Theatre 89
Rivera, José, *Another Word for
    Beauty* 196
Robb, J. Cooper 132, 136
Rockwell, John 160
Rohd, Michael 44, 74
Rolfing and Esalen regimens 72
Roosevelt, Franklin D. 25
    "four freedoms" 26
Rosenfeld, Alix 144
Rosenfield, Wendy 144
Rothenberg, Dan 121–6, 130–2, 135–7, 139,
    141–4, 146
Rotten, Johnny (né Lydon) 160, 162–3
Rubin, Ben 97
Rude Mechs company 42, 44, 49, 53, 64, 73,
    147–9, 158
    B. Beaver Animation 169
    Cherrywood: The Modern Comparable
        164
    collaborative creations 152–5, 159,
        165–6
    Contemporary Classics series 169
    COPADs 150, 155–6, 159, 164, 166
    Crucks 156–7
    "Crushing Austin" 147
    *curst & Shrewd: The Taming of the Shrew
        Unhinged* 152–5, 160, 166
    Dionysus in 69 165, 169
    *don b's snow white: Lost Among the
        Dwarves* 158
    Faminly Trilogy 157
    Field Guide 147, 165, 170

Index

Fixin' King John 170
Fixin' Timon of Athens 170
Fixin' Troilus and Cressida 170
Grageriart 170
Grrl Action program 158–63
High Crimes: The Impeachment of the Worst President in US History 170
I've Never Been so Happy 56, 165
Lipstick Traces: A Secret History of the Twentieth Century 81, 159–63, 166
Lust Supper 150, 155, 157
The Method Gun 166–9
A Midsummer's Night Dream 150
new members 164–5
as nonhierarchical ensemble 150–2
Not Every Mountain 170
Now Now Oh Now 165
Pale Idiot 151
Prometheus Unbound 156
Requiem for Tesla 163
Rude Fusion program 170
Salivation 157
Too Much Light Makes the Baby Go Blind 155
Ubu Roi 155
workshops 170
Ruiz-Sapp, Mildred 92
Rushdie, Salman 111
Russell, Mark 48, 51, 68, 92
Russia 3, 15, 18, 24, 137

Saint-Denis, Michel 123
Salas, Jo 90
Sanchez, Sonia 54
Sanders, Bernie 13, 33
Sandford, Mariellen R. 213
Sanford, Sarah 134–6, 140–2, 145
San Francisco Mime Troupe (SFMT) company 35, 72–3, 123
Sapp, Steven 92
Savran, David 58, 78, 175
  consecrated avant-garde 46
Schechner, Richard 42, 73, 116, 149–50, 164
  conservative avant-garde 46
Schneider, Rebecca 63
school shootings 6, 19. *See also* crimes
Scorsese, Martin 46
Seattle Fringe Festival 67
self-producing companies 93
Selvaratnam, Tanya 105–6, 119
Sex Pistols (band) 159

Here's the Sex Pistols 161
Never Mind the Bollocks 161
"Who killed Bambi?" 161
Shakespeare at Winedale program 148
Shakespeare, William 123, 131–2, 138–9, 148, 151–4, 159, 169–70
Shange, Ntozake 54, 89
Shaplin, Adriano 69, 134, 136
Shaw, Peggy 159
Shed company 67
Shelby County v. Holder 3
Shelley, Percy, *Prometheus Unbound* 156
Sherman, Stuart 86
Sholette, Gregory 62
Showcase Beat Le Mot company 72
Sibiu Fest 224
Sides, Shawn 73, 148–52, 156–9, 167, 169
  curst & Shrewd: The Taming of the Shrew Unhinged 152–5, 160
silent majority strategy 1–2
Silovsky, Joseph 173, 182–3
Silverstone, Michael 217–24, 226, 229, 231–2, 234–7
Simpson, Michael 156
Sinclair, Harry 118
SITI (Saratoga International Theatre Institute) Company 42, 58–9, 67, 149, 152, 156–7, 164, 167
  Small Lives/Big Dreams 152
Situationist International (S.I.) 160, 182
600 Highwaymen 56, 218–22
  Death of a Salesman 224, 228
  Employee of the Year 217, 223, 229
  The Fever 217, 221, 223, 230–8
  The Following Evening 217
  The Record 217, 229
  risks and experiments 225–8
  Rite of Spring 231
  This Great Country 224–30
  Three Days of Rain 217
  The Total People 217
  Viral Performance: Contagious Theatres from Modernism to the Digital Age 236
  Waiting for Godot 220–2, 221
Smart, Annie 73
Smith, T. Ryder 161, 163
Sobelle, Geoff 127–8, 131–2, 136–7, 140–2, 145
Sobule, Jill, *Times Square* 196
Soch, Adam 91

social art 51, 88, 93
social media 2–3, 13, 32, 95, 108. *See also* *specific companies*
social turn 42–3, 45, 77, 81, 239 n.2
SoHo Think Tank 134
Sojourn Theatre company, *Waiting for You on the Corner Of . . .* 44
Soloski, Alexis 206
Sontag, Susan 96, 115
South Coast Repertory company 53
Southern, Eric 221, 227
specialist model 60–1
Spolin, Viola, *Improvisation for the Theatre* 72
Stage Right Theatrics 69
Staniewski, Włodzimierz 122
St. Anne's Warehouse 51
Stein, Deborah 47, 132, 134, 136, 139
Stewart, Ellen 66, 149
stop and frisk policies 19
Stopschinski, Peter 166, 170
storytelling 92, 193, 200, 225
Strange Attractor company 84
Strike Anywhere rock band 58
Studio Theatre 203
subprime mortgages 10, 81
Sugg, James 129–30, 132, 134–6, 140, 142
   L'Homme de l'Orchestre/One-Man Band 129
Sundance Theatre Lab 203
Suzuki, Tadashi 156–7, 162
Svich, Caridad 116

Tati, Jacques, *Playtime* 116
Taylor, Mike 173–4
Taylor, Robert D., *Theatre: Art in Action* 168
Technicolor 109–10
Tectonic Theater Project 194
Tectonic Theatre, *The Laramie Project* 42
telecommunications legislation 5
terrorism, war and 2, 6, 8, 32
   9/11 attack 6–8
   right-wing 24
Thatcher, Margaret, "There is no alternative" (TINA) 27
Theatre Communications Group (TCG) 51, 54, 92
Théâtre de la Jeune Lune 123–5, 127
Theatre Development Fund 52
Theatre Exile company 146

The Theatre of the Emerging American Moment (The TEAM) 44, 54, 66, 69, 81, 85–6
Theatre Times 78
Theatre X company 42, 56, 66
Thread Waxing Space gallery 98
Timbers, Alex 81
Time-Warner Corporation 5
Tipton, Jennifer 97, 99, 101
Tocqueville, Alexis de 172, 176, 179, 191, 242 n.1 (Chapter 6)
Tomlin, Liz 63, 65, 78–9
Torra, Alex 142
Total Quality Management (TQM) 60
Toyotaist economy 30
transgender 2, 12, 202, 209
Trans-Pacific Partnership 15
Tricycle Theatre 193, 242 n.2 (Chapter 2)
Troubled Asset Relief Program (TARP) 10, 12
Trump, Donald 2, 8, 11–13, 17–18, 21, 93, 237
   actions during COVID-19 pandemic 22–3
   campaign strategy 2
   and evangelicals 16
   impeachment against 1, 16, 18
   Make American Great Again (MAGA) 13
   populist 13–14, 16
   sexual violence 14
   violation of pandemic guidelines 23
   vs. Clinton (votes) 14
Tuan, Alice 91
Twitter 3, 13, 17, 108
Two Trees company 64
Tzara, Tristan 162

Under the Radar Festival 51, 217–18, 223, 230, 232
unemployment 3, 25–6
"Unfinished Histories" website 37
United Nations Climate Summit 211
"Unite the Right" rally 16
Universes company 53, 91–2
   Party People 56
University of Buffalo 77
University of Southern California 77
University of Texas at Austin 147
   Shakespeare at Winedale program 148
University of Wisconsin 77

Index

university-trained artists 80
Uno, Roberta 91
Uptown theatre 55
Urban Bush Women 90
Urbaniak, James 161
U.S. Association of Fringe Festivals 69,
    240 n.15

Valentine, Clyde 68
Valk, Kate 48
Vampire Cowboys company 38
van Reigersberg, Dito 121–6, 129, 131,
    136–7, 140–2, 145
Vawter, Ron 46
    Jack Smith/Roy Cohn 96
V-Girls art group 96, 101
video gaming 13
Vilar, Jean 66
Vimeo 78
Vineyard Theatre 203
Virgin Megastore 105
Virilio, Paul 86, 103
Virno, Paolo 85
Vogel, Paula, *How I Learned to Drive* 207
Vujanović, Ana 57, 65

Walden Theatre 164
Walker Art Center 53, 223
Walker, Jillian 54
Wang, Meiyin, "The Theatre of the
    Future" 52
Washburn, Anne 195–6
    Mr. Burns: A Post Electric Play 197, 213
Waters, Les 73, 200–1
Webster, Jeff 97, 106
Web 2.0 technology 12–13
Weems, Marianne 95–104, 108, 111, 113–17
    The Builders Association 116
Weller, Alison 203
Wesleyan University 77
West, Darrell L. 163
Wexner Center at Ohio State University 67,
    77, 95

Wexner Center for the Arts 223
Wilder, Thornton 86
Williamson, Telory 121
Wilma company 146
Wilson, James Andrew 44
Wilson, Robert 40, 47, 66, 96
Wirth, Andrzej 72
Without Walls Festival 67
Witness Relocation company 217
Wolcott, Brendon 221
Woolly Mammoth Theatre Company
    53, 197
Wooster Group theatre company 35, 40,
    46–9, 55–6, 58–9, 66, 70, 78, 95–6,
    149, 173–4, 195
    The Crucible 96
    House/Lights 46, 175
    L.S.D. 46, 96, 98
    Nayatt School 46–7
    A Pink Chair 46
    Poor Theatre 46
    Rhode Island Trilogy 175
    Since I Can Remember 46–7
    The Town Hall Affair 46
    To You, the Birdie! 175
World Bank 32
World Trade Center/Twin Towers (9/11),
    attack of 6–8, 65
World Wide Web 5
Worrall, Kristin 173

Yale Boundaries Fest 67–8
Yale Repertory Theatre 53, 147
Ybarra, Patricia 161
Youth Speaks company 91
YouTube 13, 78, 91

Ziegfeld, Florenz, Jr. 111
Zinoman, Jason 117
zombie neoliberalism 33
Z Space company 52, 145, 203
Zürcher Theatre Spektakel 224

CPSIA information can be obtained
at www.ICGtesting.com
Printed in the USA
LVHW051126120221
679142LV00006B/191